THE RATIONAL... ... ...HEISM

Which is more reasonable: believing in God or not believing in God? Can any of the usual arguments actually show that God does or does not exist?

The Rationality of Theism is a controversial collection of brand-new papers by thirteen outstanding philosophers and scholars. Its aim is to offer comprehensive theistic replies to the traditional arguments against the existence of God, offering a positive case for theism as well as rebuttals of recent influential criticisms of theism.

Part One addresses foundational issues about religious language and epistemology. Part Two focuses on the traditional arguments for God's existence, including the ontological, the cosmological and the teleological arguments, and miracles. In Part Three, the contributors turn their attention to the two main arguments against theism: the alleged incoherence of the divine attributes and the problem of evil.

Overall, the book contends that theism rather than atheism offers the more rationally plausible and defensible explanatory viewpoint. It will be of serious interest to anyone studying or working in philosophy of religion.

Contributors: William P. Alston, David K. Clark, Paul K. Moser, Robert C. Koons, Stephen T. Davis, William Lane Craig, Robin Collins, Paul Copan, R. Douglas Geivett, J. P. Moreland, Francis J. Beckwith, Charles Taliaferro, Gregory E. Ganssle.

Paul Copan has a Ph.D. in philosophy from Marquette University and is Visiting Associate Professor at Trinity International University, Illinois. He is editor of *Will the Real Jesus Please Stand Up?* and author of *That's Just Your Interpretation*. **Paul K. Moser** is Professor and Chairperson of Philosophy at Loyola University of Chicago. He is the author of *Philosophy After Objectivity* and *Knowledge and Evidence*, and the editor of *A Priori Knowledge* and *Rationality in Action*.

Joshua Clark
(404) 422. 1133

THE RATIONALITY OF THEISM

Edited by
Paul Copan and Paul K. Moser

Routledge
Taylor & Francis Group

LONDON AND NEW YORK

First published 2003
by Routledge
11 New Fetter Lane, London EC4P 4EE

Simultaneously published in the USA and Canada
by Routledge
29 West 35th Street, New York, NY 10001

Routledge is an imprint of the Taylor & Francis Group

Typeset in Sabon by
Prepress Projects Ltd, Perth, Scotland
Printed and bound in Great Britain by
MPG Books Ltd, Bodmin, Cornwall

British Library Cataloguing in Publication Data
A catalogue record for this book is available from the British Library

Library of Congress Cataloging in Publication Data
The rationality of theism / [edited by] Paul K. Moser and Paul Copan
p. cm.
Includes bibliographical references (p.) and index.
1. Theism. I. Moser, Paul K., 1957- II. Copan, Paul
BD555 .R38 2003
211'.–dc21   2002038166

ISBN 0-415-26331-X (hbk)
ISBN 0-415-26332-8 (pbk)

CONTENTS

CONTENTS

CONTENTS

CONTENTS

CONTRIBUTORS

William P. Alston is Professor of Philosophy Emeritus at Syracuse University, New York. His most recent books are *Perceiving God: The Epistemology of Religious Experience* (1991), *The Reliability of Sense Perception* (1993), *A Realist Conception of Truth* (1993), and *Illocutionary Acts and Sentence Meaning* (2000).

Francis J. Beckwith is Madison Research Fellow in Constitutional Studies and Political Thought in the James Madison Program in American Ideals and Institutions, Princeton University. His books include *Affirmative Action: Social Justice or Reverse Discrimination?* (1997), *The Abortion Controversy 25 Years After Roe v. Wade: A Reader*, 2nd edn (1998), *Relativism: Feet Firmly Planted in Mid-Air* (1998), *Do the Right Thing: Readings in Applied Ethics and Social Philosophy*, 2nd edn (2002), and *Law, Darwinism, and Public Education: The Establishment Clause of the First Amendment and the Challenge of Intelligent Design* (2002).

David K. Clark is Professor of Theology and Dean of the Center for Biblical and Theological Foundations at Bethel Seminary, Minnesota. He is the author of several books on apologetics, and his most recent works are *When Someone You Love Is Dying* (1998) (coauthored with Peter Emmett) and *To Know and Love God* (2003).

Robin Collins is Associate Professor of Philosophy at Messiah College, Pennsylvania. He is currently working on a book entitled *The Well-Tempered Universe: God, Fine-tuning, and the Laws of Nature*, which argues that the basic structure of the universe strongly points to the existence of a Designer.

Paul Copan is Visiting Associate Professor at Trinity International University, Illinois. He is author of *True for You, But Not for Me* (1998) and *That's Just Your Interpretation* (2001) and editor (with Craig A. Evans) of *Who Was Jesus? 'A Jewish–Christian Dialogue* (2001).

CONTRIBUTORS

William Lane Craig is Research Professor of Philosophy at Talbot School of Theology, California. His most recent publications are *Reasonable Faith* (1994), *The Tensed Theory of Time: A Critical Examination* (2000), *The Tenseless Theory of Time: A Critical Examination* (2000), and *Time and Eternity: Exploring God's Relationship to Time*.

Stephen T. Davis is Professor of Philosophy at Claremont McKenna College, California. He is the author of *The Debate About the Bible: Inerrancy Versus Infallibility* (1977), *Faith, Skepticism, and Evidence: An Essay in Religious Epistemology* (1978), *Logic and the Nature of God* (1983), *Risen Indeed: Making Sense of the Resurrection* (1993), and *God, Reason, and Theistic Proofs* (1997).

Gregory E. Ganssle is Lecturer in Philosophy at Yale University, based at the Rivendell Institute for Christian Thought and Learning. He has published several academic papers in philosophical journals and is co-editor (with David M. Woodruff) of *God and Time: Essays on the Nature of God* (2002).

R. Douglas Geivett is Associate Professor of Philosophy at Talbot School of Theology, California. He is the author of *Evil and the Evidence for God* (1993), co-editor of *Contemporary Perspectives on Religious Epistemology* (1992) and *In Defense of Miracles* (1997).

Robert C. Koons is Professor of Philosophy at University of Texas at Austin. He is the author of *Paradoxes of Belief and Strategic Rationality* (1992), which received the Aarlt Prize from the Council of Graduate Schools in 1994. His latest book is *Realism Regained: Applications of an Exact Theory of Causation, Teleology and the Mind* (2000).

J. P. Moreland is Distinguished Professor of Philosophy at Talbot School of Theology, California. He has authored or co-authored many books including *Christianity and the Nature of Science* (1989), *Scaling the Secular City* (1987), *Does God Exist?* (1990), *Immortality: The Other Side of Death* (1997), *The Life and Death Debate: Moral Issues of Our Times* (1990), *Body and Soul* with Scott Rae (2000), and *Love Your God with all Your Mind* (1997).

Paul K. Moser is Professor and Chairperson of Philosophy at Loyola University of Chicago, Illinois. He is the author of *Philosophy after Objectivity* (1999), *Knowledge and Evidence* (1989) and *Empirical Justification* (1985).

Charles Taliaferro is Professor of Philosophy at St Olaf College, Minnesota, and is the author of *Consciousness and the Mind of God* (1994) and the *Evolution of Modern Philosophy of Religion* (forthcoming), and is co-editor of *The Companion to Philosophy of Religion* (1997).

INTRODUCTION

Paul Copan and Paul K. Moser

God remains one of the best-kept secrets within the walls of academia. A velvet revolution, however, has been taking place in the Western academy. The rumors of God's death have been greatly exaggerated. Acknowledgment of God's reality flourishes and multiplies in the academic world.

Some writers overlook the revolution under way. For instance, John Searle alleges that religion has declined among "educated members of society" because "the world has become demystified."[1] He suggests that, in earlier generations, "books like [his] would have had to contain either an atheistic attack on or a theistic defense of traditional religion."[2] Searle adds: "Nowadays nobody bothers, and it is considered in slightly bad taste to even raise the question of God's existence. Matters of religion are like matters of sexual preference: they are not to be discussed in public, and even the abstract questions are discussed only by bores."[3]

We contributors to this book bring up the subject of God, even unashamedly. The topic of God's reality is taken seriously by some of the most carefully reflective people alive. These people ably support the cognitive rationality of theism, and there is no sign of retreat on this front. We recommend that dissenters reconsider, with due care, the available evidence of God's reality.

Candidly, Thomas Nagel remarks that he *wants* atheism to be true. Not only that, according to Nagel, "I . . . am made uneasy by the fact that some of the most intelligent and well-informed people I know are religious believers."[4] Perhaps more proponents of atheism would likewise feel uneasy if they reflected on what was happening in the world of philosophy. The relatively recent emergence and growth of the Society of Christian Philosophers (with its journal *Faith and Philosophy*) and the Evangelical Philosophical Society (with *Philosophia Christi*) attest to a remarkable shift in the intellectual landscape. Books such as *Philosophers Who Believe*[5] and *God and the Philosophers*[6] tell firsthand the stories of some leading philosophers whose commitment to God informs and directs how they think and live. The change of tone in philosophy toward theism is evidenced by the shift from *hostility* toward theism in Paul Edwards's *Encyclopedia of Philosophy*[7] (1967)

1

to *sympathy* toward theism in the more recent *Routledge Encyclopedia of Philosophy*.[8]

Quentin Smith has lamented the "desecularization" of academia.[9] Beginning with Alvin Plantinga's book *God and Other Minds* in 1967, "realistic theism" has recently increased its influence in American universities. Much to Smith's dismay, it became clear that "realist theists were not outmatched by naturalists in terms of the most valued standards of analytic philosophy: conceptual precision, rigor of argumentation, technical erudition, and an in-depth defense of an original world-view." All the while, naturalists have "passively watched" as the influence of theistic philosophy has soared: "perhaps one-quarter or one-third of philosophy professors are theists, with most being orthodox Christians." Smith concedes: "God is not 'dead' in academia; he returned to life in the late 1960s and is now alive and well in his last academic stronghold, philosophy departments."

The explanatory power of theism

The contributors to this book are realist theists. They believe that God truly exists. Their belief *in* God (and not merely belief *that* God exists) owes its truth and rationality to the fact that God is an actually existing self-revealing being. They believe in the God who, according to St Paul, has not left human beings without a witness (Acts 14:17). This is the God who is "not far from each one of us," desiring that we "seek him and perhaps reach out for him and find him" (Acts 17:27).

Through various means of self-revelation, God personally convicts us of our own moral inadequacy, grants us a sense of our own limitations in light of human frailty and mortality, and gives us a sense of awe at the beauty of the natural world around us. Such self-revelation often yields salient evidence of God's existence. Faith and evidence (or reason) are not opposed at all. Citing Hebrews 11:3 and connecting faith with a future, presently unseen hope, some people infer that faith is a leap in the dark, a commitment made in the absence of evidence. Genuine faith in God, however, is primarily *person directed* or relational ("belief in" or "trust in") and secondarily *propositional* or doctrinal ("belief that"). Like a true marriage, faith in God has two primary components – *commitment* toward God and *trust* in God. Such person-directed commitment and trust can be based on good evidence, or reasons, even if they are irreducible to such reasons and extend into the future in a manner that goes *beyond* past and present evidence. You may have good reasons, for instance, to believe that you should marry a particular person. The personal step, however, of entrusting and committing yourself to that person ("belief in" that person) will go *beyond* your good reasons, but not against them. Like any faithful relationship, your relationship of trusting God involves volitional, will-based factors that go beyond propositions believed to be true. It requires commitment to follow a faithful God of redemptive promise, even into an unknown future.

Cognitively rational belief in God is not simply a matter of pragmatic, psychological, or prudential considerations. Belief in God is not cognitively justified simply because it "works" or fills one with a sense of peace or security. Cognitively justified belief in God aims at truth, at an accurate portrayal of reality. Accordingly, the apostle Paul writes, with regard to God's vindication of His Son, "If for this life only we have hoped in Christ, we are of all people most to be pitied" (1 Corinthians 15:19, NRSV, New Revised Standard Version). Paul assumes that his message of the resurrection of Jesus is true, not just useful or comforting. He assumes likewise for his conviction that the God who raised Jesus from the dead is real. Cognitively rational beliefs are supported by truth-indicators. Truth-indicators can be fallible and merely probabilistic (rather than logically entailing), and they can be supplied by experiences and beliefs irreducible to experiences (so long as the latter beliefs are themselves grounded in truth-indicators).

A theistic worldview, according to most of the chapters in this book, better resolves major philosophical questions than do its alternatives, including its most influential intellectual rival, *naturalism*. Many distinctive features of the world – the universe's temporal origination and fine-tuning, the remarkable emergence of life and of consciousness, objective moral values and obligations, libertarian freedom, human dignity and rights, and even the existence of evil[10] – fit easily and understandably within the context of a theistic universe. By contrast, explanations from naturalism for these features are not readily available. In many cases, naturalism is joined with commitments to materialism – a thesis of all causation as efficient – and reductionism, but such commitments make it difficult to find room for the aforementioned distinctive features. As Jaegwon Kim notes, naturalism is "imperialistic; it demands 'full coverage' . . . and exacts a terribly high ontological price."[11]

Religious belief systems are not cognitively equivalent. Each must be taken on its own cognitive merits. Various world religions, of course, have many good things to say about ethical living, and some exhibit certain similarities (for example, acknowledgment of the need for forgiveness and moral purification of some sort). Once we shift, however, to discussing *tenets* of belief and the nature of the *object* of religious devotion and attention, we see radical differences concerning the following:

- the nature of the Ultimate Reality (non-existent, impersonal, or personal);
- the nature of the human problem (ignorance, desire, or alienation from God);
- the solution to the human problem (attaining knowledge, eliminating desire, or being reconciled to God);
- the nature of the afterlife (non-existence, dissolution of personal identity, or union with God without eliminating individual identity).

3

If the Ultimate Reality is impersonal or beyond good and evil, how do we ground personhood or moral categories? If, as the Advaita Vedanta school of Hinduism maintains, there is no distinction between individual human beings and Brahman, on what basis do we ground individual human rights and dignity? Not all religions are created equal.

By using inference to the best available explanation, theists have a natural context for explaining important features of our world such as rationality, consciousness, human rights, objective moral values, and the origin and fine-tuning of the universe. Theists can affirm this in light of a position free of the explanatory deficiencies of reductionism and materialism. They can also preserve our common acknowledgment of human rationality, dignity, freedom, and moral obligation. As Alvin Plantinga notes, theism "offers suggestions for answers to a wide range of otherwise intractable questions."[12] In other words, considerations about our best available explanation of various data underwrite the cogency of theism.

Should theistic belief be psychoanalyzed?

Influenced by Ludwig Feuerbach's views on religion as wish-fulfillment, Sigmund Freud wrote in his *Future of an Illusion*: "Religious ideas have arisen from the same need as have all other achievements of civilization: from the necessity of defending oneself against the crushing superior force of nature."[13] Religious beliefs are thus "illusions, fulfillments of the oldest, strongest and most urgent wishes of mankind . . . the benevolent rule of a divine Providence allays our fears of the dangers of life."[14] Theistic belief is allegedly a crutch for the weak-minded and pathetic.[15]

Peter Railton has suggested that we may view the relation of theism to ethics in a Feuerbachian manner: "Rather than seeing ethics as resting on religion, one might attempt to see religion as resting to a significant degree on ethics."[16] Railton proposes that we explain the gods "to whom we have given life" as having characteristic features that centrally figure into morality and its justification. Rather than our having been made in *God's* image, we have made God in *our* image.

Is belief in God for the weak-minded, for those who cannot handle life intellectually and emotionally? This noncognitive explanation of theistic belief is a common *ad hominem* argument marshaled by skeptics. Its merits have been weighed, however, in the philosophical scales and have been found wanting.

Peter L. Berger speaks about making a "gigantic joke on Feuerbach."[17] He suggests that what we observe within human societies may actually be the *inversion* of what Feuerbach, Marx, and Freud claimed (namely, that human beings have made God in *their* image). According to Berger, "What appears as a human projection in one [frame of reference] may appear as a

reflection of divine realities in another."[18] That is, the common human longing for the Transcendent may reflect that we have been divinely designed for
such longing. Perhaps "God has set eternity in [our] hearts" (Ecclesiastes 3:
11, New International Version, NIV).

Problems with psychoanalyzing theistic belief are legion. First, the
"Freudian analysis" of religion itself has no clinical evidence to support it.
Freud, who was influenced by Ludwig Feuerbach, admitted that his analysis
was his own personal view, but he had little psychoanalytic experience with
genuinely religious believers.[19]

Second, the Freudian analysis commits the *genetic fallacy* – drawing an
inference about the truth or falsity of a proposition believed from considerations about the origin of the belief. One's autobiography of belief – including motivations and other noncognitive factors – does not settle the issue of
whether it is true that God exists. You may arrive at a correct solution to a
complex mathematical problem even though how you did so was develop-
mentally, or genetically, flawed – true answer, defective source. Similarly, believing in God as a result of flawed motivations does not entail that it is false
that God exists. In dealing with psychoanalysis of theistic belief, we must
distinguish between the *truth* or *falsity* of theistic belief and the *psychological origin* of such belief. For example, Christianity stakes its veracity on
Jesus' bodily resurrection from the dead: "If Christ has not been raised, your
faith is futile" (1 Corinthians 15:17), and many of the New Testament writers offer reasons for taking this event as real.[20] No matter how comforting
Jesus' resurrection may be to some, the Christian faith is illusory, fundamentally false, if Jesus was not raised bodily from the dead. The reality of bodily
resurrection and the cognitive reasons for acknowledging such resurrection
are distinct from any comfort that belief in resurrection could bring.

Third, a belief that brings comfort and solace should not be considered
necessarily false. We find comfort in human relationships, and this is perfectly normal, reasonable, and healthy, at least in routine cases. It would be
implausible to presume that our finding comfort in something is automati-
cally cognitively defective or otherwise wrong.

Fourth, as suggested earlier, the fact that humans tend to be deeply re-
ligious may reflect that they have been made for a relationship with God.
Just because many people long for the Transcendent does not entail that a
transcendent Being exists. Many people long for things that do not exist.
Even so, human longing for God may be suggestive of the reality of a divine
Being. Perhaps we do need God after all, and perhaps God really exists.
Freud's analysis does not establish a contrary position.

Fifth, Freud's skeptical argument (however fallacious) can be turned on
its head. Perhaps atheists *do not want* a father figure in their lives, and
perhaps they subconsciously blame God for something they dislike. Why is
theistic belief the presumed object of psychoanalysis, but atheistic belief is

not? As long as Freud's argument is alive, it may be relevant that many of the most hard-nosed skeptics or atheists in the past – David Hume, Friedrich Nietzsche, Bertrand Russell, Jean-Paul Sartre – had negative or non-existent relationships with the father figures in their lives.[21]

Psychoanalytic arguments against theistic belief are deficient with regard to the truth of such belief. In addition, the very features of theistic belief deprecated by skeptics – finding God to be a comfort, strength, and foundation for life – may turn out, when viewed from another angle, to be pointers in the direction of theism. That is, certain phenomena found *within* our "natural" reality may serve as signposts, pointing *beyond* it toward the Transcendent.

Natural revelation and theistic arguments

The Judeo-Christian scriptures acknowledge signs of God's existence through what has been created, including the human conscience. God's Spirit can use what has been created to awaken us, draw us, and influence us in a God-ward direction. Theologians call this *general*, or *natural*, revelation – God's self-revelation generally, or naturally, available to all human beings. The first three verses of Psalm 19 beautifully express the available revelation of God in nature:

> The heavens are telling of the glory of God;
> And their expanse is declaring the work of His hands.
> Day to day pours forth speech,
> And night to night reveals knowledge.
> There is no speech, nor are there words;
> Their voice is not heard.
> Their line [or sound] has gone out through all the earth,
> And their utterances to the end of the world.
> (New American Standard Bible, NASB)

The witness to God's existence is not only external to us but also internal to us. Romans 2:14 reads: "For when Gentiles who do not have the Law [i.e. the Law of Moses] do instinctively the things of the Law, these, not having the Law, are a law to themselves, . . . their conscience bearing witness and their thoughts alternately accusing or else defending them" (NASB).

Special revelation through the scriptures, for instance, is much more powerful and captivating than natural revelation. Natural revelation is minimalistic and modest; special revelation is robust and clarifying.[22] In both cases (but to varying degrees), God is personally revealed through a manifestation of creative beauty and power or of human moral failure; God thereby confronts a person and invites a response. Even if many suppress or ignore divine revelation, it may still be genuinely available through nature and conscience. Natural theology builds on divine natural revelation, seeking to formulate sound arguments that yield convincing true conclusions about the existence and nature of God.[23] Even so, knowledge of God – whether naturally or specially revealed – is a gift to be received by humans, not an object to be mastered. Divine grace thus operates even in the cognitive domain.

Some natural theologians get into philosophical trouble. First, they assume the demonstrable certainty of their arguments (as "proofs") instead of their having greater plausibility than their denials (as "better arguments"). Second, some have assumed that the theistic arguments point to a single personal God. Skeptics ask, however: why not acknowledge instead many gods (as in polytheism), some abstract nonpersonal Principle, a Deistic God (who winds up the universe and thereafter lets it "tick" on its own), or even an evil deity? The standard theistic arguments are, in general, incomplete. To cite Demea in Hume's *Dialogues Concerning Natural Religion*: "Zealous defenders of religion allow that the proofs of a Deity fall short of perfect evidence!"[24]

Third, some natural theologians have overstated what their arguments can warrant. Using one strand of evidence in a theistic argument, some natural theologians have inferred the existence of a full-blown omniscient, omnipotent, omnipresent, omnibenevolent, self-sufficient, and self-explanatory divine Cause. Some philosophers find such an inference by Aquinas in his famous Five Ways:

> this [being] everyone understands to be God.
> to which everyone gives the name God.
> this all men speak of as God.
> this we call God.
> this being we call God.[25]

Many philosophers have recognized that typical formulations of the cosmological argument do not show the First Cause or Prime Mover to be good or wise – or all-powerful, for that matter. Some inferences can be made regarding this Being's personality and creative power, but we must be guided by the strength of the argument itself.

We may respond briefly to these considerations. First, the existence of an all-loving God plausibly allows for a certain mystery or obscurity in light of the main goal of such a God (filial love among all) and the kind of beings we are (having the capacity to respond freely to God's love or to reject it). An all-loving God seeks to have us learn to love as God loves. This learning process often calls for subtlety and elusiveness on God's part in order to challenge our wayward tendencies, such as selfish pridefulness and indifference. God, in any case, does not typically overwhelm us with divine fireworks or other entertaining manifestations.

Natural theology is wisely offered in terms of good reasons rather than mathematical proofs. Used by God's Spirit, it offers reflective humans plausible reasons for believing that God is real. Stephen Davis has presented a range of options regarding the conclusions of successful theistic arguments:

(a) possibly true;
(b) known to be possibly true;
(c) more reasonable or plausible than their denials;
(d) known to be more reasonable or plausible than their denials;
(e) reasonable or plausible;
(f) known to be reasonable or plausible;
(g) true;
(h) known to be true;
(i) necessarily true; or
(j) known to be necessarily true.[26]

According to Davis, the advisable *goal* or *purpose* of a natural theological argument is to yield conclusions characterized by (c) and (d). That is, such arguments should aim for conclusions that are "more reasonable or plausible than their denials" or are "known to be more reasonable or plausible than their denials." The advisable aim of a natural theological argument is to provide cognitively good grounds for theistic belief, thereby offering such belief as cognitively more reasonable or plausible than its denials.

Second, many atheists and skeptics are uncritically dismissive of evidence for God's existence. They sometimes suggest: "If natural theological arguments fail to show, with deductive conclusiveness, that the maximally great Creator of the universe exists, then I'm not interested." If natural theological arguments are minimally successful, however, then we still live in what Dallas Willard calls an "ontologically haunted universe."[27] This would call for further probing, even whole-hearted seeking, rather than casual dismissal. Much is at stake, including our own futures, in the perennial issue of God's reality.

Suppose, if only for the sake of argument, that full-blown theism does not emerge from natural theological arguments. Even so, the aforementioned alternative suggestions (acknowledging the many gods of polytheism, an abstract nonpersonal Principle, a deistic God, or an evil deity) do not necessarily win by default. Successful natural theological arguments for traditional monotheism would rebut such alternatives. For instance, polytheism can be plausibly eliminated on the basis of explanatory simplicity. We should not postulate many gods when one will suffice for explaining the data in need of explanation. Polytheism becomes explanatorily and thus, theoretically, superfluous. The familiar thesis that a commitment to *no* God is theoretically simpler than a commitment to *one* God is true only in the numerical sense – namely, $1 > 0$. It does not follow that explanation is enhanced. In fact, removing God from our explanatory resources *reduces* our explanatory power in terms of accounting for the fact of the existence of the contingent material world. In addition, the proposal of an evil deity would fail on conceptual grounds, if the term "God" is (as we maintain) a title connoting a being worthy of worship. An evil deity would be unworthy of worship and thus of the maximally honorific title "God."

In terms of the Ultimate Reality's being an abstract nonpersonal principle (and thus not an intelligent agent), one serious problem is clear. It is difficult to see how such an entity – which has no causal or productive powers – could generate, sustain, or develop the universe. Abstractions *do* nothing, from a causal standpoint. If, moreover, the universe came into existence a finite time ago from no previously existent matter (as Big Bang cosmology supports), then a personal cause – rather than an abstraction – is the far more plausible explanation.

A methodological point is noteworthy. *Theistic arguments must be considered not in isolation from, but in combination with, one another.* A holistic approach to these arguments – one typically ignored by critics of theism – would furnish us with a more robust theism and would even more successfully challenge alternative positions. For example, while one version of the cosmological argument may involve nothing more than a deistic God who creates and then withdraws, an additional moral argument would undermine deism. A deistic God is, by any plausible ethical standard, morally inferior to a caring God involved in human history.

One might claim that from each available (and successful) theistic argument a distinct being is to be inferred – one from each. If, however, the beings inferred from each of the theistic arguments do *not* possess mutually conflicting attributes, then there seems to be no good reason to posit more entities than necessary. The *simpler* alternative would be to opt for one Being rather than multiple beings. This seems especially plausible in the absence of evidence calling for multiple beings.

Bracketing the ontological argument (for a maximally great Being), one may infer from a successful cosmological argument a very powerful *personal* Cause of the universe's existence. From a successful teleological argument, one may infer an *intelligent* designing, and thus *personal*, Agent, who intends certain orderly ends for creation. (It does not follow, of course, that *all* of creation is orderly; order can, and now does, exist alongside disorder.) From a successful moral argument, one may infer a personal Being who is *good* rather than a nonpersonal monistic One beyond all distinction, even beyond good and evil. In addition, a successful argument from consciousness points to a superhuman conscious personal Being rather than some abstract principle or force. If, moreover, there is good reason for explaining certain events (such as the resurrection of Jesus) as supernatural or miraculous rather than merely natural, then we have resources for challenging the hypothesis of a deistic God. Veridical religious experiences could reinforce and increase the evidentiary weight of such natural theological arguments.

Natural theological arguments typically fall short of the intricate portrait of God offered in the Judeo-Christian scriptures. Still, successful natural theological arguments would be adequate to warrant a personal response to the Creator and even to hold human beings accountable to their Creator. Even if the specifics about God are not clearly or fully known by successful natural theological arguments, such arguments would offer at least *sufficient reasonable basis* for humans' responding to God's claim upon human lives.

One might quickly dismiss natural theological arguments on the ground that they do not add up to warranted belief in the Judeo-Christian God. This move would be too quick. A wiser response would be to examine the interrelations between the lessons of natural theology and the offerings of special revelation. Rather than stopping, for instance, with the observation that the designer of the universe might not be omnipotent or omniscient, one might be well advised to examine the distinctive characteristics of the designer, particularly in connection with the offerings of special revelation. One might pay close attention to how special revelation illuminates the findings of natural theology.

According to the Judeo-Christian scriptures, the encounter of God's self-revelation through nature and conscience is sufficient for us to recognize God as Creator. In addition, this encounter reveals that this God has a claim upon our lives. Jeremiah 10:10–12 refers to Yahweh as the true God who made the heavens and the earth – in contrast to idols, or false gods. Isaiah 45: 18 announces that it is Yahweh who created the heavens and is thus "God." According to Psalm 90:2, the one who formed the mountains and the earth is fittingly called "God." When biblical writers speak of the Creator, they avowedly speak of the one true God, who is worthy of worship.

Overview

This book is divided into three parts. Part I looks at some preliminaries. In Chapter 1, William Alston discusses the question of whether God-talk or religious language is a meaningful category. He concludes that it is indeed cognitively meaningful, and that the strongest verificationist arguments offered by leading atheists against its intelligibility fail. In Chapter 2, David Clark examines questions of foundationalism and knowledge as they pertain to theistic belief. The common evidentialist demand (e.g. by W. K. Clifford) is often invoked by the skeptic, but it fails to grasp the nature of biblical faith and the place of properly basic beliefs. Evidence has its place, but this must be qualified with respect to properly basic beliefs, background knowledge, and the very possibility of God's existence and, thus, our personal experience of Him. In Chapter 3, Paul Moser warns of the dangers of our having false expectations of the kind of evidence an all-loving God would supply. The Judeo-Christian scriptures clearly affirm that one can know *that* God exists but still resist the divine will in one's life. Moser examines the volitional preconditions for cognitive inspiration from an all-loving God, in particular, for knowing God via receiving God's Spirit. In Chapter 4, Robert Koons argues that theism and science are harmonious rather than in conflict. He assesses the standard accusations that theism is unscientific, and shows that positivistic and materialistic assumptions cannot themselves withstand scrutiny. In fact, modern science owes much to a theistic worldview for its origin and success.

Part II examines positive reasons for belief in God. Some preliminaries about atheism and agnosticism will set the context.

Atheism entails that there is no God, and thus that the proposition that God exists is false. Atheism, however, does not win by default in the absence of evidence for theism. Even if all arguments for God's existence were to fail, this would not establish God's non-existence. As Kai Nielsen observes, "All the proofs of God's existence *may* fail, but it still may be the case that God exists."[28] In addition, reasonable endorsement of atheism demands good reasons for affirming that God does not exist. Contrary to the suggestions of some philosophers, the Judeo-Christian God should not be considered on the model of Santa Claus, mermaids, fairies, and gremlins.[29] We have very good, positive reasons to hold that the last four do not exist. It is not that we simply do not have evidence for their existence. Things are relevantly different regarding God's existence. Alleged defeaters for God's existence – such as the alleged incoherence of the idea of God and the problem of evil – are actually quite difficult to establish, and simply rebutting theistic arguments (as just noted) is insufficient to establish atheism.

Atheism differs from agnosticism. Atheism entails *dis*belief; agnosticism, *un*belief. As Scott Shalkowski writes: "if there were no evidence at all for belief in God, this would legitimize merely agnosticism unless there is evidence *against* the existence of God."[30] Even so, this would be an *open/soft* agnosticism (having the attitude of truly desiring to know if God exists) as opposed to *closed/hard* agnosticism (entailing that one *cannot* know if God exists). Like the atheist, the closed agnostic offers a strong claim in need of cognitive justification.

Part II contains an array of arguments supporting God's existence, arguments making God's existence more plausible than not. The *ontological argument*, despite its many detractors (including many theists), continually resurfaces as an argument for God's existence in certain versions, and Stephen Davis argues for its rational integrity in Chapter 5. William Craig defends a version of the *cosmological argument* in Chapter 6, and offers scientific support for the beginning of and contingency of the universe. Regarding the *argument from design*, Robin Collins states, in Chapter 7, that "the fine-tuning of the cosmos offers us significant reasons for preferring theism over atheism, where atheism is understood as not simply the denial of theism, but as also including the denial of any sort of intelligence behind the existence or structure of the universe." In Chapter 8, Paul Copan presents a version of the *moral argument* for theism. He contends that belief in objective moral values and human dignity is properly basic, and that these facts point us to a good Being in whose image we have been created. Unlike theism, naturalism is simply inept at accounting for objective moral values. And the much-touted Euthyphro argument is inept at overturning objective values rooted in the divine character.

In Chapter 9, Douglas Geivett identifies the evidential value of properly grounded *religious experience* as part of a "cumulative case" for theistic belief. Religious experience is indeed one supporting component of a broader evidential structure undergirding theism. The chapter relates the evidence of religious experience to other topics in the book. J. P. Moreland presents "The argument from consciousness" in Chapter 10, arguing that "mental entities are recalcitrant facts for naturalists" but fit quite well into a theistic context. Although some naturalists feel forced to admit to the irreality of the mental (e.g. Jaegwon Kim), the theist does not have to pay such a high philosophical price to be consistent. In Chapter 11, Francis Beckwith examines two of the strongest contemporary arguments employed to support the view that believers in *miracles* are never within their epistemic rights in believing that a miraculous event has occurred. He argues that these arguments fail owing to their question-begging nature – namely, in light of their unconvincing philosophical commitment to naturalism.

Part III looks at potential defeaters for theism. Unlike the arguments in Part II, where their failure would secure only a soft agnosticism, the atheistic arguments in this section, if successful, would show that atheism is likely to be true. It is doubtful, however, that the atheistic arguments succeed. In Chapter 12, Charles Taliaferro addresses the coherence of the divine attributes. God's attributes should not be treated in isolation but as an integrated whole for a proper understanding of what it means for God to be maximally great, and there exists a good range of options regarding the specific nature and integrity of the divine attributes. In Chapter 13, Greg Ganssle addresses the problem of evil in its various forms, focusing on recent criticisms of theism by William Rowe and Paul Draper. Ganssle shows that such criticisms do not undermine theism.

Conclusion

At the start of the movie *Gladiator*, the Roman army general Maximus tells his poised troops: "What we do in time echoes in eternity."[31] Indeed, if a personal, loving God exists, what we do with God in this life spills over into the next. The direction our lives take on earth – whether Godward or not

– has post-mortem ramifications. If God exists, then God cannot simply be the topic of armchair conversations. God does not exist for the purposes of our intellectual stimulation or entertainment. If God exists and is a self-revealing Being, and if we have been designed for a loving relationship with God, then a searching, thoughtful, and humble heart is fitting as we commence the examination. As Blaise Pascal writes: "My whole heart strains to know what the true good is in order to pursue it: no price would be too high to pay for eternity."[32] The arguments of this book recommend that we go and do likewise.

Notes

1 John Searle, *Mind, Language, and Society: Philosophy in the Real World* (New York: Basic Books, 1998), 34.
2 Ibid.
3 Ibid.
4 Thomas Nagel, *The Last Word* (New York: Oxford University Press, 1997), 130.
5 Kelly Clark (ed.) *Philosophers Who Believe* (Downers Grove, IL: InterVarsity Press, 1993).
6 Thomas Morris (ed.) *God and the Philosophers: The Reconciliation of Faith and Reason* (New York: Oxford University Press, 1994).
7 Paul Edwards (ed.) *Encyclopedia of Philosophy* (New York: Macmillan, 1967). A supplement, edited by Donald M. Borchert, was added in 1996, including entries more sympathetic to theism.
8 Edward Craig (ed.) *Routledge Encyclopedia of Philosophy* (London: Routledge, 1998). See Charles Taliaferro, "A Hundred Years With the Giants and the Gods," *Christian Scholar's Review* 29 (2000), 700, 706.
9 Taken from Quentin Smith, "The Metaphilosophy of Naturalism," *Philo* 4, 2 (2001) (on-line at www.philoonline.org/library/smith_4_2.htm).
10 For naturalism's inability to account for deep, horrendous evils (and how the hope offered by the Christian narrative does so), see Gordon Graham, *Evil and Christian Ethics* (Cambridge: Cambridge University Press, 2001).
11 Jaegwon Kim, "Mental Causation and Two Conceptions of Mental Properties." Paper presented at the American Philosophical Association Eastern Division Meeting (December 1993), 2–23.
12 Alvin Plantinga, "Natural Theology," in *Companion to Metaphysics*, Jaegwon Kim and Ernest Sosa (eds) (Cambridge: Basil Blackwell, 1995), 347.
13 Sigmund Freud, *Future of an Illusion*, J. Strachey (ed. and trans.) (New York: Norton, 1961), 30.
14 Ibid.
15 Richard Dawkins has called religious belief a *virus* of the "mind" – a kind of defect arising in the evolutionary process. See his "Viruses of the Mind," *Free Inquiry* (Summer 1993), 34–41. Dawkins believes, however, that we all "dance" to the "music" of our DNA [*River Out of Eden: A Darwinian View of Life* (New York: Harper Collins, 1995), 133]. If this is so, it is unclear why Dawkins should think that his viewpoint is any more rational or knowable than the theist's, since both are "dancing to their DNA."
16 Peter Railton, "Some Questions About the Justification of Morality," *Philosophical Perspectives* 6 (1992), 45.

17 Peter Berger, *A Rumor of Angels*, 2nd edn (New York: Doubleday, 1990), 50.
18 Ibid., 51.
19 See Paul C. Vitz, *Faith of the Fatherless* (Dallas: Spence, 1999), 8–9.
20 See William Lane Craig, *Assessing the New Testament Evidence for the Resurrection of Jesus* (Lewiston, NY: Mellen, 1989); Stephen T. *Davis, Risen Indeed: Making Sense of the Resurrection* (Grand Rapids, MI: Eerdmans, 1993); Paul Copan (ed.) *Will the Real Jesus Please Stand Up?* (Grand Rapids, MI: Baker, 1998); Paul Copan and Ronald Tacelli (eds) *Jesus' Resurrection: Fact or Figment?* (Downers Grove, IL: InterVarsity Press, 2000).
21 See, for further discussion, Paul Vitz, *Faith of the Fatherless*.
22 See Paul Helm, *The Divine Revelation* (Westchester, IL: Crossway, 1982), 16–18.
23 See Stephen Davis, *God, Reason, and Theistic Proofs* (Grand Rapids, MI: Eerdmans, 1997), ix.
24 David Hume, *Dialogues Concerning Natural Religion* (New York: Hafner, 1948), II, 19.
25 Thomas Aquinas, *Summa Theologica* in *Introduction to St Thomas Aquinas*, Anton Pegis (ed.) (New York: Modern Library, 1948), I.2.3:
   et hoc omnes intelligunt Deum.
   quam omnes Deum nominant.
   quod omnes dicunt Deum.
   et hoc dicimus Deum.
   et hoc dicumus Deum.
26 Stephen Davis, *Reason, God and Theistic Proofs*, 4.
27 Dallas Willard, "Language, Being, God, and the Three Stages of Theistic Evidence," in J. P. Moreland and Kai Nielsen (eds) *Does God Exist? The Great Debate* (Nashville: Thomas Nelson, 1990), 207.
28 Kai Nielsen, *Reason and Practice* (New York: Harper and Row, 1971), 43.
29 Cf. Michael Martin, *Atheism: A Philosophical Justification* (Philadelphia: Temple University Press, 1990), 11, 361.
30 Scott Shalkowski, "Atheological Apologetics," *American Philosophical Quarterly* 26 (1989), 7.
31 This film by Ridley Scott was produced under the banner of DreamWorks and Universal Pictures. It was released on 4 May 2000.
32 Blaise Pascal, *Pensées* (no. 429) various editions.

Part I

FOUNDATIONAL CONSIDERATIONS

1

RELIGIOUS LANGUAGE AND VERIFICATIONISM

William P. Alston

In this chapter I shall consider the challenge to the factual meaningfulness of attempted statements about God posed by the *verifiability criterion of factual meaningfulness*. I shall first lay out the criterion and something of its history, and then shape it into its most coherent form. I shall consider what can be said for and against it. Then I shall examine its application to talk about God. This will involve considering both whether attempted statements about God must satisfy the criterion in order to be factually meaningful, and also whether (some) statements about God do satisfy it. The overall conclusion will be that the verifiability criterion poses no serious threat to the factual *meaningfulness* of what is said about God.

The criterion, its history, and the most coherent form of the theory

In the early decades of the twentieth century, a number of philosophers in Vienna began a group for the discussion of issues in the philosophy of science, a group that became known as the Vienna Circle. Among its leading members were Moritz Schlick, Rudolf Carnap, Otto Neurath, Friedrich Waismann, and Herbert Feigl. The group was concerned with the logic of mathematics and science and with giving philosophy a scientific orientation. The movement was labeled "logical positivism." Its influence spread to Britain, especially from the influence of A. J. Ayer's *Language, Truth, and Logic*, and to the United States, to which several of the Vienna Circle, including Carnap and Feigl, emigrated after the rise of Hitler.

The logical positivists felt that traditional philosophy had reached a dead end and that it needed a fresh start. The main weapon they wielded in the negative part of their endeavor – to discredit traditional metaphysics, epistemology, and ethics – was *verificationism*, the "verifiability theory of meaning," according to which a statement is genuinely "factually meaningful" only if it is capable of empirical verification or falsification. Since, in their view, most traditional philosophical theses failed this test, they were deemed not to be what they professed to be – true (or even false) claims about

17

objective reality. This chapter is specifically concerned with the application of verificationism to religious statements. But to come to grips with this, we must do some fine-tuning of the verifiability theory itself.

First, there is the difference between verifiability as a *theory* of meaning and as a *criterion* of meaningfulness. The former can be formulated thus: "the meaning of a proposition is the method of its verification." In other words, "the meaning of a proposition can be given only by giving the rules of its verification in experience."[1] This is a reductively empiricist account of meaning: there is no meaning to a factual assertion except what would be involved in verifying it. It amounts to an unrestricted generalization of the position in philosophy of science known as "operationalism," according to which, say, the meaning of "temperature" is exhaustively given by a specification of how temperature is measured. But as a *criterion* of meaningfulness, the principle makes no attempt to say *what* the meaning of a factual assertion is. Instead, it confines itself to laying down a necessary condition of its meaningfulness – that it is, in principle, capable of being empirically verified or falsified. The concern here is with the criterion form of the view.

There are still a number of loose ends to tie down before we are in a position to discuss what happens when we submit attempted religious assertions to this criterion.

1   If the claim is that possible empirical verifiability is required for any kind of linguistic meaning, the position is wrecked before it leaves port. It makes no sense to speak of "verifying" interrogative, imperative, or expressive utterances. What would it be to verify "What time is it?" or "Please go to the bank for me" or "Thanks a lot"? To have a chance of being acceptable, the criterion must be limited to declarative sentences that are usable to make statements that have truth-values. This point is recognized by the more sophisticated versions of the position, in which this kind of meaning is called "cognitive meaning," or "factual meaning."

2   But this raises the more difficult question of *what sort of entity* is declared to have cognitive meaning only if it is empirically verifiable. The problem is that it is sentences (and their meaningful constituents) that are said to have or lack cognitive, or any kind, of *meaning*, whereas it is not sentences, but the statements they are used to make, or the propositions they express, that have truth-values and are subject to verification or falsification. We can see that truth-values and empirical testing do not apply, in general, to sentences by considering sentences containing indexical terms or proper names. Is the sentence "I'm hungry" true or false? What would count as empirical evidence for or against *it*? It all depends on who utters it and at what time. This very same sentence can be uttered by many people at many different times, and the truth-value of what they say is sometimes true and sometimes false. The same is true with "Jim is at home." Many people are named "Jim," and so

18

some utterances of that sentence will be saying something true and some something false. Such examples make it clear that what is true or false, verified or falsified (in the primary, straightforward sense), is not a sentence but what is stated or asserted by uttering the sentence by a certain speaker on a certain occasion, a certain place, etc. Not all sentences exhibit this kind of variation. "Lemons are sour" does not. But for a general formulation the point holds that it is *statements* – not *sentences* – that have truth-values and are susceptible to empirical testing. But then we have to reconstrue what empirical verifiability is a criterion for. If we are still to think of it as a criterion for a certain kind of sentence meaning, we have to relate verifiability of statements to a semantic status of sentences. This is not difficult to do, but we lack a snappy way of putting it. Non-snappily, the point is that a sentence must have the potentiality for being used to make statements that are verifiable or falsifiable in order to be factually meaningful. By switching the semantic status to a *potentiality* for making statements that are verifiable or falsifiable, we allow for sentences that have this status to be usable for making many different statements that vary in their truth-values. The verifiability criterion will then read:

(a)   A sentence is cognitively meaningful only if the statements it can be (standardly) used to make are, in principle, empirically verifiable or falsifiable.

3   It will not have escaped notice that in (a) the term "in principle" preceded "verifiable or falsifiable." That is meant to contrast with "in practice." To have factual meaning, a sentence need not be usable to make statements that we are, at present, able to subject to empirical testing. In the early days of logical positivism, the standard example of a genuine factual statement that could not be tested was: "There are mountains on the other side of the moon." As with many philosophical illustrations, this one has succumbed to the progress of science and technology. But it is easy to find more stable examples. Take "It was raining at this spot on the earth precisely 2 million years ago." That is verifiable or falsifiable in principle, e.g. by an observer at that spot at that time, but not by anyone now. The "in principle" requirement is sometimes put by saying that we can describe a verification or falsification. The only trouble with that restatement is that it raises the question of whether that description is factually meaningful, thus raising the specter of an infinite regress. But many such descriptions, like the one above, cannot sensibly be suspected of factual meaninglessness.

4   The early formulations of the criterion made serious use of the terms "verifiability" and "falsifiability," thus requiring the possibility of a decisive, maximally conclusive establishing of truth or falsity. But it

was soon realized that this would rule out all or most of the scientific hypotheses and theories that the logical positivists took as paradigms of factual meaningfulness. For scientific evidence is never so conclusive as to rule out the possibility that the hypothesis supported is false. Enumerative induction is universally recognized to establish only a higher or lesser probability. As for high-level theories, their support comes from their ability to explain and predict empirical data. But for any such theory there is always a potentially indefinitely large number of alternative theories that can do that same job. Moreover, we can never be sure that new data will not pop up which our favored theory cannot handle satisfactorily, as happened in the last 150 years with Newtonian mechanics, which for a very long time was a paradigm of a scientific position that was conclusively established. Hence, there has been a retreat to a more modest form of the criterion that requires only the possibility of empirical data that *confirm* or *disconfirm* – support or weaken – the statement in question *to a certain extent*. In other words, the requirement is that it is possible for some empirical data to tell for or against the statement. This entails another revision of the criterion.

(b) A sentence is factually meaningful only if the statements it can be (standardly) used to make are, in principle, empirically confirmably or disconfirmable.

Here, "confirmable" and "disconfirmable" are *not* to be read with the qualifier "conclusively."

5   The next step in firming up the criterion is to probe into just what it takes for empirical data to tell for or against the acceptability of a statement. This divides up into (a) what counts as empirical data and (b) how such data have to be related to a statement to tell for or against it. These questions get us into all the problems of confirmation theory and, more generally, the epistemology of perception and the epistemology of beliefs and statements that go beyond the directly perceivable. Here I can just skim the surface of all this.

   The first point is that to introduce a reasonable degree of precision into talk of empirical confirmation and prevent it from wallowing in a morass of purely intuitive judgments about when the results of observation bear on the acceptability of a hypothesis, we have to explicate the notion in terms of logical relations between the hypothesis and statements that report the observations. As a first approximation, for a hypothesis to be supported by a possible observation is for it, usually together with other premises, to entail a statement reporting the observation. And for a given hypothesis to be weakened by a possible observation is for that hypothesis, together with other premises, to entail the negation of a statement reporting that observation. Thus if the hypothesis (with other premises) entails that a certain liquid will turn cloudy within 10 minutes, an observation of its doing so will support the hypothesis, whereas an observation of its not doing so will weaken it. In neither case does this amount to conclusive confirmation or dis-confirmation: not the *former*, for there are other possible explanations of the observed event; not the *latter*, for since there are generally other premises involved in the deduction, the trouble might be with some of them rather than with the hypothesis under investigation.

Note that this account presupposes that we can separate out a class of "observation statements" that are confirmed or disconfirmed directly by observation, not indirectly as with the hypothesis just mentioned. There has been much criticism of this assumption in recent times. It is claimed that all perception is shaped by "theory" that we bring to it and that nothing untouched by that is "given" to us in perception. This leads to "reports of observation" themselves being treated as hypoth-eses that are to be evaluated by how well they explain the data. If those data also turn out to be hypotheses, we are off on an infinite regress or we are forced into a coherentist epistemology, in which the only stan-dard of acceptability is the way a given belief or statement fits into a background system, which itself is to be evaluated solely by its internal coherence.

However all this may be, it is not at all clear that a distinction be-tween what is directly justified by experience and what is, at most, indi-rectly so justified cannot be maintained, provided we content ourselves with relatively modest claims for the former. This would involve a dis-avowal of certainty and conclusive verification for perceptual beliefs as well as the higher-level ones. This means that perceptual experience will be taken to give only a prima facie justification of perceptual reports – justification that is, in principle, vulnerable to being canceled by suf-ficient contrary reasons. With that caution, we can still take such state-ments as "The liquid is cloudy" to be directly justified by a visual pre-sentation, and take a hypothesis of chemical constitution of the liquid to be assessed in terms of how it, along with the larger system in which it figures, explains and predicts correct observational reports. This is the way the matter is generally construed by advocates of the verifiability criterion, and I shall continue to discuss the matter in these terms.

The exposition just given reflects the fact that the verifiability crite-rion restricts "experience" to sensory experiences and, correspondingly, restricts "observation" to sense perception and empirical data to sense perceptual reports. These restrictions will turn out to have an important bearing on the application of the criterion to talk about God.

An early objection to the verifiability criterion is that it *failed its own re-quirement* for factual meaningfulness and thus was self-refuting. For it does not seem to be empirically confirmable, nor does it satisfy the only other alternative recognized by logical positivists for truth-value, namely being analytically true or self-contradictory. In response to this difficulty, a number of positivists advocated taking the criterion as a "proposal" for using the term "factually meaningful" rather than as a statement of fact. This takes some of the bite out of the position. Moreover, if the claim that empirical confirmability is required for factual meaningfulness is given up as a factual claim, what can be said for the proposal to suppose that it is so? Hence, I shall continue to treat the position as a truth claim about a requirement for factual meaningfulness.

An examination of the verifiability criterion's application to talk about God

It is now time to consider the application of the verifiability criterion to what seems, for all the world, to be (true or false) statements about God. The bare bones of the usual application by verificationists can be stated simply. Such alleged statements are not empirically verifiable or falsifiable and hence are not what they seem to be – genuine factual statements. But different espousals of this line stem from different stages in the development of the criterion sketched above.

In a much-quoted article, "Theology and Falsification," Antony Flew posed the following challenge to theists: "What would have to occur or to have occurred to constitute for you a disproof of the love of, or of the existence of, God?"[2] This formulation is in terms of the "falsification" disjunct. And if read strictly, the term "disproof" indicates that Flew was thinking of the criterion as requiring the possibility of a *conclusive* proof or disproof. As we have seen, this strong form of the criterion was abandoned early in the development of logical positivism, since it soon came to be realized that most scientific hypotheses and theories fail to satisfy it. But it took a while for this realization to trickle down to some of the positivistically minded philosophers of religion. Kai Nielsen deploys a more up-to-date version of the criterion:

> The operative principle here is that a statement would never unequivocally count as a factual statement unless it were at least in principle confirmable or infirmable, i.e. unless at least some conceivable, empirically determinable state of affairs would count against its truth and some at least conceivable, empirically determinable state of affairs would count for its truth.[3]

In this discussion, I will be thinking in terms of Nielsen's formulation. Now for the claim that statements about God fail the test: Nielsen (followed in this by Martin)[4] is also to be given credit for recognizing that at least some statements about objects of religious worship will satisfy the criterion. Here is a formulation by Martin:

> the unsophisticated discourse of believers in an anthromorphic God is not meaningless; it is merely false. Consider the view that God is a large and powerful spatio-temporal entity that resides somewhere high in the sky. A sentence expressing this is not factually meaningless. We understand what it means and . . . know in the light of the evidence that the statement it expresses is false. What troubles Nielsen is the discourse of the sophisticated believer who says, for example, that God transcends space and time, has no body, and yet performs actions that affect things in space and time. He maintains that this sort of discourse is factually meaningless and therefore neither true nor false.[5]

But the situation is much more complex than this. Leave aside the notion that God is timeless, a view that carries with it special problems of its own, and retain the rest of the above picture of the "sophisticated believer's" conception of God. It is not clear that all talk about such a God is immune from empirical test. One thing that this depends on is the larger theological-religious setting in which such a concept of God is operative. For example, a crucial part of traditional Christianity, found, for example, in the Nicene Creed, is that Christ (the incarnate second person of the divine Trinity) will return to earth at some point in glory to judge mankind. The creeds are not explicit about just how all this will be observable, but the doctrine would make no sense unless it were assumed to be manifest to humanity generally at some time. After all, this is supposed to be a BIG DEAL, the biggest deal in human history. So at least that part of the theology is disconfirmed if this never happens. This does not put us in an ideal position to carry out a test, for no date is specified, not even a "no later than ___" specification. This puts a crimp in the possibility of a conclusive falsification, which is not required anyway in the weaker form of the criterion with which we are working. But it does insure the possibility of a conclusive empirical verification, and, in Nielsen's terms it specifies to some extent observations that "could count for or against the statement." This goes significantly beyond no possible empirical evidence at all.

There are many other possibilities for bringing empirical evidence to bear on Christian doctrine involving God, although they all stop short of a possibility of conclusive verification and falsification in the same way. More than once in the New Testament Jesus is credited with saying that under certain conditions God will give a person what she prays for. These conditions include such things as "with faith" or "if you keep my commandments" – conditions for the satisfaction of which there is no conclusive test. But this is also often the case in the less exact sciences like psychology, and again it makes some provision for an observation statement, "I prayed for X and X did (not) occur" to count for or against the theological claim.

One more example: in Jesus' farewell discourse in the Gospel of John, he promises his disciples that after his death God will send the Holy Spirit to instruct them, to which is added in the Pauline epistles and elsewhere other functions of the Holy Spirit, including sanctification and inspiration. Here too these terms do not carry with them precise criteria for their application, and there can be debate over when they apply. But we can understand instruction and sanctification well enough to have some basis for determining the extent to which these promises are fulfilled.[6]

Thus far I have been restricting myself to sense perceptual observations that would be recognized as such by my positivist opponents. But when we raise the question of whether empirical evidence should be restricted in this way, more putative possibilities for empirical confirmation and disconfirmation are opened up. I will approach this gradually by first introducing a kind of case that, at least partially, involves ordinary sense perception. Consider life after death as a doctrine of theistic religion. And if a connection with God is needed, consider that in Christianity this is promised by Jesus Christ, the incarnation of the second person of the divine Trinity. Although it is highly controversial, many people, including many eminent philosophers and other intellectuals, believe that we have empirical evidence from mediumistic seances and other attempts to communicate with the dead for survival of death. The reports of seances are, of course, reports of what has been visually, tactually, and auditorily observed. Other alleged empirical evidence is of a more *outré* sort, involving paranormal, extra-sensory perception of various sorts. I cannot go into all this here, but it would have to be explored in a comprehensive discussion of whether "sophisticated" religious beliefs are capable of empirical test.

But the most controversial possibility concerns the direct experience of the presence and activity of God in people's lives that enormous numbers of people take themselves to have had. Many reasons have been given for discrediting reports of such experiences as having any real bearing on the truth of beliefs about the existence, nature, and activity of God. For example, Nielsen is typical of atheists in dismissing such experiences as being purely subjective and having no claim to be an experience of a transcendent deity.[7] I have carried out an extensive treatment of the issues involved and have concluded that it is reasonable to take such experiences as providing a significant degree of support for the beliefs their subjects take them to support[8] (see also Chapter 9). For a larger sample of the data than I have in my book, I refer the reader elsewhere.[9]

This is only the tip of the iceberg, but it should be enough to indicate that the question of whether what Nielsen and Martin consider "sophisticated" beliefs about God are capable of some empirical confirmation and disconfirmation is a very complex one, the answer to which is by no means obvious.

Various construals of God-talk

If one is convinced that no utterances about God, as construed in developed theistic religion, are factually meaningful, how will one construe them? There are a number of alternatives here. The simplest one is to avoid the necessity of any reconception by ignoring them altogether or, in Hume's memorable phrase, "consigning them to the flames." But if one is sufficiently motivated to retain God-talk, there are a number of ways to do so while avoiding any reference to a transcendent deity. These can be divided into two main groups. One seeks to preserve the statemental character by giving a purely natural-world meaning to God-talk. The other chooses to interpret putatively statemental talk about God as expressive of feelings, attitudes, commitments, and the like.

Here are two examples of the first alternative. The American theologian Henry Nelson Wieman defines "God" in naturalistic terms as "that interaction between individuals, groups, and ages which generates and promotes the greatest possible mutuality of good."[10] This preserves the beneficence of God, but the personal being is completely lost. In defense of his suggestion Wieman says:

> Can men pray to an interaction? Yes, that is what they always pray to, under any concept of God? Can men love an interaction? Yes, that is what they always love. When I love Mr. Jones, it is not Mr. Jones in the abstract, but the fellowship of Mr. Jones. Fellowship is a kind of interaction.[11]

Another naturalistic reinterpretation of theistic talk is found in the English biologist Julian Huxley's book *Religion without Revelation*.[12] He identifies God the Father with the forces of nonhuman nature (the "creator"), God the Holy Spirit as the ideals for which men, at their best, are striving, and God the Son as humanity itself, which is, more or less, utilizing the forces of nature in the pursuit of those ideals. Thus he gives us a naturalistic Trinity. He even includes the unity of the three persons in one God under the guise of the essential unity of all these aspects of nature.

The second group is extremely varied. The early twentieth-century Spanish American philosopher, George Santayana, took religious doctrines as primarily symbolic of value commitments and attitudes. In his *Reason in Religion*,[13] he distinguished two components of a religious doctrine, or "myth" as he preferred to say. There is (a) an evaluation of some sort, which is (b) expressed in the form of a picture or story. For example, the Christian "myth" of God's incarnation in Jesus Christ and his sacrificial and unmerited death on the cross to atone for the sins of men can be regarded as a symbol of the moral value of self-sacrifice. That moral conviction can be expressed much more forcefully and effectively by the story than by just saying "Self-sacrifice is a noble thing." Santayana also considers religious myths to have the function of guiding our lives in certain directions. Braithwaite also emphasizes this directive function. He takes religious statements "as being primarily declarations of adherence to a policy of action, declarations of commitment to a way of life."[14] We also find such an approach in the work of the American theologian Gordon Kaufman: "Living in relation to God is living in the world-view that has God as its focus. There is no need to posit a particular existent being, 'God.'"[15] He says that the question of the existence of God is a question of the viability and appropriateness of an orientation, a true or valid understanding of human existence.[16]

It is clear that much speech about God does have these expressive and directive functions, and if we have discarded the truth claims that are ordinarily taken to undergird those functions, the former will be all that is left. But we will be forced into these reconstruals by the verifiability criterion only if more traditionally construed statements about God are not empirically confirmable, and only if empirical confirmability is a necessary condition of factual meaningfulness. I have presented reasons for doubting the former in the previous section, and I will now proceed to consider whether we should accept the latter.

The verifiability criterion and its problems

I will first look at what can be said for the verifiability criterion and then at some reasons to reject it. Some, but not all, of the latter considerations will emerge in my critical remarks about the pro-side.

The original logical positivists did not give a great deal of attention to defending the criterion. Being struck with what they took to be the unprogressive state of philosophy in contrast with science, and with what they considered to be the puzzling nature of typical philosophical pronouncements, they took it as obvious that the reason for the contrast of traditional philosophy with science in these respects stemmed from the fact that the statements of the former were not, as scientific hypotheses were, subject to empirical confirmation or disconfirmation. And since they took science, along with its roots in commonsense empirical thought and discourse, to be the paradigm of factual meaningfulness, it seemed apparent to them that capacity for empirical confirmation and disconfirmation was what factual meaningfulness amounted to. But this line of argument naturally carried no conviction to those who were not prepared to restrict factual statements to science and its prescientific roots, and to whom it seemed equally obvious that it was to be found elsewhere – in metaphysics, ethics, and religion.

Kai Nielsen, seconded again by Michael Martin, rests his case for the verifiability criterion primarily on the claim that it is precisely what distinguishes "clear cases" of factual meaningfulness from clear cases of factual meaninglessness.[17] Armed with these credentials, it can then be used in application to less clear controversial cases like those of metaphysics and religion. Unfortunately for this line of argument, there is as much controversy over what counts as clear and unclear cases of the presence or absence of factual meaningfulness as there is over the verifiability criterion for this. With respect to our central concern here, it seems to a great many – both theists and atheists – that sentences such as

> God exercises providence over human affairs.
> It is God's purpose that we love one another.
> The physical universe depends for its existence on an omnipotent spiritual being.

are clear cases of factual claims that are objectively true or false. And if they are not subject to empirical test, then *so much the worse for the verifiability criterion*. Similar points can be made about empirically unverifiable statements in metaphysics such as "Properties have a mode of existence that is independent of their being exemplified" and "A human being is made up of two substances – one material and one immaterial."

A more substantive argument depends on considerations of the crucial role of perceptual experience in learning and using a language. It seems clear that first-language learning is heavily dependent on social reinforcement of associations between perceived features of the environment and words for those features. These have to be publicly observable features; otherwise, the parent or other "reinforcer" would not be able to provide positive or negative reinforcement at the appropriate junctures. Thus it seems that at the base of a first language is a set of observation sentences that are fitted to make statements that are directly verified or falsified by sense perception – "That is an apple" or "That is a chair." In this way the foundation of a language clearly satisfies the verifiability criterion. If the further development of the child's grasp of language into higher, more complex levels, inherits this empirical testability, this is a strong argument for the verifiability criterion. Add to this the point that unless statements in the more complex upper stories of the linguistic edifice were also responsible to empirical testing, it would be impossible for anyone to know whether the speaker was using language correctly or not.

Though this line of argument raises serious issues about language and meaning into which I cannot enter here, I will mention some reasons for thinking that the situation is not quite so rosy for the positivist as the above exposition makes it appear. The main difficulty is this: once the speaker of a language has a base of empirically established terms (plus some grasp of syntax), it is well within human cognitive powers to put these materials and their derivatives into complexes that transcend the possibilities of empirical testing. For example, having learned the meanings of *power*, *knowledge*, *more*, *limit*, *not*, *person*, and *exist*, it takes only normal human intelligence to be able to construct the sentence, "There exists a person with unlimited power and knowledge" and wonder whether the statement that sentence can be used to make is true. And even if the statement is beyond the possibility of empirical testing, it seems clear that by the procedure just sketchily described, the speaker who asserts it is making a genuinely factual claim to truth.

This is not a peripheral difficulty; rather, it indicates a *deep defect* in verificationism. The position concentrates on a holistic feature of the statemental potential of a declarative sentence and ignores the crucial point that the semantic status of a linguistic complex like a sentence is some function of the meanings of its meaningful constituents plus facts about its grammatical structure. By restricting its sights to the question of whether a statement that the sentence is standardly usable to make can be empirically tested, the position ignores the point (brought out in the last paragraph) that the way a sentence is built up from its components can result in usability to make a factual statement, with an objective truth-value, regardless of whether we can specify a possible empirical test for it. We will see another, related, case of shortsightedness in the next section.

The chief argument against the verifiability criterion

Apart from the criticism just leveled, the main argument against the verifiability criterion stems from a feature of empirical confirmation that was reflected in the setting out of the notion in the section "The criterion, its history, and the most coherent form of the theory," but not emphasized there. This is the fact that it is logically impossible to deduce one or more observation statements from a statement in non-observational terms without using auxiliary premises – "bridge principles" that contain both observational and non-observational terms – thereby making possible a logical implication of the purely observational conclusions from the whole set of premises. Thus laws of thermodynamics, when conjoined with principles that spell out how to measure the temperature of a substance, can be tested by such measures. For this reason, no statement that is not itself a purely observation statement carries any "empirical content," any set of observational consequences all on its own. It does so *only in the context of a larger body of theory*, which, whatever else it includes, must contain one or more bridge principles. Thus empirical testing of claims not directly testable by experience is much more complex than any simple confrontation with the results of observation.

Why does this make trouble for verificationism? The reason is that no one has been able to put restrictions on bridge principles that will let in non-observational statements the verificationists want to treat as empirically testable and rule out those they do not. Here is a simple example of the latter. We can take any non-observational statement, say, "God is perfectly good," and make it subject to empirical test by conjoining it with a hypothetical statement like, "If God is perfectly good, then it will rain here tomorrow." This conjunction implies "It will rain here tomorrow," and this makes an observation of the weather have a bearing on the justification of the theological statement. No doubt, it would be absurd to accept this bridge principle. But bridge principles in science itself often have no independent plausibility. Here is the way it typically goes. Prior to the development of precise measures of temperature, people could, of course, make rough judgments of hotter and colder as we all do in everyday life. But that was not good enough for testing mathematically precise laws of thermodynamics. For that we need bridge principles that specify observable conditions under which a temperature will have a certain numerical value. And that means ways have to be developed to measure temperature. Confining this brief illustration to the simplest levels, consider the development of mercury thermometers. It was a rough common observation that heat tends to expand substances, especially liquids. Some observations of mercury under what seemed to be different temperatures suggested that the height of mercury in a glass cylinder might provide a good measure of temperature. That was tried and with successive refinements it turned out that this way of measuring temperatures (within certain ranges) gave results that provided strong empirical confirmation for a number of useful laws.

Two things are to be noted about this process. First, at the outset there was no strong confirmation of the bridge principle that connected different temperature values with the height of a column of mercury; it was a plausible hunch based on rough everyday experience. Second, such confirmation as was eventually obtained for the validity of this way of measuring came from the way in which it fitted in with a complex body of theory, no part of which had any confirmation independent of the complex to which the bridge principle itself belongs along with various law-like hypotheses, the testing of which it made possible.

What this indicates is something important about how we distinguish between cases of connecting non-observational hypotheses with observations so as to make empirical testing of the former possible that are scientifically acceptable from those that are not. We do so on the basis of the fruitfulness of a large complex of hypotheses, theories, bridge principles, and observations, fruitfulness for the development of science. The distinction is not made on the basis of any formal logical criteria. That could be done only if a formal logical criterion could be developed for distinguishing acceptable from unacceptable bridge principles, and despite a great deal of effort no one has been able to do this. The above discussion reveals that this is no accident. It has not been done because the distinction depends on what pans out in a complex research program and what does not. My earlier example concerning God's goodness and rain tomorrow strikes one as absurd just because it does not hook up with success in an ongoing research program the way my thermodynamics example does (or would if properly extended). And this is not a formal logical difference. It is true that my theological example was not set in a larger complex the way the other one was, but we could easily do this by multiplying theological propositions and bridge principles to any given extent. It still would not look like anything that hooks up high-level theological principles with empirical data in a way that is of any value from any point of view.

Where does this leave us? It shows us that no formal logical criteria of empirical confirmability will distinguish positivistically approved cases from positivistically disapproved cases. And more than that, it shows that such criteria do not even distinguish obviously factually meaningful sentences from nonsense sentences. My earlier example of "God is good" could be repeated and elaborated upon just as well with the hypothesis "Friday is intelligent" – something that is uncontroversially without factual meaning. But, and this is a point that is often neglected, that does not by itself show that factual meaningfulness does not require empirical confirmability. It could be that the problem is with the attempt to give a formal logical account of the latter. And these considerations do at least show that no purely logical criterion can bring out what it is for a hypothesis to be empirically confirmable. But that leaves standing the possibility that factual meaning requires empirical confirmability. Since the failure of the usual purely logical way of explaining that the latter does not work, its failure to bring out what constitutes factual meaning does not show that factual meaning does not amount to empirical confirmability.

But even though it does not show that, we are still without any good reason for supposing that empirical confirmability is required for factual meaningfulness. The preceding discussion shows that to go further into the issue we will have to abandon any purely logical account of empirical confirmability and proceed on the basis of more intuitive judgments about when we have empirical confirmability and about when we have something that is factually meaningful. I will now present a couple of considerations that seem to me to make it extremely plausible that there are factual claims that have objective truth-values – whether or not they are empirically testable.

First, it is not hard to find examples in which it is extremely difficult to avoid recognizing that a certain statement is making a genuine truth claim even if it is not susceptible to empirical confirmation. Many people both within and outside religion have been seriously concerned with whether certain religious statements are true. Take, for example, the statement that the physical universe owes its existence to the creative activity of a supreme, spiritual personal being, or that such a being exercises active providence over our lives, or that such a being is concerned with bringing us into a loving relationship with him/herself. For many people it has been a major preoccupation in their lives to decide whether such statements are true. Not even the most hard-core positivist doubts that many people take such language to express genuine truth claims; that is why they are so concerned to determine whether they are true. Is this because they are confusing factual statements with other uses of language? Are they all simply failing to distinguish factual statements from expressions of emotional reactions or commitments to programs of action or certain ways of looking at human life? No doubt, people not infrequently are confused about such distinctions. But it strains credulity to suppose that all the people who are seriously – even desperately – worried about whether such statements are true are simply chasing a will-o'-the-wisp. And this is especially incredible in the light of what we have seen to be the absence of any strong reasons for denying the factual meaningfulness of such sentences.

The same sort of point could be made by attending to those for whom such statements express firm beliefs confidently held. It is typical for such people to orient their lives around these convictions. Their sense of their place in the world, of the purpose of their lives, their priorities for the disposition of their time and energies, what they take to be the ultimate fulfillment at which they aim, is intimately tied up with what they take to be their relationship with God in the light of what they believe to be the case about God, His purposes, His activities, His program for our lives, and His promises to them. Thus the whole organization of their lives depends on what they believe to the truth about God and His relations with human beings. How can it be doubted that when they formulate some of these beliefs, they are making genuine truth claims? Surely we must take their supposition that this is what they are doing to be correct until it is shown otherwise; and, so far as I can see, attempts to show otherwise are complete failures.

Another consideration pointing in the same direction can be drawn from a different quarter – the history of science. Scientific hypotheses (e.g. the atomic hypothesis concerning the constitution of matter) were originally put forward without anyone as yet having any idea how they could be empirically tested. Eventually the atomic hypothesis was brought into effective connection with empirical tests. But unless the hypothesis was understandable *as a factual claim* at the earlier stages, those developments would have been impossible. If the utterance "All matter is made up of tiny invisible particles" were functioning in some way other than as a statement of fact that is objectively either true or false depending on whether all matter is so constituted, then there could have been no problem of how it could be subjected to an empirical test, and the various scientific developments that made this possible would never have occurred. Thus the expression of the initial hunch must have already been functioning as a truth claim before it was discovered how to put it to empirical test. This history is typical of the development of scientific theories, in which the earliest stage is a creative invention of interesting speculations, which are then (sometimes) followed by a successful search for ways of bringing them into effective connection with modes of empirical testing. We can find many such examples in chemistry, in biology, and in psychology.

This point is intimately connected with the discussion in the last section of the way in which non-observational hypotheses need to be connected with bridge principles in order to be logically related to observation statements. Put in those terms, the above point is that hypotheses in non-observational terms are typically formulated *before* they become married to bridge principles. And it is absurd to think that they are miraculously transformed from some non-factual status to factual statements at the moment of that marriage. That would imply an incredible dissociation between an aim and its fulfillment. If the successful yoking of hypothesis to bridge principles were not the outcome of an aim to find some way of finding out whether the (true or false) hypothesis were true, the entire process would make no sense at all.

Conclusion

Thus, as I take it, verificationism is but a paper tiger, in philosophy of religion as elsewhere. It poses no threat to the apparently obvious truth that talk of God contains many statements about God that have objective truth-values – whether we can determine what they are or not. Even if the verifiability criterion were unassailable as a necessary condition for truth claims, it has not been shown that this condition is violated by all or most alleged statements about God in theistic religion, however sophisticated it may be. As indicated above, there are many uneliminated possibilities for perceptual reports to count for or against theological statements. But, and most decisively, the criterion is far from unassailable. Such reasons as have been offered in its support do not begin to make it rationally acceptable. And there are strong reasons for denying that empirical confirmability-disconfirmability is necessary for an utterance's having an objective truth-value. And so those who are concerned with the truth-value of claims about God need not worry that they are chasing a will-o'-the-wisp, at least not because of problems about empirical testability.

This conclusion by no means implies that there are not serious problems about how to understand predicates applied to God. There certainly are, and these problems even raise questions about how determinate statements about God can be. These problems have been discussed within theistic religions from the earliest times, and there is no sign that the discussion is at an end. I cannot go into the issues properly at the tag end of this article, which has been concerned with other matters, but here is a brief presentation of the main source of the problems.[18] Since we are in no position to develop a special repertoire of theological predicates (for lack of an inter-subjectively reliable way of telling when a person is perceiving God as exhibiting one or another property or activity), we are forced to borrow terms from our talk of creatures – primarily human beings – in speaking of God. The action terms (*make*, *speak*, *command*, *forgive*, *punish*), the psychological-state terms (*knows*, *intends*, *purposes*, *chooses*), and the property terms (*good*, *powerful*, *loving*, *just*) were all originally learned in their application to creatures. But God, as construed in developed theistic religion, is so radically different from any creatures that it is impossible to use the terms with exactly the same sense (univocally) in application to God as they bear in application to creatures. Hence they must be altered in some way to make them appropriate for divine application, to make it at least possible that they are true of God. If we could modify the creaturely sense so as to produce terms with meanings that fit God exactly, there would be no problem. But there are a variety of reasons for doubting that this is possible. For one thing, we are limited to forms of assertion that require us to distinguish between a property and what has that property (reflecting the distinction between the subject and predicate of the assertion), as well as between different properties we attribute to the same subject. But Aquinas and other leading medieval theologians and philosophers held that God is so absolutely simple that there are no real distinctions of any kind within his being, and hence that any mode of speech that implies distinctions (and that includes all human speech) is bound to misrepresent God to some extent. Aquinas and other advocates of divine simplicity did not think that all assertions about God are false, much less meaningless. Aquinas held that certain terms we apply to God (such as *good* and *omniscient*) fit God well with respect to the "perfection signified," but that they all fall short with respect to the "mode of signification," which inevitably implies multiplicity in the Divine Being.[19] This being the case, although we can reasonably suppose that the terms we apply to God signify some analogy with the Divine Being, the fact that none of them is perfectly adequate for the purpose prevents us from being completely explicit about what the points of analogy are – in just what way the things originally signified by the terms do and do not enjoy a commonality with the Divine Being.

And even if one rejects absolute divine simplicity, there are other reasons for supposing that none of our terms fits God adequately. Just what these are depends on our basic conception of God. For one more example, take the view, much more prevalent in ancient and medieval than in modern times, that God enjoys an atemporal mode of being, that He does not live through a temporal succession of moments, but lives in an "eternal now." Talk of creatures is so permeated with temporal distinctions that many have despaired of modifying creaturely terms so as to make them truly applicable to an atemporal being, though the matter is controversial.[20]

In any event, as noted, I cannot go into these issues properly here and now. The foregoing will have to suffice as a brief indication that even when we dismiss the challenge of verificationism, as I have sought to do here, we are by no means home free with respect to the status of talk about God. I believe that the problems briefly adumbrated in this section can be handled without abandoning genuine truth claims about God, but that is a topic for another occasion.

Notes

1 Moritz Schlick, "Meaning and Verification," in *Readings in Philosophical Analysis*, Herbert Feigl and Wilfrid Sellars (eds) (New York: Appleton-Century-Crofts, 1955), 148.
2 Antony Flew, "Theology and Falsification," in *New Essays in Philosophical Theology*, Antony Flew and Alasdair Macintyre (eds) (London: SCM Press, 1955), 99.
3 Kai Nielsen, *Contemporary Critiques of Religion* (New York: Herder & Herder, 1971), 57. Cf. Michael Martin, *Atheism: A Philosophical Justification* (Philadelphia: Temple University Press, 1990), 49–50.
4 Martin, *Atheism*, 40–78.
5 Ibid., 45.
6 For an extended discussion of this kind of issue see William P. Alston, "The Fulfillment of Promises as Evidence for Religious Belief," *Logos* 12 (1991), 1–26.
7 Nielsen, *Contemporary Critiques of Religion*, 23, 46–53.
8 William P. Alston, *Perceiving God* (Ithaca, NY: Cornell University Press, 1991).
9 William James, *The Varieties of Religious Experience* (New York: The Modern Library, 1902), and Timothy Beardsworth, *A Sense of Presence* (Oxford: Oxford Religious Experience Research Unit, 1977).
10 Henry Nelson Wieman, in *Is There a God?*, D. C. MacIntosh, and Rudolph Otto (eds) (Chicago: Willett, Clark, 1932), 15.
11 Ibid., 17.
12 Julian Huxley, *Religion Without Revelation* (New York: The New American Library, 1957).
13 George Santayana, *Reason in Religion* (New York: Charles Scribner's Sons, 1905).
14 R. G. Braithwaite, *An Empiricist's View of the Nature of Religious Belief* (Cambridge: Cambridge University Press, 1955), 80.
15 Gordon Kaufman, *In Face of Mystery: A Constructive Theology* (Cambridge, MA: Harvard University Press, 1993), 8.
16 Ibid., 35–46.
17 Nielsen, *Contemporary Critiques of Religion*, 65–71.
18 For more extended discussion, see Ian Crombie, "Theology and Falsification" in *New Essays in Philosophical Theology*; Ian Crombie, "The Possibility of Theological Statements," in *Faith and Logic*, Basil Mitchell (ed.) (London: George Allen & Unwin, 1957); and Ian G. Barbour, *Myths, Models, and Paradigms* (New York: Harper & Row, 1974).
19 For a presentation and critical discussion of Aquinas on this topic, see William P. Alston, "Aquinas on Theological Predication: A Look Backward and a Look Forward," in *Reasoned Faith*, Eleonore Stump (ed.) (Ithaca, NY: Cornell University Press, 1993), 145–78.
20 See Brian Leftow, *Time and Eternity* (Ithaca, NY: Cornell Univesity Press, 1991).

2

FAITH AND FOUNDATIONALISM

David K. Clark

Mark Twain famously defined "faith" as "believing something you know ain't so." Although that is clearly tongue in cheek, people of faith do say quite seriously that they believe something because they "take it by faith." This common phrase, as used by Christian believers, means holding some belief even without specific evidence for that particular belief. Is that a problem? Can someone hold religious beliefs without evidence to support them?

Believing without evidence

Naturalists commonly argue that believers cannot know a religious doctrine unless they can give evidence to support it. Any doctrinal claim or religious belief – say, "God exists" or "God has forgiven me" – needs evidence to support it. Some non-religious epistemologists promote a principle that requires religious people to produce objectively testable, empirical, or evidential reasons to support what they believe. This requirement is the heart of evidentialism. Philosophers associate evidentialism most closely with W. K. Clifford (1845–79).[1] Today, thinkers like Michael Martin and Kai Nielsen are Clifford's philosophical cousins. From an evidentialist stance, it follows – or seems to – that it is (virtually) never right to hold religious doctrines or to ground theological beliefs by faith.

Many kinds of believing count as "taking it by faith." What these have in common is their *lack* of an evidential basis. The positive reasons to hold beliefs that lack evidence can vary considerably. Religious people ground beliefs that are not based on evidence in different ways. So the set of all cases of "taking it by faith" has diverse members.

One kind of "taking it by faith" is holding something as true because it comes from an authoritative religious source. This involves taking the word of another. By trusting experts, the knower accepts their testimony. Anyone who accepts the experts say-so will ride their epistemic coattails. All people learn much of what they know from others. But that is not my focus here.

Another kind of "taking it by faith," or believing without evidence, is holding a religious belief as "properly basic." A *basic* belief forms in a person when that person knows it directly without inferring or deducing it from other beliefs. If a basic belief forms rightly – if nothing in the belief-forming process goes haywire – then it is *properly* basic. As I talk with Simon, the belief emerges in my mind that Simon is an actual person, a mind, and not just a robotic body that I detect with my five senses. I do not *infer* my belief from anything. I do not build an argument using premises rooted in my observation of his body movements and leading to a conclusion that Simon is an actual person. I just know Simon is more than a body. The belief is basic. In the same direct way, I can come to know God's existence – so some religious epistemologists claim.

Still another form of "taking it by faith," for Christians at any rate, is knowing directly by way of trusting the inner witness of the Holy Spirit (*sensus divinitatis*). This kind of knowing is by way of a divine enabling. This is a special case of properly basic believing. The witness of the Spirit has special meaning in the Reformed theological tradition of John Calvin. Calvin taught that believers know the Bible is God's Word – that God, by His inspiration, is an author of the Bible – because the Holy Spirit teaches them. The Bible says that the Spirit witnesses to believers that they are God's children (Romans 8:16). Now if these are possible, then perhaps believers can know certain other things directly from God.

These are examples of "taking it by faith." But notice that in the Bible, "faith" does not mean "accepting an idea as true without evidence." How does the Bible connect being "saved by faith" (see Ephesians 2:8–9) to the idea of "knowing by faith"? In English, "faith" functions grammatically only as a noun. In New Testament Greek, *pisteō,* "[to have] faith" or "to believe," is a verb that denotes personally trusting in, faithfully relying upon, or committing oneself to, a person. Faith is most like the "I do" of the wedding ceremony. It is not primarily a process of thinking or knowing. It is more a promise of loyalty along with a life of faithfully fulfilling that promise.

The Reformers helpfully distinguished *notitia*, *assensus*, and *fiducia*. *Notitia* denotes the content of the faith, the great doctrines of the Bible. *Assensus* indicates the mental act of accepting those teachings as true. And *fiducia* signifies the believer's whole-soul act of personally committing to, trusting in, and promising loyalty to the divine personal Being described in those doctrines. The truths of *notitia* denote the divine personal Being – God – and the believer accepts these truths in *assensus*. But the key is this: salvation – relationship to God – happens as the believer goes beyond mental assent to personal trust and loyalty. Biblically, faith is intricately *connected to* believing central truths about God (some of which believers will take by faith), but faith is definitely not *identical to* believing them.

This chapter is about *assensus*. Naturalists often insist that if *assensus* by faith is allowed, epistemic chaos follows. They typically say that if non-evidential beliefs are legitimate, this opens the gates to all sorts of epistemic chicanery. Suppose I claim that I can rightly take it by faith that God loves me. What is to keep just anyone from claiming to know anything by faith? Would this not imply that the members of the Heaven's Gate cult believed rationally, in a basic way, that they would ride through Heaven's Gate to the Upper Level on the Hale–Bopp comet?

Naturalist Michael Martin makes this criticism in several places. Alvin Plantinga, a Christian, states that essential Christian beliefs "are a proper *starting point* for thought." Christian thinking can *begin with* religious ideas. It is not necessary to infer all religious ideas from non-religious ideas.[2] But Martin thinks that is wrong. He describes as faulty Plantinga's assertion that religious belief can rightly form the basis or starting point for thinking. It is a "radically relativistic" view that puts any belief that functions at this basic level "beyond rational appraisal."[3] William Lane Craig, a contributor to this book, asserts that Christians can rightly know that God exists "by the self-authenticating witness of God's Holy Spirit."[4] Again, Martin thinks not. He complains, "Since people have all sorts of experiences that seem true to them and are not, it behooves Craig to explain why the experience of the Holy Spirit is any different. He fails to do this."[5]

Different projects in epistemology

To sort this out, notice that the question points us back to a tension between two different projects that lie at the core of epistemology. The goal of the knowing process is to understand truly. This goal has two prongs. On the one hand, people want and *need* to know what is true:

1   How can I believe, in a legitimate way, as many true beliefs as possible?

One way to respond to question 1 is to believe anything and everything. But there is a downside. That strategy produces many true beliefs. But, like the proverbial needles in the haystack, they would be mixed with a lot of epistemic straw. It could lead one to accept far too many illegitimate or false beliefs.

So, on the other hand, to understand the world truly, human beings also want and *need* to escape error:

2   How can I avoid believing as many false beliefs as possible?

One way to answer question 2 is to adopt a global skepticism. If someone believes nothing at all, she shall surely believe nothing false. But of course, using that procedure, she would overlook many beliefs that are both true and important. So the human need to know the world truly requires a balance of questions 1 and 2. These goals mutually govern each other, just as the three branches of the United States government put checks and balances on each other. Balancing questions 1 and 2 challenges a knower to maximize the number of important, well-warranted true beliefs she holds and to minimize the number of false beliefs she holds.

In seeking to fulfill this goal, epistemologists address at least two very different issues:

3   What do I mean by 'knowledge'?

The point here is to give an account, develop a theory, or offer a description of the concept of knowledge. If *x* is any case of genuine knowledge, then for any *x*, what are its essential features?

But this is very different from the following:

4   How can I identify particular instances of knowledge and cases of error?

The point here is to catalog, evaluate, and coordinate procedures to pick out instances of genuine knowledge. If someone wishes to evaluate whether *x* is really a case of knowledge, what coordinated set of strategies can he employ? This is the attempt to specify tactics for locating knowledge. The distinction between these two projects is critical.

Foundationalism and its alternative

A traditional way to answer question 3 is this: an instance of knowledge is an idea that has three features. First, it is true. Second, someone believes it. And third, some fact legitimates the belief in question for that person. But why is it wrong to define "knowledge" as "true belief"? Because one can hold true beliefs completely by accident. And that is *not* knowledge. If I guess the winning lottery number when I buy the ticket on Monday, I might convince myself on the next Friday when I win that *I really did know* the number on Monday. My guess was a true belief, as it turns out. But I could hardly say that on Monday I actually had genuine knowledge. I was guessing! Knowledge requires some kind of "legitimating fact" that distinguishes merely true belief (like lucky guesses) from actual knowledge. This third factor is very controversial (not to say that the other two points are simple).

How exactly can one understand and locate this "legitimating fact"? One important way to think about the "legitimating fact" that turns merely true belief into genuine knowledge is called foundationalism. The word "foundationalism" has several different connotations. Some thinkers, especially in contemporary theology, identify a *holistic method* or a *complex authoritative truth source* as a foundation. To denote this approach, I use the phrase "source-foundationalism." In this kind of foundationalism, the foundation of knowledge is some transcultural logic or language, some universal method like science, or an authoritative religious tradition or book like the Qur'an. Source-foundationalism is that typically modernist notion that "knowledge is the reflection of truth and that we can discover a stable foundation for it in God, History or Reason."[6] From a postmodern viewpoint, source-foundationalism did not produce the liberty and progress it promised. Ironically, according to postmodern critique, the modern thirst for human freedom, by means of objectivity in truth and certitude in knowledge, led toward an absolutist philosophical style that enslaves more than ever.

By contrast, belief-foundationalism, the subject of this chapter, is a class of theories about the *relationships between individual beliefs* within a person's belief system. It says that the relationships between individual beliefs are like a house where a concrete foundation supports the rest of the building. Within the structure of a person's beliefs, basic beliefs (the concrete foundation) ground non-basic beliefs (the building). Though a person knows basic beliefs directly, she knows non-basic beliefs *indirectly* or *inferentially*. I know, for instance, that the 1995 Chevy truck I just bought will get about 15 miles per gallon (mpg) because I read in *Consumer Reports* that trucks like mine generally get about 15 mpg. That makes this belief non-basic. Any theory of epistemology that distinguishes basic (directly grounded) and non-basic (indirectly inferred) beliefs is a member of the class that I am calling belief-foundationalism.

In belief-foundationalism, the "legitimating fact" – that quality that turns merely true belief into genuine knowledge – can *transfer* from a basic belief to a non-basic belief. Say, for example, that I am driving down the road in Minnesota in January, and I look out and see the local chapter of the Polar Bear Club standing in their bathing suits, chopping a hole in the ice on a lake. Inside my toasty car, I feel warm. But I infer from some basic beliefs I form in my mind (plus other background beliefs – I know how cold January gets in Minnesota) that they are *really* cold (and also *crazy*). The basic belief gives me reason to believe the non-basic belief. Now foundationalism implies that basic beliefs provide the "legitimating fact" for the non-basic ones. But it *does not work the other way around*. The "legitimating fact" only travels in one direction, not in both directions. This is a key feature of any belief-foundationalism.

Now why think this way? Essentially, belief-foundationalism is a way to block an infinite regress. If a knower must back up every belief with other beliefs, then he is quickly off and running on an infinite chain. If belief x needs the backing of y, and y needs the backing of z, and z needs the backing of . . ., well, this could go on forever. So somewhere, if he knows anything at all, a knower must find some beliefs to start with, some beliefs that are not backed up by other beliefs. Such beliefs, without the knowing process will never get started. Every inference begins with premises. Without some premises that are independent of prior premises, one could never get an argument going. So "if there is any knowledge at all then there must be some source of knowledge other than argumentation."[7]

Belief-foundationalism is subject to critique, of course. Those who object to belief-foundationalism (but still hold a realist account of knowledge) often opt for a main competitor, coherentism. "Coherentism" denotes a class of theories according to which the "legitimating fact" arises entirely from the logical fit of various beliefs with each other. That is, belief x implies y, y implies z, and z implies x. Here, all beliefs are part of a large circular argument, or better, an interlocking web. In this scenario, beliefs x, y, and z do not relate in a single circular chain, but rather as a highly integrated network. In both cases, however, the connection between beliefs does not merely *transfer* the "legitimating fact," as in belief-foundationalism, but *generates* it. The "legitimating fact" travels in both directions. In coherentism, satisfying the principle of coherence is *necessary and sufficient* for knowledge.

Laurence BonJour once defended coherentism strongly, and Martin intimates that BonJour's coherentism clears the hurdles that foundationalism trips over.[8] Two features of coherentism seem correct. The first is that avoiding incoherence is a *necessary* feature of any true set of beliefs. The second is that coherentism correctly emphasizes the *independence principle*: non-basic beliefs that are legitimized by connection to larger numbers of independent – but mutually coherent – beliefs are more adequately grounded than those legitimized by few beliefs.[9]

Despite these advantages, however, coherentism suffers two fatal difficulties. First is the "input problem." If coherence alone legitimizes beliefs, this seems to make experience (for example, perception) unnecessary. But that seems wrongheaded. Surely, beliefs about the natural world gain their "legitimating fact" from the actual experience of perception. When I see a bird with blue feathers, the "legitimating fact" that grounds my knowledge arises from the fact that I am looking at the bird with my eyes, not from the fact that my belief, "That's a bluebird," fits coherently with other things I believe.

Second is the "alternative coherent systems problem." Coherentism makes coherence not just *necessary* to a true set of interconnected beliefs, but *sufficient* as an indicator of truth. Coherentism goes beyond making the principle of coherence a *criterion* for truth. Coherence ends up *constituting* what is true. Assuming a unity of truth, any set of true beliefs is necessarily coherent, of course. But it does not follow that the coherence of a set of beliefs is *sufficient* to justify their truth. It is possible to construct an infinite number of sets of beliefs where the sets are each internally coherent, but mutually exclusive of each other. Coherentism leaves us with no way to adjudicate among these sets.

Coherentism gives a thumbs-up to an absurdly large number of sets of false propositions. So naturalists who commit to coherentism are vulnerable. It is coherentism that leads to "radically relativistic" beliefs. Coherentism makes beliefs "absurdly easy to warrant." Indeed, for reasons like these, BonJour himself, the one-time champion of coherentism, has now extricated himself from what he called the "barren labyrinths of coherentism" and has adopted foundationalism.[10]

Refining belief-foundationalism

Belief-foundationalism needs refinement. One question is this: what sorts of beliefs may I rightly construe as basic? How stringent are the criteria for properly basic beliefs? One answer is found in classical foundationalism, a particularly stringent form of belief-foundationalism. Like every kind of belief-foundationalism, classical foundationalism sees some beliefs grounded in other, more basic beliefs. But unlike other versions of belief-foundationalism, it defends very strict rules about what kinds of beliefs are legitimately seen as basic. In one version of classical foundationalism, basic beliefs need to be *self-evident* (3 + 4 = 7) or *incorrigible* ("I feel thirsty").

In contrast, other forms of belief-foundationalism are more modest. Modest foundationalism is any member of a set of views that has looser criteria for proper basicality. One kind of modest foundationalism is Reformed epistemology, associated with Alvin Plantinga, William Alston (a contributor to this volume), Nicholas Wolterstorff, and many others.[11] Reformed epistemology (in one version) insists that even religious beliefs (such as "God exists") are rightly construed as properly basic for certain people. And people for whom the belief "God exists" is properly basic regarding warrant are rightly said to *know* that God exists even though they have no evidence or argument for that belief. In a sense, they know by faith that God exists. And there is nothing inherently defective about knowing in that way. Given a Christian view of these things, knowers are committing no epistemic sins. They form their belief through reliable belief-forming processes. But assertions like these stir up naturalists' ire.

A second question is the following: if knowledge is distinguished from merely true belief by some "legitimating fact," must the knowers have clear knowledge of that fact? Or is it enough that a "legitimating fact" exists? Very roughly, those who say that knowers must know the "legitimating fact" will hold internalism. In general, an internalist uses the word "justification" to denote the "legitimating fact." This forms the backdrop for a classic view of these matters – "knowledge" means *justified true belief*. Speaking generally, internalist accounts of epistemology place some sort of duty on knowers to figure out what justifies their beliefs. Knowers have an obligation to ferret out the thing that distinguishes their genuine knowledge from coincidentally true beliefs. If they do not do their duty, it is wrong to say that they know. Now evidentialism is a kind of internalism in which evidence justifies belief. A knower must find the evidence that turns his merely true belief into knowledge.

Those who say it is enough that a "legitimating fact" exists (though knowers are not aware of it) will adopt externalism. Typically, an externalist uses the word "warrant" to denote the "legitimating fact." In one such view, a true belief formed through a reliable process of belief-formation possesses warrant, and so it counts as genuine knowledge. Externalist theories say that some warrant must exist in order for a belief to count as knowledge. But they do not insist that in every case of genuine knowing, the knower himself must investigate or become aware of that fact. Now there is little agreement on the exact nature of the distinctions between justification and warrant or between internalism and externalism. (That is an understatement.) But something like the distinction I have sketched out roughly is at the crux of the discussion.

Why do religious believers think it is right in certain cases, to believe – *assensus* – by faith? In his version of Reformed epistemology, Plantinga argued that if God exists, then knowledge of God's existence can be properly basic.[12] He sees knowledge as true belief formed by reliable belief-forming mechanisms or processes. Obviously, this is an externalist account. If God exists and has created humans with reliable belief-forming processes attuned to his existence, then knowledge can form through the processes. Knowledge of God is grounded in direct experience with God. If Plantinga is right, this is an instance of legitimate knowing of a foundational belief by faith in the sense of "believing in God without evidence."

Naturalists who criticize such theories about religious knowing say that this account of "knowing by faith" just does not carry the necessary epistemic freight. The sorts of complaints illustrated by Michael Martin's comments make the following general point: the procedures that religious believers follow, especially when they claim to know something by faith, are inadequate to separate true beliefs from false. If a Christian believer says, "I know I've sinned because I sense the conviction of the Holy Spirit," naturalists might respond, "But the Heaven's Gate cult members followed that same procedure, and surely you don't think they acquired genuine knowledge!"

Naturalists, therefore, press toward the conclusion that religious knowing of this sort just does not accomplish the goal of epistemology – to balance questions 1 and 2. It fails to find as many true, well-warranted beliefs as possible while minimizing false beliefs, for it allows far too many false ideas to sneak in. Religious believers who think that "taking it by faith" is epistemically legitimate tend to maximize question 1, but fail miserably at question 2. Surely, therefore, religious believers have a duty to produce something beyond a subjective assertion like "the Holy Spirit spoke to me."

That "something more," say the evidentialists, is evidence. Religious claims to knowledge typically lack that evidence. So they should (almost always) be abandoned. In the absence of evidence, naturalists argue, good philosophers will presume that theism and its related claims are false.

Evidentialism as a universal principle

The question comes down to this: is it reasonable to require that religious believers possess evidence for every belief? One way to rebut evidentialism is a frontal attack. Evidentialism is subject to crushing difficulties. Plantinga argued that the only reason to hold evidentialism is that it is an entailment of classical foundationalism. But classical foundationalism is clearly wrong, and for two reasons. Take this as a simple example of a statement of criteria such as are typical of classical foundationalism:

5   A belief is properly basic if and only if it is *self-evident* or *incorrigible*.

The critique explores the reason to believe statement 5. Plantinga argues that statement 5 itself is neither self-evident nor incorrigible. Nor can one infer statement 5 from premises that are. Altering details does not solve the problem. Like statement 5, any near cousins will set up criteria *that they themselves fail*. Thus, classical foundationalism is self-referentially incoherent and is in no position to lend any weight to evidentialism. And in a parallel way, evidentialism is similarly self-refuting. Taken as a universal epistemic principle, evidentialism fails to meet its own demands. Just as there are no evidential arguments that lead to classical foundationalism, so also there are no evidential arguments that could demonstrate evidentialism. The second part of the critique is this: classical foundationalism created strict, rigid standards of knowledge in trying to ensure that no errors creep into anyone's structures of thought. But these overly strict standards are much too limiting. Classical foundationalism eliminates much of what people normally and legitimately know. In fact, it takes skepticism far too seriously.[13] For instance, if classical foundationalism's standards are right, I cannot know that I drank coffee this morning (memory beliefs) or that my Mom really loves me (knowledge of other minds). But surely I do know these things. So classical foundationalism must be false. Observing how people actually do come to know about the world, it is clear that their knowing processes are much more open and flexible than classical foundationalism allows for.[14] So again, therefore, classical foundationalism is not in a position to give aid and comfort to evidentialism. And again, by the way, evidentialism cannot account for many things people rightly know either. Evidence, therefore, just is not the *sine qua non* of knowledge.

Knowing God by faith

The failure of evidentialism means it cannot knock out a particular case of religious knowledge just because a knower cannot support it with evidence. But what is the positive account of "knowing by faith"? Is it legitimate for the Christian to say, "I know God exists for I heard his voice"?[15] Although it sounds counter-intuitive to tough-minded skeptics, many philosophers argue in the affirmative. Consider the following. My Mom lives in Florida. Say that she calls up one morning and says, "Hi, Hon. It's Mom!" Now I immediately form the belief, "I'm talking to Mom." I would not go through any reasoning process from premise to conclusion. I would just know it was she, and talk. "I'm talking to Mom" is properly basic for me.

Although I would jump right to the meat of our conversation, others might need more convincing. If a demented FBI agent thinks my Mom is plotting a crime (which is ridiculous – she is a very sweet person), then he could get his FBI buddies to tape our phone conversation. He could develop an evidentially based argument to prove that I really was talking with my Mom. His electronics buddies could use computerized voice analysis equipment to turn Mom's voice into a visual pattern. They could compare that with other samples of Mom speaking. This might convince our demented FBI agent that the call I received really was from my Mom.

Even though all that FBI work is possible, obviously, that is not how *I* know that I am talking to Mom. I know immediately, without any specific evidence, that it is she. It would not occur to me to think that I should look for evidence. I would never even imagine that I ought to pass some kind of test – fulfill some sort of duty – before I could get on with the conversation. I would pretty much ignore epistemic issues. I would look through them, like a driver looking through a windshield, at Mom. To say that I must provide evidence that my Mom really is talking to me before I know enough to start telling her about my week is at least odd. Evidentialism, if applied universally, would disallow my knowledge that I was talking to my Mom until I produce the proper evidence.

This example gets at (part of) why Christian believers say the things they do. Religious believers claim to know God. They recognize his voice. As Jesus taught, the sheep who belong to the Good Shepherd "follow him because they know his voice" (John 10:4). When God speaks, believers listen. Now psychologists interested in studying the paranormal with their electronic equipment (the equivalent of the FBI agent) may feel a need to do evidential testing. They might look for distinctive brain wave patterns when believers are in prayer, for example. Now these experimental psychologists might or might not locate and record such brain patterns. But either way, the religious believer should not have to wait for the results of that study before he can commune with God. It is just odd to think I should wait for a FBI report before concluding that I am really talking to Mom. Similarly, it is implausible to insist that believers wait to see print outs of a brain scan – or some other evidentially oriented research – before counting their beliefs as knowledge. Even without evidence, believers can say, "I heard God's voice."

It is critical to get right one point. This previous discussion responds to question 3: what do I mean by the word "knowledge"? Does my believing that Mom's on the phone, without any evidential confirmation I am aware of, count as knowledge? Obviously, yes. A large part of what I know is not supported by evidence, and yet it is rightly called knowledge. Reformed epistemology says a believer who knows God and discerns his voice is perfectly right to form rather directly the belief, "God is speaking to me right now," as a case of genuine knowledge.

What is the "legitimating fact" that makes this person's belief a case of genuine knowledge? Reformed epistemology, as exemplified in Plantinga, says that what is rightly called knowledge is any case of true belief where a person knows that belief through a reliable belief-forming process, *even if the person is not aware of or thinking about that process*. The *belief*, not the *believer*, has warrant. Here is Plantinga's account. If a belief is "produced in [person] S by cognitive faculties functioning properly (subject to no dysfunction) in a cognitive environment that is appropriate for S's kind of cognitive faculties, according to a design plan that is successfully aimed at truth," then that belief has warrant for S.[16] This is not a precise set of necessary and sufficient conditions. Since there are various analogical extensions and levels of exactness in human beliefs, it seems unlikely that one could ever specify such a universal set of such conditions. But, in general, if these features are present when I am forming the belief, "It's my Mom on the phone," then my belief that I am talking to Mom counts as genuine knowledge. Similarly, if these features are present when I take some religious truth by faith, then what I possess counts as knowledge.

Again, the issue here – and this is very important – is not question 4: what strategies will point to cases of knowledge and weed out error? Naturalists often focus on question 4. Note Martin's complaint: "to consider belief in God as a basic belief seems completely out of keeping with the spirit and intention of foundationalism. Whatever else it was and whatever its problems, foundationalism was an attempt to provide critical tools for objectively appraising knowledge claims and provide a nonrelativistic basis for knowledge."[17] Clearly, "appraising knowledge claims" is about question 4. But the approach I am describing is responding to question 3: what is the meaning of the word "knowledge"?

Question 4 demands a rather large epistemic toolbox. This toolbox does not contain just one tool: in order to know x, a knower must give evidence for x. Of course, no sophisticated naturalist would put it quite this simply. But the point is that when the issue is identifying truth and eliminating error, people use a very wide range of strategies. In gathering and assessing knowledge, if knowers are limited to the one major tool that evidential-ism requires, then human knowing is unnecessarily severely restricted. A consistent application of an evidentialist requirement wipes out all sorts of things that are rightly known. It tends to maximize question 2, but question 1 fades into the background. It would imply that knowing that God exists does not count as knowledge. If God does exist, however, any epistemologi-cal strategy that precludes knowledge of that fact is deeply flawed. So if God exists, the evidentialist requirement is too strong.

The power of background knowledge

The evidential principle just is not a non-negotiable feature of every case of knowledge. It wipes out much of what is rightly called knowledge. (In fact, it wipes itself out!) But it does contain a grain of truth. To get at that grain, change the scenario a bit. What if I know that Mom passed away last year? I remember being at the funeral, and I have a video of the service. I know we buried Mom's body, and I can take you to see her grave marker. Suppose all that is true, and then, out of the blue, I get a call from a woman who says, "Hi, Hon. It's Mom!" Initially, I'd quickly form the belief, "This isn't happening. I'm *not* talking to my Mom." This belief is basic for me; I would form it instantly. Again, I would not go through lots of inferential steps or deductive argumentation. I would just know the falsity of the claim, "I'm talking to Mom on the phone right now." I would know it, because background facts that give evidence for my belief that Mom died last spring conjoined with another important and well-warranted belief: dead people do not make phone calls.

For religious believers, knowledge that someone takes by faith – whether it is gained in a natural, but basic way or learned from the Holy Spirit – de-pends on a variation of the principle of credulity. Here is one version:

6   When something seems to someone to be true, it probably is true, and she may take it as true, unless she knows of some special disqualifying circumstances or evidence to show that what *seems* true is not *actually* true.[18]

This applies to knowledge rooted in sense experience, for example. If I seem to see a marching band performing in front of me on the street, it is proba-bly true that the band is really in the street. If I am driving a car on the same street, I should do something to avoid hitting the flutes, drums, and tubas. I could be wrong about the band, but it would be a disaster to demand abso-lute proof. Similarly, statement 6 also applies to things I take by faith.

Naturally, good reasons can sometimes count against particular knowl-edge claims even when they are grounded in evidence produced by the senses. And the same is true if I know by way of the witness of the Spirit or in some direct and basic way. "Special disqualifying information" may eliminate my believing what I thought I knew. "Special disqualifying information" is a defeater. In general, a defeater is evidence, reasoning, or experience that leads one to think that an original belief is not warranted or true after all. Defeaters come in two flavors. *Undercutting* defeaters dissolve or undermine the warrant for previously held beliefs. *Rebutting* defeaters give additional evidence to override or reject previously held beliefs.[19] I take everyday beliefs as knowledge only to find later that they are defeated. I use the same strategy in matters of faith. I take teachings of the faith as true, since, if God exists, they are produced in normally reliable ways. But then I stay open to defeaters that can correct me if I am wrong.

Now even if I *think* that Mom is dead, it is possible – remotely, maybe, but still possible – that I *really am* talking to Mom. Maybe the woman we buried last spring was not actually Mom. Stranger things have happened; Christians believe that Jesus actually arose from the dead. I would be open (at least intellectually; my emotions will catch up later) to hearing any the counter-evidence that could undermine my thinking. I would be looking for someone to undercut my reasons – to prove that the video and grave marker do not count as valid evidence. If that undercutting defeater were compelling, I might correct my belief that Mom is dead. I would also investigate a rebutting defeater – new evidence to overturn my belief that Mom died last year. I would buy a plane ticket to Florida to meet the woman who called me. If I interacted with the woman who called me and discerned that she really is my Mom, that would rebut my thinking that she had died.

A limited role for an evidentialist principle

One problem with the evidentialist strategy is the confusion of questions 3 and 4. When I am trying to discover the truth of a claim for which I have some counter-evidence, it is right in some cases to look for available evidential confirmation. This is question 4: how can I identify a particular instance of knowledge? If John claims that his new Dodge Dakota is really a flying hovercraft, I would probably demand evidence for his claim. The reason is obvious: I have a large pool of background knowledge about cars and hovercraft, about the forces of gravity and aerodynamics, and about Dodge Dakotas. These rebut John's claim that his Dakota can fly. My mind is designed such that this background knowledge immediately rebuts John's claim. So even if John swears his Dakota can fly, I am not buying it. To generalize, when I have well-warranted background beliefs that make some claim implausible, I rightly move to look for wider ranges of evidence to adjudicate the competing claims. But this is not the same question as that asked in question 3.

I am suggesting that when question 4 is the issue, people sometimes do rightly look for evidential illumination. Different sorts of claims do seem to require different kinds of support. In general, the more unlikely an event is, all other things being equal, the more evidence is deemed necessary. On this basis, a naturalist could say that recognizing Mom's voice does not need evidential support because it is a routine event. It is the sort of thing that everyone knows happens all the time. But, a naturalist might continue, the evidentialist requirement does apply to religious beliefs like "God has convicted me of sin." That is not the sort of thing that normally happens. So taking some belief as true by faith, without evidence, is acceptable in normal, everyday matters, but *not* (ironically) in matters of faith. In matters of religious faith, the evidentialist principle still holds.

But this track completely begs the question against religious faith. The case of the flying Dodge truck makes this clear. If I have many well-warranted and well-integrated reasons to think that pick-up trucks do not fly, then I immediately form a belief that John's claim about his truck is implausible. On the other hand, if John merely claimed that his truck gets 18 mpg (when I thought that Dodge trucks normally get 15 mpg like my Chevy), I might feel skeptical. Still, it is within the realm of possibility – the sort of thing that *could be* true. So I would be open to hearing John's evidence. I might even press him for evidence to be sure he was not just bragging.

But maybe naturalists could say that religious beliefs are different from non-religious beliefs in just this way. To think that the Holy Spirit could speak to me is radically implausible, completely out of the ordinary, and entirely contrary to everything known to be true about the world based on a wide pool of background knowledge. So no one takes seriously the claim that the Spirit speaks to people. There is very strong evidence that this cannot happen.[20] But here is the nub of the problem. How does anyone know that God's speaking to people is radically implausible, completely out of the ordinary, and entirely contrary to everything known about the world? Whose wide pool of background knowledge is at work here? Believers need to point out that from the experience base of Christian belief, there is reason to think that the Spirit speaking to people is entirely plausible, very normal, and completely consistent with what is true about the world. Given the background knowledge that naturalists accept, hearing the voice of God seems out of place. But maybe the problem here is the naturalists' restricted experience base.

Look again at the phone call from Mom. If my friend Jim is over to my house and picks up the phone when Mom calls, he is not going to recognize her as my Mom just by hearing her voice. She will have to say, "Hi Jim. It's David's Mom calling." But Jim's failure is not going to bother me in the least. He just does not know Mom; he lacks the needed experience base. Jim has a first-order capacity to get to know my Mom, but he does not have the second-order skill of actually recognizing Mom directly. Similarly, if Christians are right, every human has a first-order capacity to get to know God, but not every human has the second-order skill of recognizing him. So the fact that someone who does not know God cannot recognize his voice will not necessarily alarm believers very much.

If theism is false, of course, then claims that the Holy Spirit speaks are implausible, abnormal, and inconsistent indeed. But if the Christian faith is true, then it is very likely that God would communicate with believers. God created the belief-forming processes like human eyesight (as Jews and Christians believe). So it is not difficult to think that God created belief-forming processes that enable believers to sense his presence (as Christians also believe). As the eye perceives the physical world, knowing by way of the *sensus divinitatis* detects the spiritual world. There is nothing implausible about that, if God exists. Again, if God *does not* exist, the question shifts to a completely different continent. But this essentially leads us to conclude that the plausibility of thinking that believers can hear God's voice (or thinking they can know in a properly basic way that God exists) boils down to one question: *does God actually exist?* In other words, this is not a straightforward, neutral discussion. It is not an unbiased conversation. Whether theism is true or false makes a major difference. When asking the question whether theistic belief is epistemically defective because it fails the evidentialists' requirement, the reality of God's existence is directly relevant to the answer. If God exists, then theistic believing is very much in order.

Strategies for genuine knowledge

What do believers do with question 4, the project of picking out or identifying genuine instances of knowledge? Traditional believers are very interested in what is actually true; point 4 *is* important. For example, the apostle Paul insisted on grounding his experience with Jesus in the truth of what actually happened. He wrote, "If Christ has not been raised, our preaching is useless and so is your faith" (1 Corinthians 15:14). The story of Christ's resurrection is no legend. In front of King Agrippa and a governor named Festus, Paul described Christ's resurrection. As he did so, Festus flew into a rage:

> "You are out of your mind, Paul!" he shouted. "Your great learning is driving you insane." "I am not insane, most excellent Festus," Paul replied. "What I am saying is true and reasonable. The king [Agrippa] is familiar with these things, and I can speak freely to him. I am convinced that none of this has escaped his notice, because it was not done in a corner."
>
> (Acts 26:24–6)

Further, in offering moral instruction, Paul did not retrofit his own teachings back into the mouth of Jesus. He took great pains to separate teachings that came directly from the mouth of Jesus from his own apostolic teachings (1 Corinthians 7:10, 12).

But I think religious believers sometimes need something more than well-warranted beliefs. From an externalist viewpoint, sometimes I can come to believe a true, well-warranted belief about God, yet without focusing on its warrant at all. At other times, however, what I need is a well-warranted belief that a particular belief is well-warranted. If that sounds like double-talk, go back to my example. If Mom calls, and I just recognize her voice, I have knowledge that Mom is on the other end of the line. This is a warranted true belief. But it is a different thing if I focus *not on Mom*, but *on reasons why I believe that my belief, "It really is Mom," is well-grounded*. I believe the following:

7   It is Mom on the phone.

Belief 7 counts as knowledge as it stands because a reliable process in an epistemically fortuitous environment produces it. But it is still possible to support point 7 by a different, second-order belief. I do not normally *need* this second-order belief to warrant point 7. From an externalist viewpoint, it is enough that point 7 formed reliably. This gives it warrant. But in cases where I am challenged, I can go farther, *looking for and acquiring self-reflected knowledge for the warrant* of point 7. I could learn that:

8   Belief 7 is well-warranted.

If statement 8 is warranted for me, then, first off, I have knowledge that Mom is on the phone, and, beyond that, I have become aware of my reasons for believing Mom is on the phone. I do not need awareness of such reasons for belief 7 in order to count belief 7 as an item of knowledge. But certain evidentially conflicted situations do challenge me to find those kinds of reasons when I can.[21] In the *absence* of defeaters (like a video of her funeral), I directly take belief 7 as an item of genuine knowledge. I do not need evidence. In the *presence* of potential defeaters, I should look to what evidence or reasoning I can find in order to evaluate the defeaters and judge among conflicting claims.

Similarly, a religious believer can have knowledge of God through direct religious experience. If this believer is my 99-year-old Grandma, she is not thinking about epistemology. Like the driver looking through the windshield, she is looking *through* epistemic issues *at* God. If her belief about God does not count as knowledge until she thinks through various reasons for believing, she will never have knowledge of God. Now she *could* explore the factors that warrant her knowledge of God. She *could* thus gain a kind of reflective knowledge of God – including knowledge of God's existence plus knowledge that her knowledge of God is warranted. But that second step is not necessary to knowledge.

Two objections (at least) arise out of this. First, if belief in God can be for the religious believer foundational or properly basic regarding warrant, does this not imply that just any belief is warranted? If a direct knowing of God is acceptable, how does the Christian believer respond to the Heaven's Gate cult members? Is not the belief held by Heaven's Gate cult members that they would ride through Heaven's Gate to the Upper Level on the Hale–Bopp comet also properly basic? The critique, apparently, is that a modest version of belief-foundationalism that considers belief in God as a basic belief leads to epistemic chaos. If belief in God is properly basic, that opens the epistemic floodgates. This, it seems, is why Martin says that if Reformed epistemology were true, then religious belief is "ridiculously easy to warrant" and "radically relativistic."[22]

But a modest foundationalism does *not* entail that just anything goes. Not every belief that *initially seems* to be warranted *really is* warranted in the end. In order for a belief to be genuine knowledge, it is not enough just to make a claim. It has to *be* warranted. And if believers think or have reason to think that something is not warranted, they can challenge even their own beliefs. The point is that they are not *required* to challenge their beliefs, or to answer the challenge of our own beliefs, before they count as knowledge. At a minimum, modest foundationalism might say, for instance, that they should have no knowledge of relevant defeaters. Suppose I *do* know of a relevant defeater for something I believe and I just ignore it, that is epistemic vice. But again, I do not have some general duty to follow a set of procedures in looking for defeaters for everything I believe. Grandma does not do that.

Second, if religious beliefs are properly basic, does that not take religious beliefs out of the realm of public discussion? Does that not make theological convictions unfalsifiable – immune to criticism? It seems that when Martin raises this evidentialist criticism against a Christian who takes something by faith, he assumes that the Christian's appeal to faith is sufficient (in the Christian's mind) to end all discussion. Once a person of faith says, "I take this by faith," he is claiming a knowledge-producing strategy that is perfect, untouchable, and disconnected from evidential concerns. Martin is afraid that the Christian believer's claim to know by faith places religious claims entirely beyond critique.

Not at all! It is possible to correct a basic belief that was apparently warranted for the person who holds it. That person normally finds her belief-forming processes generating true beliefs. But lots of things can go wrong. A particular environment, for example, might not be conducive to the production of true belief. Defeaters of one sort or another might bring this to light. The fact that beliefs normally form in reliable ways does not end the conversation. New information opens up discussion. Consider the simple example of a man who views the stick bending at the water line. At first he is unaware that light refracts. Then he learns about refraction in his GED (General Educational Development) review class. The fact that his eyesight fails him in one case only means that a relevant defeater now refutes what was once a basic belief. The man is still right to trust his eyes. His eyesight is normally reliable and typically gives him genuine knowledge. No one demands that visual perceptions be perfect in order to accept what they reveal. People trust them until proven otherwise. Similarly, although we can have properly basic, foundational beliefs about the great truths of the faith, believers can also correct false beliefs as needed.

How then can religious believers honor both questions 1 and 2? How is it possible to balance the desire to gain well-warranted beliefs and the need to avoid error? Modest foundationalism, by recognizing that many religious beliefs can be properly basic for those who have them, opens a path to warranted religious truth. If God exists, then believers can acquire well-warranted knowledge of God. This is not a strategy for identifying cases of knowledge, but something of a description of what knowledge is. If God exists, knowledge of God is grounded in the experience of God. This fulfills the need for warranted beliefs – questions 1. But not every *apparently* well-grounded knowledge claim about God *really is* well grounded. There are some false beliefs that seem initially to possess warrant for the believer. Yet those beliefs are undermined by other considerations that defeat them. This answers the concern to avoid errors – question 2.

Conclusion

The question I have asked is whether it is ever right to take something by faith. One way to take something by faith is to accept a religious belief as properly basic. Foundationalism is a class of epistemic theories in which some instances of knowledge – basic beliefs – are known directly instead of through inference. A modest religious version of foundationalism, Reformed epistemology, says that religious beliefs, such as "the God of the Bible is speaking to me," can be properly basic.

To rule out false religious beliefs, naturalists who are evidentialists apply their basic rule: every belief must be supported by evidence. They demand that every religious belief (except in a few limited cases) must be supported by evidence or else abandoned. Without such a rule, naturalists seem to fear that religious epistemologists would coronate any and every religious claim as properly basic and beyond correction. But the evidentialist rule is deeply flawed. Among other things, it wipes itself out disastrously. In the end, knowers must know some things directly. If they never know anything directly, then they will never find the first premises to begin any inference to things known indirectly. If they do not know some things *directly*, they will never know *anything*. If God exists, surely religious believers rightly take some things by faith.

Christians say that taking by faith the content (*notitia*) of biblical teaching amounts to mental assent (*assensus*). This is a first step toward God. The true faith that transforms and liberates people spiritually is a second, distinct step – an existential trust in, a faithful loyalty (*fiducia*) toward God. This is faith that leads to the love of God – the very purpose of human existence. A man might find that warranted true belief about the actual existence of a particular, splendid woman is worth something. But soul-satisfying married love with her through a relationship of personal trust and mutual commitment – "I do" – is of inestimable value. The same follows for the love of God. If all this is so and God *does* exist, I could hardly imagine that direct knowledge of God is impossible. Any epistemic standard that disallows the knowledge by which human persons find the Reality they were created to love calls itself radically into doubt.

Notes

1 W. K. Clifford, "The Ethics of Belief," in *Lectures and Essays*, 2nd edn, Leslie Stephen and Frederick Pollock (eds) (London and New York: Macmillan, 1886), 339–63.

2 Alvin Plantinga, *Warranted Christian Belief* (New York: Oxford University Press, 2000), 343.

3 Michael Martin, *Atheism: A Philosophical Justification* (Philadelphia: Temple University Press, 1990), 275–6.

4 William Lane Craig, *Reasonable Faith: Christian Truth and Apologetics*, revised edn, (Wheaton: Crossway, 1994), 31.

5 Michael Martin, "Craig's Holy Spirit Epistemology," located at www.infidels.org/library/modern/michael_martin/holy_spirit.html.

6 Patricia Waugh (ed.), *Postmodernism: A Reader* (London: Edward Arnold, 1992), 6.

7 George I. Mavrodes, *Belief in God: A Study in the Epistemology of Religion* (New York: Random House, 1970), 49.

8 Martin, *Atheism*, 276–7.

9 Robert Audi, *Belief, Justification, and Knowledge: An Introduction to Epistemology* (Belmont, CA: Wadsworth, 1988), 99.

10 Laurence BonJour, "Toward a Defense of Empirical Foundationalism," in *Resurrecting Old-Fashioned Foundationalism*, Michael DePaul (ed.) (New York: Rowman & Littlefield, 2001).

11 A helpful introduction to Reformed epistemology is Kelly James Clark, *Return to Reason: A Critique of Enlightenment Evidentialism and a Defense of Reason and Belief in God* (Grand Rapids, MI: Eerdmans, 1990).

12 Alvin Plantinga, "Is Belief in God Properly Basic?" *Nous* 15 (1981), 44.

13 See Brendan Sweetman, "The Pseudo-Problem of Skepticism," in *The Failure of Modernism: The Cartesian Legacy and Contemporary Pluralism*, Brendan Sweetman (ed.) (Mishawaka, IN: American Maritain Association, 1999), 228–41.

14 Alvin Plantinga, "Reason and Belief in God," in *Faith and Rationality: Reason and Belief in God*, Alvin Plantinga and Nicholas Wolterstorff (eds) (Notre Dame, IN: University of Notre Dame Press, 1983), 59–61.

15 To be clear, the phrase "hearing God's voice" is not the same as "hearing voices." When we speak of hearing God's voice, we mean this metaphorically. God really communicates, but usually it is not audible.

16 Plantinga, *Warranted Christian Belief*, 153–61.

17 Martin, *Atheism*, 275–6.

18 Richard Swinburne, *The Existence of God* (Oxford: Clarendon Press, 1979).

19 John Pollock, *Contemporary Theories of Knowledge* (Totowa: Rowman and Littlefield, 1986).
20 See David Hume's argument against miracles. The patterns of nature are so completely aligned against miracles, argued Hume, that no amount of evidence for a miracle could ever overcome them. "Of Miracles," in *Enquiry Concerning Human Understanding*, Part X, Section II (Oxford: Clarendon, 1975 [1777]).
21 Stephen Wykstra, "Toward a Sensible Evidentialism: On the Notion of 'Needing Evidence,'" in *Philosophy of Religion: Selected Readings*, 2nd edn, William L. Rowe and William J. Wainwright (eds) (San Diego: Harcourt Brace Jovanovich, 1989), 434–7.
22 Martin, *Atheism*, 276.

3

COGNITIVE INSPIRATION AND KNOWLEDGE OF GOD

Paul K. Moser

[I]n the wisdom of God, the world through its wisdom did not
come to know God.

(1 Corinthians 1:21, NASB)

Death and life

Death looms large over human history, bearing on every human who has
lived. Are we mortals alone in the world, on our way to death? Is there
anyone who can save us from our moral and mortal predicament, including
our ethical deficiency and impending death? We do well to ask, given the
apparent finality of death. If death is final, it spells the absolute end of our
lives, including all the good features of our lives. Human love, joy, peace,
patience, gentleness, goodness, humility, and self-control will then end in
naught. The wondrous virtues of a good human life will then cease, once
and for all, with death's final blow. The evils of human life will then end
too, but this will not restore life's good features. Perhaps the finality of death
does not rob human life of *short-lived* value and meaning. It does, however,
preclude any *lasting* value and meaning of human life. This may explain
why many people try to divert attention from our impending death. If death
is final, its consequences are disturbing indeed, perhaps even psychologically
unbearable.

We mortals lack the power of our own to escape or to survive death.
Whatever our earthly fortunes, death awaits us. We might try to divert our
attention, as we often do, but death still awaits. We evidently need outside
help, beyond mortal help, if we are to overcome death. This outside help
would have to be more powerful than death itself. An all-powerful God
could save us from death. Even so, is such a God more than a mere possibility, in particular, a reality? If commitment to an all-powerful God is
merely wishful thinking, then such a God is not real and so is unable to
save us from death. If God is to rescue us from death, God must be real,
not merely possible or imaginary. God must exercise *real power* to snatch
us from death's sharp teeth. Is there really a God with such power and such
care for us?

55

God and human expectations

Answers to the question of whether it is rational to believe that God is real are predictable. Some say yes, others, no; still others, surprisingly, have nothing to say. The issue is vital; so silence is misplaced, if not negligent. The answer depends on, among other things, what the term "God" signifies. The term is maximally honorific, at least as I shall use it. It signifies that than which nothing is more honorable. It signifies a being worthy of worship. Is it rational to believe that there really is a being worthy of worship?

Worship and worthiness thereof should not be taken lightly. They call for moral excellence in any being we worship, and this excellence must not depend on the moral status of others. It must be self-possessed; otherwise, its source would merit a place in worship. Worship calls not only for veneration, adoration, and reverence, but also for whole-hearted trusting commitment toward the being worshiped. Morally deficient beings, however, do not merit such commitment toward them. Moral deficiency in a being does not underwrite full trust in that being; on the contrary, it recommends against such trust. A worshiped being should thus be without moral deficiency.

Moral excellence is not just a matter of performing right actions and refraining from wrong actions. It involves the kind of character, motivation, and will underlying actions. True moral excellence requires, in particular, unselfish love toward all, even enemies. A selfish person lacks moral excellence, as does one who arbitrarily favors some other people. However good a person is who arbitrarily favors some other people, we can imagine a morally better person who loves *all* people, enemies included. Moral excellence in a person, then, carries a burden of unrestricted love toward all people.

Since worthiness of worship requires moral excellence, only an all-loving being is worthy of worship. This considerably narrows the field of candidates, even among all the world's religions. The most likely candidate will be a God who *promises human redemption,* a God who promises reliably to give us an opportunity to be saved from our moral and mortal predicament, including our ethical deficiency and impending death. An all-loving God would seek what is morally best for us as persons and thus would give us an opportunity for such redemption. Owing to the crucial role of human free will, however, the divine project of redemption can fail, in that some people can reject it. The needed redemption, in any case, would be a redemption of *us,* thereby preserving our status as persons and preserving us ourselves, not just something else. *You* are not redeemed if you no longer survive as a personal agent.

Remarkably, human history and its religions leave us with only one serious candidate for a God of redemptive promise: the righteously gracious God of Abraham, Isaac, Jacob, and Jesus. In order to be all-loving, a God of redemptive purpose must work in actual human history to form a loving community out of otherwise divided groups from every nation. The God

56

reportedly at work in Abraham, Isaac, Jacob, Jesus, and their true follow-ers meets this basic requirement and, in doing so, has no real competitors. Some nominal disciples of this God have opposed this requirement and even portrayed God as opposing it too, but this does not itself challenge the sub-stance of God's redemptive character or promise. Unreliable disciples cast no shadow of doubt on the reality of the true God.

Our question becomes: is it rational to believe that the alleged God of Abraham, Isaac, Jacob, and Jesus is real? Many people suspect that this God, if real, is too hidden, or too obscure, to merit rational acknowledg-ment. They think that evidence favoring this God's reality is tenuous and thus inadequate for rational commitment. John Baillie has noted some ob-jections of a person with such misgivings: "You speak of trusting God, of praying to Him and doing His will. But it is all so one-sided. We speak to God, we bow down before Him and lift up our hearts to Him. But He never speaks to us. He makes no sign. It is all so one-sided."[1] It is a familiar step from this allegation of one-sidedness to the conclusion that belief in God's reality is not rational. Call this move *the Divine Inadequacy Step*. Many ag-nostics and atheists have taken precisely this step, and many tentative theists have been tempted to follow suit.

The Divine Inadequacy Step implies that it is *not rational* to believe that God is real. We do well to clarify how the term "rational" is being used here, given the many uses in circulation. Its use in the Divine Inadequacy Step requires "adequate evidence" for one to believe rationally that God is real. So far, no problem. The kind of rational belief suitable for knowledge does require adequate supporting evidence. The key question, however, is: what *kind* of "adequate evidence" is needed for rational acknowledgment of God's reality? For any kind of adequate evidence one demands, we can plausibly ask: why must acknowledgment of God's reality be supported by *that* kind of evidence? The issue can be put more directly, with regard to any kind of adequate evidence one demands: why must God, if real, supply evi-dence of *that* kind? This issue is crucial in that it cautions us against making misguided cognitive demands of God.

Our expectations of God can distort our cognitive reflections about God. Suppose I expect God to be loose and casual with indications of divine real-ity. I thus might naturally portray God (if God is real) as evidentially pro-miscuous regarding divine reality. That is, I might expect and even demand cheap and easy evidence of God's reality. Many philosophers, including Bertrand Russell and N. R. Hanson, have demanded just such evidence.[2] Since such evidence is not in fact available to us, they have recommended either agnosticism or atheism. This is a familiar instance of the Divine Inadequacy Step.

Why suppose that God would be evidentially promiscuous and thus support a kind of cognitive voyeurism regarding divine reality? We shall see that we should not suppose this, contrary to what many philosophers uncritically assume. All our expectations of God, evidential and otherwise, should conform to *God's* distinctive character and purposes. Otherwise, they may reflect more about *us* than about God. In particular, our expectations should accommodate the fact that God must be worthy of worship and thus must be all-loving. Given how foreign an all-loving character is to us (owing to our self-centeredness), we do well to settle our evidential expectations of God carefully. We need to separate irrelevant evidential expectations from expectations suited to God's actual character of moral excellence, including perfect love for all people.

God's moral excellence calls for specific features in available evidence of God's reality. As morally excellent, God would seek what is morally best for us, including our becoming loving in the way God is. This requires that God preserve our capacity for freedom in decision-making, and not rule by coercion. Genuine love for God and others cannot be coerced by God, or anyone else for that matter. So, God must abstain from offering evidence of divine reality that extinguishes our freedom. Evidence of divine reality must accommodate human freedom in God's quest to elicit love from humans.

Divine expectations and love's judgment

We do well to ask what a God of moral excellence would expect of us, at least by way of our coming to know God. Certainly, such a God would expect us to be humble, and not selfishly prideful, in receiving evidence of God's reality. A selfishly prideful attitude toward a person is incompatible with genuine love toward that person. Genuine love requires an attitude of humble service for the good of others. So, a God of moral excellence would supply a kind of evidence of God's reality that does not encourage selfish pridefulness, and perhaps even discourages it.

If the evidence of God's reality were sophisticated, many sophisticated people would easily take selfish pride in comprehending it. Many intellectually sophisticated people would then easily treat knowledge of God as a privileged possession rather than as a gracious gift to be received gratefully and humbly. This would enhance selfish intellectual pride and thereby diminish unselfish love. It would thereby misrepresent the character of the God whose reality is being revealed by the relevant evidence. So we should not expect evidence of God's reality to be sophisticated in a way that encourages selfish pride. In 1 Corinthians, chapters 1–2, Paul outlines an approach to knowledge of God that accommodates this point (see the Appendix to this chapter.) This chapter develops this approach.

An all-loving God would want us, for our own good, to be like God regarding our moral character. Such a God would also want us to have our moral character developed via a loving friendship with God, the source and sustainer of love among humans.[3] Divine love seeks friendship with all people, not with an exclusive select group. This friendship is truly loving and thus is neither harsh nor obsequious. It seeks what is genuinely good for all people, and this sometimes differs from what we actually desire. Evidence of God's reality would accommodate such divine goals. It would be sensitive to (a) our needing moral-character transformation toward God's character and (b) our needing this transformation in reliance on friendship with God. Evidence of divine reality would fit with these needs.

Our need of moral-character transformation stems from our failure to love as God would have us love. Given God's being inherently loving, this failure is the most serious possible. If we are morally honest, we will acknowledge our failure to love others as ourselves and thereby to love as God would have us love. We readily see this failure whenever we reflect on our morally negligent treatment of the poor, the elderly, and the mentally disabled (to mention just a few obvious cases). True love requires that we go beyond our own needs to attend, with genuinely unselfish care, to the needs of others, but we consistently fail on this score. This is failure in what we can call *Love's Demand*. Our conscience, if unsuppressed, convicts us of this failure, and we then experience guilt and even shame. Our self-centeredness leaves us with a troubled conscience, at least in the absence of our suppressing conscience. We are thereby judged by a divine standard of love represented by conscience. Moral honesty about ourselves requires that we acknowledge the propriety of such judgment. It requires candor from us about our violating Love's Demand.

Human moral pride resists honesty about our flouting Love's Demand. It offers a cover-up story instead, a story concocted to save our moral honor. Our moral pride suggests that we have no need of moral guilt or shame. We are, it proposes, morally in the clear on our own. So, according to our moral pride, we are not deserving candidates for moral judgment. We rather merit moral approval even from God, by the lights of our pride. Our moral pride thus opposes any place for judgment of us from Love's Demand. (For a vivid illustration of the blinding effects of moral pride, see the Parable of the Pharisee and the Tax Collector, in Luke 18:9–14.)

Our moral pride is at best a frayed paper-thin veneer, and we recognize this if we are honest. We violate Love's Demand daily, and we have salient evidence for this. Our diversionary efforts on this front do not change the available evidence for this at all. They simply lead us deeper into the dishonesty of moral pride. Our most dangerous failures before the God issuing Love's Demand include a failure of moral honesty. Our moral pride may very well stem from fear of judgment and fear of not being in charge morally.[4] Even so, dishonesty about our unloving ways is among our most harmful failures before Love's Demand. Our dishonesty about our moral status leaves us resistant to the God issuing Love's Demand. It obscures, at least in our minds, how far we have departed from Love's Demand. The God issuing Love's Demand cannot transform us toward divine love as long as we cling to moral dishonesty about our unloving ways. We need to acknowledge our need for such transformation in order to yield to it freely, willingly, and gratefully. The transformation is, after all, a gift for our own good.

In moral honesty about ourselves, we acknowledge our need of moral transformation toward divine love and thereby open ourselves to judgment by Love's Demand. We then expect judgment and even acknowledge its propriety in light of our failure to love. Even death would be a fitting judgment on us. We cannot undo our past failure to meet Love's Demand; nor can we fully compensate for this failure by satisfying Love's Demand *from now on*. Our past unloving ways are a real part of our own history; they cannot be dismissed as illusory or insignificant. These past ways underwrite our failure by the standard of Love's Demand and our need of forgiveness relative to that Demand. Having failed repeatedly by the standard of Love's Demand, we genuinely need merciful forgiveness from the God who issues that Demand, if we are to avoid guilt, shame, and condemnation.[5] We cannot revive ourselves morally.

The actual result of moral honesty regarding Love's Demand is surprising. Upon sincere request for divine help, we receive not condemnation but mercy, forgiving mercy from the God issuing Love's Demand. This God, in response to our moral honesty and our sincere call for help, comes to us not in condemnation but rather in reconciling mercy. God, in perfect love, offers forgiveness to us, and friendship too. (The life, death, and resurrection of Jesus testify to this.) All things then become new for us. Guilt and shame begin to dissolve, and freedom emerges: freedom from the bondage of moral guilt and shame. We meet a God who prefers to befriend us rather than condemn us. We meet a God who promotes freedom over bondage, life over death, and love over selfishness. We meet the God whom Jesus represented with his life, death, and resurrection. This becomes part of our actual experience and even motivates and directs our daily life. Our *moral* honesty about our failure toward Love's Demand enables our *cognitive* access to God's reality.

The exact way in which God comes in forgiveness varies among people, owing to divine sensitivity to a person's cognitive, emotional, and motivational situation. Not all people have, for instance, the kind of experience had by Saul of Tarsus on the road to Damascus. In addition, not all people classify their experience of God's presence in the same way. The descriptive classification by the prophet Isaiah (Isaiah 6:1–13), for instance, is not universally shared, even among Jewish or Christian prophets. We should also acknowledge that an all-loving God could come to people in forgiveness even when they have many false beliefs about God. This is one lesson of the book of Jonah, and the lesson recurs throughout the Jewish–Christian scriptures. We should acknowledge, furthermore, that people can, and often do, call out for God's help in different ways. This call does not occur in a vacuum; it arises from a shared human predicament of moral deficiency and impending death. The convicting role of conscience is likewise widely shared, as are various salient goods within human life. Apparent glimmers of divine reality are available and widely shared. Even so, these glimmers do not yield a means of unfailingly arguing people into an attitude of welcoming divine help. Welcoming God results from a commitment irreducible to logical inference. It can, however, be firmly anchored in supporting evidence, even revelatory evidence of a special kind.

God's Spirit in humans

The Jewish–Christian God goes beyond revelation as the imparting of information and experience. This God offers a distinctive kind of evidence of divine reality, a kind of evidence widely overlooked in philosophical and theological discussions of God's reality. The evidence is the *imparting of God's Spirit* to humans. Such evidence is reported widely in the Jewish–Christian scriptures, and receives special acknowledgment in the letters of the apostle Paul. It calls for attention, in religious epistemology, to the human conditions for receiving the Spirit of an all-loving God. Religious epistemology seldom attends to this vital area, despite its prominence in the Jewish–Christian scriptures.

In Romans 5:5, Paul writes: ". . . hope [in God] does not disappoint, because the love of God has been poured out within our hearts through the Holy Spirit who was given to us" (NASB). Through the Holy Spirit given to us, our hearts, our innermost centers, receive the love of God and are thereby changed from being selfish to receiving God's unselfish love. Paul's insight bears on our available evidence of God's reality. Our hope in God has a cognitive anchor in God's giving His Holy Spirit to us, whereby God's love changes our hearts toward the character of divine love. Paul expresses a similar insight in 2 Corinthians 1:21 in referring to the God who "has put his seal upon us and given us his Spirit in our hearts as a guarantee" (Revised Standard Version, RSV). The Spirit given to human hearts guarantees, as a down payment, that God will complete the work of transformation begun in those hearts. Such transformation is salient evidence of God's reality.

James Dunn has captured the experienced role of God's Spirit acknowledged by Paul, as follows:

> The Spirit is that power which operates on the *heart* of man – the "heart" being the centre of thought, feeling, and willing, the centre of personal consciousness. . . . The Spirit is that power which transforms a man from the inside out, so that metaphors of cleansing and consecration become matters of actual experience in daily living (1 Cor. 6:9–11). The Spirit is the source of that wave of love and upsurge of joy which overwhelms the forces that oppose from without (Rom. 5:5; 1 Thess. 1:5f.).[6]

The Spirit of God brings new *power* to a person, and this power is felt by its recipient and is even observable by others. It can be observed by someone looking for the power of unselfish love in a life. God's Spirit empowers people to love as God loves, even in the self-giving way exemplified by Jesus in his life, death, and resurrection. Evidence of God's reality arises from the power of divine self-giving love present in a human life. Our appropriating such evidence firsthand calls for our welcoming and being moved by such power. Eduard Schweizer has thus characterized the Spirit of God, in Paul's writings, as ". . . the power which involves [a person] in the saving act of God in Christ, . . . makes impossible for him all confidence in his own 'flesh' (*sarx*), and lays him open to a life of love (*agape*)."[7]

The power of God's Spirit is easily overlooked, especially if we are looking for power that coerces or subdues people or otherwise advances one person at the expense of others. Indeed, the power of God's Spirit may even seem to be foolish pseudo-power to people out of tune with the God of true love. To know God aright is to be volitionally united with God in the power of God's Spirit, and this is to be united, in love, on the cross with God's crucified Son. Schweizer thus remarks:

> At the very place where Paul writes about the demonstration of the Spirit and of power, he states he has nothing to preach but the Crucified [Jesus], which is a stumbling-block to the Jews and folly to the Greeks (1 Cor. 1:23, 2:2). Thus the power of the Spirit is demonstrated precisely where normally nothing is to be seen but failure and disintegration. What no eye has seen nor ear heard God has revealed to his own through the Spirit which "searches everything, even the depths of God": salvation in the Crucified [Jesus]. . . . Thus it is above all the Spirit that reveals . . . that the "power of God" is to be found in the Crucified [Jesus] (2 Cor. 13:4; cf. 12:10).[8]

Evidence of the divine Spirit's presence, then, involves a kind of manifested power foreign to natural expectations. This is the power of self-giving love, as manifested in the crucified Jesus and in his true followers. The Spirit of God is thus the Spirit of Jesus, the one who gave his life in self-giving, servant love. Worldly powers of coercion, oppression, and selfishness go in the opposite direction to the power of God's Spirit. In expecting evidence of God's reality to fit with worldly powers, many people blind themselves from apprehending God's reality.

God's Spirit, according to Paul's writings, reveals God and our relationship with God. In 1 Corinthians 2:12, Paul remarks that ". . . we have received . . . the Spirit who is from God, *so that* we may know the things freely given to us by God" (NASB; italics added). Only the Spirit of God knows the things of God; so, ultimately, only the Spirit of God can reveal God to us. Paul thus concludes that we are given the Spirit of God *in order* to know God and God's ways of self-giving love. By giving his Spirit, God shares himself and knowledge of himself with others. In Romans 8, Paul comments that ". . . you did not receive the spirit of slavery to fall back into fear, but you have received the spirit of sonship. When we cry, 'Abba! Father!', it is the Spirit himself bearing witness with our spirit that we are children of God. . . ." (Romans 8:15–16, RSV; cf. Galatians 4:6–7). God's Spirit thus confirms to an individual's spirit that he or she is a child of God, a child called to filial relationship with God. The same lesson of the Spirit's cognitive role emerges in 1 John 4:13: "By this we *know* that we abide in [God] and [God] in us, because he has given us his Spirit."

The Jewish–Christian God is inherently personal. So, the personal Spirit of God is the best source, including the most direct source, to confirm God's reality and our standing before God. Indeed, given God's being inherently personal, God's personal Spirit is the only self-authenticating source of evidence of God's reality. If God's own personal Spirit cannot authenticate God's reality for us creatures, then nothing else can either. Certainly nothing other than God can. In picking something other than God to authenticate God's reality, we can always plausibly ask: what is the cognitively reliable connection between *that thing* and *God's reality*? This question will leave an opening to doubt the authenticity of the supposed witness to God's reality. So, God's Spirit authenticates God's reality *directly*, with unsurpassable authority and in agreement with God's character of love. This kind of *cognitive inspiration* yields knowledge of God. It is implausible to suppose that God should, or even could, supply some other kind of direct authentication of divine reality.

What else could God supply as salient evidence of divine reality, besides his Spirit and his unique Son? They provide the best evidence imaginable and the only evidence worthy of full commitment to God. Others kinds of evidence suffer from being a questionable distance from the God in question. The next best kind of evidence comes from humans actually guided by God's Spirit. They manifest the reality of God's loving character to others, even if indirectly. Thus Paul writes: ". . . thanks be to God, who in Christ always leads us in triumph, and through us spreads the fragrance of the knowledge of him everywhere" (2 Corinthians 2:14, RSV). God, according to Paul, leads Christians in the triumph of self-giving love exemplified by Jesus, thereby making available the knowledge of Jesus and of his Father.

Paul regarded the Corinthian Christians themselves as "letters of recommendation" confirming the veracity of Paul's message of the reality of God's love in Jesus. He writes to the Corinthian Christians: "You yourselves are our letter of recommendation, written on your hearts, to be known and read by all men; and you show that you are a letter from Christ delivered by us, written not with ink but with the Spirit of the living God, not on tablets of stone but on tablets of human hearts" (2 Corinthians 3:2–3, RSV). God's Spirit, according to Paul, changes a person's heart to make that person a living sign, even breathing evidence, of the reality of God's love. Still, my full appropriation of this evidence requires that I myself be acquainted directly with God's Spirit.

The Spirit of God, according to Romans 8, empowers an individual to relate to God *as Father*, thereby bringing a person into a relationship of obedient love toward God. Knowing God *as Lord* requires such a relationship of obedient love. Thus 1 John 4:8 states: "He who does not love does not know God, for God is love." Here we see how knowledge of God is inherently volitional, and not just intellectual. It takes us beyond reflection to obedient love toward God.

Spirit, will, and knowledge

The Jewish–Christian God's self-revelation is typically sensitive to the volitional state of recipients. This God wants to engage the human will, not just the human mind, because this God seeks to befriend people for the sake of a *loving relationship*. This is no merely intellectual matter. A loving relationship is inherently volitional; it rests on a faithful *commitment of the will* toward a person loved.[9]

One important way in which knowledge of God is volitional emerges in John's Gospel. A direct connection between one's willing and one's knowing something of God arises in John 7:17, where Jesus says: "If anyone is willing to do [God's] will, he will know of the teaching [of mine] whether it is of God . . . ." In knowing God aright, we know God *as Lord*, and knowing God as Lord requires willingness to do God's will. Knowing God aright stems from one's having a will open to submission to God; it does not come in advance of one's having such a will. Indeed, one's willingness to obey God attunes one to otherwise overlooked evidence of God's reality. One then becomes sensitive to the reality of God's merciful love at work in human lives. Consider an analogy. If I am unwilling to befriend you, I may block my access to a wealth of evidence regarding the reality of your personal virtues and even the reality of who you truly are. In contrast, if I am willing to befriend you, I can put myself in a position to acquire considerable evidence of the reality of your virtues and who you truly are. My volitional stance toward you can thus bear directly on my evidence regarding you, even regarding your reality. Likewise for one's volitional stance toward God.

John's Gospel connects obedience, love, and human reception of God's self-manifestation. After promising God's Spirit to those who love him, Jesus comments:

> He who has my commandments and keeps them, he it is who loves me; and he who loves me will be loved by my Father, and I will love him and manifest myself to him. Judas (not Iscariot) said to him, "Lord, how is it that you will manifest yourself to us, and not to the world?" Jesus an-

swered him, "If a man loves me, he will keep my word, and my Father will love him, and we will come to him and make our home with him.
(John 14:21–3)

Judas is surprised that Jesus will not manifest himself to the whole world. The brothers of Jesus were similarly surprised. They protest: "No one does anything in secret when he himself seeks to be known publicly. If you do these things, show yourself to the world" (John 7:4). They overlook the important role of volitional factors in knowledge of God.

Jesus corrects the protesters. He remarks to his brothers: "The world . . . hates me because I testify of it that its deeds are evil" (John 7:7). He assumes that the world does not welcome the things of God, and that therefore a divine manifestation would not receive the loving response desired by God. God, Jesus assumes, desires not mere acknowledgment from humans but a response of love. In John 14, Jesus draws a direct connection between loving God (a matter of the will) and receiving God's self-revelation. The self-revelation is the sending of God's Holy Spirit, called "the Spirit of truth" in John 14:17. God's Spirit is dispatched to manifest the reality of Jesus and his divine Father. This manifestation is of no avail to people resisting God's ways. It will not transform their selfish wills toward the loving will of God. However much it entertains or otherwise distracts such people, it will not draw them into a loving relationship with God and others. Since such a relationship is God's chief end, God offers his self-manifestation accordingly, typically in a manner sensitive to the volitional state of people.

An all-loving God would, by nature, promote loving relationships among humans and among God and humans. He would rely on divine self-manifestation to advance such relationships. An all-loving God would find no point in a self-manifestation that merely antagonizes or repels people, leaves them indifferent, or puffs up their pride. He would thus assess human inclinations toward divine manifestation, to discern whether they are favorable, that is, welcoming, toward such manifestation. They are *un*favorable, or *un*welcoming, when God's presence elicits a clash of wills, when a human will responds with rejection of God's loving ways.

Faithful love toward God includes a readiness to put God's will first, even over one's own will. Such an attitude of love has been exemplified by Jesus in Gethsemane. In the teeth of an impending horrifying death, he prays: "Abba! Father! All things are possible for You; remove this cup from me; yet not what I will, but what You will" (Mark 14:26, NASB). The submission of one's own will to God's, even in the presence of death, is the heartbeat of obedient love toward God. It is also the best avenue to *knowledge* of God. This is not surprising. An all-loving God would intend knowledge of God to be morally transforming of knowers toward God's character of self-giving love and toward a loving relationship with God. Knowledge of God is thus no spectator sport. It demands that we love God with all our heart, soul, mind, and strength.

The giving of God's Spirit, as a basis of knowledge of God, figures centrally in the ongoing struggle between the will of unloving humans and the will of an all-loving God. The key question becomes: what ultimately empowers me in my life? Is it my own (often selfish) will, or is it the unselfish will of God's Spirit? God offers his Spirit to humans to empower them to obey God and thus to love as God loves. Otherwise, we lapse into unloving, selfish ways and thereby violate Love's Demand. As human history shows, we lack the power of our own to love as God loves. A little reflection on our own lives, particularly their bearing on others in real need (such as the poor, the elderly, and the mentally disabled) confirms this without a doubt. We must *will* to have God's Spirit empower us to love, since a loving God cannot coerce us here. Even so, the actual power to love comes from God's Spirit, not from ourselves. There is no paradox here. God's Spirit can be what actually empowers us, even if we must exercise our will in yielding to the power of God's Spirit. In willing to have God's Spirit empower us, we put ourselves in a position to acquire otherwise unavailable evidence, and even knowledge, of God's powerful reality.

Knowing God's reality

One's willingness to befriend a person, we noted, can put one in a position to acquire evidence of that person's reality. In contrast, one's unwillingness to befriend a person can block one's acquiring evidence of that person's reality. We should avoid any confusion between evidence of a *person's* reality and evidence of the reality of a person's *body*. One can have evidence of the reality of a person's body without having evidence of the reality of the person. Even so, someone might propose that evidence of a person's *reality* differs from evidence of a person's *traits*. Perhaps willingness to befriend a person gives us access to evidence about that person's traits. Still, evidence that the person is real seems to be something else and seems not to depend on willingness to befriend that person. This much is right: I can have evidence *that* a person (say, the President of the United States) is real even though I am not willing to befriend that person.

What about firsthand evidence and knowledge of a person's reality? An all-loving God would want to promote such evidence and knowledge of himself, in order to advance loving relationships among all people. He would seek to promote such relationships by means of people being directly acquainted with his Spirit. In coming to know firsthand the reality of a person, I must become acquainted with some of the personal traits of that person. I must be willing not only to apprehend those traits but also to interact with them as the traits of a person. I must be willing to attend to the personal traits in question as traits of a person rather than traits of a mere object. Knowing a person's reality firsthand thus goes beyond mere knowing *that* a person is real.

My merely knowing that a person is real is compatible with my having no direct acquaintance with that person at all. Such mere factual knowledge would not please an all-loving God. The writer of the epistle of James has something like mere factual knowledge in mind when he says, with sarcasm: "You believe that God is one? You do well: even the demons believe [this] and shudder" (James 2:19). This is not to say that factual knowledge that God is real has no importance. It is rather to say that, for the sake of pleasing an all-loving God, such knowledge must go together, and should arise together, with firsthand knowledge of God as Lord. The two should not be separated in actual knowers, even if a conceptual distinction between them exists. Our knowing God as Lord includes obedient love toward God as our merciful Father. It thus engages our wills at the deepest level, at the level of what we love most. Paul thus puts factual knowledge in its proper place: ". . . if I understand all mysteries and all knowledge . . . but have not love, I am nothing" (1 Corinthians 13:2).

In the case of God, the reality is inherently a personal all-loving Spirit who is not necessarily embodied. An all-loving God is inherently worthy of worship, and coming to know such a God is, properly, coming to know God as Lord. In addition, coming to know firsthand the reality of *God as Lord* requires a willingness to attend to God's traits (including God's expressed love and mercy) as the traits of a worship-worthy person rather than of a mere object. Our properly attending to such divine traits requires a willingness to interact with them as the traits of a person worthy of worship and thus obedience. This means that our coming to know firsthand the reality of God as Lord involves our wills. We must be willing to receive God's manifestation in a manner suited to worship and obedience. This is no matter of mere reflection. It engages our wills in terms of the directions of our lives. Will we put God's manifested will of love first, or will we cling to our own wills? Will we respond in obedience to the call of God's love, or will we languish in our own selfish willfulness? The answers to these questions rest on volitional commitment, not mere reflection. They also determine the ultimate direction of our lives.

Knowing God's reality firsthand is *direct* in the way that mere factual knowledge that God is real is not. In depending on the reception of God's Spirit, it includes a kind of direct revelation different from (but not necessarily incompatible with) the conclusions of traditional natural theology.[10] Knowing God's reality firsthand is knowing *God*, owing to acquaintance with God's Spirit. Unlike natural theology, it is not merely knowledge of propositional conclusions on the basis of propositional premises. It is *person-centered* knowing, not just propositional knowing. It comes as a gift, not as an earning. We do not merit such knowing on the basis of our intellectual skills or any other skills. Knowing God is by grace, not by works of human credit. "In the wisdom of God, the world through its wisdom did not come to know God . . ." (1 Corinthians 1:21, NASB).

The reality of knowing God firsthand is authenticated by the superhuman power of God's Spirit. Hermann Gunkel has captured the heart of Paul's position:

> The Christian possesses a force more mighty than the natural man. What the latter could not do, the former is able to do. The natural man languished under the reign of sin; the Christian has become free from it. It was impossible for the Jew to keep the Law; Christian love is the fulfillment of the Law. The demons with dark impulse led the heathen astray to dumb idols; the Christian is able to cry, "Jesus is Lord." Thus a person cannot by himself create that mode of life which seizes the Christian; he cannot attain to the power over which the Christian disposes. This power is absolutely suprahuman. Therefore, in whomever this power dwells, he "receives" it (1 Cor. 2:12; Gal. 3:2,14; 2 Cor. 11: 4; Rom. 8:15). It is "given" to him (2 Cor. 1:22; 5:5; Rom. 5:5; 1 Thess. 4:8), "supplied" (Gal. 3:5), and "sent" (Gal. 4:6). This power is "experienced" (endured: *pathein*), as are its activities (Gal. 3:4). . . . The Christian is "led" by it (Gal. 5:18; Rom. 8:14). . . . The Christian life therefore rests upon a power that would be an impenetrable mystery if it were explained in terms of human capabilities.[11]

In other words, the power of the Christian life is explained best, if not explained *only*, by the good news that God's Spirit has truly intervened in human lives, under the authority of Jesus, the dispenser of God's Spirit. This power yields a salient kind of evidence for the reality of God. It underwrites an inference to a best available explanation to recommend Jewish–Christian theism on evidential grounds.[12] Even so, our access to such evidence depends on our willingness to acknowledge it as not of our own making. It is received as a gift or not at all.

The human reception of God's Spirit is no merely subjective matter. It yields one's becoming loving (at least to some discernible degree) as God is loving. It yields salient fruit of God's Spirit, such as love, joy, peace, patience, kindness, goodness, faithfulness, humility, and self-control (see Galatians 5:22–3). These are not merely subjective phenomena. On the contrary, they are discernible by any people appropriately attentive to them. These phenomena emerge in the lives of people in ways that are readily identifiable and testable.

People are wisely advised to "test the spirits to see whether they are of God" (1 John 4:1) rather than to believe every spirit. Otherwise, people would be led away from truth and into serious error by false teachers. Jesus offers similar advice:

> Beware of false prophets, who come to you in sheep's clothing but inwardly are ravenous wolves. You will know them by their fruits. . . .

> Every sound tree bears good fruit, but the bad tree bears evil fruit. A sound tree cannot bear evil fruit, nor can a bad tree bear good fruit.
>
> (Matthew 7:15–18)

Likewise, one can know the reality of the presence of God's Spirit by means of the fruits yielded by the Spirit. This Spirit makes one loving (at least to some discernible degree) as God is loving. This is the primary fruit of the Spirit, and it is identifiable and testable in a person's life. The presence of God's Spirit thus comes with salient evidence observable by any suitably attentive person.

Conclusion

The Spirit of God serves as the cognitive anchor of firsthand knowledge of God. According to the New Testament, this Spirit is the Spirit of Jesus and thus is seen most clearly in the life, death, and resurrection of Jesus. We will apprehend this Spirit's reality only if we are *willing* to have "eyes to see and ears to hear." That is, we must open ourselves to be attuned to receive God's Spirit. Even in connection with knowing, God seeks to move our wills. The true God, being all-loving, seeks above all to have us learn to love as God loves, and that goal is irreducibly volitional. God graciously offers cognitive inspiration, even God's own Spirit, for just that reason, and that is reason enough. Knowing without loving is altogether foreign to this God.[13]

Appendix

1 Corinthians 1 (NASB)

18 For the word of the cross is foolishness to those who are perishing, but to us who are being saved it is the power of God.

19 For it is written, "I will destroy the wisdom of the wise, and the cleverness of the clever I will set aside."

20 Where is the wise man? Where is the scribe? Where is the debater of this age? Has not God made foolish the wisdom of the world?

21 For since in the wisdom of God the world through its wisdom did not (come to) know God, God was well-pleased through the foolishness of the message preached to save those who believe.

22 For indeed Jews ask for signs and Greeks search for wisdom;

23 but we preach Christ crucified, to Jews a stumbling block and to Gentiles foolishness,

24 but to those who are called, both Jews and Greeks, Christ the power of God and the wisdom of God.

. . .

27 . . . God has chosen the foolish things of the world to shame the wise,

and God has chosen the weak things of the world to shame the things which are strong. . .,

29 so that no man may boast before God.
. . .

31 . . . just as it is written, "Let him who boasts, boast in the Lord."

1 Corinthians 2 (NASB)

1 And when I came to you, brethren, I did not come with superiority of speech or of wisdom, proclaiming to you the testimony of God.
2 For I determined to know nothing among you except Jesus Christ and Him crucified.
. . .
4 . . . my message and my preaching were not in persuasive words of wisdom, but in demonstration of the Spirit and of power,
5 so that your faith would not rest on the wisdom of men, but on the power of God.
. . .
7 . . .we speak God's wisdom in a mystery, the hidden (wisdom) which God predestined before the ages to our glory.
. . .
11 For who among men knows the (thoughts) of a man except the spirit of a man which is in him? Even so the (thoughts) of God no one knows except the Spirit of God.
12 Now we have received, not the spirit of the world, but the Spirit who is from God, so that we may know the things freely given to us by God,
13 which things we also speak, not in words taught by human wisdom, but in those taught by the Spirit . . . .
14 But a natural man does not accept the things of the Spirit of God, for they are foolishness to him; and he cannot understand them, because they are spiritually appraised.

Notes

1 John Baillie, *The Idea of Revelation in Recent Thought* (New York: Columbia University Press, 1956), 137.
2 See N. R. Hanson, *What I Do Not Believe and Other Essays* (Dordrecht: Reidel, 1971), 322; Bertrand Russell, "The Talk of the Town," *The New Yorker* (February 21, 1970), 29, cited in *Bertrand Russell on God and Religion*, Al Seckel (ed.) (Buffalo, NY: Prometheus, 1986), 11; and Russell, "What is an Agnostic?," in *Russell on Religion*, Louis Greenspan and Stefan Andersson (eds) (London: Routledge, 1999), 41. For misgivings about their cognitive demands on God, see Paul Moser, "Cognitive Idolatry and Divine Hiding," in *Divine Hiddenness*, Daniel Howard-Snyder and Paul Moser (eds) (New York: Cambridge University Press, 2002), 120–48.

3 On the relationship between friendship and knowing God, see Leslie D. Weatherhead, *The Transforming Friendship* (New York: Abingdon Press, 1928).

4 See Thomas Nagel, *The Last Word* (New York: Oxford University Press, 1997), 130.

5 On the importance of forgiveness, see John Austin Baker, *The Foolishness of God* (Atlanta: John Knox Press, 1970), 400–9; Baker, *The Faith of a Christian* (London: Darton, Longman, and Todd, 1996), 125–30; and Lewis Smedes, *The Art of Forgiving* (New York: Random House, 1996). On the origin and effects of shame, see Lewis Smedes, *Shame and Grace* (San Francisco: Harper, 1993).

6 James Dunn, *Jesus and the Spirit* (London: SCM Press, 1975), 201. See also Dunn, *The Theology of Paul the Apostle* (Grand Rapids, MI: Eerdmans, 1998), 419–33.

7 Eduard Schweizer, "Pneuma," in *Theological Dictionary of the New Testament*, Vol. 6, G. Kittel and G. Friedrich (eds) (Grand Rapids, MI: Eerdmans, 1964–76); slightly edited version in *Bible Key Words*, Vol. 3, D. M. Barton, P. R. Ackroyd, and A. E. Harvey (eds) (New York: Harper and Row, 1961), 80. Cf. Schweizer, "The Spirit of Power," *Interpretation* 6 (1952), 273.

8 Eduard Schweizer, "On Distinguishing Between Spirits," *Ecumenical Review* 41 (1989), 411. See also Schweizer, *The Holy Spirit*, R. H. Fuller and I. Fuller (trans) (Philadelphia: Fortress, 1980), 78–9, 119–23. Likewise, see Tom Smail, "The Cross and the Spirit: Toward a Theology of Renewal," in *The Love of Power or the Power of Love*, Tom Smail, Andrew Walker, and Nigel Wright (eds) (London: SPCK, 1993), 23–36; and James Dunn, "The Spirit and the Body of Christ," in his *The Christ and the Spirit, Vol. 2: Pneumatology,* (Grand Rapids, MI: Eerdmans, 1998), 350–7.

9 On this theme, see Lewis Smedes, *Caring and Commitment* (San Francisco: Harper, 1998).

10 For some misgivings about traditional natural theology, see Paul Moser, "A God Who Hides and Seeks," *Philosophia Christi* 2 (2001), 119–25. On the role of natural theology in the Jewish and Christian scriptures, see James Barr, *Biblical Faith and Natural Theology* (Oxford: Clarendon Press, 1993).

11 Hermann Gunkel, *The Influence of the Holy Spirit*, R. A. Harrisville and P. A. Quanbeck (trans) (Philadelphia: Fortress, 1979 [1888]), 93–4.

12 For some of the features of inference to a best available explanation in the empirical domain, see Paul Moser, *Knowledge and Evidence* (New York: Cambridge University Press, 1989). See also Moser, "Cognitive Idolatry and Divine Hiding," in *Divine Hiddenness,* Daniel Howard-Snyder and Paul Moser (eds), 122–6.

13 I presented a shortened version of this chapter as a McManis Lecture at Wheaton College in 2002. Many thanks to the Wheaton audience, especially Bob O'Connor and Jay Wood, for helpful comments. Thanks, too, to Paul Copan for a number of helpful suggestions.

4

SCIENCE AND THEISM

Concord, not conflict[1]

Robert C. Koons

It is widely held that the belief in supernatural entities, like God and the soul, is incompatible with a modern, scientific viewpoint. However, this bit of conventional wisdom is seldom backed up by careful argument. I will do my best in this essay to reconstruct some plausible arguments for the claim that science undermines the rationality of religious belief. In response, I will examine closely the actual historical relationship between religion and science in Western history, as well as the question of whether these historical connections are merely contingent accidents or are rooted in the very essences of science and theism. I will argue that, contrary to the popular view, the past success of science supports the truth of theism, and that the future success of science will depend on the perseverance of theistic conviction.

What is science?

Before getting down to business, we shall have to clarify what exactly is at issue. I think the meaning of "theism" is relatively clear, although it clearly refers to a fairly large family of beliefs. To count as a theist, one would have to believe that there is a personal being (construed as unitarian or trinitarian) who has unlimited power and intelligence, who is fundamentally good and trustworthy, and who is responsible for the creation of the rest of reality. This personal being would have to be at least capable of making contact with us and conveying information to us. In contrast, the meaning of "science" is not nearly so clear. Who exactly are "scientists"? When did science begin? What is the essence of scientific work? There are no settled answers to these questions, making the issue we are to address elusive.

Etymologically, the word *science* is drawn from the ordinary Latin word for *knowledge* (*scientia*). If *science* simply meant *knowledge*, then there would be no justification for a separate chapter on the relationship between theism and "science" since the book is concerned with the question of whether we can know theism to be true. So, science must refer to some special form of knowledge. For our purposes, there are four definitions of science that seem most relevant:

Definition 1   Science refers to the exponential explosion in knowledge of all kinds experienced in Europe and connected parts of the world over the last several hundred years, necessitating the re-evaluation of all prior beliefs.

Definition 2   Science is a social institution that has developed in Europe and connected parts of the world over the last several hundred years, consisting of a new priesthood, a "magisterium of fact" (in Stephen Jay Gould's ominous phrase), supplanting – or at least severely limiting – the magisterial role of the Church.

Definition 3   Science represents a radically new and vastly superior way of knowing, embodied in something called "the scientific method," which was discovered or invented in Europe during the seventeenth century.

Definition 4   Science is the history of the inexorable advance of materialistic philosophy against all rivals, including theism.

I shall not dispute the reality of the fact to which definition 1 points: the breathtaking and accelerating expansion of human knowledge in recent history. Nor shall I dispute that such expansion of knowledge calls for a careful reassessment of long-held beliefs, however venerable. However, the fact that theism should be reassessed in light of recent discoveries does not entail that theism has been cast into doubt. We may find that recent discoveries have no impact on the reasonableness of theism, or even that they strengthen our theistic convictions. I shall leave the details to other contributors to this volume, but let me record my own conviction that the new knowledge we have acquired recently, including evidence of the Big Bang, anthropic coincidences, the fantastic complexity and functionality of biological systems, and the deepening intractability of naturalistic explanations for the origin of life and of consciousness, support theism. Indeed, the evidence for theism has never been so clear and strong as it is now.

It is sometimes thought that our displacement from the center of the universe by Copernicus somehow contradicted at least Christian theism, but this seems to be based on the erroneous assumption that everything believed by ancient Christians was taken by them as equally essential to their theology. Ancient Christians knew that the earth was spherical and that the universe is immensely large compared with the earth. And although they all believed (until about the fourteenth century) that the earth was the center of the universe, they did not think that there was anything special about being there, since it was hell, rather than the terrestrial surface, that lay at the very center. From the ancient perspective, it was the periphery of the cosmos, and not the center, that took pride of place. The outermost sphere was the source of all terrestrial life and motion. The center was a kind of sump in which all that was gross and base settled.[2] In fact, one could argue that it was the poet Dante, rather than the astronomers, who first displaced the earth from its position in the center, for in the last part of the *Paradiso* (from the *Divine Comedy*), it is revealed to be an illusion of our finite perspective that places the earth, rather than God Himself, at the center of things.

Definition 2 also picks out a real historical fact. There are now hundreds of thousands of professionals who call themselves "scientists," and they are organized into university departments, laboratories, research centers, and professional associations, very few of which existed a little over 100 years ago. In addition, there is a superstructure of communications and funding that makes the institution of "science" extremely powerful, perhaps uniquely so. However, we cannot pronounce doom upon theism on the basis of this fact alone. The country in which the institutions of science are most developed and well entrenched, the United States, is also one of the world's most religious countries – and a country whose religious life is overwhelmingly theistic.

Moreover, we should be concerned with not only what will be, as a matter of sociological fact, but with what should be. Organized science may be growing in cultural power, but it does not follow that it is acquiring greater authority over all questions of fact. The institutional growth of science has great potential both for good and for ill. The vast superstructure of science has enabled an accelerated advancement of learning, but it also heightens the danger of intellectual totalitarianism. A priesthood of science, increasingly hierarchical in structure and claiming a unique and unchallenged magisterium of fact, can pose a threat to freedom of thought – a threat just as dangerous as that posed by the secular power of the Church in the Middle Ages. In the interests of pluralism, we philosophers must adopt a critical – and even at times adversarial – relationship toward the pronouncements of "science" on key questions of human existence, including the existence of God. Too often philosophers have instead adopted a sycophantic attitude, acting as cheerleaders for official science rather than as sympathetic critics.

The positivist myth of the uniqueness of science

In contrast to Definitions 1 and 2, Definitions 3 and 4 are grounded not in fact but in mythology. Definition 3 presupposes that "science" is unique, a radically new and unprecedented way of knowing, codified as "the scientific method." This myth of the uniqueness of science comprises three principal theses of positivism:

Thesis 1 The scientific method was the creation of a small group of seventeenth-century investigators, who broke decisively from the Aristotelian scholastic past, and who began, for the first time, to interact with the world in a distinctively scientific way.

Thesis 2 The scientific method they discovered is uniquely objective and trans-cultural, consisting of an impersonal method – in effect, the

construction of an investigative mechanism – that reliably generates knowledge, depending in no way on the history, ideology, or
private insight of the practitioner.

Thesis 3 The credibility of this scientific method as a revealer of truth has
been abundantly validated by the pragmatic successes and technical powers it has engendered.

All three of these theses have been decisively refuted by contemporary
historians and philosophers of science. Pierre Maurice Marie Duhem, the
eminent French physicist and historian of science, discovered the medieval
and Renaissance precursors to the new physics of the seventeenth century,
especially the development of impetus theory and other alternatives to the
Aristotelian notion of natural place by Jordanus de Nemore, Jean Buridan,
Nicholas Oresme, and da Vinci, among others. Duhem's remarkable body
of work revealed the fundamental continuity that underlay the disconti-
nuities in the refinement of physical theory.[3] Historians and philosophers
of science have also discovered that the scientific method is not a timeless
and impersonal mechanism, but, instead, personal factors, such as aesthetic
judgment, cultural perspective, and the actual history of science play an
ineliminable role.[4]

Science is thus not a radically new way of knowing discovered in the
recent past. As W. V. O. Quine has observed, the difference between science and commonsense is a matter of degree, not kind.[5] Scientific theories
persuade us of their truth, when they do, by engaging our commonsense,
and not merely by an appeal to the brute fact of their pragmatic and technical successes. As Bas van Fraassen and other scientific anti-realists have
convincingly argued, pragmatic success alone is no guarantor of the truth
of scientific conjectures; the technical fruit of scientific research can be explained by seeing science as an effective search for technical fruit and not for
the truth.[6] Unlike anti-realists, I believe that science does, for the most part,
provide us with knowledge of the real world. However, this knowledge is at-
tained, as is all other knowledge, through the normal exercise of our natural
faculties of observation and reason. Defenders of a scientific theory must
marshal evidence and arguments for their claims in the public forum: they
should not expect, and we should not offer, an uncritical, mindless deference
to scientific claims. When we are simply overawed by the technical prowess
of scientific culture, we partake in a kind of superstitious cargo cult, like the
Pacific islanders who worshipped Western traders as gods.

There is no such thing as "the scientific method." There is, on the one
hand, a cache of rules of thumb, platitudes, and homely advice drawn from
commonsense and tradition, and, on the other hand, sets of specific methods
and approaches that define specific research programs in science. Examples
of the former include: subject your conjectures to rigorous testing; do not
accept authority blindly; rely where possible on firsthand observation; be

precise and careful. Examples of the latter are: batteries of statistical tests for significance; double-blind tests for medical treatments; and reliance on well-established scientific instruments – from scales and thermometers to mass spectrometers and radio telescopes. As Etienne Gilson argued in *Methodical Realism*,[7] each domain of fact calls for its own characteristic set of methods of enquiry. Just as it was inappropriate for medieval Aristotelians to apply biological methods to physics, so too is it inept for the social and biological sciences to be distorted by a "physics envy."

Much of the philosophy of science in the mid-twentieth century was taken up in a quixotic attempt to find a line of demarcation between science, on the one hand, and metaphysics and commonsense knowledge, on the other. Every such attempt to find necessary and sufficient conditions for counting something as "scientific enquiry" or as a "scientific theory" ended in utter failure. The usual candidates – verifiability, falsifiability, testability, repeatability, quantifiability, operationalizability – all turned out to be at best rules of thumb, useful guidelines to bear in mind, but far from characterizing all the scientific ideas.

At the risk of beating a dead horse, let me take just one example of these attempted demarcations – that of falsifiability – since the falsifiability criterion seems to be widely held by working scientists as the *sine* qua *non* of genuinely scientific theory. There are at least three reasons why this cannot serve as a delimiter of genuine science. First, it is clear from history that scientists, practicing good science, do not immediately throw away a well-established theory at the first sign of trouble, including even falsified predictions by the theory. It is clear, even in hindsight, that a rigid adherence to falsificationist dogma would have stymied scientific progress through the premature rejection of theories that appeared to be in conflict with experimental results. For example, the deviant orbit of Uranus appeared to contradict Newtonian predictions, until the planet Neptune was discovered and Newtonian theory vindicated.

Second, as Duhem and Quine both demonstrated, no theory is ever simply falsified by a result. Instead, each theory is tested in conjunction with a host of auxiliary hypotheses, the falsity of any of which could be responsible for a negative result. In a sense, it is not individual hypotheses but the whole body of scientific theory that is being tested with every observation and measurement. The task of finding the responsible party when a negative result is encountered can never be reduced to a mechanistic recipe. Finally, since no empirical result is ever absolutely conclusive, it is also impossible to falsify anything absolutely, since an absolute falsification would have to be based upon an absolutely conclusive foundation.

This is not to deny that there is real value to Karl Popper's bromides.[8] We really are tempted to hold on too long to familiar and cherished ideas, to resort too often to ad hoc rescues, and to insulate a favored theory against challenge by definitional monkey business. However, it is not always and absolutely wrong to cling to a theory in the face of recalcitrant results; what is wrong is lack of balance and moderation, taking a legitimate conservatism too far. A good scientist seeks an Aristotelian Golden Mean between a hidebound conservatism and an erratic instability.

By failing to take into account these subtleties, a dogmatic falsificationism can do real harm. An uncritical insistence on falsifiability introduces a bias into scientific research that favors the quantitative over the qualitative, the atomistic and analytical over the holistic and synthetic, efficient causation over final causation, and the postulation of sub-human agencies over human and superhuman ones. It can lead, worst of all, to a supercilious disdain for metaphysics.

If science really were a distinctive mode of knowing, demonstrably superior to commonsense and all other methods, we might be under a kind of intellectual duty to base all of our beliefs on science alone. However, since science cannot be demarcated from the rest of knowledge, our ordinary ways of warranting beliefs are under no such cloud of suspicion and remain innocent until proven guilty.

The materialist myth of the unity of science

Definition 4 of science assumes that the history of science, beginning with Thales and Democritus in ancient Greece and including our recent past, has been one long train of successes on the part of an increasingly materialistic and reductionistic theory of the world. Resistance to this program of explaining everything in terms of physical forces and micro-particles has been futile, as one competitor after another has been thrown out in defeat. Theism is virtually the last holdout, and theologians have been forced repeatedly into a strategic retreat, surrendering ever-greater swaths of territory to the materialists as reductionistic science brings more and more phenomena under its sway, rendering God more and more an extravagant hypothesis for which we have no need. An intelligent student of intellectual history, surveying an unbroken string of victories on the part of the materialists over their supernaturalistic opponents, cannot help but find theistic speculations incredible.

So I think it must seem to the proponent of Definition 4. But one should not believe a word of it. Such a cartoon-like and melodramatic oversimplification of the history of science impedes our understanding of its real significance. The history of science has not been a one-sided victory of materialism over all its rivals. The real story is a good deal more complicated – and more interesting.

If we look simply at very recent history, we find that the confident prediction in the 1950s of unity-of-science enthusiasts like Hilary Putnam and Paul Oppenheim has not been borne out.[9] We have not found ways to derive the laws of biology, psychology, and the other so-called "special sciences" from the master science of fundamental physics; in fact, new discoveries have made any hope that we might do so seem ever more far-fetched. Information and other nonphysical entities play an ever-larger role in biology, cognitive psychology, and linguistics. Even doctrinaire materialists within philosophy have largely abandoned any claim that mental properties and events can be reduced to physiology and physics, with various forms of "non-reductive materialism" becoming the predominant fashion.[10] Even the reductionistic strategies within the philosophy of mind that do remain – namely, the variations on Putnam–Lewis functionalism – do not respect the kind of unity of science envisaged by Putnam and Oppenheim in 1958, since they try to reduce mental properties, not to physical properties expressible in the language of real physics, but to properties expressed in a language enhanced with sophisticated logical features (like higher-order quantification) and metaphysical relations (like causation and necessity) – a language that is very remote from the actual practice of physicists.

When we step back to look at the history of science over the entirety of its course from ancient Greece to the present, we find that a materialistic tendency is only one of four major strands that have contributed substantially to the present shape of scientific theory. The four traditions are (1) a Platonic–Pythagorean mathematical realism, (2) Aristotelian teleo-mechanism, (3) neo-Platonic and hermetic speculation about occult powers and vital principles, and, finally, (4) Democritean (atomistic) and Empedoclean (non-atomistic) versions of materialism. It is by no means the case that the fourth tradition has been the predominant influence on modern science; in fact, it is arguable that the Platonic–Pythagorean mathematical realism has been far more significant, and each tradition has made indispensable contributions. For an excellent survey of the history of science that carefully follows each of these threads, I recommend Nancy Pearcey and Charles Thaxton's *The Soul of Science: Christian Faith & Natural Philosophy*.[11] Much of what I say on this subject is drawn from their insightful book.

Ancient atomism had proved a scientific cul-de-sac, effectively fruitless after the time of Archimedes, and it never produced a theory of motion. Mathematical physics became possible only when Christian thinkers, influenced by Plato's *Timaeus* and, even more importantly, by the *Wisdom of Solomon* from the Septuagint (which taught that God has "disposed all things in measure, number and weight"),[12] turned to the study of natural phenomena, with a faith in the mysterious, even mystical, power of mathematics to reveal the essence of reality. The influence of such Christian Platonism is unmistakable in the pioneering work of Roger Bacon and the other Franciscans at Merton College, Oxford,[13] as well as in the thinking of later giants, like Galileo, Copernicus, Kepler, and, ultimately, Newton. It was a common interest in neo-Platonism that led Newton to Kepler's neglected work. Prior to this audacious attempt to find mathematical order in the world, nature had seemed, not orderly, but a "buzzin', blurrin' confusion," in William James's memorable phrase. In fact, these Christian thinkers went far beyond their Platonic roots in coming to expect absolute precision in the world. Unlike Plato's demiurge, who did his best to order recalcitrant matter, the Christian God created matter itself and could, therefore, be expected to have successfully imposed a perfectly exact form upon it. Kepler's discovery of elliptical orbits, for example, depended on a difference of 8 minutes in the orbit of Mars.

Although the arteriosclerosis of Aristotelian orthodoxy did retard, for a time, the progress of physical science (as the Galileo episode illustrates), we must not overlook the positive contribution of the teleological approach to nature.[14] In medicine and anatomy, the progress achieved by Andreas Vesalius and William Harvey depended not only on their willingness to go beyond Aristotle, but also upon their continuing to build on the foundations that Aristotle had laid. Harvey discovered the circulation of the blood because he believed in a divine architect who had created all things "for a certain purpose, and to some good end."[15] Such teleological thinking has proved indispensable in biology until the present day.[16] To identify a protein as an "enzyme" or a DNA molecule as a "code" is to use irreducibly teleological concepts, as is any reference to adaptations or disease.

Even in physics, the teleological tradition lives on in the form of so-called "variational principles," including the least action principles of Leibniz and de Maupertuis and Fermat's least time principle of refraction. All of Newton's optics and mechanics can be derived from William Rowen Hamilton's formulation of least action. Both Einstein's equations of relativity and Schrödinger's equations for quantum mechanics can be derived from similar minimum-action principles.[17] In addition, modern thermodynamics owes its central concept of a stable equilibrium to Aristotle's idea of natural place. In one case after another, the teleological form of a physical theory has proved to be both simpler and more fruitful than ateleological alternatives.[18]

Neo-Platonic, hermetic,[19] and even magical and kabbalistic[20] traditions played a significant role in the rise of modern science, especially chemistry and the physics of electromagnetism. It has often been noted that the acceleration of scientific progress in the seventeenth century coincided with a new interest in magic.[21] These mystical traditions led researchers to look for hidden powers in matter, especially powers of attraction and repulsion, as illustrated by William Gilbert's early studies in magnetism. The Paracelsian tradition inspired Jean-Baptiste von Helmont (1579–1644) to make significant discoveries in chemistry, including the discovery of gas.[22] Most importantly, Newton's postulation of a universal force of attraction had unmistakable roots in this same strand of thought,[23] as is witnessed by the virulent hostility to the idea among contemporary Cartesian materialists.

A similar neo-Platonic *Naturphilosophie* made significant contributions to biology throughout the eighteenth and nineteenth centuries, as exemplified by the work of Buffon and Lamarck in biology and Hans Christian Oersted, Sir Humphry Davy, and Michael Faraday (the discoverers of electromagnetism) in physics. In fact, materialism in the modern sense was not a significant factor in Western thought until the materialist movement in Germany in the 1840s. This movement was, at least initially, crude and naïve, inspired by political and cultural factors, rather than by a profound understanding of science.[24] If the materialist myth of the unity of science were correct, the scientific revolution should have occurred in mid-nineteenth-century Germany, not in the sixteenth and seventeenth centuries.

Modern quantum mechanics displays the marks of both aspects of the Platonic heritage: the primacy of exact mathematical formalism and the rejection of the necessity for mechanistic explanation. This latter aspect of quantum theory is most evident in its embrace of causal non-locality, instantaneous action at a distance – a consequence of Bell's theorem. The distance between the atomism of Democritus and Epicurus and the mathematically rigorous, holistically intertwined world of modern quantum theory could not be greater. The four essential features of ancient materialism, namely the absence of mathematical realism, the insistence upon explanation in terms of paradigmatic physical interactions (such as collisions, pushings, pullings, and other localizable events), the rejection of teleological explanation, and a commitment to ontological pluralism (the priority of the Many over the One) are all excluded by quantum theory. This can represent the triumph of "materialism", rather than its utter annihilation, only if the term "materialism" is evacuated of all meaning. Materialists have succeeded in the misrepresentation that science has vindicated "materialism" only by repeatedly redefining the essence of materialism to fit whatever the latest scientific theories say.

In fact, the form of materialism that had the most profound effect on science was not an atheistic or agnostic materialism drawn immediately from Empedocles or Lucretius, but a specifically theistic and Christian materialism. The materialist myth overlooks the fact that, for the most part, modern materialism and theism have been allies and not adversaries. A number of Christian thinkers worried that over-reliance on the Platonic and Aristotelian approaches would undermine respect for God's freedom, sovereignty, and immediacy, all of which are prominent themes in Judeo-Christian theism. Duhem, for example, dates the beginning of the scientific revolution at March 7 1277, when Étienne Tempier, Bishop of Paris, condemned a set of theses of Aristotelian physics as wrongfully imposing limits on God's omnipotence. Duhem saw this act as a call to Christians to apply their intellects to the development of a new physics. Tempier's condemnation of Aristotle coincided with the rise of a new voluntarism in theology, which meant that Christians had to rely on observation and experiment to discover how in fact God had exercised his sovereign freedom.[25]

Boyle and Newton stood at the culmination point of this new kind of

Christian materialism. Robert Boyle saw God as the direct and free establisher of the laws of motion. These laws depended solely and perfectly on his will, without any intermediaries or prior constraints. Boyle promoted an atomistic, corporeal theory of the world because he regarded the neo-Platonic tendency to introduce intermediary spiritual forces into our picture of the world as detracting from the honor of God as the sole author and governor of nature. For Boyle, the universe was not God, but rather a perfectly consistent artifact. This theme in Boyle reflects the larger "disenchantment of the world" effected by Christianity and widely noted by sociologists and anthropologists. By seeing nature as a fellow creature of God, rather than as the habitation of the semi-divine, Boyle helped to open nature to rational investigation.

Newton echoed these sentiments. He rejected the introduction into science of the neo-Platonic or Stoic World-Soul as a potential source of confusion between God and his creation.[26] At the same time, both Newton and Boyle rejected a full-fledged materialism of the kind promoted by Cartesians, since, as was said above, real influences from the Platonic tradition of vital principles remained. In particular, Newton was influenced by the Cambridge Platonists, who looked for exact mathematical laws and evidence of super-material forces in nature. Newton saw the universe as a riddle or cryptogram set by God.[27]

Philosophically, theistic materialism is a more coherent position than atheistic materialism, for the theist has an explanation for the three central facts that atheistic materialists must accept as brute facts, in fact, as extraordinary coincidences inexplicable by their principles. First, the atheist has no explanation for the unity of the physical universe: why the stories of the various participants in the world must cohere into a single, consistent world history. Second, the atheist has no explanation for the amazing consistency, across space and time, of the relatively small number of natural kinds we observe. What makes one electron, photon, or quark so much like another at one time, when there is such a vast number of them, and what makes each so stable over long stretches of time? Finally, as I will discuss in greater length in the next section, the atheist has no explanation of how human beings come equipped to understand the physical world's fundamental principles.

The notion that there has been significant conflict between science and theistic religion is the product of propagandists of the early twentieth century, especially John William Draper[28] and Andrew Dickson White,[29] neither of whom is defended by credible historians today. In fact, the truly remarkable thing about the explosive growth of modern science is that it happened in Christian Europe in the later medieval and early modern period, rather than at other times and places, with societies that were richer, more populous, and better organized (such as Rome, China, India, central America, or the Islamic empire). Many historians have concluded that the impetus of Christian theism provides the answer to this puzzle.[30]

Theism provides a complex and subtle view of the world, in contrast to the narrow preconceptions of the materialist. Western theism exhibited a kind of genius in establishing a balance and creative tension among quite disparate traditions, maintaining the polarities of atomism and teleology, vital forces and spatial relations, reason and empiricism. This ability of the theist to weave together a more adequate science from what had in the past remained unmixable ingredients is exemplified perfectly by Leibniz. Leibniz's conception of the vivacity of matter drew equally from Platonic mathematicism, Aristotelian teleology, neo-Platonic vitalism, and corpuscular materialism, and this conception was the direct ancestor of our modern notion of energy, which has been at the center of theoretical physics ever since. Far from hindering the progress of science, theistic metaphysics has inspired its most fruitful ideas.

The dependency of science upon theism

Far from undermining the credibility of theism, the remarkable success of science in modern times is a remarkable confirmation of the truth of theism. It was from the perspective of Judeo-Christian theism – and from that perspective alone – that it was predictable that science would have succeeded as it has. Without the faith in the rational intelligibility of the world and the divine vocation of human beings to master it, modern science would never have been possible, and, even today, the continued rationality of the enterprise of science depends on convictions that can be reasonably grounded only in theistic metaphysics.

There are seven elements of Western theism, each of which provided a necessary condition for the engendering of modern science:

1   The belief in the intelligibility and mathematical exactitude of the universe, as the artifact of a perfect Mind, working with suitable material that it has created *ex nihilo*, and the closely connected Hebraic conception of God as a law-giver. The idea of a law of nature was first explicitly formulated in the fourth century by Basil of Caesarea in his *Hexaemeron* (Six Days), applying the biblical model of God as law-giver to the Greek picture of an ordered cosmos.
2   A belief in the fitness of the human mind, created in the image of God, to the task of scientific investigation, conceived of as a *vocation given by God*.[31]
3   The need for observation and experiment to discover how in fact God has exercised his sovereign freedom and absolute omnipotence in crafting and legislating for the creation, a freedom incompatible with the complete determination of the divine will by a priori constraints.

Recall Duhem's view of the significance of Tempier's condemnation of Aristotelian physics for neglecting this very thing. In addition, Duhem argues that the omnipotence of God led to medieval speculation about the possible existence of many worlds like the earth, leading the way for the Copernican and Galilean revolutions.

4   The conception of nature as a divine Book, parallel to the Bible. The two-book model was a favorite theme of Galileo, Kepler, Bacon, and others. Historians have discovered fruitful interaction between scientific theorizing and the development of biblical hermeneutics in the late Middle Ages, Renaissance, Reformation, and Counter-Reformation.[32]

5   The *dis*enchantment of the world by theism, clearing away the potentially discordant divinities and semi-divinities of polytheism and animism. This abolished the ontological gap between the heavens and the earth (Aristotle's sub-lunar and super-lunar realms), making possible Newton's unification of the explanation of motion.

6   The linear view of time, beginning with creation and passing through the unique, unrepeatable events of "the divine comedy," in place of the otherwise ubiquitous conception of a cyclical Great Year. This enabled Christian theists to conceive of the possibility of unprecedented progress in scientific knowledge and technical efficacy, in contrast to the endemic resignation and pessimism of antiquity.

7   The elevation of the dignity of matter and of manual work, a consequence of the theological doctrine of the Incarnation, especially given Jesus' occupation as a carpenter. Modern science was possible only when investigators became willing to dirty their hands in workshops and laboratories, and only when they began to see all material things, which have been created by God, as good in themselves.

The scientific materialist might respond to this by admitting that, as a matter of historical happenstance, modern science was in fact spawned by theological conviction, but all seven of these principles can now be stripped of their theological baggage and allowed to stand on their own. We now know, by sight and historical experience – and not by faith – that the universe is mathematically intelligible and that the human mind is somehow up to the job of understanding it. We are no longer haunted by visions of inexorable fate or of a pandemonium of spirits, and so science no longer requires the tutelage of religion. We have, scientifically speaking, come of age and may now put aside such childish things as theology.

However, this sanguine view does not stand up to careful philosophical scrutiny, as Alvin Plantinga has shown in his *Warrant and Proper Function*.[33] There Plantinga demonstrates that scientific materialism, without a designer who intended man to be equipped with an aptitude for truth, leads inexorably to an epistemological catastrophe, the "epistemic defeat" of all the materialist's aspirations for knowledge. I will give here only an oversimplified summary of Plantinga's argument, since it is impossible (at least for me) to be clearer or more concise than Plantinga himself. The materialist has no real option but to believe that humanity is solely the product of an undirected and unplanned Darwinian process – random changes culled by natural selection. Natural selection cares only about behavior that promotes survival and reproduction: it has no interest in truth as such. There is no good reason to believe that an aptitude for truth is the only way, or even an especially likely mechanism, for producing survival-enhancing behavior. (For example, human beings may generally come to believe that their fellow humans have intrinsic dignity and worth and that objective moral values and their attendant obligations exist. Given naturalism, these beliefs would be false – even if holding such beliefs helped humans better to survive.)[34] The knowledge that the causal pathways leading to our present beliefs lacks any intrinsic propensity to promote truth gives us a compelling and indefeasible reason for doubting all the deliverances of our cognitive faculties, whether of perception, memory, logical reasoning, or scientific inference. Hence, the scientific materialist cannot reasonably, in the end, claim to know that the results of science (or any other mode of human knowledge) are in fact true.

In an essay published in 2000,[35] I laid out an argument that resembles Plantinga's in certain respects. I argued that it is impossible, if materialism is true, for any scientifically formed belief about fundamental physics to be knowable or even to be true. The materialist must adopt a causal or information-theoretic account of the meaning of the propositions of scientific theory, and a similar account of the nature of knowledge (along the lines of the semantic and epistemological theories of Dretske, Papineau, or Millikan).[36] These accounts require a tight connection between semantics and epistemology: it is impossible for our theories to carry information about the world unless our inferences to theories are largely reliable. Since simplicity, symmetry, and other quasi-aesthetic qualities of theories play an indispensable role in our theoretical practice,[37] our inferences to scientific theory cannot be reliable unless there is a causal explanation for the connection between simplicity and truth. However, no materialistic account of such a causal connection is possible, since any causal explanation of the linkage between simplicity and truth would have to involve reference to a factor that caused the fundamental laws of the world to be simple, and any cause of the fundamental law of matter must itself be immaterial. Hence, the materialist cannot consistently believe either that science provides us with knowledge, or that our scientific theories are really about the world (in that they fairly accurately and truly correspond to nature).

The argument depends crucially on the point made earlier – that aesthetic judgments about simplicity and elegance provide a screen through which theories must pass before we can take them seriously.[38] However, the argument does not depend on supposing that the relevant standards of aesthetic judgment are entirely innate or a priori. The materialist is in trouble, even if, as Weinberg puts it, "the universe acts as a random, inefficient and in the long-run effective teaching machine . . ."[39] It is crucial that, for these aesthetic criteria to guide us reliably toward new discoveries about the fundamental laws, the fact that the undiscovered laws share learnable aesthetic characteristics with the ones we already know must not be a brute coincidence. Real reliability, as opposed to dumb luck, requires a causal mechanism that makes the mechanism reliable. In this case, such a mechanism would have to have impressed a specific, learnable aesthetic deep structure upon all the fundamental laws of nature. Such a mechanism cannot itself be a material cause, since we are supposing that something is responsible for the fundamental laws of matter, and only something supra-material could do that. This transcendent Something need not be a god, but the fact that It imposes what is recognizably a rationally ordered form of beauty (Weinberg's chapter is entitled "Beautiful Theories") surely suggests that there is something personal about this cosmic law-giver. Even a materialist as inveterate as Weinberg begins to sound quite theological at this point:

> It is when we study truly fundamental problems that we expect to find beautiful answers. We believe that, if we ask why the world is the way it is and then ask why that answer is the way it is, at the end of this chain of explanations we shall find a few simple principles of compelling beauty. We think this in part because our historical experience teaches us that as we look beneath the surface of things, we find more and more beauty. Plato and the neo-Platonists taught that the beauty we see in nature is a reflection of the beauty of the ultimate, the *nous* [Greek for the mind or understanding]. For us, too, the beauty of present theories is an anticipation, a premonition, of the beauty of the final theory. And, in any case, we would not accept any theory as final unless it were beautiful.[40]

In addition, the argument does not depend on supposing that we are infallible in our scientific judgments. All that is required is that we are (in terms of objective probability) just better than chance at picking out candidates for serious attention. Even a slightly better-than-chance aptitude for scientific truth would require a supernatural explanation.

Plantinga's argument and mine complement one another. Plantinga argues that the materialist has no adequate explanation of how we are so constituted to learn truth, whereas I argue that the materialist has no adequate explanation of how the fundamental laws of nature are so constituted as to be learnable through experience.

Our arguments do not cast doubt on the actual reliability of scientists, even materialistic scientists, at making actual discoveries of the laws of nature. Nor are we claiming that the materialistic scientist must violate the canons of Bayesian rationality. The materialist has a perfect right to use subjective priors that are biased toward simplicity, and this bias may indeed make the materialist reliable in the pursuit of truth. The problem for the materialist concerns the question of whether he can reasonably claim to know that these discoveries are genuine, to be warranted in his conclusions. Lacking any explanation for his reliability, other than appeal to dumb luck, the materialist occupies a position that is untenable for the purposes of asserting claims to scientific knowledge.

Materialism, therefore, can draw no support whatsoever from modern science, since scientific realism entails that materialism is false, and, if scientific theories are treated as mere useful fictions, science would have no bearing on the truth or falsity of materialism at all. Materialists must find support for their position elsewhere.

By contrast, theists can point to the success of science as the confirmation of their metaphysical position, the verification of a daring prediction made by theists hundreds of years ago.

Conclusion

There is a price to be paid for scientific realism, for the conviction that our scientific theories provide models of the real world, models that we have some reason to believe may be approximately correct. This price is our admission that the physical realm does not exhaust reality, but that it is instead the artifact of a reasonable God who has fitted us to the task of investigating it.

It has been argued that theism must disrupt scientific enquiry by letting a "divine foot in the door," forcing us to take seriously the possibility of the undetectable interference of supernatural agents in all experimental setups. Such worries about a ubiquitous Cartesian deceiver, it is argued, can propel the theist into exactly the sort of epistemological meltdown that Plantinga claimed is the fate of the materialist.

However, this worry is a mere bugbear. There is no reason for the theist to take seriously at all the possibility that God might be mischievously playing tricks on us in our laboratories or field studies. It is true, however, that a theist should take seriously the possibility of an exceptional miracle, an event inexplicable in terms of the finite powers and propensities we can study scientifically – not promiscuously, but only when there is good theological or philosophical reason to do so. However, opening the door to the miraculous is not the same as opening the door to rank irrationalism. It does not mean adopting an attitude of credulity to every wild and marvelous story – this was certainly not the case for the first modern scientists, who were theists. Given the rational order of the natural world, we have reason to expect that any miracles will also form a coherent and rational order. They will not be mere parlor tricks to dazzle and amuse; they would instead exhibit the same kind of economy, elegance, and rational meaning that we find elsewhere in creation. In his classic work, *Miracles*,[41] C. S. Lewis argued that the miracles of the New Testament are of exactly this character, but that is a matter for another essay.[42]

Notes

1   I would like to thank Nancy Pearcey, Benjamin Wiker, Cory Juhl, T. K. Seung, and R. J. Hankinson for their helpful comments on earlier drafts. I also want to acknowledge the support of the Graduate School and the College of Liberal Arts at the University of Texas, Austin, which enabled me to take research leave during the spring semester of 2002, during which this was completed.

2   See Dennis R. Danielson's "The great Copernican cliché," *American Journal of Physics* 69 (October 2001), 1029–35.

3   Unfortunately, most of Duhem's work has not yet been translated into English. The major works in French are *L'évolution de la Mécanique* (Paris: A. Hermann, 1903), *Les origines de la Statique* (Paris: A. Hermann, 1905–6), *Études sur Léonard de Vinci* (Paris: A. Hermann, 1906–1913), and the ten-volume *Le Système du Monde: Histoire des Doctrines Cosmologiques de Platon à Copernic* (Paris, A. Hermann, 1913–1959). Selections from these are available in the following English translations: *To Save the Phenomena: An Essay on the Idea of Physical Theory from Plato to Galileo*, Edmund Doland and Chaninah Maschler (trans.) (Chicago: University of Chicago Press, 1969); *Medieval Cosmology: Theories of Infinity, Place, Time, Void and the Plurality of Worlds*, Roger Ariew (trans.) (Chicago: University of Chicago Press, 1985); *The Evolution of Mechanics*, Michael Cole (trans.) (Alphen an den Rijn: Sijthoff & Noordhoff, 1980); *The Origins of Statics*, Grant F. Leneaux, Vicotor N. Vigliente, Guy H. Wagener (trans) (Dodrecht: Kluwer Academic, 1991). A good survey of Duhem's significance is provided by Stanley L. Jaki in *Uneasy Genius: The Life and Work of Pierre Duhem* (The Hague: Nijhoff, 1984). More recent treatments of the relationship between religion and the origin of science, such as Christopher Kaiser's *Creation and the History of Science* (Grand Rapids, MI: Eerdmans, 1991) benefit both from Duhem's pioneering work and from later refinements and corrections. For example, Duhem underestimated the importance of Robert Grosseteste, Roger Bacon and the perspectivists, and Thomas Bradwardine and the "Oxford calculators" of Merton College. See A. C. Crombie, *Robert Grosseteste, Origin of Experimental Science* (Oxford: Clarendon Press, 1953), and *Augustine to Galileo* (Oxford: Harvard University Press, 1961); Max Jammer, *Concepts of Mass in Classical and Modern Physics* (Cambridge, MA: Harvard University Press 1961), Chapter 4. See also, Carlos Steel, "Nature as Object of Science: On the Medieval Contribution to the Science of Nature," in *Nature in Medieval Thought: Some Approaches East and West*, Chumaru Koyama (ed.) (Leiden: Brill, 2000), 125–52; E. Grant, *The Foundations of Modern Science in the Middle Ages* (Cambridge, UK: Cambridge University Press, 1996); J. M. M. H. Thijssen, "Late Medieval Natural Philosophy: Some Recent Trends in Scholarship," *Recherches de Theologie et de Philosophie medievales* 67 (2000), 158–90.

4   See for instance Michael Polanyi, *Personal Knowledge: Toward a Post-critical Philosophy* (New York: Harper & Row, 1964); Thomas S. Kuhn, *The Structure of Scientific Revolutions* (Chicago: University of Chicago Press, 1966), Paul S. Feyerabend, *Against Method*, 3rd edn (London: Verso, 1993); and Imre Lakatos,

The Methodology of Scientific Research Programmes, John Worrall and Gregory Currice (eds) (New York: Cambridge University Press, 1978).

5 W. V. O. Quine, *Ontological Relativity and Other Essays* (New York: Columbia University Press, 1969), 129.

6 Bas C. van Fraassen, *The Scientific Image* (Oxford: Clarendon Press, 1980).

7 Etienne Gilson, *Methodical Realism* (Port Royale, VA: Christendom Press, 1990).

8 Karl R. Popper, *Conjectures and Refutations: The Growth of Scientific Knowledge* (New York: Harper & Row, 1965).

9 Hilary Putnam and Paul Oppenheim, "Unity of Science as a Working Hypothesis," in *Minnesota Studies in the Philosophy of Science*, H. Feigl, M. Scriven, and G. Maxwell (eds) (Minneapolis: University of Minnesota Press, 1958), 3–36.

10 Compare the Putnam–Oppenheim piece with Jerry Fodor's "Special Sciences: The Disunity of Science as a Working Hypothesis," *Synthese* 28 (1974), 97–115.

11 Nancy Pearcey and Charles Thaxton, *The Soul of Science: Christian Faith & Natural Philosophy* (Wheaton, IL: Crossway Books, 1994).

12 Wisdom of Solomon 11:21. This was the most widely quoted Scripture in the Middle Ages, according to Duhem.

13 Roger French and Andrew Cunningham, *Before Science: The Invention of the Friars' Natural Philosophy* (Aldershot, UK: Scolar Press, 1996).

14 "Teleology" refers to the assumption that some things in nature have characteristic or proper functions or purposes, e.g. hearts have the purpose of pumping blood, eyes the purpose of enabling sight, nerves the purpose of carrying sensory and motor signals, etc.

15 Quoted by Hugh Kearney, *Science and Change, 1500–1700* (New York: McGraw-Hill, 1971), 86–7.

16 See F. J. Ayala, "The Autonomy of Biology as a Natural Science," in *Biology, History and Natural Philosophy*, A. D. Breck and W. Yourgau (eds) (New York: Plenum Press, 1974), 7; Jacques Monod, *Chance and Necessity: An Essay on the Natural Philosophy of Modern Biology*, Autryn Wainhouse (trans) (New York: Knopf, 1971), 9; E. W. Sinnott, *Cell and Psyche: The Biology of Purpose* (New York: Harper & Row, 1961), 46; T. Dobzhansky, "Chance and Creativity in Evolution," in *Interrelations: The Biological and Physical Sciences*, R. T. Blackburn (ed.) (Chicago: Scott, Foresman, 1966), 159.

17 W. Yourgrau and S. Mandelstam, *Variational Principles in Dynamics and Quantum Theory*, 3rd edn (Philadelphia: Saunders, 1968).

18 Jim Hall, "Least Action Hero," *Lingua Franca* 9 (October 1999), 68.

19 The "Hermetic" tradition is embodied in an ancient text, the *Hermeticum*, attributed to Hermes Trismegistus, supposedly an Egyptian priest and mystic of the second millenium BC. Modern scholars believe the text was written by a Greek Neoplatonist between 100 and 300 AD. The hermetic text was prized by Renaissance magi, such as Marsilio Ficino, Pico della Mirandola, and Giordano Bruno.

20 The Kabbala tradition originated in Jewish circles in early medieval Spain. It was based upon the invocation of angels and other spritiual principles through the manipulation of the Hebrew alphabet.

21 See Francis A. Yates, *Giordano Bruno and the Hermetic Tradition* (New York: Random House, 1964); Charles Webster, *From Paracelsus to Newton: Magic and the Making of Modern Science* (New York: Cambridge University Press, 1982).

22 Walter Pagel, "The Position of Harvey and van Helmont in the History of European Thought," in *Toward Modern Science*, Vol. II, Robert M. Palter (ed.) (New York: Noonday Paperback, 1961), 185ff.

23 Due in part to the Cambridge Platonists, John Smith (1618–52) and Henry More (1614–87), who had a formative influence on Newton during his undergraduate years at Cambridge. In addition, Webster documents that Newton owned editions of the work of Paracelsus and van Helmont.

24 Frederick Gregory, *Scientific Materialism in Nineteenth Century Germany* (Boston: D. Reidel, 1977).

25 In *Divine Will and Mechanical Philosophy: Gassendi and Descartes on Contingency and Necessity in the Created World* (Cambridge, UK: Cambridge University Press, 1994), Margaret Osler argues that Gassendi's empirical approach to nature was grounded in just such theological voluntarism.

26 Eugene M. Klaaren, *Religious Origins of Modern Science* (Grand Rapids, MI: Eerdmans, 1977), 135–51.

27 John Maynard Keynes, "Newton, the Man," in *Essays in Biography*, 2nd edn, (London: Rupert Hart-Davis, 1951), 310.

28 John William Draper, *History of the Conflict between Religion and Science* (New York: D. Appleton, 1902).

29 Andrew Dickson White, *A History of the Warfare of Science with Theology in Christendom* (New York: D. Appleton, 1908).

30 Alfred North Whitehead, *Science and the Modern World* (New York: Macmillan, 1925); Michael Foster, "The Christian Doctrine of Creation and the Rise of Modern Science," *Mind* 43 (1934), 446–68; and "Christian Theology and the Rise of Modern Science I and II," *Mind* 44 (1935), 439–83, and *Mind* 45 (1936), 1–27; Christopher Kaiser, *Creation and the History of Science* (Grand Rapids, MI: Eerdmans, 1981); A. R. Hall, *The Scientific Revolution, 1500–1800: The Formation of the Modern Scientific Attitude* (Boston: Beacon Press, 1954); Joseph Needham, *The Grand Titration: Science and Society in East and West* (Toronto: University of Toronto Press, 1969), 327; Stanley L. Jaki, *The Road of Science and the Ways to God* (Chicago: University of Chicago Press, 1978); Eugene M. Klaaren, *Religious Origins of Modern Science* (Grand Rapids, MI: Eerdmans, 1977); Loren C. Eiseley, *Darwin's Century: Evolution and the Men Who Discovered It* (New York: Doubleday, 1958), 62; Margaret Osler and Paul Lawrence Barber (eds), *Religion, Science and Worldview* (Cambridge, UK: Cambridge University Press, 1985); Margaret Osler, *Rethinking the Scientific Revolution* (Cambridge, UK: Cambridge University Press, 2000).

31 Kepler: "I give you thanks, Creator and God, that you have given me this joy in creation, and I rejoice in the work of your hands. See I now have completed the work to which I was called. In it I have used all the talents you have lent to my spirit." Quoted in *Kaiser, Creation and the History of Science*, 127.

32 See Peter Harrison, *The Bible, Protestantism and the Rise of Natural Science* (Cambridge, UK: Cambridge University Press, 1998), and Kenneth J. Howell, *God's Two Books: Copernican Cosmology and Biblical Interpretation in Early Modern Science* (Notre Dame, IN: University of Notre Dame Press, 2002).

33 Alvin Plantinga, *Warrant and Proper Function* (New York: Oxford University Press, 1993). On this, see Chapter 10.

34 See Chapter 8 by Paul Copan on the moral argument in this volume.

35 Robert Koons, "The Incompatibility of Naturalism and Scientific Realism," in *Naturalism: A Critical Appraisal*, William Lane Craig and J. P. Moreland (eds) (London: Routledge, 2000), 49–63. See also Chapter 15 and section 17.5 of my book, *Realism Regained: An Exact Theory of Causation, Teleology and the Mind* (New York: Oxford University Press, 2000).

36 Fred I. Dretske, *Naturalizing the Mind* (Cambridge, MA: MIT Press, 1995); David Papineau, "Representation and Explanation," *Philosophy of Science* 51 (1984), 550–72; David Papineau, *Philosophical Naturalism* (Oxford: Basil Blackwell, 1993); Ruth Garrett Millikan, "Biosemantics," *Journal of Philosophy* 86 (1989): 281–97.
37 See, for example, Steven Weinberg's discussion of the role of such criteria in recent developments in physical theory: Steven Weinberg, *Dreams of a Final Theory: The Scientist's Search for the Ultimate Laws of Nature* (New York: Vintage Books, 1993), 133–65. See also Mark Steiner, *The Applicability of Mathematics as a Philosophical Problem* (Cambridge, MA: Harvard University Press, 1998) for other examples of the remarkable fruitfulness in science of aesthetic and purely mathematical analogies
38 Weinberg says exactly this in *Dreams of a Final Theory*, 148–9, 165.
39 Ibid., 155.
40 Ibid., 165.
41 C. S. Lewis, *Miracles: A Preliminary Study* (New York: Macmillan, 1947).
42 See Chapter 11 in this volume for Francis Beckwith's discussion of miracles.

Part II

ARGUMENTS FOR GOD'S EXISTENCE

5

THE ONTOLOGICAL ARGUMENT

Stephen T. Davis

Introduction

The so-called ontological argument for the existence of God (OA) is one of the most fascinating, as well as controversial, pieces of natural theology in the history of philosophy. Invented by Anselm (1033–1109), it appears in many versions and has been attacked and defended many times. Rather than try to survey the numerous criticisms that have been raised against it, I have decided instead to focus on the arguments of one contemporary critic of the OA (and indeed of Christian theism) – Michael Martin. His objections seem to be fairly representative of what many atheists and religious skeptics have to say about the OA.

In Chapter 3 of *Atheism: A Philosophical Justification*,[1] Martin discusses the OA. He considers five versions of it – those of Anselm, Malcolm, Hartshorne, Kordig, and Plantinga – and finds them all wanting. He concludes by admitting that he is tempted to agree with Schopenhauer's claim that the OA is nothing but a "charming joke." That is, he finds the OA entirely unsuccessful as an attempt to prove the existence of God.

Now the OA is unlike many of the other issues discussed in this book in that it will not particularly damage theism even if Martin is correct that all versions of the argument fail as theistic proofs.[2] As Martin will agree, God might exist even if the OA is a total failure. Indeed, it is safe to say that few theists place much apologetic emphasis on the OA; perhaps most theistic scholars agree with Martin that the OA is unsuccessful. But despite the fact that the soundness of the OA may not be crucial to theism, my own view is that Martin has not made his case. I find his critiques of the OAs of Malcolm, Hartshorne, and Kordig to be convincing; I too reject those versions of the OA, and for many of the reasons that Martin cites. But his criticisms of the OAs of Anselm and Plantinga can in my view be answered. Those versions of the OA still stand. To show that this is true is the main aim of this chapter.

The Anselmian ontological argument

I look first at Anselm's version. But before turning to Martin's criticisms of the argument, let me mention two closely related points where Martin misconstrues it. First, like many other critics, Martin sees the OA as "an attempt to prove the existence of God by simply analyzing the concept of God."[3] This oft-repeated claim is relatively harmless, but is nevertheless quite mistaken. It is true that Anselm's definition of God – "that being than which no greater can be conceived" – is crucial to his argument. We can call this being the "Greatest Conceivable being" (GCB). But merely analyzing that concept will get one nowhere in proving the existence in reality of anything. One must also bring into consideration what Anselm surely took to be certain necessary truths (e.g. *a thing is greater if it exists both in the mind and in reality than if it exists merely in the mind* and *the existence of the GCB is logically possible*). These claims are essential aspects of the OA, and do not follow merely from an examination of any concept of God.

Second, Martin avers that Anselm claims that the person who says, "God does not exist," contradicts himself. But this is also slightly misleading. Again, "God does not exist" only turns out to be necessarily false in conjunction with certain necessary truths such as those just listed. Anselm need not be committed to the claim that the bare sentence, "God does not exist," is self-contradictory, which it certainly is not. To be sure, Anselm held that the atheist's position can be shown to be necessarily false. It is so because that position is inconsistent with the definition of God, together with certain other necessary truths.

It is important that I lay out a version of Anselm's argument that I think can be defended against Martin's criticisms. I do not claim that the argument I shall express here is the only argument that can be drawn from the text of *Proslogion II*; indeed, just about everybody who talks about Anselm's argument has her own favorite version of it. I only claim that the argument stated below is the argument that seems to me to flow from Anselm's wording in *Proslogion* II, and that this version of the OA can be defended against Martin's criticisms.

1 Things can exist in only two ways: in the mind and in reality.
2 The GCB can possibly exist in reality, i.e. is not an impossible thing.
3 The GCB exists in the mind.
4 Whatever exists only in the mind and might possibly also exist in reality might have been greater than it is.
5 The GCB exists only in the mind.
6 The GCB might have been greater than it is.
7 The GCB is a being than which a greater is conceivable.
8 It is false that the GCB exists only in the mind.
9 Therefore, the GCB exists both in the mind and in reality.

Obviously, much of this needs explaining. So far as premise 1 is concerned, Anselm meant the expression "x exists in the mind" to mean simply that somebody imagines x, defines x, or conceives of x. The expression "x exists in reality" means that x exists as a concrete individual thing and exists quite independently of anyone's ideas or concepts of it. Thus there are four modes of existence; x might exist

- both in the mind and in reality (e.g. George W. Bush);
- in the mind but not in reality (e.g. unicorns, or Stephen Davis's ninth daughter);
- in reality but not in the mind (e.g. some as yet undiscovered but existing chemical element); and
- in neither way (e.g. nuclear power in the year AD 1550).

Premise 2 simply means that there is no contradiction or other sort of incoherence in the term "Greatest Conceivable Being." If so, the GCB is a being that can possibly exist (this does not mean that it *does* exist, of course), unlike impossible things like square circles or married bachelors. Premise 3 simply means that someone – Anselm, you the reader, or whoever – has conceived of the GCB; the GCB exists in the mind of that conceiver. Thus the GCB must have one of two of our four modes of existence (i.e. two of the four have been eliminated): it either exists like George W. Bush (i.e. both in the mind and in reality), or else it exists like my ninth daughter (i.e. just in the mind).

Premise 4 is sometimes called Anselm's "hidden premise." This is because he nowhere explicitly states it in *Proslogion II*, although it is perfectly clear that his argument needs it. The basic idea is that things are greater if they exist both in the mind and in reality than they would be if they existed merely in the mind. Paul Bunyan, the legendary woodsman, would be greater than he actually is had he existed in reality as well as in the mind. The space shuttle *Columbia* would be less great than it actually is if it were only the figment of some engineer's imagination. So, if we take "greater" to mean "more powerful" (I will explain this point below), Anselm should accordingly be taken as implying that things that exist both in the mind and in reality are more powerful, freer, more able to do things than they would be if they existed only in the mind.

Now premises 1, 2, 3, and 4 constitute Anselm's basic assumptions. Like any deductive argument, the soundness of the OA depends on the truth of its assumptions. If any of them is false, then the OA fails. (As indicated above, I think Anselm considered them to be not only true but necessarily true, but all that the OA strictly requires is that they be *true*.) Premise 5 is a premise that Anselm introduced in order to refute it by *reductio ad absurdum*. He believed that assuming the non-existence of the GCB, together with the earlier assumptions, will lead to a contradiction.

95

The next three premises constitute the logical outworking of Anselm's assumptions. This is where Anselm shows that premise 5 is unacceptable because it is responsible for producing a contradiction and thus is to be negated. If premises 5, 2, and 4 are true, then premise 6 follows. If the GCB is a mere concept (like my ninth daughter) and not an existing thing (like George W. Bush), then the GCB might have been greater than it is. Mere concepts presumably have some powers and abilities – they can sometimes help stimulate us to think more clearly or act in a certain way, for example – but not nearly so many powers and abilities as existing things. Existing things are greater than the mere concepts of them. If the GCB were a mere concept, then it would still be true that the possibly existing thing that we are calling the GCB could possibly exist (just as unicorns and my ninth daughter could possibly exist); and that if it did exist, it would be greater than it (the mere concept) in fact is.

Now premise 6 is at least implicitly contradictory; it says that "the greatest conceivable being might have been greater than it is." Another way of making this same point, and one that is directly entailed by premise 6, is premise:

7   The GCB is a being than which a greater is conceivable.

Now since premise 7 is an explicit contradiction, then by *reductio ad absurdum*, we must search for whatever premise above it in the argument is responsible for producing the contradiction. Realistically, this means inspecting the argument's assumptions, i.e. premises 1, 2, 3, 4, and 5. Anselm would argue that since the first four are all necessary truths (or at least truths), the culprit premise must be 5. We are allowed, then, by *reductio ad absurdum*, to negate premise 5.

The negation of premise 5 is premise 8. Now we know by premise 1 that things can exist in only two ways, in the mind and in reality. And we know by premise 3 that the GCB exists (at least) in the mind. And we know by premise 8 that it is false that the GCB exists only in the mind. Thus it follows that

9   the GCB exists both in the mind and in reality,

which was what we were trying to prove.

Thus far I have not tried to defend the OA against objections. I have only been trying to explicate Anselm's argument, or at least a version of it that can plausibly be taken from the text of *Proslogion II*. There are very many criticisms that have been made of Anselm's argument over the centuries. Obviously, I cannot address them all. But I can show that Anselm's version of the OA can be defended against the objections raised by Michael Martin.

Criticisms of Anselm's ontological argument

Is "exists" a predicate?

Let us then turn to Martin's three criticisms of Anselm's OA. The first criticism is this: is "exists" a predicate? Martin's version of my premise 4 is, "An entity is greater if it exists in reality than if it exists only as a mental object." He then points out that this sentence has been challenged, e.g. by Kant's claim that "exists" is not a "real predicate," i.e. not a real property of things.[4] Martin does not argue that Kant is correct; he merely points out that Kant's argument makes the OA controversial, and thus not a "clearly sound argument." Well, if a *sound* argument is a valid argument whose premises are true, then I suppose a *clearly sound* argument is a clearly valid argument whose premises are clearly true. Does the mere existence of Kant's argument in the history of philosophy make the OA controversial? Well, the answer to that question is surely yes, especially given the great influence that Kant's objection has had in subsequent discussions of the OA. But philosophers who defend the OA will not mind admitting that Anselm's argument is controversial; unless they have kept their head inside a bag throughout their career, they know that already. But does the existence of Kant's objection make the OA not clearly sound? Well, perhaps it does that too; I have no desire to deny it, in any case. So let us agree that the OA is not a clearly sound argument. But the crucial point here is that the OA does not have to be *clearly sound* for it to be an entirely successful theistic proof. It need only be *sound*.[5]

Martin points out that even if defenders of the OA can show that "exists" is a property of things, this is not enough for the needs of the OA. They must also show that "exists" is a property of things *that adds to the greatness of things that have it*. And Martin is correct about that. The existence of a thing may be neutral as to its greatness, he says; it may even detract from its greatness. And, so far as God is concerned, Martin says, "the assumption that God does not exist does not seem to take away from His perfection [Martin should have said 'greatness']."[6]

Is this a good objection to Anselm's version of the OA? I do not think so. But while something is clearly amiss in the neighborhood here, part of the blame lies with Anselm not Martin. Sadly, in the *Proslogion* Anselm never tells us exactly what "great" means or what it is for one thing to be "greater" than another. That constitutes a large lacuna in Anselm's argument. And it is left to interpreters of Anselm to ask something that Martin did not bother to ask, namely what did Anselm mean by "greater"? That is, what notion of greatness *did* Anselm have in mind in order to give the OA a chance of being a successful theistic proof?

There are at first glance a host of things that we might mean by "greater"; the term might mean "faster" or "taller" or "more red-headed," for example. But clearly the OA cannot possibly work on those meanings. This is for the obvious reason that there logically can be no such thing as the "fastest conceivable being" or the "tallest conceivable being" or the "most red-headed conceivable being." Now there is some textual evidence that Anselm wanted to understand greatness in terms of goodness.[7] But let me explain further a suggestion made above, one that I do not claim is Anselm's intended notion of "greater" (although it is very much in the spirit of the view of God that Anselm works with in all his writings); I merely claim that it is a coherent notion of "greater," and at least has a chance of making the OA work.

Suppose we read greatness as *power, ability, freedom of action*. This will accomplish several things that the OA needs. *First*, things will be comparable with respect to greatness: coyotes are greater (freer, more powerful, more able to do things, etc.) than stones, humans are greater than collies, the president of the United States is greater than the governor of South Dakota. This is important because some possible ways of understanding "greater" do not allow for commensurability (e.g. if we understand it as meaning *being more of a prime number*: no prime number can be more of a prime number than another prime number). *Second*, greatness, understood in this way, admits of a maximal degree. All things will be less great than the GCB, where the GCB is understood roughly to be an omnipotent or all-powerful being, and where an omnipotent being is understood to be a being that has the property of being able to bring about any state of affairs that it is not logically impossible for it to bring about. That is a degree of power, of freedom of action, that logically cannot be bested. *Third*, greatness understood in this sense is intuitively a great-making property. Red-headedness is probably not; suppose there are two beings, exactly alike in as many of their properties as possible, except that one is red-headed and the other is blond; we would not necessarily feel that the red-headed one is greater. But this is not true of power or freedom of action. We do intuitively feel that an alarm clock is a greater thing than a toothpick; a raccoon a greater thing than an amoeba; a human being a greater thing than a cow.

Is "exists" a property (or, as Kant would have it, a real predicate)? It certainly is an unusual property. As Kant correctly says, if we add "and x exists" to a list of assertions about x, this does not expand or increase our knowledge of x. (Or at least – as I will argue – this is correct in *some* cases.) This is clearly the point of Norman Malcolm's question in support of Kant (cited by Martin): "What could it mean to say that [my future house] will be a better house if it exists than if it does not?"[8] If a property or a real predicate is something that appears in the predicate position of a sentence and that increases our knowledge of the subject, then "exists" sometimes does fail to be a property or real predicate.

But it seems to me that this will only be true in cases where the existence of the thing is already presupposed in the conversation. We often do tacitly

Knowing something exists adds to our knowledge about that thing.

is this an equivocation on what it means to know about something?

limit our conversation to the set of existing things. Thus the oddity of the following conversation:

> Do you own a car?
> Yes, I do.
> Does your car run?
> Yes.
> Is your car a Honda?
> Yes.
> Do you drive your car to work?
> Yes.
> But does your car exist?

The problem here is that the car's existence was apparently presupposed throughout the conversation; thus the strangeness of the concluding question. If the reply to it were to be, "Yes, of course my car exists," this would not (as Kant would surely say) change or expand our concept of the car. We were assuming an existing car all along. Here Kant is apparently correct.

But sometimes we broaden the ontological horizons of our language and talk about things that are, or possibly are, non-existent – things that are, say, mythical, extinct, legendary, dead, or fictional. And in those cases it might well add to our knowledge of a thing to say that it does (or does not) exist. In such cases, "exists" appears to be a property or real predicate. The statement that Malcolm implicitly questions ("My house will be a better house if it exists than if it does not") sounds fishy because talk about one's future house would normally be embedded in a conversation that takes for granted its real (future) existence. But suppose we are not taking that for granted. Then his question can make perfect sense. I would certainly prefer to have a house that actually exists – will really give shelter from the weather, for example – than a non-existent house that appears, say, only in a novel. In linguistic situations in which we are wondering whether the house is fictional or a legend, it will indeed increase our knowledge of the house if we are truthfully told and come to believe that it exists.

But even if this is true, Martin insists, it still needs to be shown that "exists" is a property *that adds to the greatness of a thing*. And Martin is correct that this is a quite separate point from showing that "exists" is a property. But here is where the definition of "greater" becomes crucial. Doubtless on some notions of "greater," to exist is not necessarily to be greater than not to exist. That is, exists is not a great-making property. But on the notion of greatness that I am defending, to exist in reality *is* to be greater than not to exist in reality. Existing things are more powerful, freer, more able to do things than those things would be if they did not exist, than for example the mere concepts of them. Mere concepts, extinct animals, dead generals, mythical woodsmen, fictional islands, unachieved ideals – such things are able to do some things. As noted, they can provide examples, help us tell stories, even stimulate us to act. But beyond that, their powers are strictly limited. An imaginary house can keep imaginary rain off our backs, but not real rain. A God that truly exists is far greater than that same God would be if it did not exist.

Martin quite misleadingly fiddles with Anselm's notion of "greater," suggesting that it be replaced by such notions as "is more valued" or "is more prized" or "is more desirable." He then points out that desirability is a relative notion, and that there will be many people who will not find the actual existence of God at all desirable. That is certainly true (one suspects that Martin himself would not find it desirable), but it has no relevance whatsoever to the success of the OA as a theistic proof. As long as there is a notion of "greater" (like the notion of power or freedom of action or ability to do things) that is coherent and makes the OA succeed (i.e. according to which it will be true that "a thing is greater if it exists in the mind and in reality than if it exists merely in the mind"), it will not matter one bit whether there are folk who find the existence of God undesirable. The logic of the situation is this: it is unfair for critics of Anselm to supply their own notions of greatness, notions that cannot possibly allow the OA to succeed. This is surely true of Martin's notion of "more desirable." Since Anselm, as noted, does not supply us with his own notion or definition of greatness, fair-minded interpreters of the OA must ask what notion of greatness (a) is consistent with Anselm's views about God and (b) has a chance of allowing Anselm's argument to succeed.

Anselm's point, then, is that existing things are greater than the mere concepts of them. So if the fool were correct and the GCB was a mere concept (if it existed, as Anselm says, only in the mind), it would still be true that the non-existing thing described by the concept "Greatest Conceivable Being" could possibly exist, and that if it did exist it would be greater than it (as non-existing) in fact is. There are surely lots of difficulties that could be and have been raised against the OA at this point.[9] But I have said enough to show that Anselm's argument can be defended against Martin's first objection.

Lost islands and greatest evil beings

Martin's second main criticism of Anselm's argument is his appeal to what I will call "parallel OAs." (Martin calls them parodies of the OA.) That is, Martin follows the strategy laid out by Gaunilo centuries ago in arguing that the basic logic of the OA (a *reductio ad absurdum* argument based on a definition of a thing involving the term "greatest conceivable," together with certain necessary truths) can be used to "prove" the existence of all sorts of bizarre entities that we know good and well do not exist. These are entities such as (using Gaunilo's own example) *"the greatest conceivable lost island*" (GCLI) or "the absolute evil one." (This is Martin's term; he should, of course, have said, "the Greatest Conceivable Evil Being" (GCEB) or perhaps "the *Most Evil* Conceivable Being"; since "the absolute evil one" is not necessarily the greatest conceivable member of any set, no parallel OA in which this terms appears will be able to advance toward the desired *reductio*.) What you do is simply remove the term "GCB" from the OA and systematically replace it with some other term like "GCLI" or "GCEB"; what results will be a parallel OA; and if the OA is a successful argument (so it is argued), so will be the parallel OA. But we know that the parallel OA is fallacious (we know, for example, that no GCLI exists); ergo, the OA itself must equally be fallacious. Moreover, Martin says, the GCB and the absolute evil one cannot both exist, since they are "mutually exclusive." "Clearly," he says, "something is wrong."[10]

Anselm himself replied to Gaunilo's objection. His response was brief and rather flippant, and Martin finds it unhelpful (it consists, he says, of "little more than insisting that the reasoning used in the argument can only be applied to God"). But I will argue that Anselm's reply was more incisive that Martin admits. Anselm said:
than

> Now I promise confidently that if any man shall devise anything exist-
> ing either in reality or in concept alone (except that than which a greater
> cannot be conceived) to which he can adapt the sequence of my reason-
> ing, I will discover that thing, and will give him his lost island, not to
> be lost again.

In other words, Anselm wanted to argue, as Martin notices, that the OA is a sound argument and that Gaunilo's parallel OA containing the term GCLI is not.[11]

How might Anselm argue, and not just assert, that his own argument is sound and Gaunilo's is not? The crucial point concerns premise 2 of the OA, which says:

2   The GCB can possibly exist in reality, i.e. is not an impossible thing.

And in Gaunilo's parallel OA, the counterpart premise would be:

2a The GCLI can possibly exist in reality, i.e. is not an impossible thing.

Now some philosophers have argued that premise 2 is false; they hold that the concept of God is contradictory or otherwise incoherent. But my own view is that these arguments have never amounted to much. (Chapter 12 by Charles Taliaferro answers certain arguments on this point.) Moreover, we are, strictly speaking, considering the concept of the GCB, not God (even though Anselm, along with most readers of the OA, took them to be the same), which I am interpreting as the most powerful conceivable being. The GCB, I would argue, is surely a possible thing. And, as noted above, the GCB has something like this property: it is able to bring about any state of affairs that it is logically possible for it (the GCB) to bring about.

But is premise 2a true? That is, is the concept of the GCLI a coherent concept? Anselm apparently thought not. Much depends here on what is meant by the word "conceivable" – that is, it depends on how widely we draw the limits of conceivability. We might draw them narrowly or widely. To draw them narrowly is to say that conceivability equals logical possibility, i.e. logically impossible things are inconceivable. To draw them widely is to say that conceivability is broader than logical possibility (i.e. that it is possible to conceive of logically impossible things). How Anselm will respond to Gaunilo-type objections to the OA will depend on which route the objector takes.

Suppose the objector wants wide limits. We can conceive, then, of logically impossible things like square circles, married bachelors, and contingent things possessing unlimited perfections. Then there is a big problem with premise 2a: the greater we make the GCLI in conception, the less it will resemble an island. Now we have seen that more powerful things are greater than less powerful things; moreover (as Anselm explicitly says in *Proslogion III*), necessary things are greater than contingent things. It follows, then, that the GCLI will be a necessary and omnipotent being. It will be everlasting, will depend for its existence on nothing else, and will be able to solve equations, write poetry, and manufacture carburetors. Now there is no problem with the GCB being an omnipotent, necessary being – that is just what we would expect. But surely islands are essentially contingent and non-omnipotent things. They depend for their existence on geological, oceanographic, and other forces. There are things that they cannot do. That is why the GCLI cannot possibly exist and why premise 2a is false. On a wide understanding of conceivability, the GCLI, i.e. a necessary and omnipotent island, is logically impossible.

At this point a defender of Gaunilo will opt for retiring to the narrower notion of conceivability, where what is conceivable equals what is logically possible. If so, we will have to conceive of the GCLI in terms of the great-making properties that islands can possibly have, properties like the temperature, the beauty of the scenery, the height of the surf, the number of palm trees, the taste of the coconuts, etc. Thus the term GCLI will no longer name an impossible being. Now Martin grasps this point. He says: "But if one means by 'the greatest conceivable island' a perfect island, it will not have an unlimited number of coconut trees but only the *right* number of coconut trees, whatever that may be."[12]

But there is a big problem here as well, and Martin has walked right into it: there is no "way that it may be" or "way that it is" here. These sorts of great-making properties have no intrinsic or objective criteria of greatness.

102

How do we decide which of two beautiful scenes is more beautiful, or which taste of coconuts is better, or how high the surf should be? These items seem to be matters of taste – do we vote? Moreover, these sorts of great-making properties have no intrinsic maximums or discernible limits. Thus there logically can be no "great*est* conceivable lost island." Thus, again, even on the narrower way of understanding conceivability, premise 2a is false.

It appears, then, that no matter how we understand the term "conceivable," Gaunilo's parallel OA will be unsound because it will contain at least one false premise, i.e. premise 2a. The GCLI cannot possibly exist in reality. Accordingly, Anselm was right in insisting that the term GCLI cannot be adapted to the sequence of his reasoning. The "lost island" objection to the OA accordingly fails.

Then what about Martin's "absolute evil one" ("the *Greatest Evil Conceivable Being*" or GECB)? Does this concept constitute a counter-example to Anselm's argument? Not at all – and for the same reason. In Martin's imagined parallel OA, the parallel premise to the OA's premise 2 would be:

2b The GECB can possibly exist in reality, i.e. is not an impossible thing.

And of course all the same problems come up. There is no intrinsic maximum to the degree of heinousness of the deeds a given being can do. Just as there logically can be no "tallest conceivable human being," so there logically can be no GECB. For every evil deed that we imagine an evil being as doing, we can always imagine a being who does one more evil deed. No matter how terrible the deeds we imagine an evil being as doing, we can always imagine a being who does deeds even more terrible. Thus premise 2b is false; Martin's imagined parallel OA fails; and Anselm's argument emerges wholly unscathed from Martin's second criticism.

Now Martin might want to claim that the same sorts of games can be played with the concept of the GCB. That is, surely Anselm thought that some such concept as "supremely morally good" was part of the greatness of the God. And I would agree with Anselm at that point. But in the OA we are talking not about God but the GCB (even though these terms may in the end have the same referent), and I am unable to produce a version of the OA that makes moral goodness a great-making property. Thus as noted I recommend a different notion of "great," one that leaves open the moral character of the GCB, to be decided wholly on other grounds.

Mackie's criticism

Finally, Martin repeats against Anselm a criticism of J. L. Mackie.[13] Mackie's basic point, which is a neighbor of a point also made by Gaunilo,[14] is that it is impossible to prove the existence of any concrete reality by an entirely a priori procedure, i.e. merely by examining concepts or definitions. The fool only contradicts himself, Martin says, if the fool's concept is *a non-existent being than which no greater can be conceived*. But the fool should only be conceiving of *a being than which no greater can be conceived*. There is no contradiction in the fool claiming that such a being does not exist – that is, that the concept has no instantiation in the real world. Understood that way, the fool can even grant Anselm's claim that "exists" is a great-making property and thus that existence is part of the concept of the GCB. The fool will simply insist that the concept is not an instantiated concept. *Definitionally*, the GCB would exist (must be conceived as existing) in reality (just as the concept "an existing Loch Ness monster" must be conceived as existing). And the statement, "The GCB does not exist" would indeed be contradictory. But that would not show that the GCB exists in fact (i.e. that the concept "GCB" is instantiated).

But it must be insisted at this point that nowhere has Anselm defined the GCB as existing in reality, or even assumed that the GCB exists in reality. It is possible to come up with an a priori theistic proof that goes something like this. For example:

10 "God" is an existing omnipotent and omniscient and loving being.
11 Therefore, God exists.

But that argument – formally valid as it is – is intellectually uninteresting and unworthy of serious consideration because it egregiously begs the question. It assumes in premise 10 exactly what it purports to prove in premise 11. But there is no such strategy in Anselm.

Perhaps at heart Martin's objection is to the very idea of using an a priori procedure to prove the existence in reality of something. But we certainly can prove some things about what exists or does not exist in reality by purely a priori procedures (i.e. without empirically looking around or counting or experimenting). For example, it can be shown that married bachelors ("unmarried adult males who are married") and square circles ("plane four-sided geometrical figures all of whose points are equidistant from the center") cannot and thus do not exist in reality. Similarly, it can be shown by purely a priori procedures that there exists at least one prime number between six and ten. The point is not that Anselm's GCB is like a number, but that a priori procedures can prove the existence in reality of certain sorts of things.

But the most important point here is that it is question-begging simply to insist against Anselm that "you cannot do that," i.e. that no a priori proofs of the existence of something can possibly be successful. The OA itself will have to be examined to see whether it does succeed. If it does not, the precise reason that it fails will have to be shown.

Accordingly, Martin's criticisms of Anselm's *Proslogion II* OA are entirely unsuccessful in overturning it. Anselm's argument may or may not constitute a sound theistic proof, but Martin has not shown that it does not.

Plantinga's modal ontological argument

It is now time to consider Martin's critique of Alvin Plantinga's version of the OA, what has come to be called the Modal OA (MOA). Here is Martin's version of Plantinga's argument (with the numbers of the premises changed so that they conform with the numbering in this chapter). Plantinga here defines *maximal greatness* as entailing maximal excellence in every possible world, and *maximal excellence* as entailing omniscience, omnipotence, and moral perfection in every possible world.

12   There is a possible world where maximal greatness is exemplified.
13   There is some possible world in which there is a being that is maximally great (from premise 12).
14   Necessarily, a being that is maximally great is maximally excellent in every possible world (by definition).
15   Necessarily, a being that is maximally excellent in every possible world is omniscient, omnipotent, and morally perfect in every possible world (by definition).
16   Therefore, there is in our world and in every world a being that is omniscient, omnipotent, and morally perfect (from premises 13, 14, and 15).

Martin correctly notes that Plantinga does not take the MOA as a conclusive demonstration of the existence of a maximally excellent being since Plantinga knows that rational people can deny premise 12. But since Plantinga thinks that premise 12 is not contrary to reason, the MOA demonstrates the rational acceptability of belief in God.

Now since Martin says nothing about accessibility relations among possible words, let me add a few introductory remarks about the MOA.[15] The MOA is based on the modal logical system S5, whose characteristic theorem is:

17   $\blacklozenge \Box p \rightarrow \Box p$.

Also crucial to the S5 system is the symmetry condition on the accessibility relations between possible worlds. Let us say that one possible world x is *accessible* from another possible world y if and only if x is possible in y. And let us say that an accessibility relation R has the property of *symmetry* if and only if when any possible world x is accessible to another possible world y, it follows that y is accessible to x.

Now take the property "unsurpassable greatness" (UG). If this property is possibly instantiated, then there exists a possible world x, in which a certain being instantiates UG. But given Plantinga's definition of UG, a being that instantiates UG is such that if it exists in any possible world, then it is necessary that it exists in that world. Ergo, it is necessary that a being instantiates UG in x. And since we are assuming that symmetry holds, it follows that a being that instantiates UG will exist in every world that is accessible to x. But since the actual world is obviously one of the worlds accessible to x, it follows that a being instantiates UG in the actual world as well. Thus the semantics of S5, especially the symmetry condition, allows Plantinga to postulate the existence of a being instantiating UG in a merely possible world and thereby establish that being's existence in the actual world.

Martin offers three criticisms of the MOA. First, following J. L. Mackie, he argues that the S5 modal system is inappropriate. Second, he argues that the use Plantinga makes of Leibniz's Law (which I will explain soon) is a poor example. Third, he argues as above with Gaunilo that Plantinga's MOA can be parodied. Let us considers these points in turn.

Is S5 appropriate?

So far as the first point is concerned, Martin does not develop it at length. He simply says that

> technical questions can be raised about the use of possible world semantics and modal logic in [Plantinga's] proof. In particular, it may be wondered if the system of modal logic used in Plantinga's proof is appropriate and if Plantinga has provided adequate truth conditions for modal sentences.[16]

And Martin specifically refers to published arguments by Mackie and Michael Tooley. Martin's worry here is not easy to grasp, especially since nearly every philosopher who discusses the MOA agrees that the S5 modal system is entirely appropriate in this context. Indeed, Plantinga himself has answered Mackie's criticisms about S5, in my view rather decisively.[17]

What exactly is Martin's concern? Perhaps he wants to dispute premise 17. But premise 17 seems intuitively obvious to many people, including me, and powerful arguments can be suggested in its favor. Let us call the set of all possible worlds "p." Now let us arbitrarily pick any possible world within p and call it "w." Question: if $\Box p$ is true, what is the truth value of $\Box p$ in w? Obviously, $\Box p$ has the truth value *true* in w. This is because in w, the proposition $\Box p$ asserts that p is true both in w and in every other possible world. But whatever is true of any arbitrarily selected possible world is true of *every* possible world. Thus, if it is possible that p is necessarily true in some world, then p is necessarily true. And that is just what premise 17 asserts.

106

Here is another argument for the same point. Clearly, a proposition and its contrapositive are logically equivalent. If "If p then q" is true, then so is "If not q then not p." The contrapositive of premise 17 is:

18   $\sim \Box p \rightarrow \sim \blacklozenge \Box p$.

To some people, premise 18 might have even more intuitive appeal than premise 17, since, obviously, if a proposition p does not have the property of being true in all possible worlds, then it follows that it is not even possible that p be true in all possible worlds. That is, it is false that in some worlds it is true that p is true in all worlds. So if p is not necessarily true, then it is not possible that p be necessarily true. Now if this seems correct, then premise 18 is true. And if premise 18 is true, then so is its contrapositive premise 17.[18]

Now another characteristic formula of the S5 system of modal logical is:

19   $\blacklozenge p \rightarrow \Box \blacklozenge p$.

Perhaps premise 19 constitutes Martin's worry about S5. And premise 19 simply says that if p is true in at least one possible world, then the proposition, "p is true in at least one possible world" is true in all possible worlds. In other words, a proposition's modal status – whatever it is – is always necessary. And maybe Martin is suspicious of premise 19.

But premise 19 seems eminently plausible. Look at the cost of denying it. To deny that $\blacklozenge p$ implies $\Box \blacklozenge p$ is to assert that p may have the property of *being true in at least one possible world* even though the assertion that it has this property is not true in every possible world (i.e. is *false* in at least one possible world). But this is simply false. Let p stand for the proposition

20   There will be a nuclear war within the next decade.

Now I do not know whether premise 20 is true (I *hope* not), but it is certainly *possibly* true. Thus, returning to premise 19, its antecedent is true for this particular substitution instance of p. But in order for Martin to deny premise 19, he must hold that there is a possible world in which it is *false* that premise 20 is logically possible. That is, he must hold that there is a possible world in which premise 20 is logically impossible. But surely there is no such world; any possible world in which premise 20 is logically impossible will itself be a logically impossible world. Accordingly, one cannot affirm the antecedent and deny the consequent of premise 19.

Again, this point seems plausible. How could some proposition q be true in some possible world and yet fail to be logically possible in some other possible world? If it is possible that q is true, then there is a possible world

– call it "w" – in which q is true. But then it follows that "q is true in w" is true in every possible world. That is, it is necessary that it is possible that q is true in w.[19] So Martin's objection to the S5 system of modal logic does not amount to much. If we are to believe that there is a serious objection to the MOA somewhere in the neighborhood, Martin is going to have to say a great deal more.

Plantinga's use of Leibniz's Law

As part of his argument for the truth of premise 12, which he admits that rational people can deny, Plantinga makes reference to Leibniz's Law (LL). He points out that we have no proof of LL, but we are justified in accepting it. But Martin objects that the analogy between premise 12 and LL is tenuous. He identifies LL as:

(LL) For any objects x and y and property P, if $x = y$, then x has P if and only if y has P.

He then says, "(LL) is a free English translation of a theorem of first-order predicate calculus with identity, but [premise 12] is not a translation of a theorem of any standard logic. Disputes about (LL) in the history of philosophy, unlike disputes about [premise 12], seem to be metalinguistic and not over the truth value of (LL)."[20]

This point seems to me to be Martin's best argument against Plantinga, but in the end it goes nowhere. Plantinga might happily admit that there are disanalogies between LL and premise 12, maybe even that his example was poorly chosen, and proceed merrily on his way. Even if Martin is entirely correct, this does nothing to weaken the MOA. Plantinga might well find better examples of philosophical propositions that we rationally accept without proof. Clearly, what Plantinga had pre-eminently in mind is the fact that both premise 12 and LL are either necessarily true or necessarily false. Other positions in philosophy that are either necessarily true or necessarily false and which many people rationally accept without proof are realism on universals, nominalism, actualism, serious actualism, and David Lewis's modal realism.

Parodies of the MOA

Finally, Martin argues that Plantinga's OA, like Anselm's, can be refuted by parody or (as I prefer) by a parallel OA. He claims that the MOA

can be parodied by using an argument with the same form to show the rational acceptability of fairies, ghosts, unicorns, and all manner of strange creatures. One *reductio* of this mode of argument proceeds as follows: "Let us define the property of being a special fairy so that it entails the property of being a fairy in every possible world. Let us define the property of being a fairy so that it entails the property of being a tiny woodland creature with magical powers in every possible world."[21]

Martin then goes on to state his parallel MOA, using the concept "special fairy" in place of "maximally excellent being." (Again, the numbers of Martin's premises have been changed.)

21 There is one possible world where the property of being a special fairy is exemplified.
22 There is one possible world where there is a special fairy (from premise 21).
23 Necessarily, a being that is a special fairy is a fairy in every possible world (by definition).
24 Necessarily, a being that is a fairy in every possible world is a tiny woodland creature with magical powers in every possible world (by definition).
25 Therefore, there is a tiny woodland creature with magical powers in our world and in every world.

Martin argues that premise 22 is "no more contrary to reason" than premise 12 of the MOA, and thus that premise 25 is just as acceptable as the conclusion of the MOA. The moral is supposed to be, as before with Gaunilo and Anselm, that something is clearly defective about the MOA.

But this argument collapses almost before it can even get going. Premise 22 is the culprit. It is about as clear as it could be that there can be no such thing as a *necessarily existent fairy*. Fairies, presumably, are physical objects (or are at least essentially connected to physical objects). And no physical object can be a necessary being, since it is possible that there be no material objects at all. But since Plantinga's Maximally Excellent Being (like Anselm's GCB) is not necessarily a physical object, this objection to Martin's parallel MOA has no relevance to the MOA. Moreover, physical or not, the very idea of a necessarily existent fairy is, if not explicitly contradictory, at least deeply problematical. We saw above in our discussion of Gaunilo that no island can be a necessary being, and surely the same is true of fairies. It is difficult to imagine a tiny woodland creature with magical powers as anything other than a contingent being.

The conclusion is that Martin's criticisms not only do not refute the MOA but leave it virtually unscathed. Plantinga's version of the OA – even given its admitted limitation that rational people can deny premise 12 – still stands as a successful piece of natural theology. It shows that rational people can rationally believe in the existence of a maximally excellent being.

Conclusion

It is not surprising that Michael Martin, an atheist, would reject the OA in all its versions. For the OA is a "knock-down" argument. If it is a formally and informally valid argument, and if its premises are true, then the being whose existence is being proven does indeed exist. That is, the OA is not a probabilistic argument or an argument based on making broad inferences from huge sets of data. If the OA succeeds, then God exists, and that is the end of the matter. Perhaps this is one reason that the OA has always been so disturbing to so many atheists, agnostics, and even some theists (who reject the OA but believe in God on other grounds).

This is related to a phenomenon I have often observed in students who study the OA. Not infrequently, some of them describe themselves as being unable to refute the argument but being deeply suspicious of it. For one reason or another, they are unable to accept the conclusion of the OA, and so they say, "But something *must* be wrong with it." Well, perhaps there is something wrong with the OA. But even if so, Michael Martin has not located what is wrong. So far as his criticisms are concerned, the OA still stands.[22]

Notes

1 Michael Martin, *Atheism: A Philosophical Justification* (Philadelphia: Temple University Press, 1990).
2 In this way, it is also quite unlike my own previous debates with Martin on the resurrection of Jesus. See, for example, Michael Martin, "Why the Resurrection Is Initially Improbable," *Philo*, 1, 1 (1998). See also Stephen T. Davis, "Is Belief in the Resurrection Rational? A Response to Michael Martin" and Michael Martin, "Reply to Davis," both in *Philo* 2, 1 (1999). See also Stephen T. Davis, "The Rationality of Resurrection for Christians: A Rejoinder" and Michael Martin, "Christianity and the Rationality of Resurrection," both in *Philo* 3, 1 (2000).
3 Martin, *Atheism*, 79.
4 See Immanuel Kant, *The Critique of Pure Reason*, Norman Kemp Smith (trans.) (New York: St Martin's Press, 1965), 500–7.
5 See the discussion of the criteria of success for theistic proofs in my *God, Reason, and Theistic Proofs* (Edinburgh: Edinburgh University Press, 1997), 1–14, 176–93.
6 Martin, *Atheism*, 81.
7 He occasionally used the term *melius* ("better") instead of *maius* ("greater"). See also *Monologion II* and *Proslogion V*, where he said to God: "Therefore, thou art just, truthful, blessed, and whatever it is better to be than not to be."
8 Martin, *Atheism*, 81.
9 Many of them are explored more fully in my *God, Reason, and Theistic Proofs*, 79–95.
10 Martin, *Atheism*, 82.
11 Anselm did follow a blind alley in responding to Gaunilo: he was at great pains to show that the GCLI is not the same thing as, and is less great than, the GCB. That much is true, but need hardly bother Gaunilo. Gaunilo's point was not that

the GCLI *is* the GCB; his point was rather that if the OA (containing the term GCB) is a sound argument, then so is his own parallel OA (containing the term GCLI). Surely – so he would have argued – in any valid argument substitutions can be made for the terms that appear in the argument; and if the substitutions are made carefully, the resulting argument will also be valid. Thus, (1) All men are mortal; (2) Jimmy Durante is a man; (3) therefore, Jimmy Durante is mortal.

12 Martin, Atheism, 83.
13 It is found in J. L. Mackie's *The Miracle of Theism* (Oxford: Clarendon Press, 1982), 52–3.
14 See Anselm, *Basic Writings*, 149–50.
15 I have been influenced here by R. Kane's essay, "The Modal Ontological Argument," *Mind* 92 (1984), 336–50.
16 Martin, *Atheism*, 93–4.
17 Alvin Plantinga, "Is Theism Really a Miracle?," *Faith and Philosophy* 3/2 (April 1986), 109–34. See also James F. Sennett, "Universe Indexed Properties and the Fate of the Ontological Argument," *Religious Studies* 27/1 (March 1991), 65–79.
18 See again Kane, 342.
19 For this argument, see Raymond Bradley and Norman Swartz, *Possible Worlds: An Introduction to Logic and Its Philosophy* (Indianapolis: Hackett, 1979), 223.
20 Martin, *Atheism*, 94.
21 Ibid.
22 I would like to thank Susan Peppers, Alvin Plantinga, and Colin Ruloff for their helpful suggestions on earlier versions of this paper.

6

THE COSMOLOGICAL ARGUMENT

William Lane Craig

Introduction

It has become conventional wisdom that in light of the critiques of Hume and Kant there are no good arguments for the existence of God. But insofar as we mean by a "good argument" an argument which is formally and informally valid and consists of true premises which are more plausible than their negations, there do appear to be good arguments for God's existence, and there are on the contemporary scene many philosophers who think so. Indeed, it would be fair to say that the rise of analytic philosophy of religion has been accompanied by a resurgence of interest in natural theology – that branch of theology which seeks to offer cogent arguments or reasons for God's existence apart from the resources of authoritative divine revelation. In this chapter I shall focus on the so-called cosmological argument for the existence of God.

The cosmological argument is a family of arguments which seeks to demonstrate the existence of a *sufficient reason* or *first cause* of the existence of the cosmos. The roll of the defenders of this argument reads like a *Who's Who* of Western philosophy: Plato, Aristotle, ibn Sina, al-Ghazali, Maimonides, Anselm, Aquinas, Scotus, Descartes, Spinoza, Leibniz, and Locke, to name but some. The arguments can be grouped into three basic types: the *kalam* cosmological argument for a First Cause of the beginning of the universe, the Thomist cosmological argument for a sustaining Ground of Being of the world, and the Leibnizian cosmological argument for a Sufficient Reason why something exists rather than nothing.

The *kalam* cosmological argument derives its name from the Arabic word designating medieval Islamic scholasticism, the intellectual movement largely responsible for developing the argument. It aims to show that the universe had a beginning at some moment in the finite past and, since something cannot come out of nothing, must therefore have a transcendent cause, which brought the universe into being. Classical proponents of the argument sought to demonstrate that the universe began to exist on the basis of philosophical arguments against the existence of an infinite, temporal regress of past events. Contemporary interest in the argument arises largely out of the startling empirical evidence of astrophysical cosmology for a beginning of space and time. Today, the controlling paradigm of cosmology is the standard Big Bang model, according to which the space-time universe originated *ex nihilo* about 15 billion years ago. Such an origin *ex nihilo* seems to many to cry out for a transcendent cause.

By contrast the Thomist cosmological argument, named for the medieval philosophical theologian Thomas Aquinas, seeks a cause which is first, not in the temporal sense, but in the sense of rank. Aquinas agreed that "If the world and motion have a first beginning, some cause must clearly be posited for this origin of the world and of motion."[1] But since he did not regard the *kalam* arguments for the past's finitude as demonstrative, he argued for God's existence on the more difficult assumption of the eternity of the world. On Aquinas's Aristotelian-inspired metaphysic, every existing finite thing is composed of essence and existence and is therefore radically contingent. A thing's essence is an individual nature which serves to define what that thing is. Now if an individual essence is to exist, there must be conjoined with that essence an act of being. This act of being involves a continual bestowal of being, or the thing would be annihilated. Essence is in potentiality to the act of being, and therefore without the bestowal of being the essence would not exist. For the same reason no substance can actualize itself; for in order to bestow being upon itself, it would have to be already actual. A pure potentiality cannot actualize itself but requires some external cause. Now although Aquinas argued that there cannot be an infinite regress of causes of being (because in such a series all the causes would be merely instrumental and so no being would be produced, just as no motion would be produced in a watch without a spring even if it had an infinite number of gears), and that therefore there must exist a First Uncaused Cause of being, his actual view was that there can be no intermediate causes of being at all, that any finite substance is sustained in existence immediately by the Ground of Being. This must be a being which is not composed of essence and existence and, hence, requires no sustaining cause. We cannot say that this being's essence includes existence as one of its properties, for existence is not a property but an act, the instantiating of an essence. Therefore, we must conclude that this being's essence just *is* existence. In a sense, this being has no essence; rather it is the pure act of being, unconstrained by any essence. It is, as Thomas says, *ipsum esse subsistens*, the act of being itself subsisting. Thomas identifies this being with the God whose name was revealed to Moses as "I AM" (Exodus 3:15).

The German polymath Gottfried Wilhelm Leibniz, for whom the third form of the argument is named, sought to develop a version of the cosmological argument from contingency without the Aristotelian metaphysical underpinnings of the Thomist argument. "The first question which should rightly be asked," he wrote, "is this: why is there something rather than nothing?"[2] Leibniz meant this question to be truly universal, not merely to apply to finite things. On the basis of his Principle of Sufficient Reason, that "no fact can be real or existent, no statement true, unless there be a sufficient reason why it is so and not otherwise,"[3] Leibniz held that this question must have an answer. It will not do to say that the universe (or even God) just exists as a brute fact. There must be an explanation why it exists. He went on to argue that the Sufficient Reason cannot be found in any individual thing in the universe, nor in the collection of such things which comprise the universe, nor in earlier states of the universe, even if these regress infinitely. Therefore, there must exist an ultra-mundane being which is metaphysically necessary in its existence, that is to say, its non-existence is impossible. It is the Sufficient Reason for its own existence as well as for the existence of every contingent thing.

The Leibnizian cosmological argument

In evaluating these arguments, let us consider them in reverse order. A simple statement of a Leibnizian cosmological argument might run as follows:[4]

1 Every existing thing has an explanation of its existence, either in the necessity of its own nature or in an external cause.
2 If the universe has an explanation of its existence, that explanation is God.
3 The universe is an existing thing.
4 Therefore the explanation of the existence of the universe is God.

Is this a good argument? One of the principal objections to Leibniz's own formulation of the argument is that the Principle of Sufficient Reason as stated in *The Monadology* seems evidently false. There cannot be an explanation of why there are any contingent states of affairs at all; for if such an explanation is contingent, then it, too, must have a further explanation, whereas if it is necessary, then the states of affairs explained by it must also be necessary.

Some theists have responded to this objection by agreeing that one must ultimately come to some explanatory stopping point which is simply a brute fact, a being whose existence is unexplained. For example, Richard Swinburne claims that in answering the question "Why is there something rather than nothing?" we must finally come to the brute existence of some contingent being. This being will not serve to explain its own existence (and, hence, Leibniz's question goes unanswered), but it will explain the existence of everything else. Swinburne argues that God is the best explanation of why everything other than the brute Ultimate exists because as a unique and infinite being God is simpler than the variegated and finite universe.

But the above formulation of the Leibnizian argument avoids the objection without retreating to the dubious position that God is a contingent being. For premise 1 merely requires any existing *thing* to have an explanation of its existence, either in the necessity of its own nature or in some external cause. This premise is compatible with there being brute *facts* or *states of affairs* about the world. What it precludes is that there could exist things – substances exemplifying properties – which just exist inexplicably. This principle seems quite plausible, at least more so than its contradictory, which is all that is required for a successful argument. On this analysis, there are two kinds of being: necessary beings, which exist of their own nature and so have no external cause of their existence, and contingent beings, whose existence is accounted for by causal factors outside themselves. Numbers might be prime candidates for the first sort of being, whereas familiar physical objects fall under the second kind of being.

Premise 2 is, in effect, the contrapositive of the typical atheist response to Leibniz that on the atheistic worldview the universe simply exists as a brute contingent thing. Atheists typically assert that, there being no God, it is false that everything has an explanation of its existence, for the universe, in this case, just exists inexplicably.[5] In so saying, the atheist implicitly recognizes that if the universe has an explanation, then God exists as its explanatory ground. This seems quite plausible, for if the universe, by definition, includes all of physical reality, then it is hard to see how it could have an explanation, or at least a better one, other than its being caused by God.

Finally, premise 3 states the obvious, that there is a universe.[6] Since the universe is obviously an existing thing (especially evident in its very early stages when its density was so extreme), possessing many unique properties such as a certain density, pressure, temperature, space–time curvature, and so on, it follows that God exists.

It is open to the atheist to retort that while the universe has an explanation of its existence, that explanation lies not in an external ground but in the necessity of its own nature; in other words, premise 2 is false. The universe is a metaphysically necessary being. This was the suggestion of David Hume, who demanded, "Why may not the material universe be the necessarily existent being . . .?" Indeed, "How can anything, that exists from eternity, have a cause, since that relation implies a priority in time and a beginning of existence?"[7]

This is an extremely bold suggestion on the part of the atheist. It runs precisely counter to the conviction driving the Swinburnian formulation of the argument, namely that there must be some ultimately inexplicable contingent being. Even if we reject that assumption, we have, I think we can safely say, a strong intuition of the universe's contingency. A possible world in which no concrete objects exist certainly seems conceivable. We generally trust our modal intuitions on other matters with which we are familiar;[8] if we are to do otherwise with respect to the universe's contingency, then the atheist needs to provide some reason for such scepticism other than his desire to avoid theism.

The Thomist cosmological argument

Still, it would be desirable to have some stronger argument for the universe's contingency than our modal intuitions alone. Could the Thomist cosmological argument help us here? If successful, it would show that the universe is a contingent being, causally dependent upon a necessary being for its continued existence. The difficulty with appeal to the Thomist argument, however, is that it is very difficult to show that things are, in fact, contingent in the special sense required by the argument. Certainly, things are naturally contingent in that their continued existence is dependent upon a myriad of factors including particle masses and fundamental forces, temperature, pressure, entropy level, and so forth, but this natural contingency does not suffice to establish things' metaphysical contingency in the sense that being must continually be added to their essences lest they be spontaneously annihilated. Indeed, if Thomas's argument does ultimately lead to an absolutely simple being whose essence is existence, then one might well be led to deny that beings are metaphysically composed of essence and existence if the idea of such an absolutely simple being proves to be unintelligible.[9]

The *kalam* cosmological argument

But what about the *kalam* cosmological argument? An essential property of a metaphysically necessary being is eternality, that is to say, being without beginning or end. It has been countered that a being with a temporal beginning or end could, nonetheless, be metaphysically necessary in that it is caused to exist in all possible worlds. But this understanding of metaphysical necessity fails to take tense seriously and is therefore inadequate. Metaphysicians have in recent years begun to appreciate the metaphysical importance of whether time is tensed or tenseless, that is to say, whether items in the temporal series are ordered objectively as past, present, or future, or whether, alternatively, they are ordered merely by tenseless relations of *earlier than*, *simultaneous with*, and *later than*.[10] Possible worlds semantics is a tenseless semantics and so is incapable of expressing the significance of one's view of time. In particular, it is evident that a truly necessary being, one whose non-existence is impossible, must exist at every moment in every world. It is not enough for it to exist at only some moment or moments in every possible world, for the fact that there exist moments in various worlds at which it fails to exist shows that its non-existence is not impossible. By the same token, a truly metaphysically necessary being must exist either timelessly or sempiternally in any tensed world in which it exists, for otherwise its coming into being or ceasing to be would again make it evident that its existence is not necessary.[11] If the universe is not eternal, then, it could not be, as Hume suggested, a metaphysically necessary being.

But it is precisely the aim of the *kalam* cosmological argument to show

116

that the universe is not eternal but had a beginning. It would follow that the universe must therefore be contingent in its existence. Not only so; the *kalam* argument shows the universe to be contingent in a very special way: it came into existence out of nothing. The atheist who would answer Leibniz by holding that the existence of the universe is a brute fact, an exception to the Principle of Sufficient Reason, is thus thrust into the very awkward position of maintaining not merely that the universe exists eternally without explanation, but rather that for no reason at all it magically popped into being out of nothing, a position which might make theism look like a welcome alternative. Thus, the *kalam* argument not only constitutes an independent argument for a transcendent Creator but also serves as a valuable supplement to the Leibnizian argument.

The *kalam* cosmological argument may be formulated as follows:

5   Whatever begins to exist has a cause.
6   The universe began to exist.
7   Therefore, the universe has a cause.

Conceptual analysis of what it means to be a cause of the universe then helps to establish some of the theologically significant properties of this being.

Whatever begins to exist has a cause

Premise 5 seems obviously true – at the least, more so than its negation. It is rooted in the metaphysical intuition that something cannot come into being from nothing. Moreover, this premise is constantly confirmed in our experience. The conviction that an origin of the universe requires a causal explanation seems quite reasonable, for, on the atheistic view, there was not even the *potentiality* of the universe's existence prior to the Big Bang, since nothing is prior to the Big Bang. But then how could the universe become actual if there was not even the potentiality of its existence? It makes much more sense to say that the potentiality of the universe lay in the power of God to create it.

Nevertheless, a number of atheists, in order to avoid the argument's conclusion, have denied premise 5. Sometimes it is said that sub-atomic physics furnishes an exception to premise 5, since on the sub-atomic level events are said to be uncaused. In the same way, certain theories of cosmic origins are interpreted as showing that the whole universe could have sprung into being out of the sub-atomic vacuum. Thus the universe is said to be the proverbial "free lunch."

This objection, however, is based on misunderstandings. In the first place, not all scientists agree that sub-atomic events are uncaused. A great many physicists today are quite dissatisfied with this view (the so-called Copenhagen Interpretation) of sub-atomic physics and are exploring deterministic theories like that of David Bohm. Thus, sub-atomic physics is not a proven exception to premise 5. Second, even on the traditional, indeterministic interpretation, particles do not come into being out of nothing. They arise as spontaneous fluctuations of the energy contained in the sub-atomic vacuum, which constitutes an indeterministic cause of their origination. Third, the same point can be made about theories of the origin of the universe out of a primordial vacuum. Popular magazine articles touting such theories as getting "something from nothing" simply do not understand that the vacuum is not nothing but is a sea of fluctuating energy endowed with a rich structure and subject to physical laws. Thus, there is no basis for the claim that quantum physics proves that things can begin to exist without a cause, much less that universe could have sprung into being uncaused from literally nothing.

Other critics have said that premise 5 is true for things *in* the universe, but it is not true *of* the universe itself. But, first, this objection misconstrues the nature of the premise. Premise 5 does not state merely a physical law like the law of gravity or the laws of thermodynamics, which are valid for things within the universe. Premise 5 is not a physical principle. Rather, premise 5 is a metaphysical principle: being cannot come from non-being; something cannot come into existence uncaused from nothing. The principle therefore applies to all of reality, and it is thus metaphysically absurd that the universe should pop into being uncaused out of nothing.

Second, until the premise's detractors are able to explain the relevant difference between embedded moments of time and a first moment of time, there seems to be no reason to think it more plausible that things can come into being uncaused at a first moment than at a later moment of time. What is the relevant difference between something's coming into existence within time and something's coming into existence at the beginning of time? Indeed, given a dynamic or tensed view of time, every moment of time is a fresh beginning, qualitatively indistinguishable from a first moment of time, for when any moment is present, earlier moments have passed away and do not exist. Thus, if the universe could exist uncaused at a first moment of time, it could exist uncaused at any moment of time. It follows that if the latter is metaphysically impossible, so is the former.

Third, the objection stifles scientific exploration of cosmological questions. The absolute beginning of time predicted by the Standard Friedman–Lemaître Big Bang model was the crucial factor in provoking not only the formulation of the Steady State model of continuous creation, but a whole series of subsequent models all aimed at avoiding the origin *ex nihilo* of our universe predicted by the Standard Model. Both philosophers and physicists have been deeply disturbed at the prospect of a beginning of time and an absolute origination of the universe, and so have felt constrained to posit the

THE COSMOLOGICAL ARGUMENT

existence of causally prior entities like quantum vacuum states, inflationary domains, imaginary time regimes, and even timelike causal loops. The history of twentieth-century astrophysical cosmology would be considerably different if there were thought to be no need of a causal explanation of the origin of time and the universe. The theist cannot be similarly accused of stifling science because the theist's identification of the cause of the universe as a being of religious significance comes only with the conceptual analysis of the argument's conclusion, and he will in any case welcome attempts to falsify his theistic hypothesis in hopes of corroboration of his preferred hypothesis by the failure of such naturalistic explanations.

Recently some critics of the argument have denied that in beginning to exist the universe *became actual* or *came into being*. They thereby focus attention on the theory of time underlying the *kalam* cosmological argument. On a static or tenseless view of time, the universe does not in fact come into being or become actual at the Big Bang; it just exists tenselessly as a four-dimensional, space-time block which is finitely extended in the *earlier than* direction. If time is tenseless, then the universe never really comes into being, and therefore the quest for a cause of its coming into being is misconceived. Although Leibniz's question "Why is there *(tenselessly)* something rather than nothing?" should still rightly be asked, there would be no reason to look for a cause of the universe's beginning to exist, since on tenseless theories of time the universe did not truly begin to exist in virtue of its having a first event, any more than a meter stick begins to exist in virtue of having a first centimeter. In affirming that things which begin to exist need a cause, the proponent of the *kalam* cosmological argument assumes the following understanding of that notion, where "x" ranges over any entity and "t" ranges over times, whether instants or moments of non-zero finite duration:

A x begins to exist at t iff x comes into being at t.
B x comes into being at t iff (1) x exists at t, and the actual world includes no state of affairs in which x exists timelessly, (2) t is either the first time at which x exists or is separated from any $t' < t$ at which x existed by an interval during which x does not exist, and (3) x's existing at t is a tensed fact.

The key clause in B is (3). By presupposing a dynamic or tensed theory of time, according to which temporal becoming is real, the proponent of the *kalam* cosmological argument justifiably assumes that the universe's existing at a first moment of time represents the moment at which the universe came into being. Thus, the real issue separating the proponent of the *kalam* cosmological argument and critics of the first premise is the objectivity of tense and temporal becoming.

119

The universe began to exist

Premise 2 may be supported by both deductive, philosophical arguments and inductive, scientific arguments.

First argument

The first argument I shall consider is the argument based on *the impossibility of the existence of an actual infinite*. It may be formulated as follows:

8   An actual infinite cannot exist.
9   An infinite temporal regress of events is an actual infinite.
10 Therefore an infinite temporal regress of events cannot exist.

In order to assess this argument, it will be helpful to define some terms. By an actual infinite, I mean any collection having at a time *t* a number of definite and discrete members that is greater than any natural number {0, 1, 2, 3, . . .}. This notion is to be contrasted with a potential infinite, which is any collection having at any time *t* a number of definite and discrete members that is equal to some natural number but which over time increases endlessly toward infinity as a limit. By "exist," I mean "have extra-mental existence," or "be instantiated in the real world." By an "event," I mean any change occurring within the space-time universe. Since any change takes time, there are no instantaneous events. Neither could there be an infinitely slow event, since such an "event" would in reality be a changeless state. Therefore, any event will have a finite, non-zero duration. In order that all the events comprising the temporal regress of past events be of equal duration, we arbitrarily stipulate some event as our standard, and, taking as our point of departure the present standard event, we consider any series of such standard events ordered according to the relation *earlier than*. The question is whether this series of events comprises an actually infinite number of events or not. If not, then since the universe is not distinct from the series of past events, the universe must have had a beginning, in the sense of a first standard event. It is therefore not relevant whether the temporal series had a beginning *point* (a first temporal instant). The question is whether there was in the past an event occupying a non-zero, finite temporal interval which was absolutely first, that is, not preceded by any equal interval.

Premise 8 asserts, then, that an actual infinite cannot exist in the real, spatio-temporal world. It is usually alleged that this sort of argument has been invalidated by Georg Cantor's work on the actual infinite and by subsequent developments in set theory. But this allegation misconstrues the nature of both Cantor's system and modern set theory, for the argument does not in fact contradict a single tenet of either. The reason is this: Cantor's system and set theory may be taken to be simply a universe of discourse, a mathematical system based on certain adopted axioms and conventions. The argument's defender may hold that while the actual infinite may be a fruitful and consistent concept within the postulated universe of discourse, it cannot be transposed into the spatio-temporal world, for this would involve counter-intuitive absurdities. One can try to show this is by way of concrete examples, like the famous Hilbert's Hotel,[12] that illustrate the various absurdities that would result if an actual infinite were to be instantiated in the real world. I am quite happy to grant the coherence and consistency of infinite set theory and transfinite arithmetic, while denying that the actual infinite can exist in reality. In any case, should the intuitionists turn out to be right in allowing only potential infinites to exist even in the realm of mathematics, I shall not weep for infinite set theory. But my argument does not require so strong a thesis as the incoherence of infinites in mathematical theories. It is the real existence of the actual infinite which I reject.

It is sometimes thought that the existence of abstract objects provides a decisive counter-example to the claim that an actual infinite cannot exist. But I see no reason to accept this counter-example, for it begs the question by assuming Platonism or realism to be true. But why make this assumption? In order to defeat this putative defeater, all the defender of the *kalam* argument has to do is deny that Platonism has been shown to be true. In other words, the burden of proof rests on the objector to prove that realism is true before his counter-example can even be launched. A conceptualist understanding of abstract objects combined with the simplicity of God's cognition is at least a tenable alternative to Platonism. Indeed, historically, this has been the mainstream theistic tradition, from Boethius through Ockham. In fact, theists had better hope that there is such an alternative to Platonism, since the latter entails a metaphysical pluralism which leaves God as but one being among an unimaginable plenitude of beings existing independently of Him, in contradiction to divine aseity and the doctrine of *creatio ex nihilo*.

Sometimes it is said that we can find counter-examples to the claim that an actually infinite number of things cannot exist, so that premise i must be false. For instance, is not every finite distance capable of being divided into $1/2$, $1/4$, $1/8$, . . . , on to infinity? Does that not prove that there are in any finite distance an actually infinite number of parts? The defender of the argument may reply that this objection confuses a potential infinite with an actual infinite. Although one can continue to divide any distance for as long as one wants, such a series is merely potentially infinite, in that infinity serves as a limit which one endlessly approaches but never reaches. If one assumes that any distance is *already* composed of an actually infinite number of points, then one is begging the question. The objector is assuming what he is supposed to prove, namely that there is a clear counter-example to the claim that an actually infinite number of things cannot exist.

Finally, it is sometimes objected that God's existence entails the existence of an actual infinite. But this seems far from inevitable. In general, God's infinity is a qualitative, not a quantitative, notion. It has nothing to do with an infinite number of definite and discrete finite particulars. Attributes like omnipotence, moral perfection, timelessness, aseity, omnipresence, and so on just are not quantitative notions.[13] Even omniscience need not entail that God has an actually infinite number of true beliefs if, with William Alston and in line with Christian tradition, we take God's knowledge to be non-propositional in nature, though represented by us finite cognizers as knowl-edge of individual propositions.[14] In short, the objections typically lodged against the premise 8 are less than decisive.

Premise 9 states that *an infinite temporal regress of events is an actual infinite.* Premise 9 asserts that if the series or sequence of changes in time is infinite, then these events considered collectively constitute an actual infinite. The point seems obvious enough, for if there has been a sequence composed of an infinite number of events stretching back into the past, then an actually infinite number of events has occurred. If the series of past events were an actual infinite, then all the absurdities attending the real existence of an actual infinite would apply to it.

In summary: if an actual infinite cannot exist in the real, spatio-temporal world and an infinite temporal regress of events is such an actual infinite, we can conclude that an infinite temporal regress of events cannot exist – that is to say, the temporal series of past events had a beginning. And this implies premise 6 of the original syllogism of the *kalam* cosmological argument.

Second argument

The second argument which we shall consider is the argument based on *the impossibility of forming an actual infinite by successive addition.* It may be formulated as follows:

11 The temporal series of events is a collection formed by successive addi-tion.
12 A collection formed by successive addition cannot be an actual infinite.
13 Therefore, the temporal series of events cannot be an actual infinite.

Here one does not assume that an actual infinite cannot exist. Even if an actual infinite can exist, it is argued that the temporal series of events cannot be such, since an actual infinite cannot be formed by successive addition, as the temporal series of events is.

Premise 11 presupposes once again a tensed theory of time. On such a theory the collection of all past events prior to any given event is not a col-lection whose members all tenselessly co-exist. Rather, it is a collection that is instantiated sequentially or successively in time, one event coming to pass on the heels of another. Since temporal becoming is an objective feature of the physical world, the series of past events is not a tenselessly existing manifold, all of whose members are equally real. Rather the members of the series come to be and pass away one after another.

Premise 12 asserts that a collection formed by successive addition cannot be an actual infinite. Sometimes this is described as the impossibility of traversing the infinite. In order for us to have "arrived" at today, temporal existence has, so to speak, traversed an infinite number of prior events. But before the present event could arrive, the event immediately prior to it would have to arrive; and before that event could arrive, the event immediately prior to it would have to arrive; and so on *ad infinitum*. No event could ever arrive, since before it could elapse there will always be one more event that had to have happened first. Thus, if the series of past events were beginningless, the present event could not have arrived, which is absurd.

This argument brings to mind Bertrand Russell's account of Tristram Shandy, who, in the novel by Sterne, writes his autobiography so slowly that it takes him a whole year to record the events of a single day. Were he mortal, he would never finish, asserts Russell, but if he were immortal, then the entire book could be completed, since to each day there would correspond a year, and both are infinite. Russell's assertion is untenable on a tensed theory of time, however, since the future is in reality a potential infinite only. Though he write forever, Tristram Shandy would only get farther and farther behind, so that instead of finishing his autobiography, he will progressively approach a state in which he would be *infinitely* far behind. But he would never reach such a state because the years and hence the days of his life would always be finite in number though indefinitely increasing.

But let us turn the story about: suppose Tristram Shandy has been writing from eternity past at the rate of one day per year. Should not Tristram Shandy now be infinitely far behind? For if he has lived for an infinite number of years, Tristram Shandy has recorded an equally infinite number of past days. Given the thoroughness of his autobiography, these days are all consecutive days. At any point in the past or present, therefore, Tristram Shandy has recorded a beginningless, infinite series of consecutive days. But now the question inevitably arises: *which* days are these? Where in the temporal series of events are the days recorded by Tristram Shandy at any given point? The answer can only be that *they are days infinitely distant from the present*. For there is no day on which Tristram Shandy is writing that is finitely distant from the last recorded day.[15]

But now a deeper absurdity bursts into view. For if the series of past events is an actual infinite, then we may ask, why did Tristram Shandy not finish his autobiography yesterday or the day before, since by then an infinite series of moments had already elapsed? No matter how far along the series of past events one regresses, Tristram Shandy would have already completed his autobiography. Therefore, at no point in the infinite series of past events could he be finishing the book. We could never look over Tristram Shandy's shoulder to see if he were now writing the last page. For at any point an actually infinite sequence of events would have transpired and the book would have already been completed. Thus, at no time in eternity will we find Tristram Shandy writing, which is absurd, since we supposed him to be writing from eternity. And at no point will he finish the book, which is equally absurd, because for the book to be completed, he must at some point have finished. What the Tristram Shandy story really tells us is that an actually infinite temporal regress is absurd.

Sometimes critics indict this argument as sleight of hand, like Zeno's paradoxes of motion. Even though Achilles must pass through an infinite number of halfway points in order to cross the stadium, somehow he manages to do so! But such a response fails to reckon with two crucial disanalogies of an infinite past to Zeno's paradoxes: whereas in Zeno's thought experiments the intervals traversed are *potential* and *unequal*, in the case of an infinite past the intervals are *actual* and *equal*. The claim that Achilles must pass through an infinite number of halfway points in order to cross the stadium is question-begging, for it already assumes that the whole interval is a composition of an infinite number of points, whereas Zeno's opponents, like Aristotle, take the line as a whole to be conceptually prior to any divisions which we might make in it. Moreover, Zeno's intervals, being unequal, sum to a merely finite distance, whereas the intervals in an infinite past sum to an infinite distance. Thus, it remains mysterious how we could have traversed an infinite number of equal, actual intervals to arrive at our present location.

It is frequently objected that this sort of argument illicitly presupposes an infinitely distant starting point in the past and then pronounces it impossible to travel from that point to today. But if the past is infinite, then there would be no starting point whatever, not even an infinitely distant one. Nevertheless, from any given point in the past, there is only a finite distance to the present, which is easily "traversed." But in fact no proponent of the *kalam* argument of which I am aware has assumed that there was an infinitely distant starting point in the past. (Even the Tristram Shandy paradox does not assert that there was an infinitely distant first day, but merely that there were days infinitely distant in the past.) The fact that there is *no beginning* at all, not even an infinitely distant one, seems only to make the problem worse, not better. To say that the infinite past could have been formed by successive addition is like saying that someone has just succeeded in writing down all the negative numbers, ending at –1. And, we may ask, how is the claim that from any given moment in the past there is only a finite distance to the present even relevant to the issue? The defender of the *kalam* argument could agree to this happily. For the issue is how the *whole* series can be formed, not a finite portion of it. Does the objector think that because every *finite* segment of the series can be formed by successive addition the whole *infinite* series can be so formed? That is as logically fallacious as saying because every part of an elephant is light in weight, the whole elephant is light in weight. The claim is therefore irrelevant.

In summary, if a collection formed by successive addition cannot be an actual infinite, then since the temporal series of events is a collection formed by successive addition, it follows that the temporal series of events cannot be an actual infinite. This implies, of course, that the temporal series of past events is not beginningless.

Third argument

The third argument for the universe's beginning is an inductive argument based on *the expansion of the universe*. In 1917, Albert Einstein made a cosmological application of his newly discovered gravitational theory, the General Theory of Relativity (GTR). In so doing, he assumed that the universe exists in a steady state, with a constant mean mass density and a constant curvature of space. To his chagrin, however, he found that the GTR would not permit such a model of the universe unless he introduced into his gravitational field equations a certain "fudge factor" in order to counterbalance the gravitational effect of matter and so ensure a static universe. Unfortunately, Einstein's static universe was balanced on a razor's edge, and the least perturbation would cause the universe either to implode or to expand. By taking this feature of Einstein's model seriously, the Russian mathematician Alexander Friedman and the Belgian astronomer Georges Lemaître were able to formulate independently in the 1920s solutions to the field equations which predicted an expanding universe.

In 1929 the astronomer Edwin Hubble showed that the red shift in the optical spectra of light from distant galaxies was a common feature of all measured galaxies and was proportional to their distance from earth. This red-shift was taken to be a Doppler effect indicative of the recessional motion of the light source in the line of sight. Incredibly, what Hubble had discovered was the isotropic expansion of the universe predicted by Friedman and Lemaître on the basis of Einstein's GTR.

According to the Friedman–Lemaître model, as time proceeds, the distances separating galactic masses become greater. It is important to understand that as a GTR-based theory, the model does not describe the expansion of the material content of the universe into a pre-existing, empty space, but rather the expansion of space itself. The ideal particles of the cosmological fluid constituted by the galactic masses are conceived to be at rest with respect to space but to recede progressively from one another as space itself expands or stretches, just as buttons glued to the surface of a balloon would recede from one another as the balloon inflates. As the universe expands, it becomes less and less dense. This has the astonishing implication that as one reverses the expansion and extrapolates back in time, the universe becomes progressively denser until one arrives at a state of "infinite density"[16] at some point in the finite past. This state represents a singularity at which space-time curvature, along with temperature, pressure, and density, becomes infinite. It therefore constitutes an edge or boundary to space-time itself. The term "Big Bang" is thus potentially misleading, since the expansion cannot be visualized from the outside (there being no "outside," just as there is no "before" with respect to the Big Bang).

The Standard Big Bang Model, as the Friedman–Lemaître model came to be called, thus describes a universe that is not eternal in the past, but which came into being a finite time ago. Moreover – and this deserves underscoring – the origin it posits is an absolute origin *ex nihilo*. For not only all matter and energy, but space and time themselves, come into being at the initial cosmological singularity. There can be no natural, physical cause of the Big Bang event, since, in Quentin Smith's words, "It belongs analytically to the concept of the cosmological singularity that it is not the effect of prior physical events. The definition of a singularity . . . entails that it is *impossible to extend the spacetime manifold beyond the singularity* . . . . This rules out the idea that the singularity is an effect of some prior natural process."[17] Sir Arthur Eddington, contemplating the beginning of the universe, opined that the expansion of the universe was so preposterous and incredible that "I feel almost an indignation that anyone should believe in it – except myself."[18] He finally felt forced to conclude, "The beginning seems to present insuperable difficulties unless we agree to look on it as frankly supernatural."[19]

Sometimes objectors appeal to non-standard models of the expanding universe in an attempt to avert the absolute beginning predicted by the Standard Model. But while such theories are possible, it has been the overwhelming verdict of the scientific community than none of them is more probable than the Big Bang theory. The devil is in the details, and once we get down to specifics we find that there is no mathematically consistent model which has been so successful in its predictions or as corroborated by the evidence as the traditional Big Bang theory.[20] For example, some theories, like the Oscillating Universe (which expands and re-contracts forever) or the Chaotic Inflationary Universe (which continually spawns new universes), do have a potentially infinite future but turn out to have only a finite past. Vacuum Fluctuation Universe theories (which postulate an eternal vacuum out of which our universe is born) cannot explain why, if the vacuum was eternal, we do not observe an infinitely old universe. The Quantum Gravity Universe theory propounded by the famous physicist Stephen Hawking, if interpreted realistically, still involves an absolute origin of the universe even if the universe does not begin in a singularity, as it does in the Standard Big Bang theory. In sum, according to Hawking, "Almost everyone now believes that the universe, and *time itself*, had a beginning at the Big Bang."[21]

Fourth argument

The fourth argument for the finitude of the past is also an inductive argument, this time on the basis of *the thermodynamic properties of the universe*. According to the Second Law of Thermodynamics, processes taking place in a closed system always tend toward a state of equilibrium. Now our interest in the law is what happens when it is applied to the universe as a whole. The universe is, on a naturalistic view, a gigantic closed system, since it is everything there is and there is nothing outside it. What this seems to imply then is that, given enough time, the universe and all its processes will run down, and the entire universe will come to equilibrium. This is known as the heat death of the universe. Once the universe reaches this state, no further change is possible. The universe is dead.

There are two possible types of heat death for the universe. If the universe will eventually re-contract, it will die a "hot" death. As it contracts, the stars gain energy, causing them to burn more rapidly so that they finally explode or evaporate. As everything in the universe grows closer together, the black holes begin to gobble up everything around them, and eventually begin themselves to coalesce. In time, all the black holes finally coalesce into one large black hole that is coextensive with the universe, from which the universe will never re-emerge.

On the other hand if, as is more likely, the universe expands forever, then its death will be "cold," as the galaxies turn their gas into stars, and the stars burn out. At 10^{30} years the universe will consist of 90 percent dead stars, 9 percent supermassive black holes formed by the collapse of galaxies, and 1 percent atomic matter, mainly hydrogen. Elementary particle physics suggests that thereafter protons will decay into electrons and positrons so that space will be filled with a rarefied gas so thin that the distance between an electron and a positron will be about the size of the present galaxy. Eventually all black holes will completely evaporate and all the matter in the ever-expanding universe will be reduced to a thin gas of elementary particles and radiation. Equilibrium will prevail throughout, and the entire universe will be in its final state, from which no change will occur.

Now the question that needs to be asked is this: if given enough time the universe will reach heat death, then why is it not in a state of heat death now, if it has existed forever, from eternity? If the universe did not begin to exist, then it should now be in a state of equilibrium. Like a ticking clock, it should by now have run down. Since it has not yet run down, this implies, in the words of one baffled scientist, "In some way the universe must have been *wound up*."[22]

Some people have tried to escape this conclusion by adopting an oscillating model of the universe that never reaches a final state of equilibrium. But even apart from the physical and observational problems plaguing such a model, the thermodynamic properties of this model imply the very beginning of the universe that its proponents sought to avoid. For entropy

increases from cycle to cycle in such a model, which has the effect of generating larger and longer oscillations with each successive cycle. Thus, as one
traces the oscillations back in time, they become progressively smaller until
one reaches a first and smallest oscillation. Hence, the oscillating model has
an infinite future, but only a finite past. In fact, it is estimated on the basis
of current entropy levels that the universe cannot have gone through more
than 100 previous oscillations.

Even if this difficulty were avoided, a universe oscillating from eternity
past would require an infinitely precise tuning of initial conditions in order to
last through an infinite number of successive bounces. A universe rebound-
ing from a single, infinitely long contraction is, if entropy increases during
the contracting phase, thermodynamically untenable and incompatible with
the initial low entropy condition of our expanding phase. Postulating an entropy decrease during the contracting phase in order to escape this problem
would require us to postulate inexplicably special low entropy conditions
at the time of the bounce in the life of an infinitely evolving universe. Such
a low entropy condition at the beginning of the expansion is more plausibly accounted for by the presence of a singularity or some sort of quantum
creation event.

So, whether one adopts a re-contracting model, an ever-expanding
model, or an oscillating model, thermodynamics suggests that the universe
had a beginning. According to P. C. W. Davies, the universe must have been
created a finite time ago and is in the process of winding down. Prior to the
creation, says Davies, the universe simply did not exist. Even though we
may not like it, he concludes, we must say that the universe's energy was
somehow simply "put in" at the creation as an initial condition.[23]

The universe has a cause

From the *kalam's* first premise (5) – that *whatever begins to exist has a cause*
– and its second premise (6) – that *the universe began to exist* – it follows
logically that *the universe has a cause*. This conclusion ought to stagger us,
to fill us with awe, for it means that the universe was brought into existence
by *something* which is greater than and beyond itself.

But what is the nature of this first cause of the universe? A conceptual
analysis of what properties must be possessed by such an ultra-mundane
cause enables us to recover a striking number of the traditional divine attributes. An analysis of what it is to be cause of the universe reveals that

14 If the universe has a cause, then an uncaused, personal Creator of the
universe exists, who *sans* the universe is beginningless, changeless, immaterial, timeless, spaceless, and enormously powerful.

As the cause of space and time, this entity must transcend space and time and therefore exist atemporally and nonspatially, at least *sans* the universe. This transcendent cause must therefore be changeless and immaterial, since timelessness entails changelessness, and changelessness implies immateriality. Such a cause must be beginningless and uncaused, at least in the sense of lacking any antecedent causal conditions. Ockham's Razor will shave away further causes, since we should not multiply causes beyond necessity. This entity must be unimaginably powerful, since it created the universe out of nothing.

Finally, and most strikingly, such a transcendent cause is plausibly to be regarded as personal. Three reasons can be given for this conclusion. First, as Swinburne points out, there are two types of causal explanation: scientific explanations in terms of laws and initial conditions, and personal explanations in terms of agents and their volitions. A first state of the universe *cannot* have a scientific explanation, since there is nothing before it, and therefore it can be accounted for only in terms of a personal explanation. Second, the personhood of the cause of the universe is implied by its timelessness and immateriality, since the only entities we know of which can possess such properties are either minds or abstract objects, and abstract objects do not stand in causal relations. Therefore, the transcendent cause of the origin of the universe must be of the order of mind. Third, this same conclusion is also implied by the fact that we have in this case the origin of a temporal effect from a timeless cause. If the cause of the origin of the universe were an impersonal set of necessary and sufficient conditions, it would be impossible for the cause to exist without its effect. For if the necessary and sufficient conditions of the effect are timelessly given, then their effect must be given as well. The only way for the cause to be timeless and changeless but for its effect to originate anew a finite time ago is for the cause to be a personal agent who freely chooses to bring about an effect without antecedent determining conditions.

From premises 7 and 14, it follows that

15   Therefore, an uncaused, personal Creator of the universe exists, who *sans* the universe is beginningless, changeless, immaterial, timeless, spaceless, and enormously powerful.

Thus, we are brought, not merely to a transcendent cause of the universe, but to its Personal Creator. He is, as Leibniz maintained, the Sufficient Reason why anything exists rather than nothing.

Notes

1   *Summa contra gentiles*, Vol. 1, Anton C. Pegis (trans.) (Notre Dame, IN: University of Notre Dame Press, 1975) 1.13.30.

2 G. W. Leibniz, "The Principles of Nature and of Grace, Based on Reason," in *Leibniz Selections*, P. Wiener (ed.) (New York: Charles Scribner's Sons, 1951), 527.

3 Leibniz, "The Monadology," in *Leibniz Selections*, 539.

4 Cf. Stephen T. Davis, "The Cosmological Argument and the Epistemic Status of Belief in God," *Philosophia Christi* 1 (New series) (1999), 5–15.

5 Recall Russell's response to Copleston in their famous BBC exchange: "I should say the universe is just there, and that's all." Bertrand Russell and F. C. Copleston, "A Debate On The Existence of God," reprinted in *The Existence of God*, Introduction by John Hick (New York: Macmillan, 1964), 175.

6 I do not mean to pronounce here on ontological debates about what constitutes an object, but merely to claim that the universe is just as much a thing as are other familiar entities which we recognize to have causes, such as chairs, mountains, planets, and stars.

7 David Hume, *Dialogues concerning Natural Religion*, with an Introduction by Norman Kemp Smith, Library of Liberal Arts (Indianapolis: Bobbs-Merrill, 1947), pt. IX, 190.

8 See Charles Taliaferro's *Auseindersetzung* with Peter Van Inwagen's modal skepticism in Charles Taliaferro, "Sensibility and Possibilia: In Defense of Thought Experiments," *Philosophia Christi* 3, 2 (New series) (2001), 403–20. Especially noteworthy for the present discussion is Van Inwagen's own rejection of Spinozism. Taliaferro proposes the following principle: if one can conceive that a state of affairs obtain, and one has carefully considered whether the state of affairs is internally coherent (self-consistent at a minimum) and consistent with what one justifiably believes, then one has prima facie reason to believe it is possible for the state of affairs to obtain.

9 To say that God does not have distinct properties seems patently false: omnipotence is not the same property as goodness, for a being may have one and not the other. To respond that these properties differ in our conception only, as manifestations of a single divine property, just as, say, "the morning star" and "the evening star" have different senses but both refer to the same reality, namely Venus, is inadequate. For being the morning star and being the evening star are distinct properties both possessed by Venus; in the same way that being omnipotent and being good are not different senses for the same property (as are, say, being even and being divisible by two) but are clearly distinct properties. Moreover, if God is not distinct from His essence, then God cannot know or do anything different than what he knows and does, in which case everything becomes necessary. To respond that God is perfectly similar in all logically possible worlds which we can imagine but that contingency is real because God stands in no real relation to things is to make the existence or non-existence of creatures in various possible worlds independent of God and utterly mysterious. To say that God's essence just is His existence seems wholly obscure, since then there is in God's case no entity that exists; there is just the existing itself without any subject. For further critique, see Christopher Hughes, *On a Complex Theory of a Simple God* (Ithaca, NY: Cornell University Press, 199); Thomas V. Morris, *Anselmian Explorations* (Notre Dame, IN: University of Notre Dame Press, 1987), 98–123.

10 For discussion and bibliography see both Robin LePoidevin (ed.) *Questions of Time and Tense* (Oxford: Oxford University Press, 1998) and my companion volumes *The Tensed Theory of Time: A Critical Examination* (Dordrecht: Kluwer Academic Publishers, 2000) and *The Tenseless Theory of Time: A Critical Examination* (Dordrecht: Kluwer Academic Publishers, 2000).

11 Thus, considerations of tense disclose the inadequacy of possible worlds semantics for dealing with metaphysical questions related to necessary existence. One might also question whether true metaphysical necessity is compatible with being caused to exist, even at all times in all possible worlds, for this leaves open the option that such a being is the causal product of some contingent being in one world and of another in another world, which seems incompatible with its being truly necessary. Only if the being were caused to exist by a truly necessary being could its being caused seem even plausibly compatible with its being metaphysically necessary. But even in such a case the demonstration that the universe began to exist shows that it is either contingent in its existence or else necessary *ab alio* in being necessarily caused by some greater necessary being. If, as Aquinas held, such a regress cannot go on to infinity, then there must be an absolutely necessary being that has its necessity per se. In a sense, then, the Thomist argument returns to supplement the *kalam* argument, just as the latter reinforces the Leibnizian argument.

12 For an account of Hilbert's Hotel, see my *Reasonable Faith* (Wheaton, IL: Crossways, 1994), 95–6.

13 On the divine attributes, see the Introduction and selections in *Philosophy of Religion: A Reader and Guide*, William Lane Craig (ed.) (Trenton: Rutgers University Press, 2002), Section III, particularly the piece "Maximal Power," dealing with omnipotence.

14 See William Alston, "Does God Have Beliefs?" *Religious Studies* 22 (1986), 287–306. Notice that divine cognitive simplicity does not, on Alston's view, commit one to full-blown simplicity.

15 In fact, the recession into the past of the most recent recordable day can be plotted according to the formula (present date – n years of writing) + n – 1 days. In other words, the longer he has written the further behind he has fallen. But what happens if Tristram Shandy has, *ex hypothesi*, been writing for an infinite number of years? The most recently recorded day of his autobiography recedes to infinity, that is to say, to a day infinitely distant from the present.

16 This should not be taken to mean that the density of the universe takes on a value of $\aleph_0$, but rather that the density of the universe is expressed by a ratio of mass to volume in which the volume is zero; since division by zero is impermissible, the density is said to be infinite in this sense.

17 Quentin Smith, "The Uncaused Beginning of the Universe," in *Theism, Atheism, and Big Bang Cosmology*, by William Lane Craig and Quentin Smith (Oxford: Clarendon Press, 1993), 120.

18 Arthur Eddington, *The Expanding Universe* (New York: Macmillan, 1933), 124.

19 Ibid., 178.

20 See discussion in my "Naturalism and Cosmology," in *Naturalism: A Critical Appraisal*, W. L. Craig and J. P. Moreland (eds) (London: Routledge, 2000), 215–52.

21 Stephen Hawking and Roger Penrose, *The Nature of Space and Time* (Princeton, NJ: Princeton University Press, 1996), 20.

22 Richard Schlegel, "Time and Thermodynamics," in *The Voices of Time*, J. T. Fraser (ed.) (London: Penguin, 1948), 511.

23 P. C. W. Davies, *The Physics of Time Asymmetry* (London: Surrey University Press, 1974), 104.

7

THE TELEOLOGICAL ARGUMENT[1]

Robin Collins

Introduction and historical background

My contention in this essay will be that discoveries in physics and cosmology, along with developments in philosophy, particularly in the logic of inference, have significantly bolstered the traditional teleological argument, or argument from design. Today, I contend, the evidence from physics and cosmology offers us significant, well-formulated reasons for believing in theism.

The design argument has a long history, probably being the most commonly cited argument for believing in a deity. Before the eighteenth century, design arguments typically appealed to the idea that the universe is orderly, or appears to be ordered toward some end. In ancient India, for instance, the argument from design was advanced by the so-called Nyāya (or logical-atomist) school (100–1000 CE), which argued for the existence of a deity based on the order of the world, which they compared both to human artifacts and to the human body.[2] In the West, the design argument goes back at least to Heraclitus, who attempted to account for the order in the universe by hypothesizing that the universe was directed by a principle of intelligence or reason. Related arguments were offered by Plato, Aristotle, and the Stoics. This sort of argument was further elaborated upon by Thomas Aquinas, in his famous Fifth Way. According to Aquinas, nature appears to be directed toward an end, yet it lacks knowledge to direct itself. Thus, Aquinas claimed, "some intelligent being exists by whom all natural things are directed to their end; and this being we call God." From the perspective of our modern scientific understanding of the world, one outstanding problem with Aquinas's argument is that it is unclear in what sense nature is "directed toward an end," other than that it simply appears to be orderly.

More generally, since the rise of the scientific revolution, these versions of the teleological argument that simply appealed to the orderliness of the universe lost much of their force as philosophers and scientists became increasingly contented with appealing to the laws of nature as a sufficient explanation of the regular operation of the universe, although God was still appealed to by some as the explanation of the existence of these laws. The version of the design argument that began to take its place was one based on the *intricate* ordering of various natural systems for some end, not the mere regularity of some aspect of the world. In William Paley's famous presentation of the design argument, the intricate organization of the organs of the body – such as an eye – is compared to the intricate ordering of the parts of a watch for the apparent purpose of telling of time. Since, Paley argues, upon finding such an object on a heath (or somewhere else), one would attribute it to some intelligence, the same should be done for the intricate structure of plants and animals. As skeptical philosophers such as David Hume pointed out, however, there is an important disanalogy between the universe or plants and animals and the case of watches that seems to undercut the argument: we know from experience that the watches are produced by minds, but we have no experience of animal life or universes being created by minds.

In the view of many, however, the real blow to Paley's argument came from a different quarter: Darwin's theory of evolution. Before Darwin, the problem facing atheists was to offer some alternative explanation for the extraordinarily complex and well-ordered biological systems in animal and plant life. One could raise philosophical doubts about the validity of the inference to design, as Hume did, but without an alternative explanation the impression of design remained overwhelming. After Darwin, however, one no longer needed to appeal to some transcendent intelligence as responsible for the apparent design of plants and animals, but could appeal to the "blind watchmaker" (to use one of Richard Dawkins's phrases) of evolution by chance plus natural selection. In his *Natural Theology*,[3] however, Paley presented another design argument that was not subject to the "evolution objection." This was the argument that in order for life to exist, the laws of nature and the physical environment of the earth must also be well designed. Partly because of the lack of detailed physical and astrophysical knowledge at the time, this version of Paley's argument was never considered particularly strong.

In recent decades, however, this version of the argument has become much more convincing. Scientists have increasingly come to realize how the initial conditions of the universe and the basic constants of physics must be balanced on a razor's edge for intelligent life to evolve – something known in the literature as the "fine-tuning" of the cosmos for (intelligent) life. Calculations show that if the constants of physics – such as the physical constant governing the strength of gravity – were slightly different, the evolution of complex, embodied life-forms of comparable intelligence to ourselves would be seriously inhibited, if not rendered impossible. These calculations added an important quantitative element to the argument from design: instead of simply appealing to a qualitative impression of the intricate ordering of nature for some end, as in Aquinas's Fifth Way, one could now give "hard" numerical content to these qualitative impressions. Because of this new quantitative data, along with developments in the logic of inference during the twentieth century, the design argument can be cast into a much more rigorous form then in the past, as I will now elaborate. We will begin by looking at the evidence for the fine-tuning of the cosmos for intelligent life.

The evidence of fine-tuning

Many examples of the fine-tuning for intelligent life can be given, a few of which we will briefly recount here.[4] One particularly important category of fine-tuning is that of the *constants* of physics. The constants of physics are a set of fundamental numbers that, when plugged into the laws of physics, determine the basic structure of the universe. An example of such a constant is the gravitational constant G that is part of Newton's law of gravity, $F = GM_1M_2/r^2$. G determines the strength of gravity between two masses. If one were to double the value of G, for instance, then the force of gravity between any two masses would double.

So far, physicists have discovered four forces in nature: gravity, the weak force, electromagnetism, and the strong nuclear force that binds protons and neutrons together in an atom. As measured in a certain set of standard dimensionless units,[5] gravity is the weakest of the forces, and the strong nuclear force is the strongest, being a factor of 10^{40} – or ten thousand billion, billion, billion, billion – times stronger than gravity.

Various calculations show that the strength of each of the forces of nature must fall into a very small life-permitting region for intelligent life to exist. As just one example, consider gravity. Compared with the total range of forces, the strength of gravity must fall in a relatively narrow range in order for complex life to exist. If we increased the strength of gravity a billion-fold, for instance, the force of gravity on a planet with the mass and size of the earth would be so great that organisms anywhere near the size of human beings, whether land-based or aquatic, would be crushed. (The strength of materials depends on the electromagnetic force via the fine-structure constant, which would not be affected by a change in the strength of gravity.) Even a much smaller planet of only 40 feet in diameter – which is not large enough to sustain organisms of our size – would have a gravitational pull of 1000 times that of earth, still too strong for organisms of our brain size, and hence level of intelligence, to exist. As astrophysicist Martin Rees notes, "In an imaginary strong gravity world, even insects would need thick legs to support them, and no animals could get much larger."[6] Other calculations show that if the gravitational force were increased by more than a factor of 3000, the maximum life-time of a star would be a billion years, thus severely inhibiting the probability of intelligent life evolving.[7] Of course, a 3000-fold increase in the strength of gravity is a lot, but compared with the total range of the strengths of the forces in nature (which span a range of 10^{40}, as we saw above), it is very small, being one part in a billion, billion, billion, billion.

134

Similarly, if the strong force were slightly increased or decreased, the existence of complex life would be seriously inhibited, if not rendered impossible. For instance, using the latest equations and codes for stellar evolution and nucleosynthesis, Heinz Oberhummer *et al.* showed that a small increase or decrease in the strong force – by as little as 1 percent – would drastically decrease, by 30- to 1000-fold, the total amount of either carbon or oxygen formed in stars.[8] Since the carbon and oxygen on planets comes from previous stars that have exploded or blown off their outer layers, this means that very little oxygen would be available for the existence of carbon-based life. At the very least, this would have a life-inhibiting effect given the many important, and seemingly irreplaceable, roles both carbon and oxygen play in living processes.[9]

There are other cases of the fine-tuning of the constants of physics besides the strength of the forces, however. Probably the most widely discussed – and esoteric – among physicists and cosmologists is the fine-tuning of what is known as the *cosmological constant*, which influences the expansion rate of the universe. If the cosmological constant were not fine-tuned to within one part in 10^{53} or even 10^{120} of its natural range of values, the universe would expand so rapidly that all matter would quickly disperse, and thus galaxies, stars, and even small aggregates of matter could never form.[10]

Besides the constants of physics, however, there is also the "fine-tuning" of the laws. If the laws of nature were not just right, life would probably be impossible. For example, consider again the four forces of nature. If gravity did not exist, masses would not clump together to form stars or planets; if the electromagnetic force did not exist, there would be no chemistry; if the strong force did not exist, protons and neutrons could not bind together and hence no atoms with atomic number greater than hydrogen would exist; and if the strong force were a long-range force (like gravity and electromagnetism) instead of a short range force that only acts between protons and neutrons in the nucleus, all matter would either almost instantaneously undergo nuclear fusion and explode or be sucked together forming a black hole. Each of these consequences would seriously inhibit, if not render impossible, the existence of complex intelligent life.

Similarly, other laws and principles are necessary for complex life: as prominent Princeton physicist Freeman Dyson points out,[11] if the Pauli-exclusion principle did not exist, which dictates that no two fermions can occupy the same quantum state, all electrons would occupy the lowest atomic orbit, eliminating complex chemistry; and if there were no quantization principle, which dictates that particles can only occupy certain discrete quantum states, there would be no atomic orbits and hence no chemistry, since all electrons would be sucked into the nucleus.

Finally, in his book *Nature's Destiny*, biochemist Michael Denton extensively discusses various higher-level features of the natural world, such as the many unique properties of carbon, oxygen, water, and the electromagnetic spectrum, that are conducive to the existence of complex biochemical systems. As one of many examples that Denton presents, both the atmosphere and water are transparent to electromagnetic radiation in a thin band in the visible region, but nowhere else except in radio waves. If, instead, either of them absorbed electromagnetic radiation in the visible region, the existence of terrestrial life would be seriously inhibited, if not rendered impossible.[12] These higher-level coincidences indicate a deeper-level fine-tuning of the fundamental laws and constants of physics.

As the above examples indicate, the evidence for fine-tuning is extensive, even if one has doubts about some individual cases. As philosopher John Leslie has pointed out, "clues heaped upon clues can constitute weighty evidence despite doubts about each element in the pile."[13] At the very least, these cases of fine-tuning show the truth of Freeman Dyson's observation that there are many "lucky accidents in physics,"[14] without which our existence as intelligent embodied beings would be impossible.

The argument formulated

Now it is time to consider the way in which the fine-tuning supports theism. In this section, I will argue that the evidence of fine-tuning primarily gives us a reason for preferring theism over what could be called the atheistic single-universe hypothesis – that is, the hypothesis that there is only one universe, and it exists as a brute fact. We will examine the typical alternative explanation of the fine-tuning offered by many atheists – what I call the "many-universes hypothesis" – in the section 'The many-worlds hypothesis' below.

Although the fine-tuning argument against the atheistic single-universe hypothesis can be cast in several different forms – such as inference to the best explanation – I believe that the most rigorous way of formulating the argument is in terms of what I will call the *prime principle of confirmation* (PPC), and which Rudolph Carnap has called the *"increase in firmness"* principle, and others have simply called the *likelihood principle*.[15] The PPC is a general principle of reasoning that tells us when some observation counts as evidence in favor of one hypothesis over another. *Simply put, the principle says that whenever we are considering two competing hypotheses, an observation counts as evidence in favor of the hypothesis under which the observation has the highest probability (or is the least improbable).* (Or, put slightly differently, the principle says that whenever we are considering two competing hypotheses, H_1 and H_2, an observation, O, counts as evidence in favor of H_1 over H_2 if O is more probable under H_1 than it is under H_2.) Moreover, the degree to which the evidence counts in favor of one hypothesis over another is proportional to the degree to which the observation is more probable under the one hypothesis than the other.[16] To illustrate, consider a case of finding a defendant's fingerprints on the murder weapon. Normally, we would take such a finding as strong evidence that the defendant was guilty. Why? Because we judge that it would be *unlikely* for these fingerprints to be on the murder weapon if the defendant was innocent, but *not unlikely* if the defendant was guilty. Then by the prime principle of confirmation, we would conclude that the fingerprints offered significant evidence that the defendant was guilty.

Using this principle, we can develop the fine-tuning argument in a two-step form as follows:

1   The existence of the fine-tuning is not highly improbable under theism.
2   The existence of the fine-tuning is very improbable under the atheistic single-universe hypothesis.[17]

We can conclude from premises 1 and 2 and the prime principle of confirmation that the fine-tuning data provide significant evidence to favor of the design hypothesis over the atheistic single-universe hypothesis.

At this point, we should pause to note two features of this argument. First, the argument does not say that the fine-tuning evidence proves that the universe was designed, or even that it is likely that the universe was designed. Indeed, of itself it does not even show that we are epistemically warranted in believing in theism over the atheistic single-universe hypothesis. In order to justify these sorts of claims, we would have to look at the full range of evidence both for and against the theistic hypothesis – something I am not doing in this essay (but note the range of essays in this volume). Rather, the argument merely concludes that the fine-tuning significantly *supports* theism *over* the atheistic single-universe hypothesis. (I say significantly supports, because presumably the ratio of probabilities for the fine-tuning under theism versus the atheistic single-universe hypothesis is quite large. See note 16.)

In this way, the evidence of the fine-tuning argument is much like fingerprints found on a gun: although they can provide strong evidence that the defendant committed the murder, one could not conclude merely from them alone that the defendant is guilty; one would also have to look at all the other evidence offered. Perhaps, for instance, ten reliable witnesses claimed to see the defendant at a party at the time of the shooting. In this case, the fingerprints would still count as significant evidence of guilt, but this evidence would be counterbalanced by the testimony of the witnesses. Similarly the evidence of fine-tuning significantly supports theism over the atheistic single-universe hypothesis, but it does not itself show that, everything considered, theism is the most plausible explanation of the fine-tuning or the world.

The second feature of the argument we should note is that, given the truth of *the prime principle of confirmation*, the conclusion of the argument follows from the premises. Specifically, if the premises of the argument are true, then we are guaranteed that the conclusion is true: that is, the argument is what philosophers call *valid*. Thus, insofar as we can show that the premises of the argument are true, we will have shown that the conclusion is true. Our next task, therefore, is to attempt to show that the premises are true, or at least that we have good reasons to believe them.

Support for the premises

Support for premise 1

Premise 1 is easy to support and somewhat less controversial than premise 2. The argument in support of it can be simply stated as follows: *since God is an all good being, and it is good for intelligent, conscious beings to exist, it not highly surprising or highly improbable that God would create a world that could support intelligent life.* Thus, the fine-tuning is not highly improbable under theism.

Support for premise 2

Upon looking at the data, many people find it very obvious that the fine-tuning is highly improbable under the atheistic single-universe hypothesis. And it is easy to see why when we think of the fine-tuning in terms of various analogies. In the "dart-board analogy," for example, the theoretically possible values for fundamental constants of physics can be represented as a dart-board that fills the whole galaxy, and the conditions necessary for life to exist as a small inch-wide target. Accordingly, from this analogy it seems obvious that it would be highly improbable for the fine-tuning to occur under the atheistic single-universe hypothesis – that is, for the dart to hit the target by chance.

Now some philosophers object to claim that the fine-tuning is highly improbable under the atheistic single-universe hypothesis by arguing that since there is only one universe, the notion of the fine-tuning of the universe being probable or improbable is meaningless. Ian Hacking, for instance, claims that a probability could only be meaningfully assigned to the fine-tuning if we had some model of universe generation which implied that a certain percentage of universes would turn out to be fine-tuned.[18] Given such a model, and given that a single-universe is generated, we could then assign the universe a certain probability of being fine-tuned. Keith Parsons raises similar objections.[19]

Although I do not have space to provide a full-scale response to this objection, I will briefly sketch an answer. The first is to note that the relevant notion of probability occurring in the fine-tuning argument is a widely recognized type of probability called *epistemic probability*.[20] Roughly, the epistemic probability of a proposition can be thought of as the degree of confidence or belief that we rationally should have in the proposition.

THE TELEOLOGICAL ARGUMENT

Further, the conditional epistemic probability of a proposition R on another proposition S – written as P(R/S) – can be defined as the degree to which the proposition S *of itself* should rationally lead us to expect that R is true. Under the epistemic conception of probability, therefore, the statement that *the fine-tuning of the cosmos is very improbable under the atheistic single-universe hypothesis* is to be understood as making a statement about the degree to which the atheistic single-universe hypothesis would or should, *of itself*, rationally lead us to expect cosmic fine-tuning.

The phrase "*of itself*" is important here. The rational degree of expectation should not be confused with the degree to which one should expect the constants of physics to fall within the life-permitting range if one believed the atheistic single-universe hypothesis. For even those who believe in this atheistic hypothesis should expect the values of the constants of physics to be life-permitting since this follows from the fact that we are alive. Rather, the conditional epistemic probability in this case is the degree to which the atheistic single-universe hypothesis *of itself* should lead us to expect the values of the constants of physics to be life-permitting. This means that in assessing the conditional epistemic probability in this and other similar cases, one must exclude contributions to our expectations arising from other information that we have, such as that we are alive. In the case at hand, one way of doing this is by means of the following sort of thought experiment. Imagine a disembodied being with mental capacities and a knowledge of physics similar to that of the most intelligent physicists alive today, except that the being does not know whether the values of the constants of physics allow for embodied, intelligent life to arise. Further, suppose that this disembodied being believed in the atheistic single-universe hypothesis. Then, the degree that being should rationally expect the values of the constants of physics to be life-permitting would be equal to our conditional epistemic probability, since its expectation is solely a result of its belief in the atheistic single-universe hypothesis, not other factors such as its awareness of its own existence.

Given this understanding of the notion of conditional epistemic probability, it is not difficult to see that the conditional epistemic probability of a constant of physics having a life-permitting value under the atheistic single-universe hypothesis will be much smaller than under theism. The reason is simple when we think about our imaginary disembodied being. If such a being were a theist, it would have some reason to believe that the values of the constants would fall into the life-permitting region. (See the argument in support of premise 1 above.) On the other hand, if the being were a subscriber to the atheistic single-universe hypothesis, it would have no reason to think that the values would be in the life-permitting region instead of any other part of the "theoretically possible" range of values. Thus, the being has more reason to believe that the constants would fall into the life-permitting region under theism than the atheistic single universe hypothesis – that is, the epistemic probability under theism is larger than under this atheistic hypothesis. How much larger? That depends on the degree of fine-tuning. Here, I will simply note that it seems obvious that in general the higher the degree of fine-tuning – that is, the smaller the width of the life-permitting range is to the "theoretically possible" range – the greater the surprise under the atheistic single-universe hypothesis, and hence the greater the ratio of the two probabilities. To go beyond these statements and to assign actual probabilities under the atheistic single-universe hypothesis – or to further justify these claims of improbability – would require appealing to the probabilistic principle of indifference, which is beyond the scope of this essay.

Objections to the argument

As powerful as the fine-tuning argument against the atheistic single-universe hypothesis is, several major objections have been raised to it by both atheists and theists. In this section, we will consider these objections in turn.

Objection 1: more fundamental law objection

One criticism of the fine-tuning argument is that, as far as we know, there could be a more fundamental law under which the constants of physics *must* have the values they do. Thus, given such a law, it is not improbable that the known constants of physics fall within the life-permitting range.

Besides being entirely speculative, the problem with postulating such a law is that it simply moves the improbability of the fine-tuning up one level, to that of the postulated physical law itself. As astrophysicists Bernard Carr and Martin Rees note, "even if all apparently anthropic coincidences could be explained [in terms of some grand unified theory], it would still be remarkable that the relationships dictated by physical theory happened also to be those propitious for life."[21] A similar sort of response can be given to the claim that the fine-tuning is not improbable because it might be *logically necessary* for the constants of physics to have life-permitting values. That is, according to this claim, the constants of physics must have life-permitting values in the same way that 2 + 2 must equal 4, or the interior angles of a triangle must add up to 180 degrees in Euclidian geometry. Like the "more fundamental law" proposal above, however, this postulate simply transfers the improbability up one level: of all the laws and constants of physics that conceivably could have been logically necessary, it seems highly improbable that it would be those that are life-permitting.[22]

Objection 2: other forms of life objection

Another objection people commonly raise against the fine-tuning argument is that, as far as we know, other forms of life could exist even if the constants of physics were different. So, it is claimed, the fine-tuning argument ends up presupposing that all forms of intelligent life must be like us. One answer to this objection is that many cases of fine-tuning do not make this presupposition. If, for example, the cosmological constant were much larger than it is, matter would disperse so rapidly that no planets, and indeed no stars could exist. Without stars, however, there would exist no stable energy sources for complex material systems of any sort to evolve. So, all the fine-tuning argument presupposes in this case is that the evolution of intelligent life requires some stable energy source. This is certainly a very reasonable assumption.

Of course, if the laws and constants of nature were changed enough, other forms of embodied intelligent life might be able to exist of which we cannot even conceive. But this is irrelevant to the fine-tuning argument since the judgment of improbability of fine-tuning under the atheistic single-universe hypothesis only requires that, given our current laws of nature, the life-permitting range for the values of the constants of physics (such as gravity) is small compared with the *surrounding* range of non-life-permitting values.

Objection 3: anthropic principle objection

According to the weak version of the so-called *anthropic principle*, if the laws of nature were not fine-tuned, we would not be here to comment on the fact. Some have argued, therefore, that the fine-tuning is not really *improbable or surprising* at all under atheism, but simply follows from the fact that we exist. The response to this objection is simply to restate the argument in terms of our existence: our existence as embodied, intelligent beings is extremely unlikely under the atheistic single-universe hypothesis (since our existence requires fine-tuning), but not improbable under theism. Then, we simply apply the prime principle of confirmation to draw the conclusion that *our existence* significantly confirms theism over the atheistic single-universe hypothesis.

To further illustrate this response, consider the following "firing-squad" analogy. As John Leslie points out, if fifty sharp shooters all miss me, the response "if they had not missed me I wouldn't be here to consider the fact" is not adequate. Instead, I would naturally conclude that there was some reason why they all missed, such as that they never really intended to kill me. Why would I conclude this? Because my continued existence would be very improbable under the hypothesis that they missed me by chance, but not improbable under the hypothesis that there was some reason why they missed me.[23] Thus, by the prime principle of confirmation, my continued existence strongly confirms the latter hypothesis.

Objection 4: the "Who designed God?" objection

Perhaps the most common objection that atheists raise to the argument from design, of which the fine-tuning argument is one instance, is that postulating the existence of God does not solve the problem of design, but merely transfers it up one level, to the question of who designed God. In fact, philosopher J. J. C. Smart claims that hypothesizing God as an explanation for the order and complexity of the universe makes us explanatorily worse off:

> If we postulate God in addition to the created universe we increase the complexity of our hypothesis. We have all the complexity of the universe itself, and we have in addition the at least equal complexity of God. (The designer of an artifact must be at least as complex as the designed artifact) . . . . If the theist can show the atheist that postulating God actually reduces the complexity of one's total world view, then the atheist should be a theist. [24]

In response, we can first note that even if Smart is correct in claiming that God exhibits enormous internal complexity, it still would be the case that the fine-tuning provides evidence in favor of theism over the atheistic single-universe hypothesis. The reason is that the above argument only relies on comparison of probabilities of fine-tuning under the two different hypotheses, not on whether the new hypothesis reduces the overall complexity of one's worldview. As an analogy, if complex, intricate structures (such as aqueducts and buildings) existed on Mars, one could conclude that they would support the hypothesis that intelligent, extraterrestrial beings existed on Mars in the past, even if such beings are much more complex than the structures to be explained. Second, however, for reasons entirely independent of the argument from design, God has been thought to have little, if any, internal complexity. Indeed, medieval philosophers and theologians often went as far as advocating the doctrine of divine simplicity, according to which God is claimed to be absolutely simple, without any internal complexity. So, atheists who push this objection have a lot of arguing to do to make it stick.

The many-worlds hypothesis

In response to the theistic explanation of the fine-tuning, many atheists have offered an alternative explanation, what I will call the *many-universes hypothesis*, but which in the literature goes under a variety of names, such as many-worlds hypothesis, the many-domains hypothesis, the world-ensemble hypothesis, the multi-universe hypothesis, etc. According to this hypothesis, there are a very large – perhaps infinite – number of universes, with the constants of physics varying from universe to universe.[25] Of course, in the vast majority of these universes, the constants of physics would *not* have life-permitting values. Nonetheless, in a small proportion of universes they would, and consequently it is no longer improbable that universes such as ours exist that have life-permitting values for their constants.

Further, usually these universes are thought to be produced by some sort of physical mechanism, which I call a many-universe generator. The universe generator can be thought of as analogous to a lottery ticket generator: just as it would be no surprise that a winning number is eventually produced if enough tickets are generated, it would be no surprise that a universe fine-tuned for life would occur if enough universes are generated.[26]

Most many-universes models are entirely speculative, having little basis in current physics. However, many physicists, such as Steven Weinberg, have proposed a model that does have a reasonable basis in current physics – namely, inflationary cosmology. Inflationary cosmology is a currently widely discussed cosmological theory that attempts to explain the origin of the universe, and which has recently passed some preliminary observational tests. Essentially, it claims that our universe was formed by a small area of pre-space being massively blown up by a hypothesized *inflation* field, in much the same way as a soup bubble would form in an ocean full of soap. In chaotic inflation models – widely considered the most plausible – various points of the pre-space are randomly blown up, forming an enormous number of bubble universes.[27]

In order to get the initial conditions and constants of physics to vary from universe to universe, as they must do if this scenario is going to explain the fine-tuning, there must be a further physical mechanism to cause the variation. Such a mechanism *might* be given by superstring theory, one of the most hotly discussed hypotheses about the fundamental structure of matter, but it is too early to tell. Other leading alternatives to string theory being explored by physicists, such as the currently proposed models for Grand Unified Theories (GUTs), do not appear to allow for enough variation (e.g. they only give a dozen or so different values for the constants, not the enormous number needed to account for the fine-tuning).[28]

Although at present these theories are highly speculative (for example, superstring theory has no experimental evidence in its favor),[29] I do not believe that simply rejecting the many-universe generator hypothesis is an adequate response. Not only does the inflationary/superstring scenario have some plausibility, but God could have created our universe via some many-universe generator, just as God created our planet by the Big Bang – a sort of many-planets generator. A better response is to note that the "many-universe generator" itself, whether that given by chaotic inflationary models or some other type, seems to need to be "well-designed" in order to produce life-sustaining universes. After all, even a mundane item like a bread machine, which only produces loaves of bread instead of universes, must be well designed to produce decent loaves of bread. If this is right, then, to some extent, invoking some sort of many-universe generator as an explanation of the fine-tuning only kicks the issue of design up one level, to the question of who designed the many-universe generator.

For example, the inflationary scenario discussed above only works to produce universes because of the prior existence of the inflaton field, and the peculiar nature of the central equation of general relativity, that is Einstein's equation.[30] Without either factor, there would neither be regions of space that inflate nor would those regions have the mass–energy necessary for a universe to exist. If, for example, the universe obeyed Newton's theory of gravity instead of Einstein's, the inflaton field would at best simply create a gravitational attraction causing space to contract, not to expand. Moreover, as mentioned above, one needs a special underlying physical theory – such as perhaps superstring theory – that allows for enough variation in the constants of physics among universes.

Further, the inflationary many-universe generator can only produce life-sustaining universes if the right background laws are in place. For example, without the Pauli-exclusion principle, electrons would occupy the lowest atomic orbit and hence complex and varied atoms would be impossible; or, without a universally attractive force between all masses, such as gravity, matter would not be able to form sufficiently large material bodies (such as planets) for life to develop or for long-lived stable energy sources such as stars to exist. The universe generator hypothesis, however, does not explain these background laws.

Finally, I would argue, the many-universes generator hypothesis cannot explain other features of the universe that seem to exhibit apparent design whereas theism can. For example, many physicists, such as Albert Einstein, have observed that the basic laws of physics exhibit an extraordinary degree of beauty, elegance, harmony, and ingenuity. Nobel Prize winning physicist Steven Weinberg, for instance, devotes a whole chapter of his book *Dreams of a Final Theory* (Chapter 6, "Beautiful Theories") to explaining how the criteria of beauty and elegance are commonly used to guide physicists in formulating the right laws.[31] Indeed, one of most prominent theoretical physicists of this century, Paul Dirac, went so far as to claim that "it is more important to have beauty in one's equations than to have them fit experiment."[32] Now such beauty, elegance, and ingenuity make sense if the universe was designed by God; I would contend, however, that apart from some sort of design hypothesis, there is no reason to expect the fundamental laws to be elegant or beautiful. Thus theism makes more sense of this aspect of the world than atheism, whether that atheism is of the single-universe or many-universe variety.[33]

Conclusion

In this chapter, I argued that the fine-tuning of the cosmos for life provides strong evidence for preferring theism over the atheistic single-universe hypothesis. I then argued that although one can partially explain the fine-tuning of the constants of physics by invoking some sort of many-universes generator, we have good reasons to believe that the many-universe generator itself would need to be well designed, and hence that hypothesizing some sort of many-universes generator only pushes the case for design up one level. The arguments I have offered do not prove the truth of theism, or even show that theism is epistemically warranted or the most plausible position to adopt. To show this would require examining all the evidence both for and against theism, along with looking at all the alternatives to theism. Rather, the arguments in this essay were only intended to show that the fine-tuning of the cosmos offers us significant reasons for preferring theism over atheism (where atheism is understood as not simply the denial of theism but as also including the denial of any sort of intelligence behind the existence or structure of the universe). As with the design argument in general, by itself the fine-tuning argument cannot get one all the way to theism. Other arguments or considerations must be brought into play to do that. Thus, although quite significant, it only constitutes one part of the case for theism, other parts of which are explored in this book.

Notes

1 A full-scale treatment of the fine-tuning argument, and related design arguments, will be presented in a book I am currently working on tentatively entitled *The Well-Tempered Universe: God, Fine-tuning, and the Laws of Nature*. Some parts of this paper were adapted from previous articles and book chapters: "The Fine-Tuning Design Argument" in *Reason for the Hope Within*, Michael Murray (ed.) (Grand Rapids, MI: Eerdmans, 1999); "The Argument from Design and the Many-Worlds Hypothesis," in *Philosophy of Religion: a Reader and Guide*, William Lane Craig (ed.) (Tronten: Rutgers University Press, 2001); "God, Design, and Fine-tuning" in *God Matters: Readings in the Philosophy of Religion*, Raymond Martin and Christopher Bernard (eds) (New York: Longman Press, 2002); "The Evidence for Fine-tuning," in *God and Design: The Teleological Argument and Modern Science*, Neil Manson (ed.) (London: Routledge, 2003). Work on this topic was made possible by a year-long fellowship from the Pew Foundation, several grants from the Discovery Institute, and a grant from Messiah College.
2 Ninian Smart, *Doctrine and Argument in Indian Philosophy* (London: George Allen and Unwin, 1964) 153–4.
3 Paley, William, *Natural Theology* (Boston: Gould and Lincoln, 1852 [1802])
4 For an up-to-date analysis of the evidence for fine-tuning, with a careful physical analysis of what I consider the six strongest cases, see my "The Evidence for Fine-Tuning," in *God and Design*, Neil Manson (ed.) (London: Routledge, forthcoming); more detailed treatments of the cases of fine-tuning cited below are presented in that chapter, along with more detailed references to the literature. Other useful references are John Barrow and Frank Tipler, *The Anthropic Cosmological Principle* (Oxford: Oxford University Press, 1986); Paul Davies, *The Accidental Universe* (Cambridge: Cambridge University Press, 1982); John Leslie, *Universes* (London: Routledge, 1989); B. J. Carr and M. J. Rees, "The Anthropic Cosmological Principle and the Structure of the Physical World," *Nature* 278 (1979), 605–12; Martin Rees, *Just Six Numbers: The Deep Forces that Shape the Universe* (New York: Basic Books, 2000).
5 Barrow and Tipler, *Anthropic Cosmological Principle*, 292–5.
6 Rees, *Just Six Numbers*, 30.

7 For the actual calculations, see my "The Evidence for Fine-tuning."
8 H. Oberhummer, A. Csoto, and H. Schlattl, "Fine-Tuning of Carbon Based Life in the Universe by Triple-Alpha Process in Red Giants," *Science* 289 (2000), 88.
9 Michael Denton, *Nature's Destiny: How the Laws of Biology Reveal Purpose in the Universe* (New York: The Free Press, 1998), 19–47, 117–40.
10 The fine-tuning of the cosmological constant is widely discussed in the literature. See Davies, *The Accidental Universe*, 105–9; Rees, *Just Six Numbers*, 95–102, 154–5. For an accessible, current discussion, see my " The Evidence for Fine-Tuning."
11 Freeman Dyson, *Disturbing the Universe* (New York: Harper and Row, 1979), 251.
12 Denton, *Nature's Destiny*, 56–7.
13 John Leslie, "How to Draw Conclusions From a Fine-Tuned Cosmos," in *Physics, Philosophy and Theology: A Common Quest for Understanding*, Robert Russell, Nancy Murphy, and C. J. Isham (eds) (Vatican City State: Vatican Observatory Press, 1988), 300.
14 Dyson, *Disturbing the Universe*, 251.
15 See Rudolph Carnap, *The Logical Foundations of Probability* (Chicago: University of Chicago Press, 1962). For a basic, but somewhat dated, introduction to confirmation theory and the prime principle of confirmation, see Richard Swinburne, *An Introduction to Confirmation Theory* (London: Methuen and Co. Ltd, 1973). For literature specifically casting design arguments as likelihood comparisons, see A. W. F. Edwards, *Likelihood* (Baltimore: Johns Hopkins University Press, 1992).
16 For those familiar with the probability calculus, a precise statement of the degree to which evidence counts in favor of one hypothesis over another can be given in terms of the odds form of Bayes's Theorem: that is, $P(H_1/E)/P(H_2/E) = [P(H_1)/P(H_2)] \times [P(E/H_1)/P(E/H_2)]$. The general version of the principle stated here, however, does not require the applicability or truth of Bayes's theorem.
17 To be precise, the fine-tuning refers to the joint fact that the life-permitting values of the constants of physics are small compared with the "theoretically possible" ranges for those values *and* the fact that the values actually fall in the life-permitting range. It is only this latter fact that we are arguing is highly improbable under the atheistic single-universe hypothesis.
18 Ian Hacking, "Coincidences: Mundane and Cosmological," in *Origin and Evolution of the Universe: Evidence for Design*, John M. Robson (ed.) (Montreal: McGill-Queen's University Press, 1987), 128–30.
19 Keith Parsons, "Is There a Case for Christian Theism?" In *Does God Exist? The Great Debate*, J. P. Moreland and Kai Nielsen (eds) (Nashville: Thomas Nelson, 1990), 182.
20 For an in-depth discussion of epistemic probability, see Swinburne, *An Introduction to Confirmation Theory*; Ian Hacking, *The Emergence of Probability: A Philosophical Study of Early Ideas About Probability, Induction and Statistical Inference* (Cambridge: Cambridge University Press, 1975); and Alvin Plantinga *Warrant and Proper Function* (Oxford: Oxford University Press, 1993), Chapters 8 and 9.
21 Carr and Rees, "The Anthropic Cosmological Principle and the Structure of the Physical World," 612.
22 Those with some training in probability theory will want to note that the kind of probability invoked here is what philosophers call *epistemic probability*, which, as we discussed above, is a measure of the rational degree of belief that we should have in a proposition. Since our rational degree of belief in a

necessary truth can be less than 1, we can sensibly speak of it being improbable for a given law of nature to exist necessarily. For example, we can speak of an unproven mathematical hypotheses – such as Goldbach's conjecture that every even number greater than 6 is the sum of two odd primes – as being probably true or probably false given our current evidence, even though all mathematical hypotheses are either necessarily true or necessarily false.

23 Leslie, "How To Draw Conclusions from a Fine-Tuned Cosmos," 304.

24 J. J. C. Smart, "Laws of Nature and Cosmic Coincidence," *The Philosophical Quarterly* 35 (1981), 275–6.

25 I define a "universe" as any region of space–time that is disconnected from other regions in such a way that the constants of physics in that region could differ significantly from the other regions. A more thorough discussion of the many-universes hypothesis is presented in my essay, "The Argument from Design and the Many-Worlds Hypothesis," in *Philosophy of Religion: A Reader and Guide*, William Lane Craig (ed.) (Tronten: Rutgers University Press 2001).

26 Some have proposed what could be called a *metaphysical* many-universe hypothesis, according to which universes are thought to exist on their own without being generated by any physical process. Typically, advocates of this view – such as the late Princeton University philosopher David Lewis [*On the Plurality of Worlds* (New York: Basil Blackwell, 1986)] and University of Pennsylvania astrophysicist Max Tegmark ["Is 'the theory of everything' merely the ultimate ensemble theory?", *Annals of Physics* 270 (1998), 1–51] – claim that every possible world exists. According to Lewis, for instance, there exists a reality parallel to our own in which a duplicate of me is President of the United States and a reality in which objects can travel faster than the speed of light. Dream up a possible scenario, and it exists in some parallel reality, according to Lewis. Besides being completely speculative (and in many people's eyes, outlandish), a major problem with this scenario is that the vast majority of possible universes are ones that are chaotic, just as the vast majority of possible arrangements of letters of 1,000 characters would not spell a meaningful pattern. So, the only way that these metaphysical hypotheses can explain the regularity and predictability of our universe, and the fact that it seems to be describable by a few simple laws, is to invoke an "observer selection" effect. That is, Lewis and Tegmark must claim that only universes like ours in this respect could support intelligent life, and hence be observed. The problem with this explanation is that it is much more likely for there to exist local islands of the sort of order necessary for intelligent life than for the entire universe to have such an ordered arrangement. Thus, their hypotheses cannot explain why we, considered as generic observers, find ourselves in a universe that is highly ordered throughout.

Among others, George Schlesinger has raised this objection against Lewis's hypothesis ["Possible Worlds and the Mystery of Existence" *Ratio* 26 (1984), 1–18]. This sort of objection was raised against a similar explanation of the high degree of order in our universe offered by the famous physicist Ludwig Boltzman, and has generally been considered fatal to Boltzman's explanation [Paul Davies, *The Physics of Time Asymmetry* (Berkeley, CA: University of California Press, 1974), 103].

27 For an accessible introduction to superstring theory, see Alan Guth, *The Inflationary Universe: The Quest for a New Theory of Cosmic Origins* (New York: Helix Books, 1997).

28 Andrei Linde, *Particle Physics and Inflationary Cosmology*, Marc Damashek (trans.) (Longhorne, PA: Harwood Academic Publishers, 1990), 3; *Inflation and Quantum Cosmology* (New York: Academic Press, 1990), 6.

29 Michio Kaku, *Introduction to Superstrings and M-Theory*, 2nd edn (New York: Springer-Verlag, 1999), 17.
30 John Peacock, *Cosmological Physics* (Cambridge, UK: Cambridge University Press, 1999), 24–6.
31 Steven Weinberg, *Dreams of a Final Theory* (New York: Vintage Books, 1992), Chapter 6.
32 P. A. M. Dirac, "The evolution of the physicist's picture of nature," *Scientific American* (May 1963), 47.
33 For a further development of this argument for design from the simplicity and beauty of the laws of nature, see Part II of my "Argument from Design and the Many-Worlds Hypothesis," in William Lane Craig (ed.) *Philosophy of Religion*.

8

THE MORAL ARGUMENT

Paul Copan

Introduction

Civil rights leader Martin Luther King Jr wrote from a Birmingham, AL, jail: "One may well ask: How can you advocate breaking some laws and obeying others?" The answer, he noted, "lies in the fact that there are two kinds of laws: just and unjust."[1] King spoke of an "eternal law" or "natural law" to which we are subject.

Do objective moral values exist? If so, do they make sense in a non-theistic world? And if so, what metaphysical grounds do we have for affirming their existence? I shall contend that

1 objective moral values do exist and are properly basic;
2 they do not make sense in a non-theistic world (most time will be spent in this area, focusing primarily on naturalism, although my argument would apply to other non-theistic alternatives), but are properly grounded in a theistic worldview in which human beings have been uniquely created in God's image and thus reflect certain divine properties in important – even if limited – ways; and
3 the Euthyphro argument does not undermine the connection between God and objective moral values.

The argument undergirding my chapter is thus:

• If objective moral values exist, then God exists.
• Objective moral values do exist.
• Therefore, God exists.

Such values are inexplicable non-theistically – or, more specifically, naturalistically. This "natural law," which transcends human history and cultures, is rooted in the very nature or character of a good God. Because we humans are uniquely made in the divine image, we are capable of *recognizing* or *discovering* moral principles; we do not *invent* them.

149

Even if we cannot move inferentially from objective moral values to the omniscient and omnipotent God of Abraham, Isaac, and Jacob, at least we can say that we live in an "ontologically haunted universe."[2] Moral values serve as one of the *signals of transcendence*.[3] We humans, who have been made in God's image, are endowed with moral capacities (e.g. conscience, moral responsibility and freedom, the recognition of our need for grace and mercy in the face of moral failure) so that, at a minimum, we may infer a personal Being to whom each of us is accountable (Romans 1:19–20; 2:14–15) and with whom we must be in right relationship – even if the moral argument does not logically bring us to an all-powerful, all-knowing Being.

Moral values as properly basic

Rather than being the product of culture, individual preference, or socio-biological evolution, objective moral values do indeed exist: *kindness is a virtue and not a vice; torturing babies for fun is immoral; rape is morally reprehensible*. Most of us find such truths obvious – just as we find 2 + 2 = 4 and *modus ponens* perspicuously true. Basic moral truths exist regardless of

- the *plurality of moral beliefs* over time and across cultures (i.e. even if cultures throughout history have carried out morally reprehensible activities, this fact does *not* entail that objective moral values are non-existent); and
- the *alleged evolutionary benefit from believing certain moral tenets* (certain beliefs and actions may be right – such as self-sacrifice for others – even if such practices do not necessarily prolong my or my species' existence).

As with basic logical truths, so it is with moral truths. To deny them is to reject something fundamental about our humanness. Atheist philosopher Kai Nielsen comments on the vileness of child abuse and wife-beating:

> It is more reasonable to believe such elemental things to be evil than to believe any skeptical theory that tells us we cannot know or reasonably believe any of these things to be evil . . . . I firmly believe that this is bedrock and right and that anyone who does not believe it cannot have probed deeply enough into the grounds of his moral beliefs. [4]

Nicholas Rescher rightly notes: "If [members of a particular tribe] think that it is acceptable to engage in practices like the sacrifice of first-born children, then their grasp on the conception of morality is somewhere between inadequate and non-existent."[5] When the murderous intentions of Stalin, Hitler, or Pol Pot are applauded or deemed justifiable because "it seemed good from *their* perspective," right-thinking persons will denounce such twisted approbations.

Although culture may *influence* one's moral perceptions, it need not *dictate* them. Throughout history, civilizations have produced moral reformers such as William Wilberforce or Martin Luther King Jr, who withstood the cultural tide against them and recognized the dignity and rights of *all* human beings, who are made in the image of God. (According to the Jewish–Christian tradition, sin has brought damage to our God-given nature but has not eradicated or eclipsed its intrinsic goodness.)[6]

As Robert Audi has eloquently argued, we ought to take seriously fundamental or pre-theoretical moral intuitions that arise as we confront particular moral situations.[7] As Romans 1:20 and 2:14 indicate, we are responsible humans who are equipped with the capacity to recognize right and wrong – even if partially distorted by culture and hardening of heart. While such directly apprehended intuitions are not necessarily infallible or indefeasible (e.g. further clarification and refining may be required – just as with objects of sense perception), they can serve as a partial guide for detecting the world's moral framework.

Many of our moral beliefs are *properly basic*. That is, they are properly grounded in certain appropriate circumstances. For example, we are properly *appalled* at a man's adultery with his personal assistant and his abandoning his wife and children; there is no need to explain away our shock and horror at such actions. Even if it is impossible to prove in some scientific/positivistic fashion (a position which itself cannot be proven scientifically) that moral values exist, we probably find ourselves far more certain of the wrongness of such actions than we may be of the truth of Einstein's relativity theories or of the universe's expansion.

As with particular *epistemic* beliefs (my belief that I had chocolate-chip pancakes for breakfast last Saturday), so it is with my *moral* beliefs (the terrorist attacks on September 11, 2001, were morally reprehensible). Holding to such beliefs is properly basic, and thus rational and justifiable. That is, I am violating no epistemic norm in holding these beliefs, and, as Alvin Plantinga puts it, I am doing my epistemic duty *in excelsis*.[8] Although these prima facie beliefs may be defeasible,[9] in the absence of any decent defeaters for holding them there is just no good reason to reject them. For instance, I may be taking prescribed drugs with hallucinogenic side-effects such that I see pancakes when no pancakes are present. Similarly, many of our *moral* perceptions are so inescapable that we would do serious damage to our noetic structure in rejecting their validity.

Of course, there are relativists or social constructionists, who would have us believe that morality is relative to personal preferences or particular cultures. Of course, one wonders why moral relativists generally uphold the cardinal and universally binding standard of "tolerance"[10] and get upset when their own "rights" are violated or their property is stolen. Moral relativists are usually *selectively* relativistic – until *their* rights are violated or *their* property is stolen. That is, they tend to be armchair relativists – not practical relativists.

For the perspectivalist or social constructionist, she finds herself in the awkward position of either saying nothing at all ("this is just my perspective that it is all a matter of perspective") or contradicting herself ("it is all a matter of perspective – *except mine*, which is universally true").[11] Perspectivalism ends up being either trivial or incoherent.

It seems that the *credulity principle* is appropriate with regard to both our *sense* perceptions and our *moral* intuitions/perceptions: both are innocent until proven guilty. I am wise to accept their testimony *unless* I have an overriding reason to doubt them. Moreover, given the *logical* possibility of being morally or epistemically misguided does not entail comprehensive skepticism regarding such perceptions. There is no need to take such epistemic and moral skepticism with radical seriousness.[12] Furthermore, talk of human equality, rights, value, or worth by political philosophers (e.g. Ronald Dworkin, John Rawls) reflects a common commitment to ideals we generally take seriously. (Of course, such thinkers tend to *posit* such ideals; their refusal to offer a coherent metaphysical grounding for such rights is a glaring deficiency, as we shall see below.)

Thus there are no overriding reasons – including relativism's denial of moral values or (as we shall see below) socio-biological evolution as the basis for moral values – to deny their objectivity or applicability to all human beings.

An unnatural fit: non-theism and objective moral values

The United Nations Universal Declaration of Human Rights of 1948 declares: "All human beings are born free and equal in dignity and rights. They are endowed with reason and conscience and should act towards one another in a spirit of brotherhood." Notice how the dignity and rights of human beings are simply *posited*. What is noticeably lacking are any *grounds* or *basis* for believing this to be the case. By contrast, America's Declaration of Independence connects the "self-evident" value and "unalienable rights" of human beings to God their Creator. The Jewish–Christian Scriptures declare that human beings – both male and female – have been made "in the image of God" (Genesis 1:26–7). We have been uniquely made by God as personal, relational, volitional, moral, rational, self-aware, and spiritual beings – attributes that God has to a maximal degree. Even atheists, who deny God's existence, can hold to the same objective moral values as theists, and this is no surprise – because they have been made in the selfsame divine image and are therefore capable of moral reflection and action just as theists are. So while they, being morally sensitive human beings, believe that moral realism (i.e. *mind-independent moral truths exist*)[13] is *logically* justified, the more fundamental question of *metaphysical* justification remains.

Naturalistic moral realists (NMRs) claim such justification. David Brink puts it this way: "Ethical naturalism claims that moral facts are nothing more than familiar facts about the natural, including social, world."[14] He expands on this summary: "moral facts *are* natural and social scientific (e.g. social, psychological, economic, and biological facts)."[15] Michael Smith claims that in all respects (including the moral), we are "constrained" by the truth of naturalism, "the view that the world is amenable to study through empirical science."[16] What makes moral claims true are naturalistic features, which are themselves "posits, or composites of posits, of empirical science."[17] Moral features *are* natural features.[18]

Peter Railton claims that any charge that morality is "odd" is eliminated when we take the view that moral facts are *constituted by* natural facts.[19] (Brink claims that moral properties are *constituted by* and not *identical to*, natural properties.)[20] Railton prefers to see emergent moral properties as supervening upon – but not reducible to – physical ones.[21] This would be similar to wetness supervening on H_2O, whereas hydrogen and oxygen by themselves do not have the property of wetness. Railton does not believe that moral facts are bizzare or *sui generis*: "there need be nothing odd about causal mechanisms for learning moral facts if these facts are constituted by natural facts."[22] If moral properties supervene on one set of conditions (e.g. when a brain and nervous system are sufficiently and complexly developed – or when a certain level of social interconnectedness arises), then it is necessarily true that moral properties supervene on an identical set of conditions elsewhere or at another time. Moral properties are in the *effect* but not in the *cause*. Thus *nature*, Brink claims, is the only place we can look in an attempt to find the moral realm: "We are natural and social creatures, and I know of nowhere else to look for ethics than this rich conjunction of facts."[23]

Noted ethical theorist William Frankena claims that the theist cannot appeal to the naturalistic fallacy (the allegedly illicit shift from *is* to *ought*) without question-begging.[24] He criticizes "religionist" ethics,[25] maintaining that there is no *logical* reason that we *must* conceive ethics as a part of religion (moving from the *is* of "God loves us" to the *ought* of "we must love one another").[26] And even though ethical principles are not all logically dependent upon theology, "it does not follow that they cannot be justified in any objective and rational sense."[27]

But is this really the case?[28] Is morality as natural as granola? Did human dignity and moral obligation just emerge through the course of naturalistic evolution? I suggest that the answer is no. Rather, it is *theism* that furnishes the metaphysical resources to make sense of the instantiation of moral properties in the form of objective moral values, human dignity, human rights, and obligations. Theism actually offers us a more suitable environment and thus a more plausible explanation for the existence of objective moral values (i.e. the instantiation of moral properties).

Three considerations for a theory's explanatory superiority

Thesis: In deciding between two competing hypotheses, we should look for (a) the more natural (less ad hoc) transition from the overall theory to the entity in question, (b) the more unified theory, and (c) the more basic theory.[29]

First, the *natural fit* criterion: take hypotheses X and Y. If explanations for particular entities are repeatedly ad hoc under X but flow naturally from Y, then Y is a superior explanation. When we look at naturalism vs. theism, we must ask: is there a naturalness in flow from theory to the particular entity in question, or is the transition disjointed?

To illustrate, take the feature of *libertarian freedom*: if theism and scientific naturalism are the only games in town, the balances would be tipped in the favor of theism. After all, in contrast to naturalism's mechanistic universe in which efficient causality (under some covering law model of explanation) predominates, theism has ample room for a personal cause or agency, which involves final (and not merely efficient) causation.[30] The buck stops with the agent – not certain prior conditions and states. The agent chooses/acts with a certain goal in mind, not simply because certain impulses, motivations, and conditions direct him – even if they play an influential role.

We could similarly speak of theism's preferable explanatory power over naturalism with regard to the emergence of first life or consciousness or the existence of rationality and the correspondence of our minds to the external world. The *worldview context* is clearly an important feature in adjudicating between competing hypotheses.

The same applies to objective moral values, which flow readily from a supremely valuable Being to us as his valuable creatures. Such a smooth transition does not appear in the move from mindless, valueless, naturalistic evolutionary processes to – *voilà* – objective moral values and human dignity.

Second, the *unification* criterion: another factor worth considering is whether a worldview has some kind of *grand unifying factor for all its features* or not. Are explanations within a theory *unified* and inter-connected, or are they disparate and unrelated? Again, it seems that God's role as the unifier of the variety of features of the world – the universe's origin and fine-tuning, the emergence of life and of consciousness, the existence of rationality and of morally significant beings – is the superior explanation or grounding when contrasted with a naturalistic alternative (in which numerous, unconnected series of causes and effects bring about these features). God as the background factor serves as the natural unifier (e.g. through primary or, usually, secondary causation).

The framework of naturalistic moral realism lacks any kind of unification of the brute facts that the naturalist takes for granted. The naturalist must deal with the following hurdles – accounting for the origin of the universe, the fine-tuned nature of the universe making it fit for life, the actual emergence of first life, the emergence of consciousness, the emergence of moral and intrinsically valuable beings, etc. – in a kind of "that's just the way things worked out" perspective. We have a hodge-podge of disparate brute necessary conditions which somehow led to the existence of moral persons, yet nothing unifies them. Again, *the theist has no such problem*, with God as the unifier of these "hurdles." If one is open to the supernatural, a Grand Unified Theory or Theory of Everything is on the horizon! As Del Ratzsch notes: "When a value is produced by a long, tricky, precarious process, when it is generated and preserved by some breathtaking complexity, when it is realized against all odds, then intent – even design – suddenly becomes a live and reasonable question."[31]

To the naturalist, we put the question: would moral properties be instantiated even if humans did *not* exist? If *not*, why think that the alleged supervening moral properties have any objectivity at all or are non-arbitrary, since we could have developed differently (e.g. most humans might come to think rape is acceptable, and arguments could easily be made showing how this could be conducive to human survival)?[32] If, however, moral properties exist in a *Platonic* sense, then it is strange *in excelsis* and staggeringly coincidental that (a) these moral properties should "just exist" *and* that (b) they should correspond to beings who "just evolved" to such a point that they have emerged as intrinsically valuable. It is as though these moral properties were *just waiting* for us to evolve. In a theistic universe, these two unconnected features come together unproblematically.

The third criterion is *basicality*: if important relevant features are more basic in hypothesis Y than in Z, then Y is the preferable one.[33] Does a worldview leave us with certain brute facts and conundrums that we must simply take for granted, or does the worldview more ably furnish ontological foundations or more ultimate explanations for their existence? Take the phenomenon of consciousness. The materialist philosopher of mind Colin McGinn writes:

> How is it possible for conscious states to depend upon brain states? How can technicolour phenomenology arise from soggy grey matter? . . . How could the aggregation of millions of individually insentient neurons generate subjective awareness? We know that brains are the *de facto* causal basis of consciousness, but we have, it seems, no understanding of how this can be so. It strikes us as miraculous, eerie, even faintly comic.[34]

Is consciousness merely a surd (as with the naturalist worldview), or is there some deeper, more basic explanation to account for its existence?

Ironically, NMRs such as David Brink will commonly appeal to the emergence of the mental as a springboard for their claim justifying the supervenience of the moral. Says Brink: "Assuming materialism is true, mental states supervene on physical states, yet few think that mental states are metaphysically queer."[35] A quick reality check turns out that this naturalistic position is truly question-begging. The emergence of consciousness is deeply problematic, and to base the emergence of moral properties on an appeal to the emergence of consciousness from matter is grossly ill-conceived. Again, we cite McGinn:

> Consider the universe before conscious beings came along: the odds did not look good that such beings could come to exist. The world was all just physical objects and physical forces, devoid of life . . . . We have a good idea of how the Big Bang led to the creation of stars and galaxies, principally by force of gravity. But we know of no comparable force that might explain how ever-expanding lumps of matter might have developed into conscious life.[36]

As with consciousness, so it is with instantiated moral properties. Do moral properties *just happen to be instantiated,* or do human beings *just have* intrinsic value, or is there a more fundamental explanation for these instantiated properties? It would seem that with regard to consciousness and moral values – and other phenomena listed above – theism "offers suggestions for answers to a wide range of otherwise intractable questions."[37] As though by osmosis, naturalists readily borrow metaphysical capital from the theistic worldview.[38] Naturalism experiences a great logical difficulty of moving from *is* to *ought.* For the theist, humans are made in the divine image and thus have value by virtue of their nature. And naturalism has no *predictive value* when it comes to the instantiation of moral properties, which is not the case with theism.

A common naturalistic rejection of objective moral values

Thesis: The greater plausibility of theism with regard to the instantiation of moral properties/the existence of objective moral values is reinforced by the fact that many naturalists themselves find it difficult to account for the instantiation of moral properties such as moral values, obligations, personal dignity/rights, whereas this has not been a problem for theists.

Frankena's claim that theistic use of the naturalistic fallacy to argue for a supernatural basis as question-begging is further undermined by the claims of various naturalists of all stripes who believe the rejection of objective moral values to be the ineluctable entailment of their naturalism. In the florilegium below, note how a number of them deem objective moral values to be utterly at odds with an atheistic world.

156

- Jonathan Glover claims morality may survive "when seen to be a human creation."[39] We must "re-create ethics."[40]
- Bertrand Russell stood on the "firm foundation of unyielding despair."[41] He claimed that "the whole subject of ethics arises from the pressure of the community on the individual."[42]
- J. L. Mackie found moral properties "queer" in a naturalistic universe: "If . . . there are . . . objective values, they make the existence of a god more probable than it would have been without them. Thus we have . . . a defensible argument from morality to the existence of a god."[43]
- Jean-Paul Sartre believed that "man exists, turns up, appears on the scene, and, only afterwards, defines himself."[44] The human being "at first . . . is nothing."[45]
- Steven Weinberg asserts that "The more the universe seems comprehensible, the more it also seems pointless," and trying to understand the universe is "one of the very few things that lifts human life a little above the level of farce."[46]
- E. O. Wilson maintains that "precepts and religious faith are entirely material products of the mind."[47] Moral feeling rooted in the hypothalamus and the limbic system is a "device of survival in social organisms."[48]
- James Rachels insists that "Man is a moral (altruistic) being, not because he intuits the rightness of loving his neighbor, or because he responds to some noble ideal, but because his behavior is comprised of tendencies which natural selection has favoured."[49]
- Michael Ruse declares that we have developed an "awareness of morality – a sense of right and wrong and a feeling of obligation to be thus governed – because such an awareness is of biological worth."[50]
- Richard Dawkins declares, "The universe we observe has precisely the properties we should expect if there is, at bottom, no design, no purpose, no evil and no good, nothing but blind pitiless indifference."[51]
- Paul Draper agrees with Mackie: "A moral world is . . . very probable on theism."[52]

You get the picture. The truth of moral realism is far from clear, given naturalism. Theists, on the other hand, face no such difficulty. Theists maintain that moral realism and God's existence are ontologically connected. The reason they are connected is rooted in the concept of *personhood*.

The intrinsic connection between morality and personhood

Thesis: The reason human persons exist is because a personal God exists, in whose image we have been made. The instantiation of moral properties is internally related to (or bound up with) personhood, and if no persons existed, then no moral properties would be instantiated.

Philosopher Wes Morriston asks a Euthyphro-like question about God's goodness: "is God good because he has these [moral] properties? Or are they good because God has them?"[53] Even if Morriston showed that that there is a theological problem in God's just "happening to have" certain moral properties over which he exerted no control,[54] he *still* has not shown that there could be an instantiation of moral properties *apart from God*. God's character *may still* be the source of goodness and objective moral values, even though his being good is not something God brought about. If the instantiation of moral properties is inextricably bound up with person-hood, then it would follow that a personal God, in whose image we have been made as morally valuable, is the source of moral values (more on this below).

Take the parallel phenomenon of (self-)consciousness: to use Morriston's language, God just "happens to have" the property of (self-)consciousness over which he has no control. However, one could readily argue that if God did not exist [and thus no (self-)conscious creatures], then no property of (self-)consciousness would be instantiated either.

In addition to the instanced properties of (self-)consciousness and value, we could say the same about those of free agency, dignity, rationality, or deep relationality that human beings experience. The instantiation of these properties is necessarily bound up with personhood, and without persons, these distinctive properties would not become instantiated.

How do some naturalists ground morality metaphysically? Boyd speaks of certain "homeostatic property clusters," which he claims offer an "extremely deep insight" into the possibility of natural definitions of morality.[55] Thus even if moral properties such as goodness are *natural* properties, they are not strictly *physical* ones.[56] It should be noted, however, that this "homeostatic cluster" which defines moral goodness is *social* rather than *individual*:

> The properties in homeostasis are to be thought of as instances of the satisfaction of particular human needs among people generally, rather than within the life of a single individual . . . [the homeostatic conse-quentialist claims that] the satisfaction of those needs for one individual tends to be conducive to their satisfaction for others, and it is to the homeostatic unity of human needs satisfaction in the society generally that she or he appeals in proposing a definition of the good.[57]

According to Brink, moral facts are realized (or constituted) by "organized combinations of natural and social scientific facts and properties."[58]

Boyd asserts that there could be a parallel type of supervenience at a *social* level when an appropriate equilibrium or balance of conditions is reached. There are, first, many *human needs* – whether physical/medical, psychological, or social (e.g. love and friendship). Now, under a "wide variety" of circumstances, these human goods are "homeostatically clustered" – that is, they are mutually supportive of one another. And when this balance is supported by psychological or social mechanisms they contribute to the homeostasis.

Thus, the cluster of goods and homeostatic mechanisms which unify them *defines* moral goodness. Actions, policies, and character traits are morally good "to the extent that they foster the realization of these goods or to develop and sustain the homeostatic mechanisms upon which their unity depends."[59] Correct moral choices contribute to and even strengthen this balance.[60]

In response, why does moral goodness only emerge in the context of the *social* rather than at the *individual* level? Boyd answers: "The properties in homeostasis are to be thought of as instances of the satisfaction of particular human needs among people generally, rather than within the life of a single individual."[61] Although he does not specify, one wonders what is the ontological status of the individual *apart from* the needs and well-being of society – namely, in terms of inherent moral worth. Boyd's own utilitarian consequentialism actually undermines intrinsic dignity and views individual humans as of instrumental worth alone, bringing the greatest good to the greatest number.[62]

However, do human persons have *no* intrinsic value *until* they are part of a community in which various needs and circumstances are "balanced"? Do individual human rights develop solely in this context of equilibrium, balance, or unity? If humans are merely *instrumental* in achieving such a unity, then we deny a bedrock principle of the intrinsic dignity and rights of the human individual – a denial worthy of rejection.

If, on the other hand, the naturalist claims that intrinsic dignity somehow emerges when an organism is sufficiently neurologically complex, the same problem remains (i.e. accounting for the emergence of value or dignity). As Kant argued regarding the actual infinite, *dignity cannot be formed by successive addition*. Intrinsic value must be given at the outset; otherwise, it does not matter how many nonpersonal and nonvaluable components we happen to stack up. From valuelessness, valuelessness comes.

I would argue that a *personal* Creator, who made human *persons* in his image, serves as the ontological basis for the existence of objective moral values, moral obligation, human dignity and rights. Without the existence of a personal God, there would be no persons at all; and if no persons existed, then no moral properties would be instantiated in our world. The syllogism would look something like this:

If persons (whether human or divine) exist, moral properties are instanced.
A divine, supremely valuable personal Creator is necessary for the existence of personal – and thus intrinsically valuable – human beings.

159

Therefore, if God did not exist (and thus no human persons would either), no moral properties would be instantiated either.[63]

Without *personhood*, there would be no moral properties instantiated. Thus God is necessary to ground the instantiation of moral properties. Moral categories (right/wrong, good/bad, praiseworthy/blameworthy) get to the essence of who we fundamentally are. They apply to us *as persons* (e.g. a good architect may be good *as an architect*, but not *as a human being/person*).[64] Moral values and personhood are intertwined.

The trustworthiness of our moral faculties

Thesis: One's worldview context is critical regarding the trustworthiness of our moral (and rational) faculties: given naturalistic evolution, why should we trust these faculties if they have been shaped by processes that direct us merely toward survival and reproduction? They just are but fail to inform us about what ought to be.

The geneticist and Nobel Prize winner, Francis Crick, writes in his book, *The Astonishing Hypothesis*:

> The Astonishing Hypothesis is that "You," your joys and your sorrows, your memories and your ambitions, your sense of personal identity and free will, are in fact no more than the behavior of a vast assembly of nerve cells and their associated molecules . . . . This hypothesis is so alien to the ideas of most people today that it can truly be called "astonishing."[65]

But if Crick is right, then his book is "no more than the behavior of a vast assembly of nerve cells and their associated molecules"! Falling prey to the self-excepting fallacy, Crick gives the impression that he, unlike the rest of us, has somehow been able to evade the physiological forces that determine what the rest of us think. He gives the impression that the behavior of *his* particular nerve cells and their associated molecules had absolutely *nothing* to do with his conclusions!

Here we look at a significant objection to objective moral values – namely, the socio-biological evolutionary development of human beings. If the evolutionary process has blindly shaped and hard-wired us toward survival and reproduction, then this can lead to serious doubts about the reliability of our rational and moral faculties. The evolutionary process is interested in fitness and survival, not in true belief.[66] Darwin was deeply troubled by this:

> With me the horrid doubt always arises whether the convictions of man's mind, which has been developed from the mind of the lower

animals, are of any value or at all trustworthy. Would any one trust in the convictions of a monkey's mind, if there are any convictions in such a mind?[67]

Can we trust our minds if we are nothing more than the products of naturalistic evolution trying to fight, feed, flee, and reproduce? Perhaps we have come to believe certain ideas – moral and non-moral – simply because they help us *survive* and not by virtue of their being *true*. Naturalistic moral realism suffers from the same defects found within the naturalistic philosophy of mind: although naturalism may offer some basis for *holding moral beliefs*, it furnishes no basis for claiming they are *true*. George Mavrodes writes of the naturalist position: "morality has a survival value for a species such as ours because it makes possible continued cooperation . . . ."[68] Thus, "the existence of moral feelings" is not absurd in a naturalistic world. Rather it is "the existence of moral *obligations* that is absurd." Mavrodes continues: "It is quite possible . . . for one to feel (or to believe) that he has a certain obligation without actually having it, and also vice versa."[69]

So we may *believe* that human beings are intrinsically valuable, and this helps the *homo sapiens* species survive, but it may be *false*. We may *believe* with full conviction that we have moral obligations – but be completely wrong. We may have the belief that our wills are free and that our choices do make a difference, but, again, we may be in serious error. If we accept a "scientific" account of epistemology, then we do not have access to the *truth-status* of these beliefs. They may help us to survive, but we may be completely wrong. Daniel Dennett calls our moral bent a *mistake*. But this widespread compliance with the mistaken – but common – "rule worship" (following the voice of conscience) has the happy consequence when we tend to comply – namely, societal cohesion and flourishing.[70] If the naturalist is right, then maybe we are being *systematically deceived* in order to survive and get along in society.

Which worldview furnishes us with more solid grounding for believing that our beliefs about moral obligations and human dignity are not reducible to our being hardwired to survive and reproduce? If naturalism is true, why think we have moral *obligations*? Rather, our moral beliefs just *are* and *could have been different* (e.g. *rape* could have contributed to survival). To help us beyond brute facts and naturalistic "just so" stories, a theistic world, in which a good, rational Being has made us in his image such that we can have confidence that our belief-producing mechanism is not unreliable, so a theistic worldview inspires confidence that we can *know* moral truths – even if they do not contribute one whit to our survival. Theism gives us no reason to be skeptical about our general capacity to think rationally, about the reliability of our sense perceptions, and about a general capacity to move towards the truth. Naturalism, on the other hand, does not inspire confidence in our belief-forming mechanisms. Naturalistic morality may still be true, but there seems to be no way that we can confidently know it.

Philosopher of religion Alvin Plantinga makes this case as follows:

> From a theistic point of view, human beings, like cathedrals and Boeing
> 747s, have been designed; we might say they are divine artifacts . . ..
> furthermore, God has created us human beings in "in his own image";
> in certain crucial and important respects, we resemble him. God is
> an actor, a creator, one who chooses certain ends and takes action to
> accomplish them. He is therefore a *practical* being. But God is also,
> crucially, an *intellectual* or *intellecting* being. He apprehends concepts,
> believes truths, has knowledge. In setting out to create human beings in
> his image, then, God set out to create *rational* creatures: creatures with
> reason or *ratio*; creatures that reflect his capacity to grasp concepts, en-
> tertain propositions, hold beliefs, envision ends, and act to accomplish
> them. Furthermore, he proposed to create creatures who reflect his abil-
> ity to hold *true* beliefs. He therefore created us with that astonishingly
> subtle and articulate battery of cognitive faculties and powers . . . .
> From this perspective it is easy enough to say what it is for our faculties
> to be working properly: they are working properly when they are work-
> ing in the way they were intended to work by the being who designed
> and created both them and us.[71]

Theism offers us a better hope for firmly grounding morality. It seems
that naturalism has the potential to undermine our conviction that objective
moral values exist. If our moral *beliefs* are by-products of Darwinistic evolution, why think that we actually *have* dignity, rights, and obligations?

The facts that (a) naturalistic evolutionists such as Crick, Wilson,
Dennett, Dawkins, and their ilk, can make pronouncements they believe
to be true (as distinct from simply helping them to survive) and (b) they
believe they have drawn rational and objective conclusions from data they
have observed actually indicate that they are living as practical theists. They
demonstrate what theists have always maintained – that we live in a rational
and knowable universe because God is its designer and we have been made
in God's likeness.

The undermining of morality by its very own "scientific basis"

Thesis: What appears to be the greatest strength of current naturalistic moral realism – its "scientific" basis – ends up being undercut by the naturalistic
worldview itself. Physicalism seems to undergird naturalism, but physical
properties are radically different from moral ones. And to be consistent,
it may be simpler for the naturalist to reject the existence of moral values
rather than unnecessarily bloat his ontology.

Thomas Nagel rightly speaks of "the scientism and reductionism of our time. One of the tendencies it supports is the ludicrous overuse of evolutionary biology to explain everything about life, including everything about the human mind."[72] Science, despite its accomplishments, is highly overrated. Science may *enhance* aesthetic and moral perceptions (e.g. beauty in music has been linked to certain mathematical and logical qualities),[73] but it does not speak to the *whole* of it.

For instance, the materialist Colin McGinn wonders how consciousness, which is so *un*like matter, could have emerged from matter:

> The property of consciousness itself (or specific conscious states) is not an observable or perceptible property of the brain. You can stare into a living conscious brain, your own or someone else's, and see there a wide variety of instantiated properties – its shape, colour, texture, etc. – but you will not thereby see what the subject is experiencing, the conscious state itself.[74]

In appealing to the alleged supervenience of the mental/conscious upon non-conscious matter to justify supervenience of the moral upon the non-moral, the NMR rightly doubts that his (quasi-)physicalism (rooted in the Big Bang and the universe's evolution) is sufficient to account for the emergence of subjective awareness, which has no physical properties (color, shape, size, spatial location, and the like). There is a metaphysical canyon that one finds difficult to bridge.

Similarly, one must deny that instantiated moral properties – unlike gray matter – are, say, orange, approximately 2 inches across, of an oblong shape, rough to the touch, and somewhat elastic. But how do we move from a universe, which inexplicably originates and produces matter and energy, to objective moral values or human dignity (which have no color, shape, size, spatial location, and the like)? Again, the gap is significant for the naturalist, but there is none for the theist. For the naturalist, it seems difficult to insist that from one set of (subvening) properties emerges another set of (supervening) properties even though each set does not come close to approximating the other.

An irony supervenes upon our discussion! Physicalists chide substance dualists for not having any way of showing that soul and body could interact. Jaegwon Kim, for instance, doubts that "an immaterial substance, with no material characteristics and totally outside physical space, could causally influence, and be influenced by, the motions of material bodies that are strictly governed by physical law."[75] Allegedly, the problem of "mental causation" (i.e. the mental's effects on the physical body) doomed Cartesian dualism.[76] But what do we make of the *physical* causes and processes producing the instancing of *mental* or *moral* properties? There seems to be something of naturalistic bias at work here: *why is there a problem with a mental-to-physical causation (for the theist – or substance dualist) but not*

– or at least not much of – a problem with physical-to-mental causation (for the naturalistic property dualist)? It seems that the criticism must cut both ways, and if the naturalist can have her way, why cannot the theist (or, more specifically, the substance dualist) have his? And if God – a powerful, non-corporeal Being – exists and created the universe, then we have a precedent for a non-material agent interacting with the physical world.[77]

Another problem with the scientific account is this: *in the name of simplicity and scientism, it may have to do away with instantiated moral properties altogether.* The naturalistic philosopher or scientist typically claims that if natural processes can account for the origin of the universe, the fine-tuning of the universe, the emergence of first life, the emergence of consciousness, the emergence of rationality, and the emergence of moral, intrinsically valuable beings (an exceedingly tall order!), then, in the name of simplicity, we do not need to invoke God as an explanation.

But what if the shoe is on the other foot? What if we can use *non*-moral, natural terms to explain certain events that NMRs typically take as morally weighted? *Why not eliminate objective morality in the name of simplicity?* NMRs claim that moral facts help explain certain actions performed by individuals (e.g. "Hitler killed millions of Jews because he was morally depraved"). But it is questionable whether NMRs have adequately made their case for the explanatory *necessity* of moral facts. A non-realist could proffer this explanation:

> Hitler was a very bitter and angry person. Because of various false beliefs about Jews (most importantly his belief that Jews were responsible for Germany's defeat in World War I), he found hatred for the Jews to be a satisfying way of releasing his pent-up hostility and anger. His moral beliefs did not place any bounds or restraints on his expression of that hatred.[78]

While NMRs may argue that moral facts are *relevant* to explain Hitler's behavior, they generally fail to show that moral facts are *necessary* to explain Hitler's behavior. That is, "moral properties seem to be dispensable for explanatory purposes. Natural properties seem to be doing all of the work in the explanations in question."[79]

Further, *nothing is explained* by assuming that moral facts are constituted by natural facts: "The best explanations of human behavior available to us at the present time do not make use of claims to the effect that moral facts are constituted by natural facts . . . and it is a mystery how those properties cause or explain observable phenomena."[80] Simply to *posit* that moral properties have been instantiated is a far cry from *explaining* how this is so. One can respond to the NMR (who typically chides the theist for "unnecessarily" adding an extra entity – God – to his ontology in order to explain the instantiation of moral properties) by turning the tables: you have made your bed of parsimony; now sleep in it!

In the end, the scientific account of moral realism is primarily an *episte-mological methodology* – not an *ontological basis* for morality. Many moral realists justify their claims simply by appealing to scientific – i.e. *episte-mological* – categories (e.g. recognizing moral values, refining moral judg-ments) without offering substantial reasons for any *actual* basis of humans' intrinsic value or moral obligation. And even at the epistemological level, the scientific methodology is inadequate. In the words of Thomas Carson: "[naturalistic] moral realists have not yet proffered theories developed in sufficient detail to be very useful in explaining or predicting the relevant (moral) phenomena";[81] to date, "no [naturalistic] moralist-realist theory has anything like the explanatory or predictive power of atomic theory."[82] Robert Audi would agree:

> There is much reason to think . . . that the issue of moral realism should not be cast wholly in terms of the comparison with scientific models. It simply may not be assumed that only causal or nomic properties are real, or that moral knowledge is possible only if it is causally or nomi-cally grounded in the natural world. Our moral beliefs often concern particular persons or acts; they are responsive to observations; and, together with our wants, they explain our behavior. But this does not require that moral properties are natural, and it allows that general moral knowledge is a priori.[83]

The Euthyphro argument: dilemma or red herring?

Our discussion of the moral argument would be incomplete without ad-dressing the oft-raised Euthyphro question. In Plato's *Euthyphro* dialogue, Socrates asks: "Is what is holy holy because the gods approve it, or do they approve it because it is holy?"[84] This raises the dilemma: are God's com-mands *arbitrary* (i.e. is something good *because* God commands it – and he could have commanded an opposite imperative)? Or is there some *autono-mous moral standard* (which God consults in order to command)? [85] In oth-er words, is the ground of morality, as Bertrand Russell put it, rooted in "no reason except [divine] caprice"?[86] Or is the problem, as Robin Le Poidevin puts it, that "we can, apparently, only make sense of these doctrines [that God is good and wills us to do what is good] if we think of goodness as be-ing defined independently of God"?[87]

I believe that the ultimate resolution to this dilemma is that *God's good character/nature* sufficiently grounds objective morality; thus we need to look nowhere else for such a standard. We have been made in the divine image, without which we would neither (a) be moral beings nor (b) have the capacity to recognize objective moral values.[88] The ultimate solution to the Euthyphro dilemma focuses on the *nature* or *character* of God as the source of objective moral values. Thus, we (who have been made to resemble God

165

in certain ways) have the capacity to recognize them, and thus his commands – far from being arbitrary – are in accordance with that nature. [89]

The atheist may push the Euthyphro dilemma further by questioning
whether the very *character* of God is good because it is God's character or it
is God's character because it is good. Several responses are in order.

First, *if a good God does not exist, why think that morally responsible,
intrinsically valuable, rights-bearing beings would exist at all?* Without
God, moral properties would never be instantiated. Personhood is the lo-
cus of objective moral values, and without God, no persons would exist.
Contextually, theism favors such moral obligations and human dignity, not
naturalism.

Second, *if the naturalist is correct, then she herself cannot escape a similar dilemma; her argument offers her no actual advantage*: We can ask the
NMR: "Are these moral values good simply because they are good, or is
there some independent standard of good to which they conform?" She faces
the same alleged dilemma of *arbitrariness* or some *autonomous standard*. So
it is difficult to see why the theist's stopping point – God – is arbitrary and
the naturalist's is not. The sword cuts both ways. Le Poidevin's comment
that we must think of goodness as defined independently of God is merely
posited. But two entities are sufficient to establish relations – namely, God's
character and objective moral values; the third (some standard independent
of God) becomes superfluous.

Third, *the naturalist's query is pointless since we must eventually arrive
at some self-sufficient and self-explanatory stopping point beyond which
the discussion can go no further*. Imagine that God does not exist and that
we have a Platonic form of the Good from which all values derive. At this
point, it would appear silly to ask, "Why is the Good good?" Rather, we
have an ultimate ground for morality, and everything is good in approximation to this. Again, why is atheism any less arbitrary a stopping-point than
theism?[90]

Fourth, *God, who is essentially perfect, does not have obligations to
some external moral standard; God simply acts, and it is good as he naturally does what is good*. [91] The revised Euthyphro dilemma wrongly assumes
God has moral *obligations*. If such an external standard existed, God would
be obligated to it. But God's actions and will operate according to the divine
nature. So God's goodness should not be viewed as his *fulfilling* moral obligations but as *expressing the way he is*: "No preliminary stage of checking
the relevant principles is required."[92]

Fifth, *the idea that God could be evil or command evil is utterly contrary
to the very definition of God; otherwise, such a being would not be God
and would not be worthy of worship*. Worshiping God because of his great
power or knowledge is inadequate. A being worthy of worship must also be
essentially good. As Robert Adams states: "Belief in the existence of an evil
or amoral God would be morally intolerable."[93]

Sixth, *the acceptance of objective values assumes a kind of ultimate goal or cosmic design plan for human beings, which would make no sense given naturalism, but makes much sense given theism (which presumes a design plan)*. Objective moral values presuppose (1) a fixed human nature (all human beings have a moral nature and possess dignity/rights) and (2) that a certain kind of life is better than another and thus ought to be pursued by every human being (i.e. teleology). It is exceedingly difficult to make sense of a brute cosmic purpose for all human beings apart from a transcendental purposive Creator. The brute fact of the value of human beings and a corresponding overarching purpose for their eudaimonistic living (another brute fact) are for naturalism nothing more than, as John Rist suggests, an "ethical hangover from a more homogeneous Christian past."[94]

In light of these reasons, there seems to be no good reason to take the Euthyphro dilemma seriously.

Conclusion

Truly, the *super*natural is necessary to ground morality.[95] While objective morality appears *logical* and obvious to some naturalists, the more fundamental question is *metaphysical: can there be persons possessing inherent rights and dignity apart from a good God, in whose image they have been made*? NMRs such as Frankena wrongly frame the theological basis for moral obligation,[96] and others have simply failed to grasp the proper grounding for morality.[97]

Which hypothesis proves most resourceful when it comes to providing grounds for such an affirmation – a naturalistic one or a theistic (or supernaturalistic) one? NMRs persistently *fail to proffer any substantive metaphysic or ontology of personhood from a naturalistic vantage point to account for the intrinsic value of persons adequately – a necessary starting point for moral realism*. To my mind, it is the theistic one that does the more adequate job. The naturalistic worldview presents an inherent clash of ideals or stories. On the one hand, there is no cosmic purpose (but an unguided evolutionary process), no intelligent design, no guarantee of justice and moral rectification in the afterlife. But on the other hand, the NMR makes pronouncements about how objective moral values have emerged despite the universe's purposelessness and impersonal nature, how we *ought* to treat one another, how we *ought* to live up to moral principles even while death – yea, non-existence – stares us in the face. [98] The metaphysical chasm between the NMR's cosmic context and objective moral values is huge.

Not so with theism! It furnishes us with a grand ontological match between "our deepest moral values" and "the fundamental structures of reality."[99] Even the naturalist Richard B. Brandt concludes that there has been no significant recent advance to show how "moral/value properties are identical to (or even coextensive with) natural properties;" such attempts appear to "break down at every point."[100] Carson argues that despite the prominent versions of naturalistic moral realism available, "none is worthy of our acceptance."[101]

Ontologically, then, objective moral values would not exist if God did not. But if they exist, then we have very good reason to think God exists.

Notes

1 "Letter from Birmingham Jail" (16 April 1963) (www.stanford.edu/group/King). King added "One has not only a legal but a moral responsibility to obey just laws," King said, "but conversely, one has a moral responsibility to disobey unjust laws."
2 Dallas Willard, "Language, Being, God, and the Three Stages of Theistic Evidence," in J. P. Moreland and Kai Nielsen (eds) *Does God Exist? The Great Debate* (Nashville: Thomas Nelson, 1990), 207 (reprinted by Prometheus Press: Buffalo, NY).
3 Peter Berger, *A Rumor of Angels*, 2nd edn, (New York: Doubleday, 1990), 59.
4 Kai Nielsen, *Ethics Without God*, revised edn, (Buffalo, NY: Prometheus Books, 1990), 10–11.
5 Nicholas Rescher, *Moral Absolutes: An Essay on the Nature and Rationale of Morality*, Vol. 2 (New York: Peter Lang, 1989), 43.
6 One does not need to be a theist to acknowledge this admixture. Atheist Michael Martin admits humans (1) "seem so ungod-like" and are "morally flawed," *and* (2) have "mathematical, scientific, and technological knowledge which enables them to construct elegant mathematical systems, and to build huge skyscrapers, dams, and bridges" ["A Response to Paul Copan's Critique of Atheistic Objective Morality," *Philosophia Christi* 2 (Series 2), (2000), 88]. Also, see my reply to Martin's essay in the same issue of *Philosophia Christi*, "Atheistic Goodness Revisited," 91–104.
7 Robert Audi, *Moral Knowledge and Ethical Character* (New York: Oxford University Press, 1997), 32–65. According to Audi, moral intuitions are (1) *non-inferential* or *directly apprehended*; (2) *firm* (they must be believed as propositions); (3) *comprehensible* (intuitions are formed in the light of an adequate understanding of their propositional objects; (4) *pre-theoretical* (not dependent on theories nor are they themselves theoretical hypotheses). Audi rejects that prima facie intuitions are indefeasible; he argues for a particularist approach to intuitions (i.e. moral knowledge does not emerge from reflection on abstract principles, but it is derived from reflection on particular cases). He argues that duty still exists even if overridden in certain instances (e.g. keeping a promise is overridden by circumstances preventing me from keeping it, but I still have a duty to explain to the person why I could not keep the promise). For another defense of intuitionism, see David McNaughton, "Intuitionism" in *The Blackwell Guide to Ethical Theory*, Hugh LaFollette (ed.) (Malden, MA: Blackwell Publishers, 2000), 268–87.
8 Alvin Plantinga, "Reason and Belief in God," in *Faith and Rationality*, Alvin Plantinga and Nicholas Wolterstorff (eds) (Notre Dame, IN: University of Notre Dame Press, 1983), 16–93; idem, "Self-Profile," in *Alvin Plantinga*, Profiles 5, James Tomberlin and Peter van Inwagen, (eds) (Dordrecht: D. Reidel, 1985), 55–64.
9 Such properly basic beliefs are not ultima facie (or all-things-considered) justified, only prima facie.

10 Historically, *tolerance* has not been understood as "accepting all views as true or worthy of belief"; if this were so, then the relativist would violate his standard by rejecting moral realism. In truth, we do not tolerate chocolate or the music of Johann Sebastian Bach. Tolerance has to do with putting up with what we find false, disagreeable, or erroneous.

11 On the deep problems of perspectivalism, see Thomas Nagel, *The Last Word* (New York: Oxford University Press, 1997), 3–76. See also Curtis L. Hancock, "Social Construct Theory: Relativism's Latest Fashion," in *The Failure of Modernism: The Cartesian Legacy and Contemporary Pluralism*, Brendan Sweetman (ed.) (Mishawaka, IN: American Maritain Association, 1999), 242–58.

12 See Brendan Sweetman, "The Pseudo-Problem of Skepticism," in *The Failure of Modernism: The Cartesian Legacy and Contemporary Pluralism*, Brendan Sweetman (ed.) (Mishawaka, IN: American Maritain Association, 1999), 228–41.

13 David Brink, *Moral Realism and the Foundations of Ethics* (New York: Cambridge University Press, 1989), 17. Richard Boyd adds as a component another feature (epistemic condition) to moral realism: "Ordinary canons of moral reasoning – together with ordinary canons of scientific and everyday factual reasoning – constitute, under many circumstances at least, a reliable method for obtaining and improving (approximate) moral knowledge" ["How To Be a Moral Realist," in *Moral Discourse and Practice: Some Philosophical Approaches*, Stephen Darwall, Allan Gibbard, and Peter Railton (eds) (New York: Oxford University Press, 1997)], 105.

14 Brink, *Moral Realism and the Foundations of Ethics*, 156.

15 Ibid., 156–7.

16 Michael Smith, "Moral Realism," in *The Blackwell Guide to Ethical Theory* Hugh LaFollette (ed.) (Malden, MA: Blackwell Publishers, 2000), 23.

17 Ibid.

18 Michael Smith, "Moral Realism," 24.

19 Railton, "Moral Realism," *The Philosophical Review* 95 (April 1986), 171.

20 According to Brink, "If G actually composes or realizes F, but F can be, or could have been, realized differently, then G constitutes, but is not identical with, F", *Moral Realism*, 157. Brink calls such a constitution a "synthetic moral necessity" (166).

21 Railton urges: "moral properties supervene upon natural properties, and may be reducible to them", "Moral Realism," 165.

22 Ibid. Also, Railton urges: "moral properties supervene upon natural properties, and may be reducible to them" (171).

23 Brink, *Moral Realism*, 207.

24 William Frankena, "The Naturalistic Fallacy," in *Readings in Ethical Theory*, 2nd edn, Wilfrid Sellars and John Hospers (eds) (New York: Appleton–Century–Crofts, 1970), 54–62; see also William K. Frankena, "Obligation and Motivation in Recent Moral Philosophy," in *Perspectives on Morality: Essays by William K. Frankena*, K. E. Goodpaster (ed.) (Notre Dame, IN: University of Notre Dame Press, 1976), 49–73.

25 William K. Frankena, "Is Morality Logically Dependent Upon Religion?", in Paul Helm (ed.), *Divine Commands and Morality* (Oxford: Oxford University Press, 1981), 14–33.

26 Ibid., 16. According to the ordinary canons of logic, "a conclusion containing the term 'ought' or 'right' cannot be logically derived from premises which do not contain this term" (ibid., 18).

27 Ibid., 31.
28 Perhaps certain naturalistic moral realists are confident in their position because they have grossly misunderstood the theistic basis for ethics. One such culprit is Peter Railton: "Some Questions About the Justification of Morality," *Philosophical Perspectives* 6 (1992) 27–53. He construes the connection between God and morality in terms of: "the policing and punishing functions of God." Thus we can dispense with such a "suprahuman grader" who would "mark us down" for our failings. With the "death of God," the "universal policeman" is gone (29). Railton then proceeds to offer a comparison between this basis for morality with "divine bases" (45). We have no need for such "middlemen" between the justificatory impulse and norms of behavior. I think that rumors of God's death have been greatly exaggerated, and Railton confuses matters by bifurcating divine power and divine goodness, as though God's moral character has nothing to do with the exertion of his power.

Another failure in Railton is his utilization of the genetic fallacy (45), resorting to the Freudian canard of psycho-analyzing religious believers (as though naturalists are immune to psychoanalysis for their atheism!).

Brink believes that the theist is stuck on the two horns of the Euthyphro dilemma, *Moral Realism*, 158. However, the theist can reject the horns of the dilemma in favor of rooting moral properties in the character or nature of God.
29 I refer to such an approach in Paul Copan "Can Michael Martin Be a Moral Realist? *Sic et Non*," *Philosophia Christi* 1, 2 (Series 2) (1999), 45–72, and "Atheistic Goodness Revisited" *Philosophia Christi* 2, 1 (Series 2) (2000), 91–104.
30 See Vance G. Morgan, "The Metaphysics of Naturalism," 55 (Summer 2001), 409–31.
31 *Nature, Design, and Science* (Albany, NY: State University of New York Press, 2001), 68.
32 Randy Thornhill and Craig T. Palmer, *A Natural History of Rape: Biological Bases of Sexual Coercion* (Cambridge, MA: MIT Press, 2000).
33 See Chapter 10 by J. P. Moreland in this volume.
34 Colin McGinn, *The Problem of Consciousness* (Oxford: Basil Blackwell, 1990), 10–11.
35 Brink, "Moral Realism and the Skeptical Arguments from Disagreement and Queerness," 120. Brink offers a more detailed argument in his *Moral Realism and the Foundation for Ethics*, 156–67.
36 Colin McGinn, *The Mysterious Flame: Consciousness Minds in a Material World* (New York: Basic Books, 1999).
37 Alvin Plantinga, "Natural Theology," in *Companion to Metaphysics*, Jaegwon Kim and Ernest Sosa (eds) (Cambridge: Blackwell, 1995), 347.
38 Louis P. Pojman, "A Critique of Contemporary Egalitarianism: A Christian Perspective," *Faith and Philosophy* 8 (October 1991), 501.
39 Jonathan Glover, *Humanity: A Moral History of the Twentieth Century* (London: Jonathan Cape, 1999), 41. He speaks of the need to "start to establish a tradition" that will help us find previous atrocities "intolerable" (42).
40 Ibid., 42.
41 Bertrand Russell, "A Free Man's Worship," in *Why I Am Not a Christian* (New York: Simon and Schuster, 1957), 107.
42 Bertrand Russell, *Human Society in Ethics and Politics* (London: Allen & Unwin, 1954), 124.
43 J. L. Mackie, *The Miracle of Theism* (Oxford: Clarendon Press, 1982), 115–16.
44 Jean-Paul Sartre, *Existentialism and Human Emotions* (New York: Philosophical Library, 1957), 15.

45 Ibid.
46 Stephen Weinberg, *The First Three Minutes: A Modern View of the Origin of the Universe* (New York: HarperCollins), 154–55.
47 Edward O. Wilson, *Consilience* (New York: Random House, 1998), 269.
48 Ibid., 268.
49 James Rachels, *Created From Animals: The Moral Implications of Darwinism* (Oxford: Oxford University Press, 1990), 77.
50 Michael Ruse, *The Darwinian Paradigm* (London: Routledge, 1989), 262.
51 Richard Dawkins, *River Out of Eden: A Darwinian View of Life* (New York: Basic Books/Harper Collins, 1995), 132–3.
52 Cited in Greg Ganssle, "Necessary Moral Truths and the Need for Explanation," *Philosophia Christi* 2, 1 (Series 2) (2000), 111.
53 "Must There Be a Standard of Moral Goodness Apart from God?", *Philosophia Christi* 3, 1 (Series 2) (2001),129.
54 Various suggestions are still under discussion in this area. Alvin Plantinga raises this issue in *Does God Have a Nature?* (Milwaukee: Marquette University Press, 1980). Plantinga suggests elsewhere: "God is a necessary being who has essentially the property of thinking just the thoughts he does think; these thoughts, then, are conceived or thought by God in every possible world and thus exist necessarily" [Plantinga "How To Be an Anti-Realist," *Proceedings and Addresses of the American Philosophical Association* 56 (1982), 70]. Thomas Morris and Christopher Menzel have expanded upon Plantinga's thoughts: "Absolute Creation," in *Anselmian Explorations,* Thomas V. Morris (ed.) (Notre Dame, IN: University of Notre Dame Press, 1987), 161–78. See also Charles Taliaferro, *Contemporary Philosophy of Religion* (Oxford: Blackwell, 1998), 65–72.
55 Boyd, "How To Be a Moral Realist," 116.
56 Ibid., 119.
57 Ibid., 133n.
58 Brink, *Moral Realism,* 159; this is similar to "tableness" suvervening on properly arranged microphysical particles.
59 Boyd, "How To Be a Moral Realist,"122.
60 Ibid.
61 Ibid., 133n.
62 See Tom Regan's criticism of utilitarianism, in which individuals are like cups or receptacles, which have no value in themselves, nor are they equally valuable: "What has value is what goes into us, what we serve as receptacles for; our feelings of satisfaction have positive value, our feelings of frustration have negative value" ["The Case for Animal Rights," in *People, Penguins and Plastic Trees,* 2nd edn, Christine Pierce and Donald Van DeVeer (eds) (Belmont, CA: Wadsworth Publishing Company, 1995), 75].
63 Some theists claim that moral properties exist independently of God – for example, C. Stephen Layman, *The Shape of the Good: Christian Reflections and the Foundation of Ethics* (Notre Dame, IN: University of Notre Dame Press, 44–52; Richard Swinburne, *The Coherence of Theism* (Oxford: Oxford University Press, 1977), 204. For reasons spelled out here and elsewhere, this position has its problems. Paul Copan "Can Michael Martin Be a Moral Realist? *Sic et Non,*" *Philosophia Christi* 1, 2 (Series 2) (1999), 45–72, and "Atheistic Goodness Revisited," *Philosophia Christi* 2, 1 (Series 2) (2000), 91–104; see also Gregory E. Ganssle, "Necessary Moral Truths and the Need for Explanation," *Philosophia Christi* 2, 1 (Series 2) (2000), 105–12.
64 David S. Oderberg, *Moral Theory: A Non-Consequentialist Approach* (Malden, MA: Blackwell, 2000), 1.

65 Francis Crick, *The Astonishing Hypothesis: The Scientific Search for the Soul* (New York: Charles Scribner's Sons, 1994), 3.
66 Alvin Plantinga, *Warrant and Proper Function* (New York: Oxford University Press, 1993), 219.
67 Letter to William Graham Down, 3 July 1881, in *The Life and Letters of Charles Darwin*, Francis Darwin (ed.) (London: John Murray, 1887), 315–16 (includes an autobiographical chapter).
68 George I. Mavrodes, "Religion and the Queerness of Morality," in *Rationality, Religious Belief, and Moral Commitment*, Robert Audi and William Wainwright (eds) (Ithaca, NY: Cornell University Press, 1986), 219.
69 Ibid.
70 Daniel Dennett, *Darwin's Dangerous Idea* (New York: Simon and Schuster, 1995), 507.
71 Plantinga, *Warrant and Proper Function*, 197.
72 Thomas Nagel, *The Last Word* (New York: Oxford University Press, 1997), 131.
73 See Douglas R. Hofstadter, *Gödel, Escher, Bach: An Eternal Golden Braid* (New York: Vintage, 1980).
74 Ibid., 1.
75 Jaegwon Kim, *Philosophy of Mind* (Boulder, CO: Westview Press, 1996), 4.
76 I am not claiming here to hold to a Cartesian dualism. For an alternative, more organic substance dualism, see J. P. Moreland and Scott Rae, *Body and Soul* (Downers Grove, IL: InterVarsity Press, 2000).
77 For a defense of such a mind-body interaction, see Charles Taliaferro, *Consciousness and the Mind of God* (Cambridge: Cambridge University Press, 1994).
78 This point is taken from Thomas Carson, *Value and the Good Life* (Notre Dame, IN: University of Notre Dame Press, 2000), 194. He is utilizing an argument made by Gilbert Harman.
79 Ibid., 198.
80 Ibid., 198–9.
81 Ibid., 199.
82 Ibid.
83 Robert Audi, "Ethical Naturalism and the Explanatory Power of Moral Concepts," in *Naturalism: A Critical Appraisal*, Steven J. Wagner and Richard Warner (eds) (Notre Dame, IN: University of Notre Dame Press, 1993), 111.
84 Plato, *Euthyphro* 10a, in *Plato, The Collected Dialogues of Plato*, Edith Hamilton and Huntington Cairns (eds) Lane Cooper (trans.) (Princeton: Princeton University Press, 1961), 178.
85 These terms are taken from Mark D. Linville, "On Goodness: Human and Divine," *American Philosophical Quarterly* 27 (April 1990), 143–52.
86 Bertrand Russell, *Human Society in Ethics and Politics* (New York: Simon & Schuster, 1962), 38.
87 Robin Le Poidevin, *Arguing for Atheism* (London: Routledge, 1996), 85.
88 Thus, while there is a strong version of the divine command theory (in which God could just as easily have commanded, "Thou *shalt* murder"), the more moderate versions root divine commands in God's character: "Theists of all stripes will insist that God is perfectly just" [Philip Quinn, *Divine Commands and Moral Requirements* (Oxford: Clarendon Press, 1978), 136]. Robert Merrihew Adams asserts: "It matters what God's attributes are. God is supremely knowledgeable and wise – he is omniscient, after all; and that is very important motivationally. It makes a difference if you think of commands as coming from someone who

completely understands both us and our situation. It matters not only that God is loving but also that he is just." ["Divine Commands and Obligation" *Faith and Philosophy* 4 (July 1988), 272].

89 See Thomas V. Morris essays, "Duty and Divine Goodness" and "The Necessity of God's Goodness" in *Anselmian Explorations* (Notre Dame, IN: University of Notre Dame Press, 1987), 26–41 and 42–69; William P. Alston, "Some Suggestions for Divine Command Theorists," in *Christian Theism and the Problems of Philosophy*, Michael D. Beaty (ed.) (Notre Dame, IN: University of Notre Dame Press, 1990); Mark D. Linville, "Euthyphro and His Kin," in *The Logic of Rational Theism*, Vol. 24, William Lane Craig and Mark McLeod (eds) (Lewiston, NY: Edwin Mellen, 1990), 187–210.

90 William Alston asks this question in "Some Suggestions for Divine Command Theorists," in Michael D. Beaty (ed.) *Christian Theism and the Problems of Philosophy* (Notre Dame, IN: University of Notre Dame Press, 1990), 303–26.

91 The question is raised: why praise God for doing the good *naturally*? But as Thomas Morris rightly claims, "praise is never strictly appropriate for duty satisfactions." Rather, we rightly praise God – as we do any person – for moral acts of *supererogation* (i.e. going beyond the requirements of duty). *Why* then should God be praised? According to the Judeo-Christian tradition, God's *condescension* and *grace* – undeserved kindness – offer justifiable reasons to praise him. God was not obligated to create at all. Nor was God, having freely willed to create, obliged to make the best possible world – only a good one, but not a less-than-good one. God is also not obligated to communicate with and enter into covenant relations with his creatures. He is not morally compelled to forgive human transgression nor to give second chances to those who have defied his authority. Such actions are not the fulfillment of duty but acts of supererogation. See Thomas V. Morris, "Duty and Divine Goodness," in *Anselmian Explorations* (Notre Dame, IN: University Press, 1987), 35, 38.

92 Alston, "Some Suggestions for Divine Command Theorists," 320.

93 "Moral Arguments for Theistic Belief," in *Rationality and Religious Belief*, C. F. Delaney (ed.) (Notre Dame, IN: University of Notre Dame Press, 1979), 135.

94 John M. Rist, *Real Ethics* (Cambridge: Cambridge University Press, 2002), 2.

94 G. E. Moore did not go far enough by saying that morality is *non*-natural. H. P. Owen suggests: "although 'ought' can never be derived, or at least never wholly, from 'is' where 'is' lacks moral evaluation, any over-all moral theory of life is bound to involve a correspondingly over-all view of man and his destiny." H. P. Owen, "Morality and Christian Theism," *Religious Studies* 20 (1984), 16.

95 Surprisingly, Frankena's claim that theists, in attempting to establish a religious basis for morality, move illegitimately from "God is love" to "We ought to love others" is wrongly construed. A more adequate formulation would be:

> Human *persons* have been made in the image of a good, necessarily valuable, *personal* Being (God).
> Human *persons* are thus inherently constituted with intrinsic value, rights, and moral obligations.
> Therefore, we *ought* to treat human beings (persons) as worthy of respect, as ends in themselves (rather than means to ends), as morally responsible agents, etc.

96 For example, God as a divine policeman, whom we merely obey out of fear of punishment rather than out of love; or God as commanding arbitrarily, who could command just the opposite.

97 Thanks to Ronald Tacelli on this point.
98 Peter Byrne, *The Moral Interpretation of Religion* (Edinburgh: University of Edinburgh Press, 1998), 168.
99 Richard B. Brandt, *Facts, Values, and Morality* (Cambridge: Cambridge University Press, 1996), 183.
100 *Value and the Good Life*, 187.

9

THE EVIDENTIAL VALUE OF RELIGIOUS EXPERIENCE

R. Douglas Geivett

The emerging interest in religious experience

Less than 100 years ago, Anglo-American philosophy of religion was embroiled in a literal fight for its life. In the 1920s, a movement called logical positivism set up shop and threatened a thinly veiled challenge to religious belief by erecting a blockade to the iron horse of traditional metaphysics. It asserted that the vintage locomotive, and everything that followed down to the caboose, was – in the bright light of scientific progress – an outmoded means of transport to true and meaningful belief. Emphasis here belongs on the word "meaningful." The positivists foreswore the meaningfulness of any statement that could be neither empirically verified nor analyzed as tautological.[1] They congratulated themselves for stoking the fires with enough heat to melt the metal of metaphysics beyond recognition and recovery.[2]

One celebrated casualty was to be the edifice of theology, which had hitherto been securely strapped to a flatbed car near the locomotive itself. As Rudolf Carnap wrote, "In its metaphysical use, the word 'God' refers to something beyond experience. The word is deliberately divested of its reference to a physical being or to a spiritual being that is immanent in the physical. And as it is not given a new meaning, it becomes meaningless."[3] And A. J. Ayer, the premier British campaigner for logical positivism, declaimed: "The term 'God' is a metaphysical term. And if 'God' is a metaphysical term, then it cannot even be probable that a god exists. For to say that 'God exists' is to make a metaphysical utterance which cannot be either true or false."[4]

The bright light of science proved to be blinding. It blinded the positivists to the virility of metaphysics (and of theology) and to the conveniently accessible key to the demise of positivism itself. Chief among its numerous shortcomings was that its own requirement was self-referentially incoherent: the "verification principle" itself was neither empirically verifiable nor tautological. In retrospect, it is astonishing that the hubris puffed up by the pretensions of science could reach such proportions that it could not see its own belt buckle, much less its feet of clay. In 1967, Christian philosopher Alvin Plantinga wrote, "The fact is that no one has succeeded in stating a version of the verifiability criterion that is even remotely plausible; and by now the project is beginning to look unhopeful."[5] Less than a decade later, Malcolm Diamond and Thomas Litzenburg Jr re-printed a selection from Plantinga's book in their anthology and acknowledged that by 1967 "pessimism about verification was widespread among the empiricists who were most concerned to achieve an adequate statement of it."[6]

By mid-century, then, logical positivism had given up the ghost, so to speak, and metaphysics was back in business. So, too, was the philosophy of religion. A landmark work, signaling a new trend in the discipline, was Plantinga's book *God and Other Minds*. Seeking to vindicate the rationality of belief in God, Plantinga included a highly original reformulation of the most metaphysical of arguments in the history of philosophy: the ontological argument for the existence of God. It is with considerable irony, and a healthy measure of poetic justice, that the burial site of logical positivism was trampled with the traffic of extensive speculation about the merits of this venerable old argument. The 1960s may indeed be called the decade of the ontological argument, so far as natural theology is concerned.[7]

More recently, serious engagement with the ontological argument has subsided.[8] But interest in the evidence for theism has only intensified. Three other types of argument share the limelight today: the cosmological argument, the design argument, and the "argument" from religious experience. Unlike the ontological argument, all of these arguments have an *empirical* aspect – another of life's little ironies. This chapter is devoted to a critical but sympathetic appraisal of the third of these currently most popular arguments.[9]

Is there an argument from religious experience?

It needs to be noted from the start that it can be seriously misleading to speak of "the *argument* from religious experience." Certainly, there have been more or less straightforward arguments from religious experience to the existence of God. George Mavrodes has remarked, in a short dictionary entry on this topic, that "this can be considered a special version of the teleological argument, claiming that the widespread occurrence of religious experience, with a common phenomenological core and giving rise to a common core of interpretation, requires explanation. And it is argued . . . that the most plausible explanation involves the existence and activity of God."[10]

Carl Jung reasoned that religious experience has a life-enhancing effect. Arguably, Jung was an anti-realist about the object of religious awareness (i.e. the Archetype), and he certainly did not craft an argument of the sort I have just described. Still, he did uncover interesting psychological data that might be featured in some such argument.[11] Such an argument would, in a way, parallel what might be called the "anthropic design argument," or the argument that the laws governing the arrangement and behavior of our physical environment (from the cosmological constants to the structure of the earth's biosphere) are so precisely calibrated that they seem to be designed with the flourishing of physical organisms (i.e. humans and other animals) in mind.[12] The parallel in the psychological realm might then be that consciousness of God's presence fosters human spiritual (psychological) flourishing, and this is best explained by divine design of the human psyche as a fit receptor of stimuli caused by the presence of God.

So, in these and other respects, the phenomena of religious experience may demand an explanation. And an argument to the existence of God as the best explanation of the phenomena may be effectual. (Let us call arguments of this form *A-type* arguments.) But there is an alternative and more typical way to think of the evidential value of religious experience. Believers with firsthand religious experiences of one type or another often consider the experiences themselves to be *non-inferential* grounds for their own religious beliefs. It is the evidential value of religious experience construed in *this* way that has received the most attention and support by Christian philosophers in recent memory. And construed in this way, the fundamental question is: what evidential weight does religious experience have for those who have religious experiences?

However, closely connected with this is the question: what evidential weight does religious experience have for those who have not had religious experiences? What evidential weight do reports (individual and/or collective) of religious experience have for recipients of those reports? Here, too, it can be proper to speak of an *argument* from religious experience. If religious experience provides subjects of that experience with non-evidential grounds for belief in God, it surely does not, as such, provide similar grounds for others who are not subjects of religious experience. But it does not follow from this that the religious experiences of believers are evidentially otiose for nonbelievers. And the evidential relevance of religious experiences for nonbelievers who fail to have such experiences *may* turn on questions of explanation.[13] A subject's belief in God may be grounded in an awareness of God who is present to the subject, either directly or indirectly, in his/her experience. But a nonbelieving recipient of a report of this experiential awareness will naturally want a reason to believe that the subject's experience was a bona fide experience of God, an experience where God was actually present (directly or indirectly) to the subject, if the subject's experience is to count as evidence for the nonbelieving recipient of testimony regarding the experience. What is *non-inferential evidence* for the believing subject of a religious experience is, for the nonbelieving outside observer, data for a potential *inference* to the existence of God. Let us call arguments that parallel this pattern *B-type* arguments from religious experience.

Plan of this chapter

In "The perils of definition and classification" I make loud disclaimers about the perils of definition and classification when it comes to religious experience, and then I plunge into the swirling vortex in hope of salvaging a characterization that will serve the purposes of the remainder of the chapter. In "The standard argument for the existence of God," I describe the general pattern of prominent contemporary arguments that religious experience provides substantial non-inferential support for belief that God exists. The weave of this pattern – resulting in what I call the *standard argument* from religious experience – is especially noteworthy for three bold strands that have been subjected to vigorous criticism. If they cannot withstand criticism, the weave begins to fray. Thus, in "Objections to the standard argument" I examine a few of the strongest objections to these three features of the standard argument from religious experience. "Three additional objections" deals with additional objections of a more general nature, objections in the form of naturalistic explanations for the data of religious experience. In "A revised conception," I sketch a revised conception of the evidential value of religious experience, chastened by some lessons learned from the dialectic rehearsed in the earlier sections.

The perils of definition and classification

Anglo-American philosophers are fond of seeking rigorous definitions for concepts under investigation. The most rigorous (and therefore the most desirable) definitions are those that define a concept or specify a class of entities in terms of necessary and sufficient conditions. But this is often risky business. It is particularly so when it comes to religious experience. And yet, it is standard practice for philosophers of religion to begin the discussion of religious experience with a provisional definition of this sort. Perfectly general definitions of this sort are what I call "unrestricted definitions." They are meant to range over anything that is a religious experience. In contrast, some definitions of the rigorous sort are "restricted definitions," in that they are meant to range over a specific species of religious experience.

Unrestricted and restricted definitions may be generated in one of two ways. The purely theoretical approach seeks to answer in the abstract a question like the following from Wallace Matson: "What sort of experience might suffice to certify the existence of a god?"[14] To answer such a question in the abstract is to do so without reference to concrete cases of, or candidates for, religious experience. There is merit to such an approach, but it is faced with serious difficulties. First, the attempt to formulate an *unrestricted* definition of religious experience by asking this particular question will rule by definition that any experience that does not purport to certify the existence of a god is not a religious experience. This seems arbitrary. To yield the generality of an unrestricted definition, the question would have to be translated into something more schematic, such as: what sort of experience might suffice to certify X?, where the purported certification of X is what makes the experience religious. But now other problems arise. What sort of entity besides a god could be substituted for "a god" in the original question and still be the sort of thing the certification of whose existence by means of experience would make the experience religious? And must X be replaced by an existence claim? What about other replacements for X that have nothing to do with existence claims? Finally, must an experience purport to "certify" (i.e. count as evidence for) something or other in order to count as a religious experience? Why should this be so?

On the other hand, if the goal of the theoretical approach is to formulate a *restricted* definition of religious experience, then Matson's question is impertinent, for the question itself implies the following restricted definition of religious experience: "An experience is a religious experience (in some restricted sense, R_1) if and only if it is an experience that certifies the existence of a god."

The second way that one might generate either an unrestricted or a restricted definition of religious experience is by examining a suitable sample of cases of religious experience, or cases of experience that are good candidates for being religious experiences, for the purpose of isolating a common core of religious experience (or of religious experience types), or setting forth a complete or partial classification of religious experiences. They start with candidates for religious experience, or uncontroversial cases of religious experience, and seek to formulate a definition in terms of what they have in common. Most philosophers of religion favor this approach.

My own approach to this matter of definition and taxonomy is a little less ambitious. I begin with the obvious fact that many individuals across a wide spectrum of religious traditions have had experiences of a religious nature. Without settling the question of their veridicality,[15] these experiences may be called "religious experiences." That religious experiences occur, then, is not usually contested. What is contested is that religious experiences are sometimes veridical, or that it is reasonable to believe that some religious experiences are veridical, and hence that it is reasonable, for example, to believe on the basis of some such experiences that God exists.

I say *some* such experiences because some – not all – religious experiences are "of-God experiences." I use the term "of-God experiences" for alleged experiences of God, which again *may* or *may not be* veridical. And I use "experiences of God" more narrowly, as a label for *of-God experiences* that *are* veridical, that is experiences where God is either directly or indirectly present to the subject, in a thoroughgoing realist sense of "present."[16] This species of religious experience is of special interest for our purposes, since it is classical theism, or monotheism – what I shall call "personal theism" – that is explored and defended by the contributors to this book. And so, I

179

shall generally confine my remarks to the problem of the evidential value of of-God experiences, and address the problem of religious diversity in due course.

Recapitulating, now in terms of the dialectical context prescribed by our narrower interest in the evidential status of personal theism, there is no serious doubt about whether there are or have been of-God experiences. Skeptics about the existence of God, or about experiences of God, are generally happy to accept claims by a subject (or a group of subjects) to have had an of-God experience. The real question is whether *of-God experiences* are *experiences of God*. The usual way of treating this question is as an explanation-seeking question. Here is a phenomenon – namely, of-God experiences – whose reality is not to be denied. But what explains its occurrence? Not surprisingly, a standard objection to the evidential value of religious experience is that religious experiences can be explained as well, or better, in terms acceptable to a metaphysical naturalist. (All that needs to be noted about the nature of metaphysical naturalism is that metaphysical naturalists deny the existence of the God of personal theism. So an explanation that is acceptable to metaphysical naturalists is one that is consistent with this denial.)

The standard argument for the existence of God

The most typical conception of the positive evidential value of religious experience emphasizes the *non-inferential* grounding of religious belief by religious experience. Most proponents of this general conception endorse three claims that largely determine the pattern of the main variety of B-type argument from religious experience for the existence of God. The first claim is that the principle of credulity is a fundamental principle of rationality that applies to cases of perceptual experience (e.g. sense perception). The second is that religious experience is a species of perceptual experience that relevantly resembles sense perception. A third claim concerns the possibility of converting the non-inferential grounding of religious experience for a subject into grounds for recipients of a subject's testimony, on the basis of a principle of testimony. These three claims are central to what I call "the *standard argument* from religious experience."

The principle of credulity

As noted earlier, there are no serious opponents of the claim that many people have had of-God experiences. The main source of evidence for this claim is the testimony of subjects who have had of-God experiences. But some who accept these testimonies object to the further claim that of-God experiences count as evidence for the existence of God. And the first sort of objection to consider cuts to the chase by asserting that an of-God experience is not evidence for anything except the fact that a subject, S, has had an experience which it *seemed* to the subject involved an awareness of God. Consider the following three propositions:

1 It seems to subject S that God is present to S in S's experience.
2 God is present to S in S's experience.
3 God exists.

Let us suppose that most skeptics about experiences of God accept proposition 1 on the basis of S's testimony. S's testimony may take the form, "I had an of-God experience" (i.e. "I had an experience that seemed to be an experience of God"), or the form, "I had an experience of God." On the basis of either sort of report, one may be led to accept proposition 1.

Now, if S reports, "I had an experience of God," then we shall take it that S accepts proposition 2, and that she does so on the basis of her of-God experience. Let us also stipulate that if S reports, "I had an of-God experience," then S accepts proposition 2, although the intent of the report might not be to express S's acceptance of proposition 2.[17] Under these conditions, let us say, S accepts proposition 1 and takes proposition 1 to be evidence for proposition 2. And let us suppose that S accepts proposition 2 only if S accepts proposition 3, and hence that S accepts proposition 3. It may be, though it need not be, that the purpose of reporting S's experience is to present this as grounds for S's own acceptance of proposition 3. Further, it may be, though it need not be, that a purpose of reporting S's experience is to present this as grounds for another's acceptance of proposition 3.

The way is now clear to consider two questions. First, can the truth of proposition 1 count as adequate grounds for S's acceptance of proposition 2, and hence of S's acceptance of proposition 3? Second, can the truth of proposition 1 count as adequate grounds for another's acceptance of proposition 2, and hence of his/her acceptance of proposition 3? I am guessing that some who read this will be tempted to answer the first question in the affirmative while answering the second with an emphatic "No." This may have something to do with a desire to be tolerant toward S without feeling any compunction to believe as S does. But there may be another explanation for this sort of response to our two questions. We shall return to this in a moment.

Let us first explore why someone might think that the truth of proposition 1 provides grounds for S to accept proposition 2, and hence proposition 3. Here is where the principle of credulity comes into play. As Richard Swinburne writes, "How things seem to be is good grounds for a belief about how things are."[18] For example, the experience of it seeming to me that my keys are locked inside my car is good evidence in support of my supposing that my keys are locked inside my car. Swinburne claims that "it is a principle of rationality that (in the absence of special considerations), if it seems (epistemically) to a subject that x is present, then probably x is present; what one seems to perceive is probably so."[19] He then says that "it would seem to follow that, in the absence of special considerations, all religious experiences ought to be taken by their subjects as genuine, and hence as substantial grounds for belief in the existence of their apparent object."[20] Thus, if the religious experience in question is an of-God experience, the subject ought to take this experience as grounds for belief in the existence of God.[21]

Most of Swinburne's exposition and defense of "the argument from religious experience" (as he calls it) is devoted to spelling out the significance of this principle for cases of religious experience. Notice, Swinburne's argument from religious experience assumes that

a if the principle of credulity holds in contexts of sense perceptual experience, then it holds in other perceptual contexts as well; and
b religious experiences are perceptual experiences.

Swinburne takes care to argue for this assumption against two attempts to restrict the principle of credulity so that it does not apply in cases of religious experience.[22] In "Objections to the standard argument" below we shall look at recommended restrictions on the principle of credulity.

Notice also that Swinburne's argument allows that grounds for belief in God on the basis of having of-God experiences may be defeated by "special considerations." It is only in the absence of such special considerations that a subject ought to take of-God experiences as genuine, as substantial grounds for belief in the existence of God. This qualification is embedded in Swinburne's formulation of the principle of credulity. Swinburne delineates the "four kinds of special consideration which would defeat perceptual claims" and considers whether "they will normally be able to show that religious experiences are not to be taken at their face value."[23] We shall reflect on these matters in "Objections to the standard argument" and "Three additional objections" below.

The analogy with sense perception: the parity thesis

Swinburne introduces the principle of credulity by presenting ostensibly uncontroversial instances of the principle at work. These initial illustrations of the principle pertain to *sense* perceptual contexts: of seeming to *see* a table, and of seeming to *hear* a lecture.[24] The relevant "seemings" arise in contexts of *sense* perception. Then, in his general statement of the principle, Swinburne speaks of it seeming to a subject that x is present, of the subject seeming to perceive x. Apparently, it is paramount that the relevant context for the application of the principle of credulity is perceptual experience. Thus, if the principle of credulity is to have application to religious experience, religious experience must also be in some sense perceptual. In this limited respect at least, religious experience must be analogous to sense experience.

It does seem, however, that some discernible and appropriately strong analogy between sense experience and religious experience is needed in order to assert the transferability of the principle of credulity from the one experiential context (i.e. sense experience) to the other (i.e. religious experience). Swinburne does not develop the analogy at length; arguably, he does not develop it at all. He does argue that the types of special considerations that would defeat sense perceptual evidence for a belief do not normally obtain in contexts of religious experience. Even if this argument is successful, however, it does nothing to *show* that religious experience is a species of perception so relevantly like sense perception that the same principles of rationality can be expected to apply to both. It also assumes without argument that precisely the same four special considerations that may defeat experiential evidence in sense perception count as the potential defeaters for perception of God. Swinburne's discussion of these special conditions only shows that religious experience does not normally violate a certain principle of rationality, whether or not that principle happens to apply to religious experience.

In contrast to Swinburne, William Alston takes great pains to establish a relevantly strong analogy between sense perception and what he calls "mystical perception" (which comes close enough to what we are here calling of-God experiences).[25] Alston argues at length that "mystical experience can be construed as *perception* in the same generic sense of the term as sense perception."[26] Of-God experiences, then, are experiences of *perceiving God* (hence, the title of Alston's book).

The main benefit conferred by a strong analogy between sense perception and mystical perception is that it makes possible "a uniform treatment of the epistemology of the two modes of experience."[27] Mystical perceptions "play an important epistemic role with respect to beliefs about God importantly analogous to that played by sense perception with respect to beliefs about the physical world."[28] The strong analogy between sense perception and perception of God ensures strong epistemological parity between the evidence of sense perception in grounding beliefs about the physical world and the perception of God in grounding beliefs about God. Thus, problems with accepting the outputs of mystical perception (e.g. the belief that God exists) will be equally problematic for accepting the outputs of sense perception (e.g. the belief that there is a book before me now).[29] The latter point is critical, since it places considerable pressure on anyone who would deny the reliability of mystical perception to repudiate the reliability of sense perception as well. Or, to put it the way that Alston does in one passage, perception of God "has basically the same epistemic status" as sense perception, such that "no one who subscribes to the former is in any position to cavil at the latter."[30]

One might think, from these few remarks, that it would be a straightforward matter for Alston simply to list the various ways in which perception of God resembles sense perception. But this is not quite the way he seeks to establish epistemic parity between these two modes of perception. The basic idea is, rather, that sense perception is a species of perception from which it is possible to sort out what the generic notion of perception includes, so that if an of-God experience has this same generic structure then it, too, is a species of perception. The trick, then, is to identify the generic perceptual structure of sense perception that must be shared by any other species of perception, *however much it may differ from sense perception in other respects.*

According to Alston, an examination of sense perception reveals that its "presentational" character is the basic "phenomenological requirement for being a mode of perception." In perceptual experience, an object is presented to a subject's consciousness such that the subject is directly aware of the object. Moreover, the object appears to the subject as so-and-so; that is, it is manifest to the subject "in patterns of phenomenal qualia." In of-God experiences "the subject takes him/herself to be directly aware of God . . . the mode of consciousness involved is distinctively perceptual; it seems to the subject that something (identified by the subject as God) is directly presenting itself to his/her awareness as so-and-so."[31]

This is not the place to rehearse all of the technical details in Alston's account. It should be clear from what has been said that Alston's argument for parity is subtle and sophisticated. Failure to attend to the details of his position has led to numerous and frequent misunderstandings of the significance of important differences between sense perception and perception of God. I revisit this matter in the sections "Objections to the standard argument" and "A revised conception" below.

The principle of testimony

It is time to return to a question that we set aside earlier: why should anyone allow that the truth of proposition 1 provides grounds for S to accept proposition 2 (and therefore proposition 3], while it does not provide similar grounds for anyone to whom S reports her of-God experience? Can the truth of proposition 1, allowed by a recipient of testimony concerning S's experience, count as adequate grounds for the recipient's acceptance of proposition 2, and hence for S's acceptance of proposition 3?

Richard Swinburne thinks so. In support of his conviction, he invokes the principle of testimony: "(in the absence of special considerations) the experiences of others are (probably) as they report them."[32] This principle, combined with the principle of credulity, yields the following result: "things are (probably) as others claim to have perceived them."[33] In short, if things probably are as others have perceived them, then acceptance of their testimony about having of-God experiences should lead one to accept that these of-God experiences are experiences of God and therefore that God exists.

Summary of the argument

We have been considering two questions. First, what evidential weight do of-God experiences have for those who have them? Second, what evidential weight do of-God experiences have for those who have not had them but are recipients of subjects' reports about of-God experiences? In answer to the first question, the standard argument appeals to a fundamental principle of rationality called the principle of credulity. This strategy is buttressed with an argument for strong epistemological parity between sense experiences and of-God experiences. Given the parity between sense perception and of-God perception, and unless there are special considerations that defeat the evidence of the latter, it would seem that of-God experiences provide substantial support for a subject's belief that God exists.

In answer to the second question, the standard argument makes use of the principle of testimony. If an of-God experience provides a subject with substantial support for believing that God exists, and if a recipient accepts the authenticity of the subject's report about his/her having such an experience, then the subject's of-God experience also provides the recipient of this testimony with significant reason to believe that God exists.

Swinburne and Alston can be viewed as proponents of the standard argument. Some interpreters, however, have overlooked the close affinity between Swinburne and Alston. For example, Paul Draper distinguishes between the "argument from credulity" (which he attributes to Swinburne) and the "analogical argument" (which he attributes to Alston).[34] As we have seen, Swinburne does consider religious experience to be a species of perceptual experience, although he is more strenuously occupied with a defense of the application of the principle of credulity to religious experience. Alston, on the other hand, develops a detailed and sophisticated defense of the analogy between sense perception and perception of God and of consequent epistemological parity between the grounding of physical object-beliefs in sense perception and the grounding of God-beliefs in perception of God.[35]

Does Alston also endorse the principle of credulity? He does. In fact, he emphasizes its importance when he says that "the most important philosophical positive reason" for concluding that mystical experiences often are genuine experiences of God is that "beliefs formed on the basis of experience possess an initial credibility by virtue of their origin. They are innocent until proven guilty."[36] In his book, Alston offers carefully nuanced support for Swinburne's use of the principle and acknowledges Swinburne as an ally on the general topic of the perception of God.[37]

Naturally, this line of argument has been subjected to considerable close examination by others who remain unconvinced. It is to their protests that we turn in the next two sections.

Objections to the standard argument

The objections considered in this section all have to do with the machinery of the standard argument from religious experience to the existence of God. These can be conveniently sorted into challenges confronting the key components of the standard argument: the parity thesis, the application of the principle of credulity to of-God experiences, and the possibility of grounding belief in God on the testimony of subjects concerning their of-God experiences.

Challenges to the parity thesis

The main challenges to the parity thesis have to do with differences, or disanalogies, between sense experience and experience of God. For example, C. B. Martin observes that there are standard ways of testing for veridicality when it comes to sense experience. But "when it comes to such a case as knowing God . . . the society of tests and checkup procedures, which surround other instances of knowing, completely vanishes. What is put in the place of these tests and checking procedures is an immediacy of knowledge that is supposed to carry its own guarantee."[38] What sort of tests are used for distinguishing veridical from nonveridical sense experiences? Martin's basic worry is that "whether anything or nothing is apprehended by experiences is not to be read off from the experiences themselves."[39] He states:

> The presence of a piece of blue paper is not to be read off from my experience as of a piece of blue paper. Other things are relevant: What would a photograph reveal? Can I touch it? What do others see? It is only when I admit the relevance of such checking procedures that I can lay claim to apprehending the paper, and, indeed, the admission of the relevance of such procedures is what gives meaning to the assertion that I am apprehending the paper. *What I apprehend is the sort of thing that can be photographed, touched, and seen by others.*[40]

Martin does not insist that experiences of God be subject to precisely the same tests that we use when checking up on sense experience. But he does insist that there must be some *standard* procedures for testing the veridicality of experiences of God.[41]

As it happens, Alston acknowledges that the perception of God differs from the perception of physical objects in just the respect that Martin alleges.[42] It is not that there are no procedures at all for testing of-God experiences.[43] It is, rather, that the available procedures cannot be applied to of-God experiences with the rigor and reliability that we are accustomed to when it comes to sense experience. But there is an explanation for this: the object presented in an of-God experience is a *personal* being, whose behavior is not as predictable as the behavior of physical objects. As George

Mavrodes writes, "The world contains many things, and not all of them are as inert as a piece of paper."[44]

Does this answer the objection? Not completely. For one might say that it matters not why standard checking procedures are not available; it only matters that they are not available. But then we must ask: "Matters to what?" The answer, presumably, is that this matters to the justification of beliefs based on of-God experiences. And that may be true. But the precise bearing of this on epistemic justification needs to be spelled out. For even if it should be desirable to have an independent means of testing for the veridicality of religious experiences, and even if such means are widely available for testing sense perception, it does not follow that the availability of an independent testing procedure is *necessary* for justified belief. In the absence of standardized tests, experientially based belief will still normally be prima facie justified. What *is* critical is that there be no defeaters for the justification of experience-based belief that God exists.

There are other differences as well. Here are some that Alston explicitly recognizes:

> Sense perception is insistently and unavoidably present in all our waking hours, and the experiential awareness of God is a rare phenomenon except for a very few souls. Sense perception, especially vision, is vivid and richly detailed, bursting with information, whereas the experience of God is dim, meager, and obscure. Sense perception is shared by all human beings, whereas the experience of God, though more widely dispersed than is often supposed, is still by no means universal.[45]

Clearly, these are all differences that make an epistemological difference. Many of Alston's critics have stressed these and other differences in their attack on the parity thesis.[46]

So why are these differences not defeaters for Alston's claim regarding epistemic parity between of-God experience and sense experience? Answer: because these differences have no bearing on the "generic identity of structure" between the two modes of experience, for they do not defeat the crucial evidence-making feature of all perceptual experience. That feature is the presentational character of perceptual experience. Since this feature is the most epistemically distinguishing structural component in generic perceptual experience, it is the most epistemically relevant feature of individual species of perceptual experience, including both sense perception and perception of God.

Many objections to Alston's parity thesis come to grief because they misunderstand or neglect the specific rationale that Alston develops. This, I suspect, has quite a lot to do with the method Alston adopts in distilling the nature of generic perception, and his tireless comparison of mystical perception with sense perception. Alston derives a pristine conception of generic perception in the only way he thinks this can be done – by abstracting from the familiar practice of sense perception. And he sees greater similarities between the experience of God and sense experience than he does between experience of God and other modalities of belief formation. But there is another reason, I believe, why Alston is attracted to the notion of epistemic parity between sense experience and experience of God. As we have already seen, strong epistemic parity of this sort forces a painful choice on anyone who would prefer to deny the evidential value of religious experience:

1 allow that of-God experience is a legitimate non-inferential ground for belief that God exists;
2 acquiesce to skepticism about sense perception; or
3 repudiate both skepticism about sense perception and the reliability of experience of God, on pain of inconsistency.

Despite the attractions of the epistemic parity thesis, it is possible that it has been overdrawn.

Challenges to the principle of credulity

As I argue in 'A revised conception', the manifest differences between sense experience and experience of God do nothing to undermine the application of the principle of credulity to of-God experiences. But the application of this principle to religious experience has been challenged. Most challenges materialize as restrictions precluding application of the principle to religious experience. Let us consider three distinct attempts at restricting application of the principle.

First, William Rowe recommends the following gloss on the principle of credulity: it "presupposes that we have some understanding of what reasons there might be for questioning our experiences and some way of telling whether or not these reasons are present."[47] He reasons that "it is quite difficult to discover reasons for thinking that someone's [of-God experience] is delusive," for "it is entirely up to God whether to reveal his presence to some human being."[48]

This objection will already be familiar from our consideration of C. B. Martin's objection to thinking of experience of God as perceptual. There are additional problems with this suggestion.

1 As a gloss on the principle of credulity, Rowe's proposal is problematic. The principle of credulity enshrines the notion that belief grounded non-inferentially in perceptual experience is innocent until proven guilty. But Rowe's restriction effectively counsels the reverse attitude of guilty until proven innocent. One and the same experience cannot be both innocent until proven guilty and guilty until proven innocent.

2   Rowe's restriction, if generalized, has two deleterious effects. It launch-
es an infinite regress and it undermines the evidence of sense experience.
For any belief-forming practice, there will always be additional checks
and tests that one could conduct; an interminable regress of testing
protocols is unavoidable. And what is a restriction for one modality
of belief formation that is governed by the principle of credulity is a
restriction for any other modality that is governed by the principle of
credulity, including sense perception. But sense perception is considered
by many (rightly, I think) to be a basic source of justified belief and
knowledge.[49] On the other hand, if the restriction is not generalized, it
is arbitrary to require it only in the context of religious experience.

Second, Michael Martin has argued for a "negative principle of credulity" as the complement to the principle of credulity. He reasons that
if "experiences of God are good grounds for the existence of God," then
"experiences of the absence of God [may as well be] good grounds for the
non-existence of God."[50]

In his original statement of the argument from religious experience,
Richard Swinburne decries the significance of "negative seemings." These
are, he reasons, no evidence of how things are. He adds that "there are no
good grounds for supposing that if there is a God, the atheist would have
experienced him."[51]

The problem is that even if it is true that an atheist might not experience a God that does exist and is experienced by others, it does not follow
that negative seemings have no evidential value. For even though they are
negative, they are seemings about the way things are, and often enough it
seeming to be that something is not the case is quite good evidence that it is
not the case. For example, it now seems to me that there is no elephant in
the room with me as I write. That particular negative seeming impresses me
as very good evidence that things *are not* the way they *seem not* to be; I am
right to believe that there is no elephant in the room with me.

Furthermore, negative seemings are all the more telling when the very thing
that ought to be present under certain conditions seems not to be present under those conditions. So, sticking to the existence of God to illustrate, if we
were right to think that God's presence would be irresistibly evident to everyone, or to everyone who cared to notice him, then God's seeming not to exist
would really count for something. Or, if God's presence should be particularly
manifest to those suffering horrific pain, and it seems to the one who suffers
that God is not present, then again the negative seeming has force.

So Michael Martin must be given his due. But that means that we must
also be careful not to let him get away with too much. And he does claim
too much by asserting that negative seemings are on a par, epistemically,
with positive seemings, especially with respect to God's existence.

Sometimes even the obvious must be said, and even repeated: God is not an elephant, nor is he much like an elephant. I wonder what Martin thinks he knows about how God's presence would have to be manifest, if, contrary to fact (according to Martin), God did exist? Size is not really at issue. But perhaps it is the alleged omnipresence of God that has got Martin thinking this way. However, divine omnipresence is more a matter of the scope of God's consciousness of things than it is a matter of our consciousness of God. Furthermore, God is a personal being with a will and intentions and capacities. How and whether, or when, he chooses to disclose himself is up to him. And the criteria he uses may have to do with choices we make. After all, even experience of human persons as persons and not solely as bodies in a physical world depends on relational dynamics that include openness towards one another and a host of other attitudinal states. My wife has sometimes said to me, "It seems to me that you are not listening very carefully to what I'm saying now." In most cases she has been right, and I knew as soon as she spoke (assuming I heard her) that I not only failed to disguise my inattention, but I could not possibly have faked the sort of behavior that goes with the sort of listening she desired from me.

Finally, Jerome Gellman has responded that the negative seemings that are associated with great suffering are mistakenly taken to be especially telling.[52] He points out that in conditions of horrendous pain one is often, in the nature of the case, unable to sense the presence of God. The nature of the suffering can affect the very possibility of experiencing the presence of God. If Gellman is right, the only way that God could ensure that he is consciously present whenever a believer suffers would be to prevent certain forms of suffering altogether. But the good that would result if God should do this may be overridden by greater goods associated with God's permission of those lonelier forms of suffering. Further exploration of this theme would require extensive investigations of theodicy.[53]

A third restriction on the principle of credulity has been suggested by Paul Draper, who allows that the principle is a fundamental principle of rationality, but denies that it is a universal principle of rationality. It does not apply to "all persons in all epistemic situations"; rather, it applies only to "'epistemically immature' persons," such as "children first learning about the world." The principle of credulity comes to be "modified as we mature intellectually," so that, "as we grow older, we learn to treat different sorts of perceptual claims differently."[54] Some are met with a greater degree of initial credulity; others with a greater degree of initial skepticism.

According to Draper, four factors influence the degree of initial credulity we are prepared to allow. Perceptual experience provides relatively weak evidence if the claim purportedly supported by that evidence is (a) highly specific, (b) very significant (as opposed to trivial), (c) about extraordinary objects not otherwise known to exist and be perceivable, or (d) dependent upon an extraordinary mode of perception.[55] Draper's thesis is that "all four of these factors diminish the amount of direct evidence that theistic experiences provide for basic perceptual claims about God."[56]

How are these four factors that influence the degree of initial credulity identified? They are identified on the basis of observing actual belief-forming practices within contexts of perceptual experience. But notice, it is more precisely an examination of our habits in *sense* perception that yields this list of factors governing levels of initial credulity. But perceiving God, in the sense that we are considering, is not a form of sense perception. It is likely that differences between sense perception and the perception of God correlate with differences in initial credulity factors. Following Draper's example of observing belief-forming habits in sense perception for the purposes of specifying initial credulity factors, we should examine the actual practices of subjects having of-God experiences if we want to know what factors govern their levels of initial credulity. An examination of actual practice will reveal that not all of-God experiences are treated equally by the subjects who have them. An array of degrees of credulity will be found within this context, even if this array differs from that specified for sense perception. In the domain of religious experience, differences in *spiritual* maturity, for example, will specially account for differences in degree of initial credulity.

Even *epistemic* maturity is context relative and not just a matter of general attainment. One who is relatively epistemically mature in contexts of ordinary sense perception may not be so mature in contexts of mystical perception. Thus, Draper's restriction on the principle of credulity relative to religious experience may not be warranted; it may be too restrictive.

Challenges to the principle of testimony

For subjects of religious experience, belief that God exists may be non-inferentially grounded in their of-God experiences. The only access others have to a subject's experiential grounds is the testimony of the subjects. For this reason, the *standard argument* from religious experience requires a principle of testimony. In general, the experiences of others are probably as they report them.

There is an initial difficulty to overcome, however. Typically, the strength of justification afforded by testimony is lower than that afforded by direct experiential evidence. Swinburne is not disturbed by this. As long as the subject of an of-God experience has substantial experiential, non-inferential grounds for believing that God was or is present in the subject's experience, and there are no special reasons to distrust his/her report about his/her experience, a recipient of his/her testimony also has "quite good reason" to believe that God was present in the subject's experience, and hence to believe that God exists.

Swinburne's confidence in this matter is supported by two observations. First, a vast amount of what any of us knows is based on the testimony of others. There is no special reason why we should not trust the testimony of others when it comes to experiences of God. Second, with respect to experiences of God there is substantial testimonial evidence at our disposal. The strength of testimonial evidence regarding experiences of God is compounded by the numerous reports of having of-God experiences.

There certainly is merit to these considerations. And yet, perhaps Swinburne's optimism is excessive. First, whether or not a person is prepared to accept the testimony of others about a matter depends greatly on what is personally at stake. In matters of great human concern, standards for the acceptance of testimonial evidence will be fairly high. How high they should be relative to religious experience is to some extent a matter of personal decision. But I can imagine that for many the standards will be much higher when the question of God's existence is in the balance than it is in most other situations.

Second, one may well wonder why a question of such moment should be decided on the basis of experiences that others have had. Why should some have to rely heavily on the testimony of others, rather than enjoy immediate, non-inferential justification of their own, especially when it would seem that God is perfectly capable of presenting himself to anyone? Why shouldn't God simply appear to anyone who might benefit from an of-God experience, and especially to anyone who truly desires an experience of God and would likely believe in God on the occasion of having such an experience?

Third, of-God experiences may be numerous indeed. But the problem here is that while there is an impressive plurality of such experiences, there is an equally impressive variety of conceptual contents associated with these types of experiences as their justified outputs. This generates a twofold problem: some of this variety betrays the presence of conflicting conceptions of God arising out of experiences of God; and, where no conflict is discernable, it is nevertheless difficult to ascertain the degree to which the entity experienced in of-God experiences is the same being across experiences.[57] Furthermore, of-God experiences do not exhaust the class of religious experiences whose possible veridicality is of interest. Perhaps the strength of testimonial evidence regarding of-God experiences is vitiated by equally numerous reports of non-theistic religious experiences.

In the final section I make a few suggestions in response to the difficulties that have been raised in this section. But first we must consider briefly three more general challenges to the evidential value of religious experience.

Three additional objections

The objections we have so far considered concern the basic structure and machinery of the *standard argument* for the existence of God based on religious experience. They concern the elements of the argument itself. In this section I discuss three objections that pose challenges to any positive construal of the evidence of religious experience relative to the existence of God.

The problem of religious diversity

A particularly thorny issue for our purpose has to do with the reality of religious diversity and the way conflicting beliefs are tethered to religious experience.

First, as we shall see, background beliefs may very well contribute to the way particular subjects understand and interpret their religious experiences. If these background beliefs explain much of the disparity of perspective that we find in the world, it cannot be the singular fault of religious experience. Although background beliefs do not necessarily distort an understanding of religious experience, they certainly could.

Second, religious experience may sometimes be given a richer interpretation than the phenomenology of the experience by itself would support, because of the role played by background beliefs and expectations. On the other hand, an experience rich in conceptualizable content may not be understood by the subject in the full sense of which it is capable. This, too, may be a consequence of the operation of beliefs and attitudes in the background. This invites a distinction between of-God experiences where the subject perceives God and of-God experiences where the subject does not perceive God, but not because the experiences are not veridical. Assuming veridicality, we should perhaps speak instead of *experiences of God*, and distinguish between those where God is recognized by the subject and those where God is not recognized. The point of making this distinction is that many religious experiences may be experiences of God in the second sense. Auto-descriptions of religious experiences may be inaccurate. This may happen for various reasons, one of which would be the system of background beliefs of, and linguistic practices available to, subjects providing the descriptions.

Finally, among conflicting claims rooted to a significant degree in experience is the tradition of metaphysical naturalism. This places pretty much everyone in the same boat. The fact that religious traditions vary conceptually and doctrinally despite their respective appeals to religious experience cannot by itself be taken to vitiate the value of religious experience in favor of some amorphous naturalism. Naturalism as a commitment on the part of individuals is very seldom amorphous. It varies in form and perspective. Phenomena and explanations that seem perfectly innocuous from the perspective of some naturalists are utterly scandalous from the perspective of other naturalists.[58] This relatively rich diversity parallels the diversity of religious traditions, not only in richness of diversity, but also for the role that experience plays in the formation of naturalistic beliefs about particular matters of controversy among naturalists.

In any case, if the experiences (including the lack of of-God experiences) of naturalists are added to the mix of perspectives embraced by people, and the question is posed, "What are we to make of reality, given the diverse perspectives of people rooted in their respective experiences?", why should we privilege a non-religious perspective over a particular religious perspective?[59]

The availability of naturalistic explanations

As I noted at the outset, a B-type argument for the existence of God does take seriously an explanation-seeking question: are *of-God experiences* bona fide *experiences of God*, or do they have some other explanation? I pointed out that a metaphysical naturalist may well acknowledge the reality of of-God experiences, but he will most assuredly cavil at the suggestion that many such experiences are veridical. One standard objection to the evidential value of religious experience is that religious experiences can be explained as well or better in terms acceptable to a metaphysical naturalist. This claim is supported with specific proposals about how of-God experiences may be explained so that they are consistent with metaphysical naturalism. The most ambitious forms of this type of objection go further. They seek to demonstrate that some naturalistic explanation for of-God experiences provides a better explanation than the hypothesis that God exists and is present in the experiences.

The list of reductive strategies favored by naturalists is too long for me to take account of each individually. The more plausible-sounding strategies are wrapped in the vocabulary of science, and for good reason. Any explanation labeled "scientific" (or better yet, "medically scientific") will tend to command a measure of deference. "You cannot argue with science, right?" Sometimes, however, the measure of deference accorded a "scientific explanation" is disproportionate to the actual evidence available.

The modern world is acquainted with a profusion of psychological pathologies. These pathologies have been accorded splendiferous power to explain away religious experience. Recognized pathologies that have been credited with this vaunted explanatory power include, for starters: hyper-suggestibility (from self-induced hypnotic suggestion to brainwashing); deprivation; sexual frustration; anxiety, panic, and amorphous foreboding that tend to trigger defense mechanisms; regression; mental illness (from hysteria to delusions to manic depression); and abnormal physiological states induced by drugs.[60] With a list like that, it is easy to imagine that for every yet-to-be catalogued pathology there is a new naturalistic explanation for religious experience waiting to be commandeered for deployment against experience-of-God claims. Come to think of it, it is a wonder more naturalists do not simply invent from scratch a pathology specific to of-God experiences.

I invite naturalists with the appropriate disposition (whatever the psychological explanation for *that* might be) to sift the data pertaining to of-God experiences using "pathological personality variables" to eliminate all the demonstrably wacky cases of alleged experience of God. Let them even perform a further reduction by setting aside all cases where there is a strong presumption in favor of pathological explanation. What remains following this exercise will still be a substantial body of testimonial evidence that resists assimilation to pathological causes. With regard to this substantial residue, all the naturalist can do is suggest that the remaining cases may well be pathological as well.

Now the evidence for this more modest claim about what is possible is just the evidence of pathology in the easy cases. But what makes them easy cases is that they bear the marks of pathology on their sleeves, as it were. The remaining cases do not. So what possible bearing could identifiable pathologies passing for of-God experiences have on those of-God experiences that show no indication, in their own right, of being pathological? The best explanation for this difference may well be that experiences in the first group are artificial and experiences in the second group are veridical. There must, after all, be *some* explanation for this difference.

As a matter of fact, another sort of explanation has been proposed. This brings us to our final objection.[61]

The role of background beliefs

Some skeptics about religious experience have thought to explain the character of religious experience by emphasizing the role of background beliefs in religious experience. Very simply, the idea is that what one experiences is conditioned by what one already believes, so that if, for example, subjects already have a rich background of beliefs about the existence and character of God, they are more likely to have of-God experiences, so that their having of-God experiences can be completely chalked up to their having these background beliefs going into the experience.[62]

The first thing to notice here is that background beliefs are just as likely to illuminate an experience as they are to distort. To the extent that background beliefs do condition one's understanding of an of-God experience, it will matter whether those background beliefs enjoy an appropriate degree of justification by independent means. This means that in such cases belief in God must already have some positive epistemic standing. It would be a mistake to think that of-God experiences contribute nothing at all to the epistemic status of a belief already held and independently justified. No amount of external, public evidence for the existence of God can substitute for relationship with God, however much it may justify belief in God. If the evidence of natural theology (cosmological and design arguments for the existence of God, for example) implies (as I believe it does) that God is a personal being with a keen interest in the human condition and a desire for a relationship between Himself and human persons, then of-God experiences will not only be the vehicle of such a relationship but also tend to confirm the hypothesis supported by natural theology.

Second, quite often subjects having of-God experiences report that their experiences were the occasion of acquiring religious beliefs that they did not already have. Indeed, reluctant naturalists have sometimes converted to belief in God on the basis of what they describe as religious experience of one kind or another. Not only are these cases impressive counter-examples to the generalization embodied in the explanation under consideration, but some appropriate explanation is needed to account for the conversion of a person out of commitment to a strong naturalist package of beliefs. Others have converted from some variety of generic theism to a more robust theism like Christianity, again with experience of God playing a key role.[63]

Third, the role of background beliefs among those who do not experience God must also be taken into consideration as a factor explaining their not experiencing God. First, there is the obvious role that confident belief that God does not exist will almost certainly play in this regard. I confess, I have sometimes suspected that, however ambiguous the evidence for theism may seem to some people, anyone with a confident belief that God does not exist just is not paying attention. (And let us not forget, committed metaphysical naturalists, are, for all intents and purposes, confident of the non-existence of God.) But even if one is not an atheist, one may have in the background to one's own experiences beliefs that limit the prospects of having of-God experiences, even if God does exist and desires to be known in experience. There is the real danger that the supposed "hiddenness of God" is actually due to background beliefs and attitudes that people have about how God must be prepared to manifest himself if he exists. There is the real possibility that the chief barrier to experiencing the presence of God lies within our own noetic and attitudinal structures.[64]

A revised conception

Where does the critical discussion of the sections "Objections to the standard argument" and "Three additional objections" leave the argument from religious experience for the existence of God? What are we to make of the evidential value of religious experience in light of the difficulties treated in those sections?

First, the chief lesson to be learned from the discussion in "Three additional objections" is that the evidence of religious experience should not be quarantined from whatever evidence is available from other sources. All available evidence should be assimilated into a cumulative case for personal theism that is sensitive to the complex logical relations that hold among the various categories of evidence. The evidence of religious experience should be respected enough to foster serious enquiry into the availability of other evidences for theism. Alternatively, the evidences of cosmology, anthropic design, and human consciousness, all of which are discussed at length in this book, may be seen to support a reasonable expectation that the personal

God responsible for creating and ordering our universe, thereby arranging for our physical flourishing, and for creating us with faculties associated with immaterial minds (including aspirations for spiritual flourishing and the potential for relationship with God), also desires a relationship with us. This expectation may be tested in human experience and confirmed by of-God experiences that we have independent reason to believe are veridical.

The religious experiences of others may further elicit sympathy for the possibility of experience of God among those who have not yet had such experiences. The attitudes and dispositions that accompany this sort of sympathy may put nonbelievers in a better position to appraise all of the data for personal theism, and even to encounter God in their own experience. At the very least, if they are agnostics who appreciate the momentous nature of the religious quest and recognize the role that attitudes play in guiding appropriate pursuit of God as a possibly real being personally interested in a relationship, then they may be encouraged to engage in a devotional experiment that would lead to a personal awareness of God in their own experience.[65]

All of this suggests that there is yet a third way to incorporate the data of religious experience into an argument for personal theism. As it is best regarded as a cumulative case argument, let us call it a C-type argument. How might this argument relate to the strengths and weaknesses of the standard B-type argument explored earlier in this chapter? Here I wish to make several suggestions.

My first recommendation is that we relax the strong claim on behalf of epistemic parity that figures so prominently in the standard argument. There are disanalogies between sense perception and of-God experience; some have substantial epistemological consequences. (This is not to be lamented. Some disanalogies are religiously quite significant.) It does not serve the purposes of an argument from religious experience to the existence of God to emphasize the similarities and then have to explain repeatedly why notable dissimilarities do not undermine the basic argument. Abandoning ambitious claims on behalf of epistemic parity will help to forestall confusion about the significance of the very real similarities that do exist.

Of-God experiences are irreducibly *sui generis*. This does not mean that there are no analogies between of-God experiences and other modes of experience. Sense perception is one domain where we meet with significant analogies. All salient analogies between sense perception and "perception" of God are due to the subject–object presentational structure that they have in common. In both modes of experience, a subject is directly acquainted with an object that is presented to the subject's consciousness as existing, having some set of properties, and standing in certain relations to other objects in experience, where the object that is presented is taken to be in some way the cause of the experience.

I have no objection to characterizing perception in some generic sense in terms of this basic structure. But then other experiences will count as perceptual as well. (In fact, on some accounts, even the intuitional grasp of mathematical or logical truths may be regarded as similarly perceptual.[66]) Among perceptual experiences understood in this generic sense, of-God experiences bear the strongest resemblance to experiences of, or "encounters" with, other *persons*. If the sensory imagery that subjects often use to describe of-God experiences suggests close comparison with sense perception, other elements in their descriptions for of-God experiences point to a different comparison. The object presented in of-God experiences is presented as a personal being, and the resulting acquaintance with the object presented is personal in nature. It is typical of Christian believers, for example, to speak of having a personal relationship with God, where they mean this quite literally. The much-ballyhooed "ineffability" of so much religious experience may, in of-God experiences at least, be due to the I–Thou character of the experiences. Little wonder that language may fail a subject attempting to articulate the details of her experience of a personal deity and the knowledge that she acquires through such direct acquaintance.[67]

My second recommendation concerns the principle of credulity. If there are differences between sense perception and perception of God that undercut an ambitious claim for epistemic parity between the two modes of experience, these differences do not affect the applicability of the principle of credulity to experiences of God. This principle is far more generalizable than is acknowledged in most discussions of it. Its application ranges over a host of epistemic contexts. In fact, it is difficult to think of a context where it does not apply. Consider Swinburne's "principle of testimony." Is it anything more than a special case of a principle of credulity applied to belief based on testimony? Although Swinburne does defend the principle of credulity by drawing an analogy with sense perception, its actual defense may be more successful if it is derived from our habits across the whole range of doxastic practices.

In any event, the undeniable similarity between sense perception and experience of God *as modes of experience that have a presentational aspect*, permits an extension of the use of the principle of credulity in sense experience to its use in of-God experiences. For it is with respect to the presentational character of sense perception that the principle of credulity is germane. The "seemings" that occur in sense perception are to be taken at face value, barring the existence of contraindications. Analogous seemings also occur in of-God experiences. And for that reason there is cause for endorsing a principle of credulity in the rational appraisal of such experiences.

This affords a mitigated (scaled-down) claim to epistemic parity between sense perception and the "perception" of God. Both modes of experience are governed by similar principles of rationality. Approval of the use of fundamental principles of rationality in the domain of sense perception and disapproval of their use in the domain of religious experience suggests that the decision about proper domains of application is arbitrary. But it is not. On the other hand, consistent disapproval in all cases will land one in the "skeptical bog", as warned about by Swinburne and Alston. A modest epistemic parity thesis survives acknowledgement of epistemologically significant disanalogies between sense perception and experience of God.

Turning, finally, to the principle of testimony, I recommend a more expansive construal of the nature and significance of testimony. Testimonial evidence must be weighed relative to the credibility of the witness. Credibility of the witness is a function of the witness's perceived character and expertise. With regard to character, various virtues are relevant, but basic honesty is especially important. With regard to expertise, there must be confidence that a witness has a certain minimal ability to grasp whatever it is that her testimony pertains to and can talk about it intelligently and accurately. The moral fruits of religious experience in the lives of their subjects concern both dimensions of credibility. All of these conditions of credible testimony have been discussed in the literature on religious experience.

But there is an additional component that deserves more attention. It is arguably the most important. Transcending the particular virtues and competencies of an expert witness is the overall impression that the witness creates in others. Some individuals enjoy a stature that far outstrips the reputation of others. These individuals are without peers. Their testimony has eminently greater weight. They are the paragons.

In the realm of religious experience, there are few who would regard themselves as paragons of religious practice. Those who do advertise themselves in this way had better have impeccable credentials. Genuine models of spirituality are in short supply. Amateurs and hucksters abound. Even the most admirable figures confess their neophyte status. So far as I can tell, there is one shining exception. Those in search of a model of spiritual perceptiveness can do no better than attend respectfully to the life and teachings of Jesus Christ. He had an authoritative bearing that led a multitude to remark about it and inspired many to make it the pattern of their own highest aspirations. Of the many figures whom we admire for their spiritual devotion, whom we would be most prepared to trust for reliable testimony about of-God experiences, I dare say the preponderance of them are figures who have made Jesus their own model.

The centuries-long tradition of religious experience traceable to the effect of Jesus Christ in the lives of people across cultures should provoke a measure of curiosity about the possible veridicality of alleged experiences of God. A certain feeling of exposure by acquaintance with the person and teaching of Jesus is a commonly reported religious experience that may be shared by believers and nonbelievers alike.

I conclude, then, with the testimony of a band of men who knew Jesus most intimately. His presence in their lives was so transformational that they invoked the most exalted language they could find to give expression to it, language that linked their own personal destinies to the power of his presence. Their words are especially arresting for being a direct response to Jesus himself: "Lord, to whom shall we go? You have the words of eternal life."[68]

Notes

1 "Tautological" here means "statements whose truth is recognizable entirely on the basis of understanding the meaning of the statements themselves." Under this description, tautological statements include statements of logic and mathematics, as well as analytic statements. This was the conception of "tautological" used by Moritz Schlick, leader of the Vienna Circle, which spawned the logical positivist movement.

2 This metaphor of "stoking the fires" recalls the statement by David Hume about the proper treatment of metaphysics and theology: "If we take in our hands any volume; of divinity or school metaphysics, for instance, let us ask, *Does it contain any abstract reasoning concerning quantity or number?* No. *Does it contain any experimental reasoning concerning matter of fact and existence?* No. Commit it then to the flames: for it can contain nothing but sophistry and illusion" [David Hume, *An Inquiry concerning Human Understanding*, 3rd edn, L. A. Selby-Bigge (ed.) (Oxford: Oxford University Press, 1975), 165]. More than any other predecessor, Hume was an inspiration to the empiricism-intoxicated proponents of logical positivism.

3 Rudolf Carnap, "The Elimination of Metaphysics Through Logical Analysis of Language," in *Logical Positivism*, A. J. Ayer (ed.) (Glencoe, IL: The Free Press, 1959), 63.

4 A. J. Ayer, *Language, Truth and Logic*, 2nd edn (London: Gollancz, 1946), 115.

5 See Alvin Plantinga, *God and Other Minds: A Study of the Rational Justification of Belief in God* (Ithaca, NY: Cornell University Press, 1967), 167.

6 Malcolm L. Diamond and Thomas V. Litzenburg Jr (eds), *The Logic of God: Theology and Verification* (Indianapolis: The Bobbs-Merrill Company, 1975), 436.

7 See the following two anthologies published during the 1960s: John Hick and Arthur C. McGill (eds), *The Many-Faced Argument: Recent Studies on the Ontological Argument for the Existence of God*, (New York: Macmillan, 1967) (see especially the items listed on pages 366–8 on the bibliography), and Alvin Plantinga (ed.) *The Ontological Argument from St Anselm to Contemporary Philosophers*, (Garden City, NY: Doubleday, 1965).

8 But see the discussion of this fascinating and historically tenacious argument in Chapter 5 by Stephen T. Davis.

9 See Chapter 6 by William Lane Craig and Chapter 7 by Robin Collins for sophisticated defenses of contemporary versions of cosmological and design arguments respectively.

10 George I. Mavrodes, "Religious experience, argument for the existence of God from," in *The Oxford Companion to Philosophy*, Ted Honderich (ed.) (Oxford: Oxford University Press, 1995), 768.

11 See Carl Jung, *Psychology of the Unconscious* (New York: Dodd, Mead, & Co., 1947).

12 Again, see Chapter 7 by Robin Collins.

13 I say *may*, because there are other ways that the religious experiences of believers may frame the cognitive responsibilities of nonbelieving recipients of reports of religious experience. These will be explored in due course.

14 Wallace I. Matson, *The Existence of God* (Ithaca, NY: Cornell University Press, 1965), 14.

15 An experience is veridical, in the sense I have in mind, only if what seems to be presented in the experience actually exists and has the properties that it seems to have, given the experience.

16 It is admittedly arbitrary to employ the terms "of-God experiences" and "experiences of God" the way I do; but it is convenient to have some way of referring to the contrasting notions, and this seems to me to be as good a way as any.

17 Of course, S might report, "I had an of-God experience" without accepting proposition 2. But we are interested in the case where S reports, "I had an of-God experience" only if she accepts proposition 2. Hence, the stipulation.

18 Richard Swinburne, *The Existence of God* (Oxford: Clarendon Press, 1979), 254.

19 Ibid., 254.

20 Ibid., 254.

21 Swinburne does not distinguish, as he should, between (a) the grounding of a subject's belief by his experience, and (b) the subject's taking his/her experience to be adequate grounds for his belief. William Alston, in commenting on an early draft of this chapter, reminded me of the importance of this distinction. An experience may constitute grounds for a subject's belief even if the subject has not so much as contemplated the adequacy of those grounds. If the subject's original experiential grounds for belief are adequate, let us say that the subject's belief is non-inferentially justified. Subsequent reflection may lead the subject to consider whether the grounds for his/her belief are adequate. Here, inference will naturally play an important role.

22 See ibid., 255–60.

23 See ibid., 260–71.

24 Ibid., 254.

25 For his reasons for resisting the term "religious experience," see William P. Alston, *Perceiving God: The Epistemology of Religious Experience* (Ithaca, NY: Cornell University Press, 1991), 34–5. The basic problem is that the term is "obfuscating," which, if true, would sure enough be a reason to avoid it. For present purposes, I take no position on the matter.

26 Ibid., 66. The details are spelled out in Chapter four of Alston's book (i.e. 9–67).

27 Ibid., 66.

28 William P. Alston, "Perceiving God," *The Journal of Philosophy* 83 (1986), 655.

29 On the second point here, see Alston, *Perceiving God*, 6.

30 William P. Alston, "Religious Experience and Religious Belief," in *Contemporary Perspectives on Religious Epistemology*, R. Douglas Geivett and Brendan Sweetman (eds) (New York: Oxford University Press, 1992), 302.

31 Alston, *Perceiving God*, 67.

32 See Swinburne, *The Existence of God*, 272.

33 Ibid., 272.

34 Paul Draper, "God and Perceptual Evidence," *International Journal for Philosophy of Religion* 32 (1992), 149–65.

35 See also William J. Wainwright, *Mysticism: A Study of Its Nature, Cognitive Value, and Moral Implications* (Madison, WI: University of Wisconsin Press,

1981), Ch. 3, which defends the claim that mystical experiences are importantly like sense experiences, and William J. Wainwright, "Mysticism and Sense Perception," *Religious Studies* 9 (1973), 257–78.

36 William P. Alston, "God and Religious Experience," in *Philosophy of Religion: A Guide to the Subject*, Brian Davies (ed.) (Washington, DC: Georgetown University Press, 1998), 67.

37 See Alston, *Perceiving God*, 195. Since Alston limits his discussion of the epistemology of religious experience to questions about the evidential value of religious experiences for their subjects, it is not surprising that he does not explore the further question of whether the testimony of these subjects could provide others with adequate grounds for religious belief. But there can be little doubt from what he says here and there that Alston does countenance a role for such testimony in contributing to the justification a recipient might have for acquiring religious beliefs. This is illustrated, for example, in the remark I have just quoted from Alston, "God and Religious Experience," 67.

38 C. B. Martin, *Religious Belief* (Ithaca, NY: Cornell University Press, 1959), 70.

39 Ibid., 87.

40 Ibid., 87–88 (italics in the original).

41 Others who insist both that certifiability by independent checks is necessary and that they are not sufficiently available in the case of religious experience include Antony Flew, *God and Philosophy* (London: Hutchinson, 1966); Paul Schmidt, *Religious Knowledge* (Glencoe, IL: The Free Press, 1961); and, Ronald Hepburn, *Christianity and Paradox: Critical Studies in Twentieth-Century Theology* (London: C.A. Watts & Co., Ltd, 1958), 37.

42 Alston, "Religious Experience and Religious Belief," 299.

43 See Alston, *Perceiving God*, 209–22. See also Wainwright, *Mysticism*, 82–102, for a list of six tests employed by Christian theists seeking to distinguish between veridical and nonveridical of-God experiences; and Caroline Franks Davis, *The Evidential Force of Religious Experience* (Oxford: Clarendon Press, 1989), 71–7.

44 George I. Mavrodes, *Belief in God: A Study in the Epistemology of Religion* (New York: Random House, 1970), 79. See also Wainwright, *Mysticism*, 93–96.

45 Alston, *Perceiving God*, 36, 49, and Alston, "Religious Experience and Religious Belief," 299.

46 For a recent example, see Peter Byrne, "Perceiving God and Realism," *Philo* 3.2, available on the internet as of 12 April 2002, at www.philoonline.org/library/byrne-_3_2.htm.

47 William L. Rowe, *Philosophy of Religion: An Introduction*, 3rd edn (Belmont, CA: Wadsworth, 2001), 61.

48 Rowe, *Philosophy of Religion*, 61.

49 See Mavrodes, *Belief in God*, 76.

50 Michael Martin, "The Principle of Credulity and Religious Experience," *Religious Studies* 22 (1986), 79–93; and Michael Martin, *Atheism: A Philosphical Justification* (Philadelphia, PA: Temple University Press, 1990).

51 See Swinburne, *The Existence of God*, 254–55.

52 See Jerome I. Gellman, *Experience of God and the Rationality of Theistic Belief* (Ithaca, NY: Cornell University Press, 1997).

53 For my own response to the problem of evil, see my *Evil and the Evidence for God* (Philadelphia, PA: Temple University Press, 1993).

54 Draper, "God and Perceptual Evidence," 157–58.

55 Ibid., 158–9.

56 Ibid., 159.

57 Some of these difficulties arise quite apart from the context of testimonial evidence we are considering. But it is here, perhaps, that difficulties of this sort are most disconcerting.

58 I think, for example, of the various naturalist accounts of mind-body phenomena.

59 For a fuller treatment of the challenge of religious diversity, see Davis, *The Evidential Force of Religious Experience*, Ch. 7, and Wainwright, *Mysticism*, 107–10.

60 These examples are culled from a catalog of pathologies discussed in Davis, *The Evidential Force of Religious Experience*, 195–223.

61 For detailed discussions of reductionist strategies for dealing with religious experience, see Davis, *The Evidential Force of Religious Experience*, Ch. 8; Gellman, *Experience of God and the Rationality of Theistic Belief*, Ch. 5; Jerome Gellman, *Mystical Experience of God: A Philosophical Inquiry* (Aldershot, UK: Ashgate, 2001), Chs 4 and 5; and Keith E. Yandell, *The Epistemology of Religious Experience* (Cambridge, UK: Cambridge University Press, 1993), Chs 6 and 7. For a helpful general discussion of the proper way to study the phenomenon of religion, see Roger Trigg, *Rationality and Religion* (Oxford: Basil Blackwell, 1998), Ch. 2.

62 Perhaps the most notable proponent of this strategy is Wayne Proudfoot. See his "Explaining Religious Experience" in R. Douglass Geivett and Brendan Sweetman, *Contemporary Perspectives on Religious Epistemology*.

63 For examples of Christian philosophers for whom experience of God was an important contribution to their conversion to belief in God, see several autobiographical essays in Kelly Clark (ed.) *Philosophers Who Believe: The Spiritual Journeys of 11 Leading Thinkers* (Downers Grove, IL: InterVarsity Press, 1993); and Thomas V. Morris, *God and the Philosophers: The Reconciliation of Faith and Reason* (New York, NY: Oxford University Press, 1994). Examples of converts among intellectuals throughout history and across the disciplines further support the point being made.

64 For more on this, see Chapter 3 by Paul Moser. For more discussion of the role of background beliefs in the interpretation of religious experience, see Davis, *The Evidential Force of Religious Experience*, Ch. 6, and Wainwright, *Mysticism*, 1981, 18–33.

65 For more on these matters, see R. Douglas Geivett, "A Pascalian Rejoinder to the Presumption of Atheism," in *God Matters: An Anthology*, Christopher Bernard and Raymond Martin (eds) (Longman, 2002); Caroline Franks Davis, "The Devotional Experiment," *Religious Studies* 22 (1986), 15–28; and, H. H. Price, *Belief* (London: George Allen & Unwin, 1969), lectures 9 and 10.

66 See Laurence BonJour, *In Defense of Pure Reason* (Cambridge: Cambridge University Press, 1998).

67 See C. E. Raven, *Natural Religion and Christian Theology*, Vol. 2 (Cambridge, UK: Cambridge University Press, 1953), 47; St Teresa of Avila, *The Complete Works of Saint Teresa of Jesus*, Vol. 1, *Life*, E. Allison Peers (trans. and ed.) (London: Sheed & Ward, 1946), 326; and Davis, *The Evidential Force of Religious Experience*, 77–82. For a valiant and compelling attempt to articulate the nature of the I–Thou encounter, see Martin Buber, *I and Thou*, Walter Kaufmann (trans. and ed.) (New York: Charles Scribner's, 1970).

68 *The Gospel of John* (6:68).

10

THE ARGUMENT FROM
CONSCIOUSNESS

J. P. Moreland

Consciousness is among the most mystifying features of the cosmos. Geoffrey Madell opines that "the emergence of consciousness, then is a mystery, and one to which materialism signally fails to provide an answer."[1] Naturalist Colin McGinn claims that its arrival borders on sheer magic because there seems to be no naturalistic explanation for it: "How can mere matter originate consciousness? How did evolution convert the water of biological tissue into the wine of consciousness? Consciousness seems like a radical novelty in the universe, not prefigured by the after-effects of the Big Bang; so how did it contrive to spring into being from what preceded it?"[2] Finally, naturalist William Lyons argues that "[physicalism] seem[s] to be in tune with the scientific materialism of the twentieth century because it [is] a harmonic of the general theme that all there is in the universe is matter and energy and motion and that humans are a product of the evolution of species just as much as buffaloes and beavers are. Evolution is a seamless garment with no holes wherein souls might be inserted from above."[3]

Lyons's reference to souls being "inserted from above" appears to be a veiled reference to the explanatory power of theism for consciousness. Some argue that, although finite mental entities may be inexplicable on a naturalist worldview, they may be explained by theism, thereby furnishing evidence for God's existence. In this chapter, I shall defend this argument from consciousness (hereafter, AC) by describing two relevant issues in scientific theory acceptance, presenting a summary of AC, characterizing naturalism and showing why mental entities are recalcitrant facts for naturalists, and evaluating three explanations of consciousness that serve as rivals for AC.

Preliminary points

Two preliminaries are important. First, for two reasons I shall assume that theism and naturalism are the only worldviews relevant to the chapter: these are, indeed, the only live options for many who debate this topic; in any case, other worldviews (e.g. Buddhism) are far from univocal in their commitment to the reality of consciousness or of the cosmos itself. Second,

I shall assume a commonsense understanding of mental states such as sensations, thoughts, beliefs, desires, volitions and the selves that have them. So understood, mental states are in no sense physical since they possess *five* features not owned by physical states:

- there is a raw qualitative feel or a "what it is like" to have a mental state such as a pain;
- at least many mental states have intentionality – *ofness* or *aboutness* – directed towards an object;
- mental states are inner, private, and immediate to the subject having them;
- they require a subjective ontology – namely, mental states are necessarily owned by the first-person sentient subjects who have them;
- mental states fail to have crucial features (e.g. spatial extension, location) that characterize physical states and, in general, cannot be described using physical language.

Space considerations prevent me from arguing for these claims, but this is not necessary for present purposes, since many (but not all) critics of AC assume with it advocates a dualist construal of consciousness.[4]

Two issues in scientific theory acceptance

Although theism and naturalism are broad worldviews and not scientific theories, two issues that inform the adjudication between rival scientific theories are relevant to AC. First, there is the issue of whether some phenomenon should be taken as *basic*, for which only a description and not an explanation is required, or as something to be explained in terms of *more basic* phenomena. For example, attempts to explain uniform inertial motion are disallowed in Newtonian mechanics because such motion is basic on this view, but an Aristotelian would have to explain how or why a particular body exhibited uniform inertial motion. Thus, what is basic to one theory may be derivative in another.

Issue two is the *naturalness* of a postulated entity in light of the overall theory of which it is a part. The types of entities postulated, along with the sorts of properties they possess and the relations they enter should be at home with other entities in the theory. Some entity (particular thing, process, property, or relation) e is natural for a theory T just in case either e is a central, core entity of T or e bears a relevant similarity to central, core entities in e's category within T. If e is in a category such as substance, force, property, event, relation, or cause, e should bear a relevant similarity to other entities of T in that category.

This is a formal definition and the material content given to it will depend on the theory in question. Moreover, given rivals R and S, the postulation of e in R is ad hoc and question-begging against advocates of S if e bears a relevant similarity to the appropriate entities in S, and in this sense is "at home" in S, but fails to bear this relevant similarity to the appropriate entities in R.[5]

The issue of naturalness is relevant to theory assessment between rivals in that it provides a criterion for advocates of a theory to claim that their rivals have begged the question against them or adjusted their theory in an inappropriate, ad hoc way. And though this need not be the case, naturalness can be related to basicality in this way: naturalness can provide a means of deciding the relative merits of accepting theory R, which depicts phenomenon e as basic, vs. embracing S, which takes e to be explainable in more basic terms. If e is natural in S but not in R, it will be difficult for advocates of R to justify the bald assertion that e is basic in R and that all proponents of R need to do is describe e and correlate it with other phenomena in R as opposed to explaining e. Such a claim by advocates of R will be even more problematic if S provides an explanation for e.[6]

The argument from consciousness

AC may be expressed in inductive or deductive form. As an inductive argument, AC may be construed as claiming that given theism and naturalism as the live options fixed by our background beliefs, theism provides a better explanation of consciousness than naturalism and, thus receives some confirmation from the existence of consciousness.

AC may also be expressed in deductive form. Here is one deductive version of AC:

1   Genuinely nonphysical mental states exist.
2   There is an explanation for the existence of mental states.
3   Personal explanation is different from natural scientific explanation.
4   The explanation for the existence of mental states is either a personal or natural scientific explanation.
5   The explanation is not a natural scientific one.
6   Therefore, the explanation is a personal one.
7   If the explanation is personal, then it is theistic.
8   Therefore, the explanation is theistic.

Theists such as Robert Adams[7] and Richard Swinburne[8] have advanced a slightly different version of AC which focuses on mental/physical correlations and not merely on the existence of mental states. Either way, AC may be construed as a deductive argument.

Premises 2, 4, and 5 are the ones most likely to come under attack. We are granting premise 1 for the sake of argument.[9]

Premise 3 turns on the fact that personal explanation differs from event causal covering law explanations employed in natural science. Associated with *event* causation is a covering law model of explanation according to which some event (the *explanandum*) is explained by giving a correct deductive or inductive argument for that event. Such an argument contains two features in its *explanans*: a (universal or statistical) law of nature *and* initial causal conditions.

By contrast, a *personal* explanation (divine or otherwise) of some basic result R brought about intentionally by person P where this bringing about of R is a basic action A will cite the intention I of P that R occur and the basic power B that P exercised to bring about R. P, I, and B provide a personal explanation of R: agent P brought about R by exercising power B in order to realize intention I as an irreducibly teleological goal.

To illustrate, suppose we are trying to explain why Wesson simply moved his finger (R). We could explain this by saying that Wesson (P) performed an act of endeavoring to move his finger (A) in that he exercised his ability to move (or will to move) his finger (B) intending to move the finger (I). If Wesson's moving his finger was an expression of an intent to move a finger to fire a gun to kill Smith, then we can explain the non-basic results (the firing of the gun and the killing of Smith) by saying that Wesson (P) performed an act of killing Smith (I_3) by endeavoring to move his finger (A) intentionally (I_1) by exercising his power to do so (B), intending thereby to fire the gun (I_2) in order to kill Smith. An explanation of the results of a non-basic action (like going to the store to get bread) will include a description of an action plan. A personal explanation does not consist in offering a mechanism, but rather, in correctly citing the relevant person, his intentions, the basic power exercised, and in some cases, offering a description of the relevant action plan.[10]

Advocates of AC employ the difference between these two modes of explanation to justify premise 2. Briefly, the argument is that given a defense of premises 4 and 5, there is no natural scientific explanation of mental entities. Since both modes of explanation are *ones people use all the time*, there is no reason to take mental entities as brute facts and there is precedent for proffering a personal explanation for them.

Premise 7 seems fairly uncontroversial. To be sure, Humean style arguments about the type and number of deities involved could be raised at this point, but these issues would be intramural theistic problems of small comfort to naturalists.[11] That is, if the explanation for finite conscious minds is supernatural, then naturalism is false. Premise 4 will be examined in conjunction with two alternatives to AC that reject it: Colin McGinn's position and panpsychism.

That leaves premise 5. At least four reasons have been offered for why there is no natural scientific explanation for the existence of mental states (or their regular correlation with physical states):

a   *The uniformity of nature.* Prior to the emergence of consciousness, the universe contained nothing but aggregates of particles/waves standing in fields of forces relative to each other. The story of the development of the cosmos is told in terms of the rearrangement of micro-parts into increasingly complex structures according to natural law. On a naturalist depiction of matter, it is brute mechanical, physical stuff. The emergence of consciousness seems to be a case of getting something from nothing. In general, physico-chemical reactions do not generate consciousness, not even one little bit, but they do in the brain, yet brains seem similar to other parts of organisms or bodies (e.g. both are collections of cells totally describable in physical terms). How can like causes produce radically different effects? The appearance of mind is utterly unpredictable and inexplicable. This radical discontinuity seems like an inhomogeneous rupture in the natural world. Similarly, physical states have spatial extension and location, but mental states seem to lack spatial features. Space and consciousness sit oddly together. How did spatially arranged matter conspire to produce nonspatial mental states? From a naturalist point of view, this seems utterly inexplicable.

b   *Contingency of the mind-body correlation.* The regular correlation between types of mental states and physical states seems radically contingent. Why do pains instead of itches, thoughts or feelings of love get correlated with specific brain states? No amount of knowledge of the brain state will help to answer this question. For the naturalist, the regularity of mind-body correlations must be taken as contingent brute facts. But these facts are inexplicable from a naturalistic standpoint, and they are radically *sui generis* compared with all other entities in the naturalist ontology. Thus, it begs the question simply to announce that mental states and their regular correlations with certain brain states is a natural fact. As naturalist Terence Horgan acknowledges, "in any metaphysical framework that deserves labels like 'materialism', 'naturalism', or 'physicalism', supervenient facts must be explainable rather than being *sui generis*."[12] Since, on most depictions, the theistic God possesses libertarian freedom, God is free to act or refrain from acting in various ways. Thus, the fact that the existence of consciousness and its precise correlation with matter is contingent fits well with a theistic personal explanation that takes God's creative action to have been a contingent one. God may be a necessary being, but God's choice to create conscious beings and to correlate certain types of mental states with certain types of physical states were contingent choices, and this fits nicely with the phenomena themselves.

c   *Epiphenomenalism and causal closure.* Most naturalists believe that their worldview requires that all entities whatever are either physical or depend on the physical for their existence and behavior. One implication of this belief is commitment to the causal closure of the physical.

On this principle, when one is tracing the causal antecedents of any physical event, one will never have to leave the level of the physical. Physical effects have only physical causes. Rejection of the causal closure principle would imply a rejection of the possibility of a complete and comprehensive physical theory of all physical phenomena – something that no naturalist should reject. Thus, if mental phenomena are genuinely nonphysical, then they must be epiphenomena – effects caused by the physical that do not themselves have causal powers. But epiphenomenalism is false. Mental causation seems undeniable and, thus, for the naturalist the mental can be allowed to have causal powers only if it is in some way or another identified with the physical. The admission of epiphenomenal nonphysical mental entities may be taken as a refutation of naturalism. As naturalist D. M. Armstrong admits:

> I suppose that if the principles involved [in analyzing the single all-embracing spatio-temporal system which is reality] were completely different from the current principles of physics, in particular if they involved appeal to mental entities, such as purposes, we might then count the analysis as a falsification of Naturalism.[13]

d   *The inadequacy of evolutionary explanations.* Naturalists are committed to the view that, in principle, evolutionary explanations can be proffered for the appearance of all organisms and their parts. It is not hard to see how an evolutionary account could be given for new and increasingly complex physical structures that constitute different organisms. However, organisms are black boxes as far as evolution is concerned. As long as an organism, when receiving certain inputs, generates the correct behavioral outputs under the demands of fighting, fleeing, reproducing, and feeding, the organism will survive. What goes on inside the organism is irrelevant and only becomes significant for the processes of evolution when an output is produced. Strictly speaking, it is the output, not what caused it, that bears on the struggle for reproductive advantage. Moreover, the functions that organisms carry out consciously *could just as well have been done unconsciously.* Thus, both the sheer existence of conscious states and the precise mental content that constitutes them are outside the pale of evolutionary explanation. As Howard E. Gruber explains:

> the idea of either a Planful or an Intervening Providence taking part in the day-to-day operations of the universe was, in effect, a competing theory [to Darwin's version of evolution]. If one believed that there was a God who had originally designed the world exactly as it has come to be, the theory of evolution through natural selection could be seen as superfluous. Likewise, if one believed in a God

who intervened from time to time to create some of the organisms, organs, or functions found in the living world, Darwin's theory could be seen as superfluous. Any introduction of intelligent planning or decision-making reduces natural selection from the position of a necessary and universal principle to a mere possibility.[14]

We have looked at four reasons why many scholars, including many naturalists, hold that naturalism requires the rejection of consciousness construed along dualist lines. Speaking of the conjunction of naturalism and evolution, naturalist Paul Churchland asserts:

> The important point about the standard evolutionary story is that the human species and all of its features are the wholly physical outcome of a purely physical process . . . . If this is the correct account of our origins, then there seems neither need, nor room, to fit any nonphysical substances or properties into our theoretical account of ourselves. We are creatures of matter. And we should learn to live with that fact.[15]

The naturalistic worldview

At this point, it may be wise to look briefly at the nature of naturalism as a worldview to gain further insight into why consciousness is such a problem for naturalists. Naturalism usually includes:

- different aspects of a naturalist epistemic attitude (for example, a rejection of so-called "first philosophy" along with an acceptance of either weak or strong scientism);[16]
- a Grand Story which amounts to an etiological account of how all entities whatsoever have come to be told in terms of an event causal story described in natural scientific terms with a central role given to the atomic theory of matter and evolutionary biology;
- a general ontology in which the only entities allowed are those that bear a relevant similarity to those thought to characterize a completed form of physics.

For most naturalists, the ordering of these three ingredients is important. Frequently, the naturalist epistemic attitude serves as justification for the naturalist etiology, which, in turn, helps to justify the naturalist's ontological commitment. Moreover, naturalism seems to require a coherence among the postulates of these three different areas of the naturalistic turn. For example, there should be a coherence among third-person scientific ways of knowing; a physical, evolutionary account of how our sensory and cognitive processes came to be; and an ontological analysis of those processes themselves. Any entities that are taken to exist should bear a relevant similarity to entities that characterize our best physical theories; their coming-to-be should be intelligible in light of the naturalist causal story; and they should be knowable by scientific means.

For our purposes, it is important to say a bit more about naturalist ontological commitments. A good place to start is with what Frank Jackson calls the location problem.[17] According to Jackson, given that naturalists are committed to a fairly widely accepted physical story about how things came to be and what they are, the location problem is the task of locating or finding a place for some entity (for example, semantic contents, mind, agency) in that story. As an illustration, Jackson shows how the solidity of macro-objects can be located within a naturalist worldview. If solidity is taken as impenetrability, then given the lattice structure of atoms composing, say, a table and chair, it becomes obvious why they cannot penetrate each other. Given the naturalist micro-story, the macro-world could not have been different: the table could not penetrate the chair. Location is necessitation.

There are three constraints for developing a naturalist ontology and locating entities within it:

- Entities should conform to the naturalist epistemology.
- Entities should conform to the naturalist Grand Story.
- Entities should bear a relevant similarity to those found in chemistry and physics or be shown to depend necessarily on entities in chemistry and physics.

Regarding the naturalist epistemology, all entities should be knowable by third-person scientific means. Regarding the Grand Story, one should be able to show how any entity had to appear in light of the naturalist event causal story, according to which the history of the cosmos amounts to a series of events governed by natural law in which micro-parts come together to form various aggregates with increasingly complex physical structures. The four arguments listed above (pp. 208–9), in one way or other, claim that consciousness cannot be located in the naturalist ontology under the relevant constraints.

Given theism and naturalism as rivals, theists who employ the argument from consciousness seek to capitalize on the naturalistic failure to come to terms with consciousness by offering a rival explanation for its appearance. That failure is why most prominent naturalists (e.g. John Bishop, Daniel Dennett, D. M. Armstrong, Paul Churchland, David Papineau, and Jaegwon Kim) reject premise 1 of AC ("Genuinely nonphysical mental states exist") and either eliminate or, in one way or another, identify conscious states with physical ones.[18]

Unfortunately for naturalists, consciousness has stubbornly resisted treatment in physical terms. Consciousness has been recalcitrant for naturalists and premise 1 is hard to dismiss. Aware of this problem, various alternatives to theism and AC have been provided which accept premise 1. In this section, we shall look at the main options.

Alternatives to AC

John Searle's biological naturalism

John Searle has developed a naturalistic account of consciousness that would, if successful, provide justification for rejecting premise 5 of AC.[19] According to Searle, for 50 years philosophy of mind has been dominated by scientific naturalists who have advanced different versions of strict physicalism because it was seen as a crucial implication of taking the naturalistic turn. For these naturalists, if one abandons strict physicalism, one has rejected a scientific naturalist approach to the mind-body problem and opened oneself up to the intrusion of religious concepts and arguments about the mental.

By contrast, Searle's own solution to the mind-body problem is biological naturalism: although mental states are exactly what dualists describe them to be, nevertheless, they are merely emergent biological states and processes that causally supervene upon a suitably structured, functioning brain. Brain processes cause mental processes, which are not ontologically reducible to the former. Consciousness is just an ordinary (i.e. physical) feature of the brain and, as such, is merely an ordinary feature of the natural world.

Given that he characterizes consciousness as dualists do, why does Searle claim that there are no deep metaphysical implications that follow from biological naturalism? More specifically, why is it that biological naturalism does not represent a rejection of scientific naturalism which, in turn, opens the door for religious concepts about and explanations for the mental? Searle's answer to this question is developed in three steps.

In Step 1, he cites several examples of emergence (liquidity, solidity, features of digestion) that he takes to be unproblematic for naturalists and claims that emergent consciousness is analogous to the unproblematic cases.

In Step 2, he formulates two reasons why consciousness is not a problem for naturalists. (i) The emergence of consciousness is not a problem if we stop trying to picture or image consciousness. (ii) In standard cases (heat, color), an ontological reduction (e.g. identifying a specific color with a wavelength) is based on a causal reduction (e.g. claiming that a specific color is caused by a wavelength) because our pragmatic interests are in reality, not appearance.

In these cases we can distinguish the *appearance* of heat and color from the *reality*, place the former in consciousness, leave the latter in the objective world, and go on to define the phenomenon itself in terms of its causes. We can do this because our interests are in the reality and not the appearance.

The ontological reduction of heat to its causes leaves the appearance of heat the same. Regarding consciousness, we are interested in the appearances, and thus the irreducibility of consciousness is merely due to pragmatic considerations, not to some deep metaphysical problem.

In Step 3, Searle claims that an adequate scientific explanation of the emergence of consciousness consists in a detailed, lawlike set of correlations between mental and physical state tokens. Part of his justification for this is that some explanations in science do not exhibit the type of necessity that explains why certain things must happen (e.g. macro-impenetrability) given that other things have obtained (e.g. micro-structure). Searle cites as an example the inverse square law, which is an explanatory account of gravity that does not show why bodies have to have gravitational attraction.

Several things may be said in response to Searle's position. Regarding Steps 1 and 2, his cases of emergence (rigidity, fluidity) are not good analogies to consciousness, for the former are *easy* to locate in the naturalist epistemology and ontology but the latter are *not*. Given a widely accepted physicalist description of atoms, molecules, lattice structure, and the like, the rigidity or fluidity of macro-objects follows necessarily. But there is no clear necessary connection between any physical state and any mental state. For example, given a specific brain state normally "associated" with the mental state of being appeared to redly, inverted qualia worlds (worlds with that physical state but radically different mental states "associated" with it), zombie worlds (worlds with that physical state and no mental states at all), and disembodied worlds (worlds with beings possessing mental states with no physical entities at all) are still metaphysically possible. It is easy to locate solidity in a naturalist framework but the same cannot be said for consciousness. This is why there has been turmoil for naturalists in philosophy of mind but not in the philosophy of solidity. Searle's emergent entities follow necessarily given the naturalist Grand Story, but consciousness does not.

Further, the emergence of genuinely new properties in macro-objects that are not part of the micro-world (e.g. heat construed as warmth, color construed commonsensically as a quality) presents problems for naturalists in the same way that consciousness does and, historically, that is why they were placed in consciousness. Contrary to Searle, they were not so placed because of the pragmatics of our interests. For example, historically, the problem was that if so-called secondary qualities were kept in the mind-independent world, there was no explanation for why they emerged on the occasion of a mere rearrangement in micro-parts exhaustively characterized in terms of primary qualities.

It is this straightforward ontological problem, not the pragmatics of reduction or the attempt to image consciousness, that presents difficulties for naturalism: how do you get secondary qualities or consciousness to come to be by merely rearranging purely physical entities bereft of the emergent features?

Given their existence, why are secondary qualities and conscious states that are regularly correlated with purely physical states similarly bereft?

In fact, the emergence of mental properties is more like the emergence of normative (e.g. moral) properties than the properties of solidity or digestion. Even the atheist J. L. Mackie admitted that the emergence of moral properties provided evidence for a moral argument for God's existence analogous to AC: "Moral properties constitute so odd a cluster of properties and relations that they are most unlikely to have arisen in the ordinary course of events without an all-powerful god to create them."[20]

Regarding Step 3, "explanations" in science that do not express the sort of necessity we have been discussing are better taken as *descriptions*, not *explanations*. For example, the ideal gas equation is a description of the behavior of gases. An explanation of that behavior is provided by the atomic theory of gas. Curiously, Newton himself took the inverse square law to be a mere description of gravity and not an explanation; so Searle's own example counts against him. Further, given theism and AC, along with our earlier discussion of scientific theory acceptance, it is question-begging and ad hoc for Searle to assert that mental entities and mental–physical correlations are basic, since such entities are natural in light of theism but unnatural given philosophical naturalism.

Our current belief that there is no causal necessity to specific mind–brain correlations is not due to our ignorance of how the brain works, but to an understanding of the radical differences between mental and physical entities. As fellow naturalist Jaegwon Kim notes, the correlations are not explanations. They are the very things that need explaining, and, given a proper understanding of the real questions, no naturalistic explanation seems to be forthcoming:

> How could a series of physical events, little particles jostling against one another, electric current rushing to and fro . . . blossom into a conscious experience? . . . Why shouldn't pain and itch be switched around? . . . Why should *any* experience emerge when these neurons fire?[21]

By misconstruing the problem, Searle fails to address the real issue and, weighed against AC, his position is inadequate.

Colin McGinn's agnostic "naturalism"

Naturalist Colin McGinn has offered a different solution.[22] Given the radical difference between mind and matter as it is depicted by current or even an ideal future physics, there is no naturalistic solution that stays within the widely accepted naturalist epistemology and ontology. Darwinian explanations fail as well because they cannot account for why consciousness appeared in the first place. What is needed is a radically different kind of solution to the origin of mind, one that must meet two conditions: (1) it must be a naturalistic solution; and (2) it must depict the emergence of consciousness and its regular correlation with matter as necessary and not contingent facts.

McGinn claims that there must be two kinds of unknowable natural properties that solve the problem. There must be some general properties of matter that enter into the production of consciousness when assembled into a brain. Thus, all matter has the potentiality to underlie consciousness. Further, there must be some natural property of the brain, which he calls C^*, that unleashes these general properties.

The temptation to take the origin of consciousness as a mystery, indeed, a mystery that is best explained theistically, is due to our ignorance of these properties. However, given C^* and the general properties of matter, the unknowable link between mind and matter is ordinary, commonplace, and necessitates the emergence of consciousness. Unfortunately, evolution did not give humans the faculties needed to know these properties and, thus, they are in principle beyond our grasp. We will forever be agnostic about their nature. However, they must be there since there must be some naturalistic explanation of mind, for all other solutions have failed.

McGinn offers two further descriptions of these unknowable yet ordinary properties that link matter and mind: (i) they are not sense perceptible; and (ii) since matter is spatial and mind nonspatial, they are either in some sense pre-spatial or are spatial in a way that is itself unknowable to our faculties. In this way, these unknowable properties contain at least the potentiality for both ordinary spatial features of matter and the nonspatial features of consciousness as judged by our usual concept of space.

In sum, the mind–matter link is an unknowable mystery due to our cognitive limitations resulting from our evolution. And since the link is quite ordinary, we should not be puzzled by the origin of mind, and no theistic explanation is required.

Does McGinn's solution succeed? For at least three reasons, it must be judged a failure. First, given McGinn's agnosticism about the properties that link mind and matter, how can McGinn confidently assert some of their features? How does he know that they are non-sensory, pre-spatial, or spatial in an unknowable way? How does he know that some of these properties underlie all matter? Indeed, what possible justification can he give for their reality? The only one he proffers is that we must provide a naturalistic solution, and all ordinary naturalistic ones either deny consciousness or fail to solve the problem. But given the presence of AC, McGinn's claims are simply question-begging. Indeed, his agnosticism seems to be a convenient way of hiding behind naturalism and avoiding a theistic explanation. Given that theism enjoys a positive degree of justification prior to the problem of consciousness (see other chapters in this volume), he should avail himself of the explanatory resources of theism.

Second, it is not clear that his solution is a version of naturalism, except in name only. In contrast to other entities in the naturalist ontology, McGinn's linking properties cannot be known by employment of the naturalist epistemology, nor are they relevantly similar to the rest of the naturalist ontology. Thus, it becomes vacuous to call these properties "naturalistic." McGinn's own speculations strike one as ad hoc in light of the inadequacies of naturalistic explanations. In fact, McGinn's solution is actually closer to an agnostic form of panpsychism (see below) than to naturalism. Given AC, McGinn's solution is an ad hoc readjustment of naturalism.

Third, McGinn does not solve the problem of consciousness; he merely relocates it. Rather than having two radically different entities, he offer us unknowable properties with two radically different aspects, e.g. his links contain the potentiality for ordinary spatiality and nonspatiality, for ordinary materiality and mentality. Moreover, these radically different aspects of the linking properties are just as contingently related as they seem to be without a linking intermediary. The contingency comes from the nature of mind and matter as naturalists conceive it. It does not remove the contingency to relocate it as two aspects of an unknowable third intermediary with both.

Panpsychism

Currently, there are few serious advocates of panpsychism, but it has been suggested by Thomas Nagel and David Chalmers.[23] Roughly, panpsychism is the view that all matter has consciousness in it. Since each parcel of matter has its own consciousness, the brain is conscious since it is just a collection of those parcels. Consciousness is pervasive in nature; so its apparent emergence in particular cases is not something that requires special explanation. One can distinguish two forms of panpsychism. According to the strong version, all matter has conscious states in it in the same sense that organisms such as dogs and humans do. According to the weak form, regular matter has consciousness in a degraded, attenuated way in the form of proto-mental states that, under the right circumstances, yield conscious mental states without themselves being conscious.

The strong form is quite implausible. For one thing, regular matter gives no evidence whatever of possessing consciousness. Further, if all matter has consciousness, why does it emerge in special ways only when certain configurations of matter are present? And if conscious human beings are in some sense merely combinations of little bits of consciousness, how are we to account for the unity of consciousness and why do people have no memory of the conscious careers of the bits of matter prior to their combination to form humans? There is no answer to these questions and few, if any, hold to strong panpsychism.

What about the weak version? Given the current intellectual climate, a personal theistic or a naturalistic explanation would exhaust at least the live – if not the logical – options. It is widely recognized that weak panpsychism has serious problems in its own right, e.g. explaining what an incipient or proto-mental entity is; how the type of unity that appears to characterize the self could emerge from a mere system of parts standing together in various causal and spatio-temporal relations; and why certain physical conditions are regularly correlated with the actualization of consciousness when the connection between consciousness and those conditions seems to be utterly contingent.[24]

Moreover, panpsychism is arguably less reasonable than theism on other grounds. I cannot pursue this point here, but other chapters in this volume take up other aspects of the case for theism. In light of that case, theism enjoys positive epistemic justification prior to the issue of consciousness, but the same cannot be said for panpsychism.

Also, panpsychism is merely a label for and not an explanation of the phenomena to be explained. As Geoffrey Madell notes, "the sense that the mental and the physical are just inexplicably and gratuitously slapped together is hardly allayed by adopting . . . a pan-psychist . . . view of the mind, for [it does not] have an explanation to offer as to why or how mental properties cohere with physical."[25]

Conclusion

Prominent naturalist Jaegwon Kim has observed that "if a whole system of phenomena that are prima facie not among basic physical phenomena resists physical explanation, and especially if we do not even know where or how to begin, it would be time to reexamine one's physicalist commitments."[26] For Kim, genuinely nonphysical mental entities are the paradigm case of such a system of phenomena. Kim's advice to fellow naturalists is that they must simply admit the irreality of the mental and recognize that naturalism exacts a steep price and cannot be had on the cheap.[27] If feigning anesthesia is the price to be paid to retain naturalism, then the price is too high. Fortunately, the theistic argument from consciousness reminds us that it is a price that does not need to be paid.

Notes

1 Geoffrey Madell, *Mind and Materialism* (Edinburgh: Edinburgh University Press, 1988), 141.
2 Colin McGinn, *The Mysterious Flame* (New York: Basic Books, 1999), 13–14. See G. K. Chesterton's claim that the regular correlation between diverse entities in the world is magic that requires a Magician to explain it. See *Orthodoxy* (John Lane Company, 1908; reprinted, San Francisco: Ignatius Press, 1950), Ch. 5.

3 William Lyons, "Introduction," in *Modern Philosophy of Mind*, William Lyons (ed.) (London: Everyman, 1995), iv. In context, Lyons remark is specifically about the identity thesis, but he clearly intends it to cover physicalism in general. Similarly, alhough he explicitly mentions an entity in the category of individual – the soul – the context of his remark makes clear that he includes mental properties and events among the entities out of step with scientific materialism.

4 For defenses of dualism see William Hasker, *The Emergent Self* (Ithaca, New York: Cornell University Press, 1999); J. P. Moreland, Scott Rae, *Body & Soul: Human Nature and the Crisis in Ethics* (Downers Grove, IL: InterVarsity Press, 2000); Richard Swinburne, *The Evolution of the Soul* (Oxford: Clarendon Press, revised edn, 1997); Charles Taliaferro, *Consciousness and the Mind of God* (Cambridge, UK: Cambridge University Press, 1994).

5 For example, suppose theory S explains phenomena in terms of discrete corpuscles and actions by contact, whereas R uses continuous waves to explain phenomena. If some phenomenon x was best explained in corpuscularian categories, it would be ad hoc and question-begging for advocates of R simply to adjust their entities to take on particle properties in the case of x. Such properties would not bear a relevant similarity to other entities in R and would be more natural and at home in S.

6 For example, suppose that R is Neo-Darwinism and S is a version of punctuated equilibrium theory. Simply for the purpose of illustration, suppose further that R depicts evolutionary transitions from one species to another to involve running through a series of incrementally different transitional forms except for some specific transition e which is taken as a basic phenomenon, say, the discrete jump from amphibians to reptiles. S pictures evolutionary transitions in general, including e, as evolutionary jumps to be explained in certain ways that constitute S. In this case, given the presence of S, it would be hard for advocates of R to claim that their treatment of e is adequate against S. Phenomenon e clearly counts in favor of S over against R.

7 See Robert Adams, "Flavors, Colors, and God," reprinted in *Contemporary Perspectives on Religious Epistemology*, R. Douglas Geivett and Brendan Sweetman (eds) (New York: Oxford University Press, 1992), 225–40.

8 See Richard Swinburne, *The Existence of God* (Oxford: Clarendon, 1979), Ch. 9; *The Evolution of the Soul*, 183–96; *Is there a God?* (Oxford: Oxford University Press, 1996), 69–94; "The Origin of Consciousness," in *Cosmic Beginnings and Human Ends*, Clifford N. Matthews and Roy Abraham Varghese (eds) (Chicago: Open Court, 1995), 355–78.

9 I have already listed five features of mental properties and events that justify the claim that they are not physical properties and events. It is beyond the scope of this chapter to defend the irreducible mental nature of mental properties and events against strict physicalist alternatives. Our focus is the more limited one of comparing AC with rivals that accept premise 1. For a defense of a dualist construal of consciousness, see the sources in note 4.

10 For a more detailed defense of this premise, see J. P. Moreland, "Searle's Biological Naturalism and the Argument from Consciousness," *Faith and Philosophy* 15 (January 1998), 68–91.

11 Regarding the *number* of deities, the principle of economy would move us in the direction of one rather than a plurality of deities: why posit multiple entities when one entity will suffice? Regarding the *type* of deity, arguments for God's existence are – or should be – generally modest in what they attempt to show (e.g. the design argument is not intended to show that God is *all*-knowing nor supremely good or the Uncaused Cause). Furthermore, bringing the various arguments together furnishes us with a much less pared-down understanding of

this God, which is sufficient to render us personally accountable to this Being, and does not in any way conflict with the revealed God of Judeo-Christian theism.

12 Terence Horgan, "Nonreductive Materialism and the Explanatory Autonomy of Psychology," in *Naturalism*, Steven J. Wagner and Richard Warner (eds) (Notre Dame, IN: University of Notre Dame Press, 1993), 313–14.

13 D. M. Armstrong, "Naturalism: Materialism and First Philosophy," *Philosophia* 8 (1978), 262.

14 Howard E. Gruber, *Darwin on Man: A Psychological Study of Scientific Creativity* (Chicago: University of Chicago Press, 1974), 211.

15 Paul Churchland, *Matter and Consciousness* (Cambridge, MA: MIT Press, 1984), 21.

16 The *strong* version of scientism maintains that science provides us with the *sole* basis of knowledge; the *weaker* version claims that science furnishes us with the *most certain* basis of knowledge, even if other disciplines provide more weakly justifed beliefs or knowledge.

17 Frank Jackson, *From Metaphysics to Ethics* (Oxford: Clarendon Press, 1998), 1–5.

18 John Bishop, *Natural Agency* (Cambridge, UK: Cambridge University Press, 1989); Daniel Dennett, *Elbow Room* (Cambridge, MA: MIT Press, 1984); idem, D. M. Armstrong, *Universals and Scientific Realism*, Vol. I: *Nominalism & Realism* (Cambridge, UK: Cambridge University Press, 1978), 126–35; "Naturalism: Materialism and First Philosophy," *Philosophia* 8 (1978), 261–76; Churchland, *Matter and Consciousness*; David Papineau, *Philosophical Naturalism* (Oxford: Blackwell Publishers, 1993); Jaegwon Kim, *Mind in a Physical World* (Cambridge, MA: MIT Press, 1998); idem, *Philosophy of Mind* (Boulder, CO: Westview Press, 1996).

19 See John Searle, *The Rediscovery of the Mind* (Cambridge, MA: MIT Press, 1992).

20 J. L. Mackie, *The Miracle of Theism* (Oxford: Clarendon Press, 1982), 115.

21 Kim, *Philosophy of Mind*, 8.

22 McGinn, *The Mysterious Flame*.

23 Thomas Nagel, *The View From Nowhere* (New York: Oxford University Prerss, 1986), 49–53. David J. Chalmers, *The Conscious Mind* (New York: Oxford University Press, 1996), 293–301.

24 For a critique of panpsychism in the process of defending AC, see Stephen R. L. Clark, *From Athens to Jerusalem* (Oxford: Clarendon, 1984), 121–57.

25 Madell, *Mind and Materialism*, 3.

26 Kim, *Mind in a Physical World*, 96.

27 Ibid., Ch. 4, especially pages 118–20. Partially to justify the price paid for naturalism, Kim raises the dualist problem of causal interaction. It is doubtful, Kim argues, that "an immaterial substance, with no material characteristics and totally outside physical space, could causally influence, and be influenced by, the motions of material bodies that are strictly governed by physical law." See *Philosophy of Mind*, p. 4. Several things may be briefly said in response to this alleged problem. First, the so-called problem of causal interaction is not one that arises solely within the province of interacting substances or particulars. To the degree that it is a problem, it applies in virtue of the disparate nature of mental–physical entities, whether their category be that of substance, property, event, or relation. Second, this objection assumes that if we do not know *how* A causes B, then it is not reasonable to believe *that* A causes B, especially if A and B are different. But this assumption is not a good one. We often know that one thing causes another without having any idea of how causation takes

place, even when the two items are different. Even if one is not a theist, it is not inconceivable to believe it possible for God, if He exists, to create the world or to act in that world, even though God and the material universe are very different. A magnetic field can move a tack, gravity can act on a planet millions of miles away, protons exert a repulsive force on each other, and so forth. In these examples, we know that one thing can causally interact with another thing, even though we may have no idea how such interaction takes place. Further, in each case the cause would seem to have a different nature from the effect – forces and fields vs. solid, spatially located, particle-like entities. In the case of mind and body, we are constantly aware of causation between them. Episodes in the body or brain (being stuck with a pin, having a head injury) can cause things in the soul (a feeling of pain, loss of memory), and the soul can cause things to happen in the body (worry can cause ulcers; one can freely and intentionally raise one's arm). We have such overwhelming evidence that causal interaction takes place that there is no sufficient reason to doubt it. Third, it may even be that a "how" question regarding the interaction between mind and body cannot even arise. A question about how A causally interacts with B is a request for an intervening mechanism between A and B that can be described. One can ask how turning the key starts a car because there is an intermediate electrical system between the key and the car's running engine that is the means by which turning the key causes the engine to start. The "how" question is a request to describe that intermediate mechanism. But the interaction between mind and body may be, and most likely is, direct and immediate. There is no intervening mechanism and, thus, a "how" question describing that mechanism does not even arise. For a fuller defense of dualist interaction, see Keith Yandell, "A Defense of Dualism," *Faith and Philosophy* 12 (October 1995), 551–3.

11

THEISM, MIRACLES, AND THE MODERN MIND

Francis J. Beckwith

Introduction

Believers in the orthodox traditions of Christianity and Judaism maintain that God has performed miracles in history. Some non-theistic philosophers, however, have challenged in several ways the rationality of belief in the miraculous. This chapter will cover the arguments of Michael Martin and Antony Flew, two philosophers who have presented perhaps the most trenchant criticisms of belief in the miraculous, although the style and type of argument they present has its roots in the thought of eighteenth-century Scottish philosopher David Hume.[1] In this chapter, I will assess two of their arguments: (1) the argument from the impossibility of eliminating naturalism, and (2) the argument from a miracle's improbability.

Prior to addressing these two arguments, it is important that we define what theists generally mean by the miraculous: *a divine intervention that occurs contrary to the regular course of nature within a significant historical–religious context*. Let me clarify the three elements of this definition. First, a divine intervention refers to the action of a non-natural agent, e.g. a god, an angel. Second, that which occurs contrary to the regular course of nature refers to an event that overrides scientific laws, that cannot reasonably be accounted for either by the actions of natural agents (e.g. human beings, extraterrestrials) or by nature left to its own devices. Third, a significant historical–religious context refers to the purpose attached to the miracle because of when, where, and to (or for) whom the miracle occurs. That is, the historical–religious context of the event typically grounds the event's existential and teleological significance, and may serve as the basis by which to infer agent causation.

Consider a non-miraculous, non-religious example from the field of US Constitutional law, the case of *Yick Wo* v. *Hopkins*.[2] It concerned an ordinance in San Francisco that required the approval of the Board of Supervisors for operating a laundry in a wooden building. (A permit was not necessary if the laundry was in a brick or stone building). According to Gerald Gunther and Kathleen Sullivan, "[t]he Board granted permits to operate laundries in wooden buildings to all but one of the non-Chinese applicants, but to none of about 200 Chinese applicants. A Chinese alien who had operated a laundry for many years was refused a permit and imprisoned for illegally operating a laundry."[3] Even though the ordinance was facially neutral, its administration was discriminatory, for, according to the Court, intentional discrimination was the best explanation of the pattern of the Board's granting of permits. Consequently, the historical context, and not chance or necessity, could account for what appeared to be the agent-directed action found in the pattern of excluding every single Chinese applicant.

One can easily extend this type of analysis to an alleged miracle. Suppose that a purported miracle-worker, C, claims that he is God's chosen and that he will perform a miracle, R, a resurrection of himself from the dead at time t in order to confirm God's approval of his mission. Furthermore, C is vehemently opposed by the religious elite who insist that he is *not* God's chosen. Moreover, every person who has ever made claims similar or identical to C's has remained dead. Therefore, if C performs R at t, it seems entirely reasonable to believe that C is God's chosen one. Given its law-violating nature, its uniqueness (i.e. nobody who has made similar claims, except C, has ever performed R), C's claim that God is responsible for R, its existential[4] and teleological significance (i.e. C performed R at the particular time he predicted, t, and not at any other time), and the religious context of the event (in a certain historical and religious milieu, C performed R when his claims about himself hinged on the actuality of R occurring at time t), it becomes apparent that a particular message is being communicated through this event – namely, C *is God's chosen one*. In light of the converging nature of the facts, and the inference to a rational non-natural agent made eminently plausible by them, any appeals to coincidence or chance in this case become entirely ad hoc, a sort of naturalism-of-the-gaps.[5] It seems, then, that theists are within their epistemic rights in believing that such a contranomic event was brought about by a non-natural agent capable of suspending or overriding the laws of nature with a specific design, or purpose, in mind.

In this chapter I will be arguing against the conclusion that I believe Flew's and Martin's anti-miracle arguments are employed to support: believers in miracles are never within their epistemic rights in believing that a miraculous event has occurred. I will not be arguing that opponents of miracles are irrational if they disbelieve in the miraculous. That is another topic for another essay. In addition, I will not specifically address the question of whether a miracle can be attributed to a non-natural agent (i.e. a god). However, it seems to me, as Del Ratzsch points out, "if legitimately established, genuine *contranomicity* would constitute evidence of supernatural agent activity," and if such contranomicity would be combined with "mind correlativity or value," such a combination would "relocate the case into the area of design."[6] That is to say, if it is reasonable to believe that a genuine overriding of scientific law has occurred in a way that seems mind-correlative (i.e. its timing and historical–religious context make it difficult

222

to not see purpose or design in the event), then it is not clear why believers in miracles are not within their epistemic rights in believing that a legitimate contranomic event attributed to a supernatural agent has indeed occurred. Imagine if on the evening of September 11, 2001 – only hours after Muslim terrorists had crashed hijacked American airliners into the World Trade Center buildings and the Pentagon – the stars were arrayed in such a way that there appeared to everyone who looked up in the night sky the following unmistakable sentence: "Allah does not approve. All the hijackers are now burning in hell. Osama Bin Laden will be joining them soon enough." It seems clear to me that a believer in miracles would be within her epistemic rights in maintaining that such an event was indeed miraculous.

The argument from the impossibility of eliminating naturalism

Naturalism is the view that the entire universe and all the entities in it can be accounted for by strictly material processes without resorting to any designer, Creator or non-material entity as an explanation for either any aspect of the natural universe or the universe as a whole. That is, an exhaustive naturalistic description of the universe is in principle possible and no non-natural or supernatural entity is required in order to explain it. The reason for this is that the material universe is all there is.

Michael Martin makes a distinction between two different types of nature, $nature_b$ and $nature_n$. The former refers to "nature in its broadest sense" and "includes all entities (supernatural and natural) and their activities (determined by supernatural and natural powers) . . . . The only things not included in $nature_b$ are entities that are incapable of any causal interaction, such as numbers or sets." On the other hand, $nature_n$, or "nature in a narrow sense, . . . consists of the realm of human and subhuman entities and their powers." Thus, $nature_n$ is included in $nature_b$ but if "there are no supernatural beings or entities or powers," the two are identical.[7] For the sake of simplicity, however, I will employ the term naturalism for the view that $nature_n$ is identical to $nature_b$.

According to Martin, the defender of miracles must rule out the possibility that there will be future naturalistic explanations for miracles. Short of that, he is not justified in calling the event miraculous.[8] Writes Martin:

> The believer in miracles must give reasons to suppose that the event E, the alleged miracle, will probably not be explained by any unknown scientific laws that govern $nature_n$. Since presumably not all laws that govern $nature_n$ have been discovered, this seems difficult to do so. The advocates of the miracle hypothesis must argue the probability that E will not be explained by future science, utilizing heretofore undiscovered laws that govern $nature_n$. Given the scientific progress of the last two centuries, such a prediction seems rash and unjustified.[9]

But this argument is significantly flawed. In order to grasp properly its weakness, we must juxtapose two insightful points Martin makes in the same book in which he makes the following argument.

1   He claims that certain reports of miracles, "if accepted as accurate, cannot be explained in either commonsense or scientific terms. For example, there appears no ordinary way of explaining how Jesus raised the dead or turned water into wine . . . ."[10]
2   In reply to C. S. Lewis's famous defense of miracles, Martin writes that "the solution to this problem [of rejecting miracles a priori] is not to decide on naturalism or supernaturalism beforehand. Rather, one must attempt to reject the a priori arguments and instead base one's position on inductive considerations."[11]

If we extract from the juxtaposition of these two points what seem to be a coherent principle of investigation and a particular judgment of apparent natural inexplicability, Martin is saying that one ought not reject miracles a priori but assess them and their evidence on inductive considerations, and that certain miracle reports that are nearly 2000 years old defy any commonsense or scientific (i.e. naturalistic) explanation. Now, armed with this principle and this judgment, we are prepared to dismantle Martin's argument.

Let us first reflect on the data that one should consider when making one's inductive assessment of miracle-claims in terms of Martin's argument. Let me suggest the following considerations, which seem to be suggested by Martin as well:

Consideration 1:   "[T]he scientific progress over the last two centuries" and the nature of that progress.
Consideration 2:   The law-violating nature of the alleged miracle(s).
Consideration 3:   The nature of the miracle-claims that were later discovered to have natural explanations.

Concerning consideration 1, it is not clear why Martin believes that "scientific progress over the last two centuries" makes it more difficult for the defender of miracles to rule out the possibility that there will be future naturalistic explanations for miracles. For the nature of scientific progress over the past 200 years seems to point in the opposite direction. No particular theory, discovery, invention, etc., developed over the past 200 years casts doubt upon, or calls into question, the miraculous nature of any of the primary miracle-claims of the Christian tradition if the accounts of them are accepted as historically accurate. Thus, consideration 2, as part of our inductive assessment, is particularly relevant here, especially if we restrict our analysis to some of the miracle-claims mentioned by Martin earlier in this essay, resuscitations or Jesus' resurrection (in particular) and Jesus' turning water into wine. For these alleged miracles are more than presently inexplicable, they are prima facie not the sorts of events about which one could speculatively develop and propose ad hoc hypotheses on the basis of which one can reasonably imagine they would be explicable under a future, yet undiscovered, scientific law. They are, as Martin implicitly admits by his singling them out, qualitatively unlike a cure for cancer or a vaccine for AIDS, each of which one could imagine will occur in the future.

Now to consideration 3: the nature of the miracle-claims that later were discovered to have natural explanations. Martin offers a parade of examples:

Example 1: "[D]iseases that were considered mysterious are now under-stood without appeal to supernatural powers. Furthermore, progress seems extremely likely . . . ."[12]

Example 2: "Many so-called miracle cures of the past may one day be understood, as some have already been, in terms of psychoso-matic medicine."[13]

Example 3: We have good reason "to believe that some contemporary faith healers use fraud and deceit to make it seem that they have paranormal powers and are getting miracle cures."[14]

Example 4: There have been numerous cases of fraud and deceit in the study of parapsychology, an area of research that attempts to verify the existence of paranormal or supernatural powers.[15]

Consequently, in light of "the progress of science, the history of decep-tion and fraud connected with miracles and the paranormal, and the history of gullibility and misperceptions . . . ,"[16] Martin asks how the believer in miracles can rule out that the alleged miracles in biblical times were natural events resulting from natural causes rather than the overriding of scientific law resulting from supernatural causes. For example, people during biblical times did not have the benefit of the laboratory conditions and other precau-tions that are employed today to rule out fraud and deceit in parapsycho-logical research. Moreover, if contemporary people can be duped by faith healers and other flim-flam men, why not the followers of Jesus?

Martin raises important concerns in Consideration 3, but they are not adequate to prove his point, if he is making a case against miracles based on "inductive considerations." For each of the categories in examples 1–4 concerns apparently anomalous events later discovered to be naturally ex-plicable, but clearly the sorts of events that one could anticipate would be naturally explicable if other facts were to turn up. But the case for miracles, at least within the Christian tradition, is not based exclusively on events of that sort – isolated and transparent parlor tricks divorced from an identifi-able historical–religious context – but, rather, events that are qualitatively

225

different (e.g. resurrections, radically instantaneous healings, changing the chemical composition of liquid, all at the command of an agent) and for that reason should be assessed on the merits of the case *for them* rather than trying to find an analogy in the present in order to dismiss them without assessing that evidence. We will call these miracles *ultramiracles* in order to distinguish them from Examples 1–4. Remember that Martin claims that "[t]he advocates of the miracle hypothesis must argue the probability that E will not be explained by future science, utilizing heretofore undiscovered laws that govern nature."[17]

However, if we are to take seriously Martin's call for an *inductive*, rather than a deductive, assessment of the case for miracles, it is not clear why the believer in miracles is not within his epistemic rights in believing that these ultramiracles are legitimate miracles without any serious chance of being overturned by a future, yet undiscovered, scientific law. That is, given the naturalist's long-standing *incapacity* to provide natural explanations for ultramiracles, or even to suggest possible scientific laws or ad hoc hypotheses that could account for such events, Martin's appeal to a possible future in which they might be naturally explicable, and to compare ultramiracles to other miraculous claims that are qualitatively different (e.g. Examples 1–4), is simply to beg the question in favor of naturalism, to engage in a type of naturalism-of-the-gaps. Consequently, Martin's case is not sufficient to prove the conclusion against which I am arguing – namely, that the believer in miracles is not within her epistemic rights in believing that a miraculous event has occurred.

Of course, it is always *possible* that even ultramiracles could be scientifically explicable. But that bare logical *possibility* cannot possibly be adequate warrant for the skeptic to say that the believer in miracles is somehow not within his epistemic rights in believing that an event is truly miraculous. Consider the following example. Suppose that someone tells you that he has just seen his father, who has been dead for the past 2 days, alive and walking the streets of New York City. You would be perfectly reasonable if you thought like David Hume: "When someone tells me, that he saw a dead man restored to life, I immediately consider with myself, whether this person should either deceive or be deceived, or that the fact, which he relates should really have happened."[18] That is, per Hume and Martin, it is more probable that deception is involved than that the testimony is accurate. After all, you would have no problem believing the testimony if this man's father had never died. This is because your expectations and judgments hinge on your previous experience: dead men do not come back to life. However, let us say that there are a number of reliable witnesses who corroborate this testimony. Furthermore, the mortuary, which had embalmed the body, reports that it is missing, and police confirm that the fingerprints of the living man (which they found on a glass he had touched) correspond perfectly to the fingerprints of the dead man. Moreover, the man in question was very religious and had prayed prior to his death, asking God to resuscitate him in order to demonstrate to his atheistic relatives the truth of his religious convictions. In light of this example, it becomes apparent that Martin's (and Hume's) weighing of probabilities is highly artificial, not to mention woefully inadequate. In this case it is not a weighing of *a* probability, L (a law of nature), against *a* probability, T (a testimony claiming to have witnessed an overriding of L), but a weighing of L against what John Henry Cardinal Newman called a "convergence of independent probabilities,"[19] T, T_1, T_2, ... T_n (i.e. diverse and reliable testimonies, fingerprints, circumstantial evidence such as the missing embalmed body and his prayer to God, etc.).

As some have pointed out, just as our formulations of scientific law are based on certain regularities, our standards of evaluating testimony and evidence are based on certain regularities as well (e.g. "witnesses in such-and-such a situation are more apt to tell the truth.").[20] Because these standards do not have the same individual probative strength as a scientific law, a single piece – or even several strands – of testimonial evidence in most cases is insufficient to warrant our belief that an overriding of natural law has occurred (although a single testimony is usually sufficient to warrant belief in most everyday situations, such as "Honey, get the checkbook; the paper boy is here"). However, if the testimonial evidence is multiplied and reinforced by circumstantial considerations (as in the above example), and the explanation of the event as an overriding of scientific law connects the data in a simple and coherent fashion (just as we expect a scientific law to do),[21] and a denial of the event's occurrence becomes an ad hoc naturalism-of-the-gaps,[22] I do not see why the believer is not within her epistemic rights in believing that a miracle has occurred (based on a convergence of independent probabilities). This approach retains a healthy skepticism by taking into consideration the improbability of a miraculous event, but it has the added virtue of resisting a dogmatic skepticism – a naturalism-of-the-gaps – by taking seriously the possibility that one may have evidence for a miracle.

The argument from a miracle's improbability

In this section we shall critically assess an argument put forth by Flew, which he cogently summarizes:

> The basic propositions are: first, that the present relics of the past cannot be interpreted as historical evidence at all, unless we presume that the fundamental regularities obtained then as still obtain today; second, that in trying as best he may to determine what actually happened the historian must employ his present knowledge of what is probable or improbable, possible or impossible; and third, since *miracle* has to be

defined in terms of practical impossibility the application of these criteria precludes proof of a miracle.[23]

This can be better understood if put in the following form:

a   The believer in miracles investigates history in order to demonstrate the
     actuality of miracles.
b   Only if we assume that the regularities of the present were also true of
     the past can we hope to know anything historically.
c   In order to gain knowledge of the past, the critical historian must em-
     ploy his present knowledge of what is possible/impossible, probable/
     improbable.
d   A miracle is a highly improbable, practically impossible, event.
e   Therefore, miracles cannot be known historically.[24]

Since there is no doubt that historical investigation is necessary if one
is to show that a past miracle has occurred, the believer in miracles does
not dispute Flew's first premise. Consequently, since "without criteria there
can be no discrimination . . . and hence no history worthy of the name,"[25]
Flew's second and third premises should be left unchallenged. Concerning
his fourth premise, the believer in miracles does not disagree with Flew that
a miracle is a highly improbable or practically impossible event, although
it seems that Flew does not adequately distinguish between logical impossibility and physical impossibility (see below). Nevertheless, if an event
was not highly improbable in terms of physical law, it would not merit the
appellation of a miracle (i.e. miraculous event, M, is physically impossible
given scientific law, L, and thus could occur if and only if an agent capable
of acting contranomically brings M about).

It is evident, therefore, that the believer in miracles finds his opposition
to Flew's argument in its conclusion. That is to say, although his premises
are for the most part correct, Flew's conclusion does not *follow* from his
premises.

Flew seems to be subtly begging the question in favor of naturalism by
assuming that because criteria by which we judge the historicity of events
are based on certain regularities, thus the *object* of our historical investigation cannot be an event that overrides (or "violates") scientific regularities
(or laws). Clearly, Flew is correct when he asserts that "the critical historian,
confronted with some story of a miracle, will usually dismiss it out of hand
. . . ."[26] If Flew means by this that antecedent improbability of a miracle
makes any claim of its occurrence highly doubtful prior to the examination of the evidence, the believer in miracles does not disagree. However, as
noted above, because the criteria by which we evaluate testimony and other
evidence are also based on certain regularities (laws, so to speak), there does
not seem to be any way to rule out in principle the possibility that one may
be justified in believing that a particular miracle has occurred, based on the

convergence of distinct pieces of evidence and independent probabilities – when taken collectively. In this sense, regularity, because it is the basis and not the object of historical investigation, can yield a singularly irregular result.

Flew, nevertheless, maintains that the antecedent improbability of a miraculous event can never be outweighed by the evidence without admitting that the event was not miraculous:

> Our sole ground for characterizing the reported occurrence as miraculous is at the same time a sufficient reason for calling it physically impossible. Contrawise, if ever we became able to say that some account of the ostensibly miraculous was indeed veridical, we can say it only because we know that the occurrences reported were not miraculous at all.[27]

This is crude question-begging. For the believer in miracles, although defining a miracle as an overriding of scientific (or natural) law and hence physically impossible,[28] argues that a miracle is *not* logically impossible. That is, one can imagine, without any logical contradiction, the actuality of such events as resurrections, levitations, instantaneous healings, etc. Unlike logically impossible objects, such as married bachelors and square circles, the actuality of physically impossible events cannot be ruled out a priori.

Consequently, if an apparently contranomic event cannot be subsumed under either a current or new scientific law, it is perfectly coherent to say that in this instance the *physically impossible* is *historically actual*. Although there is considerable debate among philosophers of science as to the precise technical meaning of the term "scientific law," R. S. Walters writes that there is "agreement that a minimum necessary condition of a scientific statement proposed as lawlike is that it be a universal generalization."[29] Richard Swinburne writes that a scientific law is that which describes "what happens in a *regular* and *predictable* way."[30] Contrary to Flew's appeal "the regularities of the present," a scientific law does *not* only describe what happens in the actual course of events, but explains the actual course of events in terms of hypothetical universal (i.e. regular and predictable) formulas (e.g. if X has a certain mass, it will have a certain weight within earth's gravitational field). For if a scientific law were merely descriptive of what regularly occurs and nothing more, the term "scientific law" would be devoid of any cognitive content, similar to such assertions as "whatever will be will be." After all, scientists do revise laws because of recurring anomalies, but rarely if ever on the basis of a *single* non-recurring anomaly that is nevertheless recognized as an anomaly (which obviously does not *count against* the law violated). Hence, scientific laws must be cognitively significant assertions in which a true counter-factual is possible, whether it is an apparent violation (a singular non-analogous anomaly) or a recurring anomaly. For this reason, if "what happens is entirely irregular and unpredictable [i.e. an over-riding or 'violation'], its occurrence is not something describable by natural laws." In other words, to "say that a certain such formula is a law is to say that in general its predictions are true and that any exceptions to its operations cannot be accounted for by another formula which could be taken as a law . . . ."[31] Furthermore, a contranomic miracle is non-analogous; that is, because a miracle is the result of an agent, it should not be confused with an anomaly that occurs regularly under like natural circumstances, which is usually a good indication that the law in question should be revised, re-placed, or altered in some fashion so as to account for this anomaly under these particular circumstances.[32]

Consider the following example. Suppose we have a natural law, L, which states that when a human being has been dead for 24 hours it is phys-ically impossible for this corpse to become alive again. L is so intertwined with what has been well-established by years of anatomical, physiological, and biological study that no one doubts its status as a law; it is regular and predictable (i.e. "Given these circumstances, X, P will remain dead."). Every epitaph testifies to this reality.

Suppose that on one Sunday afternoon a certain human being, H (let us say, a recognized holy person), who has been dead for more than 24 hours, gets up and walks out of the coroner's office. If this counter-instance to L, E, cannot be subsumed under either L or a more comprehensive law and it is a non-recurring anomaly, I do not see why it is incorrect to call E a legitimate overriding of natural law without saying that L is no longer a natural law.

However, let us imagine that prior to his death H had ingested a yet-undiscovered serum that has a natural chemical ability to restore life. Furthermore, let us say that the scientists studying this serum conclude that its chemical composition fits perfectly with what we already know about life, but yet takes us far beyond this knowledge. We are then forced to alter (although not completely change) some of our natural laws in light of this new discovery confirmed by repeatable experiment and observation (i.e. "If P drinks the serum prior to his death, P will resurrect within 36 hours of his death."): L will be replaced by a new law, L_2.

But if E cannot be subsumed under a more comprehensive law such as L_2, and we have good reason to believe that E would not occur again under sim-ilar circumstances (that is, it is a non-repeatable counter-instance), it seems coherent to say that E is an overriding of natural law without saying that E counts against L. For E to be able to count against L, it would have to be an anomaly repeatable under similar circumstances (such as in the case of the serum and L_2). "For these latter reasons it seems not unnatural to describe E as a non-repeatable counter-instance to a law of nature L . . . ."[33]

Among the many examples Flew employs to defend his argument from critical history is one employed by Hume "in the footnote to the section 'Of

Miracles' where he quotes with approval the reasoning of the famous physician De Sylva in the case of Mademoiselle Thibaut":[34]

> It was impossible that she could have been so ill as was "proved" by witnesses, because it was impossible that she could, in so short a time, have recovered so perfectly as he found her.[35]

In employing this example, Flew is asserting that the miraculous nature of the event (i.e. its physical impossibility) makes it *always* unreasonable to believe that this event has occurred. However, since physical impossibility cannot be equated with logical impossibility, to discount all evidence for an event on this basis alone is to reason a priori, and hence to beg the question.

For it is certainly conceivable that an antecedently improbable event may have enough evidence in its favor to make belief in its occurrence eminently reasonable (see the above examples). This is because, as I noted above, the criteria and standards by which one weighs evidence are themselves based on regularities and probabilities. Therefore, if a number of independent probabilities converge upon an alleged miraculous event, and alternative naturalistic explanations are inadequate to explain the data (i.e. they are hopelessly ad hoc and question-begging), then it becomes entirely reasonable to believe that this miraculous event has occurred. In light of this, let us revise Flew's example by giving it a contemporary setting, a greater number of details, and placing a letter before each important fact.

Suppose that on a particular Sunday, (a) Mrs. D, a person stricken with rheumatoid arthritis for the past 10 years, is (b) instantaneously healed of her ailment, which entails the complete reconstruction of her bone structure and complete elimination of her disease, not merely the temporary disappearance of the symptoms. (c) This occurred moments after she was prayed for, in the name of a certain god, by her pastor in the presence of the entire congregation (about 500 people). (d) Given the nature of her illness and the inability for a scientific law to make the healing explicable, this occurrence is an overriding of natural law. (e) There is no doubt that Mrs. D had been diagnosed properly. She had been receiving therapy for 10 years for a condition that had been getting progressively worse: (f) she had lost the ability to walk properly, make a fist, or even grasp her husband's hand. In fact, at times, (g) she could get along only with a wheelchair. (h) And the sleepless nights of body-wrenching pain were almost unbearable. At time t, prior to the prayer, Mrs. D was experiencing all of the above symptoms. At time t_2, moments after the prayer, all of Mrs. D's symptoms had disappeared without a trace of the disease ever having been present. (i) The total elimination of the disease and the reconstruction of her entire bone structure was later confirmed the following week by a half-dozen awe-struck physicians who had treated Mrs. D scores of times for her arthritic condition.

To claim that this did not happen because miracles are physically impossible is to miss the whole point of historical investigation, and to engage in special pleading for one sort of regularity (scientific laws) while ignoring another (the basis of evidential criteria). Although the antecedent probability of the event occurring is very low, the pieces of evidence (a . . . i), which are themselves based on certain regularities (e.g. "It is highly improbable that a half-dozen doctors in this case could all be wrong in their diagnosis"), are independent probabilities that converge upon the event and make it reasonable to believe that this event has occurred. Furthermore, the radical law-overriding nature of the healing and the timing of the event make appeals to coincidence and psychosomatics appear question-begging and ad hoc.

In conclusion, regularity must be the *basis* – not the *object* – of historical investigation, unless one is willing to reduce one's historical investigations to a question-begging enterprise, and hence eliminate true but irregular events from the outset.

Conclusion

In this chapter we did not specifically offer positive arguments for miracle-claims within the Jewish–Christian worldview (e.g. the miracles of Jesus or Jesus' bodily resurrection);[36] if historically and evidentially supportable, these miracles would obviously offer support for God's existence. But we have taken the more modest approach of showing the rationality of belief in the miraculous. In doing so, we critically assessed two of the strongest contemporary arguments employed to support the view that the believer in miracles is never within her epistemic rights in believing that a miraculous event has occurred. At the end of the day, both arguments fail – not because they do not raise legitimate epistemological questions about belief in the miraculous, but rather, because they presuppose a rigid, unbending philosophical commitment to naturalism, a commitment so strong that there seems nothing in principle that may, or can, falsify it. This is, ironically, a charge often leveled against the theist by the naturalist.[37] Perhaps non-falsifiability – like original sin – is more equitably distributed than we had supposed.

Notes

1 See Francis J. Beckwith, *David Hume's Argument Against Miracles: A Critical Analysis* (Lanham, MD: University Press of America, 1989), and Francis J. Beckwith, "Hume's Evidential/Testimonial Epistemology, Probability, and Miracles," *Logos* 12 (1991), 87–104.
2 118 U.S. 356 (1886)

3 Gerald Gunther and Kathleen M. Sullivan, *Constitutional Law*, 13th edn (Westbury, NY: Foundation Press, 1997), 750.

4 It seems prima facie correct to say that it is a qualitatively greater accomplishment, because of its obvious existential significance and human impossibility, to conquer death than to perform another type of miracle. Hume, ironically, admits to the significance of death in his *Natural History of Religion*: "We are placed in this world, as in a great theatre, where the true springs and causes of every event are entirely concealed from us; nor have we either sufficient wisdom to foresee, or power to prevent those ills, with which we are continually threatened. *We hang in perpetual suspense between life and death, health and sickness, plenty and want; which are distributed among the human species by secret and unknown causes, whose operation is oft unexpected, and always unaccountable*" [David Hume, *Natural History of Religion*, in *Hume Selections*, Charles W. Hendel Jr (ed.) (New York: Charles Scribner's Sons, 1927), 262, emphasis added].

Albert Camus' sobering and profound observation serves as a gentle reminder of the Grim Reaper's deftly approaching shadow: "Likewise and during every day of an unillustrious life, time carries us. But a moment always comes when we have to carry it. We live in the future: 'tomorrow,' 'later on,' 'when you have made your way,' 'you will understand when you are old enough.' Such irrelevancies are wonderful, for, after all, it's a matter of dying. Yet a day comes when a man notices that he is thirty. Thus he asserts his youth. But simultaneously he situates himself in relation to time. He takes his place in it. He admits that he stands at a point on a curve that he acknowledges having to travel to its end. He belongs to time, and by the horror that seizes him, he recognizes his worst enemy. Tomorrow, he was longing for tomorrow, whereas everything in him ought to reject it. That revolt of the flesh is the absurd" [Albert Camus, "Absurd Walls," in *Phenomenology and Existentialism*, Robert C. Solomon (ed.) (Lanham, MD: University Press of America, 1980), 490–1].

5 This is why, for example, it strikes me as counter-intuitive Michael Martin's claim that it is not to clear to him that a so-called miraculous event is more likely uncaused than the result of a non-natural rational agent. [See Michael Martin, *Atheism: A Philosophical Justification* (Philadelphia: Temple University Press, 1990), 199]. Perhaps Martin would have a point if one were talking about an apparently random anomaly rather than an event that it does not seem obviously irrational to attribute to an agent due to its timing, historical–religious context, apparent message conveyed, and contranomic nature.

6 Del Ratzsch, *Nature, Design, and Science: The Status of Design in Natural Science* (Albany, NY: State University of New York Press, 2001), 75.

7 Martin, *Atheism*, 190.

8 Ibid., 196.

9 Ibid. (note in original omitted).

10 Ibid., 188.

11 Ibid., 193.

12 Ibid., 196.

13 Ibid., 196.

14 Ibid., 197.

15 Ibid.

16 Ibid., 199.

17 Ibid., 196.

18 David Hume, *An Enquiry Concerning Human Understanding*, 3rd edn, text revised and notes, P. H. Nidditch; intro. and analytic index, L. A. Selby-Bigge (Oxford: Clarendon, 1975 [1777]), 116.

19 As cited in John Warwick Montgomery, "Science, Theology, and the Miraculous," in his *Faith Founded on Fact* (New York: Thomas Nelson, 1978), 55.

20 See Richard Swinburne, *The Concept of Miracle* (New York: Macmillan, 1970), 41–8. Montgomery explains that legal reasoning is an example of evidential criteria based on certain regularities: "The lawyer endeavors to reduce societal conflicts by arbitrating conflicting truth-claims. Inherent to the practice of the law is an effort to resolve conflicts over legal responsibilities, and such conflicts invariably turn on questions of fact. To establish a 'cause of action' the plaintiff's complaint must allege a legal right which the defendant was duty-bound to recognize, and which he violated; at the trial evidentiary facts must be marshaled in support of the plaintiff's allegations, and the defendant will need to provide factual evidence in his behalf to counter the plaintiff's prima facie case against him. To this end, legal science, as an outgrowth of millennia of court decisions, developed meticulous criteria for distinguishing factual truth from error" [John Warwick Montgomery, *The Law Above the Law* (Minneapolis: Dimension Books, 1975), 86].

21 Richard Swinburne writes: "So then a claim that a formula L is a law of nature and a claim that testimony or trace of a certain type is reliable are established basically the same way–by showing that certain formulae connect observed data in a simple coherent way." (Swinburne, *The Concept of Miracle*, 43).
   That simplicity and coherence are values which the scientist seeks in formulating any law or theory is defended by more than a few philosophers of science. For example, see W. H. Newton-Smith, *The Rationality of Science* (London: Routledge & Kegan Paul, 1981), 226–32; Karl R. Popper, 'Truth, Rationality, and the Growth of Knowledge,' in his *Conjectures and Refutations* (New York: Harper & Row, 1963), 240–1; and Hilary Putnam, *Reason, Truth, and History* (New York: Cambridge University Press, 1981), 35.

22 A fine example of naturalism-of-the-gaps is Hume's defense of maintaining naturalism in his fictional account of Queen Elizabeth's resurrection. See Hume, *Enquiry*, 128.

23 Antony Flew, *God: A Critical Enquiry*, 2nd edn (LaSalle, IL: Open Court, 1984), 140.

24 Flew's argument may also be viewed as maintaining that the theist is inconsistent. Stephen T. Davis summarizes this interpretation in the following way: "People who offer historical or probabilistic arguments in favor of the occurrence of a given purported miracle, Flew says, themselves presuppose the very regularity of nature and reliability of nature's laws that they argue against. Their position is accordingly inconsistent" [Stephen T. Davis, "Is it Possible to Know that Jesus was Raised from the Dead?" *Faith and Philosophy*, 2 (April 1984), 149. Montgomery interprets Flew's argument in a similar way. See his "Science," 52–8].

25 Flew, *God: A Critical Enquiry*, p. 140.

26 Antony Flew, "Miracles," in *Encyclopedia of Philosophy*, Vol. 5, Paul Edwards (ed.) (New York: Macmillan/Free Press, 1967), 352.

27 Ibid.

28 R. F. Holland uses the term "conceptually impossible." He writes that "miracle, though it cannot only be this, must at least be something the occurrence of which can be categorized at one and the same time as empirically certain and conceptually impossible" [R. F. Holland, "The Miraculous," in *Logical Analysis and Contemporary Theism*, (ed.) John Donnelly (New York: Fordham University Press, 1972), 232].

29 R. S. Walters, "Laws of Science and Lawlike Statements," in *Encyclopedia of Philosophy*, Vol. 4, Paul Edwards (ed.) (New York: Macmillan & The Free Press, 1967), 410–11. See John Hospers, "Law," in *Introductory Readings in the Philosophy of Science*, E. D. Klemke, Robert Hollinger, and A. David Kline (eds) (Buffalo, NY: Prometheus Books, 1980), 104–11; Charles E. Hummel, *The Galileo Connection* (Downers Grove, IL: InterVarsity Press, 1986), 180–8; and Ernest Nagel, *The Structure of Science* (New York: Harcourt, Brace, 1961), 75–8.

30 Swinburne, *Concept*, 26 (emphasis mine). This view of scientific law as regular and predictable is echoed by Hummell, Walters, and Patrick Nowell-Smith. Hummel writes: "Since laws are based directly on experimental data, they can be tested at any time. They not only describe present natural phenomena but also precisely predict future results for a given set of conditions. Thus they also provide the basis for technology, the use of science for practical purposes." (Hummel, *Galileo*, 184). Walters asserts: "Suppose it is a law, *s*, that sodium burns when exposed to air. This law . . . can explain why a given piece of sodium burns when exposed to air and can be used to predict that a given piece of sodium will burn when exposed to air." (Walters, "Laws," 412). Patrick Nowell-Smith, whose article is written in opposition to belief in miracles, writes that "a scientific explanation is an hypothesis from which predictions can be made, which can afterwards be verified. It is the essence of such an hypothesis – a 'law' is but a well-confirmed hypothesis – that it should be capable of such predictive expansion." [Patrick Nowell-Smith, "Miracles," in *New Essays in Philosophical Theology*, Antony Flew and Alasdair MacIntyre (eds) (New York: Macmillan, 1955), 249–50].

31 Swinburne, *Concept*, 26, 27–8.

32 Of course, it is possible that an agent is responsible for a recurring anomaly, e.g. Jesus' healing different people over a 3-year period. But this sort of 'recurrence' has more in common with agent-caused events than the sort of recurring anomalies found in the history of science, e.g. Isaac Newton's attributing to God the perturbed orbit of a planet. Nevertheless, even there it is *logically possible* that God is responsible for the planet's perturbed orbit; that is, He, rather than another body's gravitational pull, moves it. However, given what we know about such recurring anomalies, it is more probable that there is an undiscovered object, e.g. a planet whose gravitational pull does in fact move the planet in question.

33 Swinburne, *Concept*, 27.

34 Flew, *God: A Critical Enquiry*, 140. Hume's original citation is found in an additional note to his *Enquiry*, 345.

35 As quoted in Flew, *God: A Critical Enquiry*, 140.

36 See Graham Twelftree, *Jesus the Miracle Worker* (Downers Grove, IL: InterVarsity Press, 1999); R. Douglas Geivett and Gary Habermas (eds) *In Defense of Miracles* (Downers Grove, IL: InterVarsity Press, 1997); William Lane Craig, *Reasonable Faith* (Wheaton, IL: Crossway, 1994). Paul Copan (ed.) *Will the Real Jesus Please Stand Up?* (Grand Rapids, MI: Baker, 1998); Paul Copan and Ronald K. Tacelli (eds) *Jesus' Resurrection: Fact or Figment?* (Downers Grove, IL: InterVarsity Press, 2000).

37 Flew, for example, has written that "it often seems to people who are not religious as if there was no conceivable event or series of events the occurrences of which would be admitted by sophisticated religious people to be sufficient reason for conceding 'there wasn't a God after all' or 'God does not really love us then'." He then poses the question to the theist: "What would have to occur or to have occurred to constitute for you a disproof of the love of, or the existence

of, God?" According to Flew, there does not seem to be any possible evidence that could disprove a believer's belief in God's existence. Hence, this belief is unfalsifiable and dies by a "death by a thousand qualifications . . ." [Antony Flew, 'Theology and Falsification,' in *New Essays in Philosophical Theology*, Antony Flew and Alasdair MacIntyre (eds) (New York: Macmillan, 1955), 98–9, 107]. The believer in miracles can raise the question by paraphrasing Flew: what would have to occur or to have occurred to constitute for you a disproof of naturalism? But it seems that for Martin and Flew there is virtually no event in principle that could falsify naturalism. Thus, they are in precisely in the same position as Flew's obstinate theist.

Part III

POTENTIAL DEFEATERS FOR THEISM

12

THE POSSIBILITY OF GOD

The coherence of theism

Charles Taliaferro

> It is one thing to describe an interview with a gorgon or a
> griffin, a creature who does not exist. It is another thing to
> discover that the rhinoceros does exist and then take pleasure
> in the fact that he looks as if he didn't.
>
> G. K. Chesterton[1]

A form of naturalism according to which reality is through and through
physical is a prominent, working assumption in much contemporary philosophy. From this vantage point, nonphysical objects like souls or immaterial minds, angels and demons, as well as abstract objects like mathematical
properties and sets, all look suspicious. More suspicious still is God who is
traditionally conceived of as a nonphysical reality. This chapter focuses on
the coherence of the idea of God in Jewish, Christian, and Islamic traditions.
Is it coherent to think there is a nonphysical, omniscient, omnipotent, eternal, good, divine reality? Pursuing this question will, in the end, involve assessing the anti-theistic philosophy embedded in contemporary naturalism.

I divide the material into three parts, the first states the case against and
then in favor of the idea that God is an incorporeal, nonphysical reality.
While there are some theists who propose that God is a physical reality
(Hobbes in early modern philosophy, Grace Jantzen today), the vast majority of theists see God as an immaterial being. If the very notion that there
could be a nonphysical, purposive being is incoherent, then subsequent
debates about God's properties – for example, arguments about whether
God can be both omniscient and omnipotent – are of little interest. Part two
looks at the debate over the coherence of the divine attributes, highlighting
current work on omniscience, eternity, and omnipotence. The final section,
"Naturalistic coherence and theistic coherence" places the debate about the
idea of God over against our general philosophical convictions about the
nature of the cosmos.

Divine incorporeality

Contra

The most extensive argument against divine incorporeality is made on the grounds of a radical form of naturalism, one that insists on a physicalist view of the cosmos and the incoherence of anything nonphysical.[2] I characterize this as *radical* to distinguish it from forms of naturalism which allow that it is possible for there to be nonphysical realities, even though we live in an exclusively physical cosmos and there are no immaterial beings. There are many non-radical or moderate naturalists, atheists who believe in a solely material cosmos but who also think that it is possible for there to be a God and other nonphysical realities (Bertrand Russell, Sydney Hook, John Searle, Michael Tooley, J. L. Mackie, K. Parsons, David Lewis, Richard Gale, etc.). In this chapter our concern is with the more ambitious challenge that, if successful, shows theism to be futile from the start.

In philosophy of religion today, there are at least four objections to the coherence of God as an immaterial being: The Problem of Observation, the Problem of Individuation, the Problem of Transcendence, and the Evidential Problem.

The entry for "Supernatural" in the Blackwell *Dictionary of Philosophy* hints at a radical naturalist outlook that sequesters or nudges the idea of a nonphysical deity off the list of live options. This entry raises in a preliminary way what may be called the Problem of Observation.

> **Supernatural** *adj., n.* Supernatural beings exist above or beyond nature, where 'nature' is to be understood in a wide sense, to take in all of space and time and everything existing within that framework, i.e. the whole of the physical universe. It is especially in the context of religious belief that the concept of the supernatural has been used.
>
> If scientists (or non-scientists) discover a new type of wave, a new force, a strange phenomenon in a remote galaxy, the very fact that it was there to be discovered makes it a natural phenomenon which may in due course be described in science textbooks. Supernatural beings run no risk of having their existence disclosed by scientific or everyday observation.[3]

In this schema the immaterial nature of God runs an ever greater risk: a risk not just of being ignored in empirical enquiry but of being exposed as a confused, incoherent idea. It has been argued that the terms employed to describe God in classical theism (God is loving, just, knows about the world, acts purposively) only have meaning when used of observable, embodied beings. We know what it is for humans to love, and to be just, and to act purposively. With God, we are on a more difficult footing. If we take away

240

material bodies, are not we left with Lewis Carroll's charming but nonsensical portrait of a cat who has no body but still has a smile? This objection has been advanced by a range of philosophers, including Gareth Moore, Kai Nielsen, Paul Edwards, Anthony Kenny, and Michael Martin.

In *Believing in God: A Philosophical Essay*, Gareth Moore offers a version of the above objection:

> We say that God is invisible, intangible, etc. These traditional attributes of God have their part to play in theology and in the spiritual life of Christians. Treating the existence of God as a hypothesis makes them look like makeshifts for the purpose of preserving the hypothesis from falsification, as if they said, "God is there all right, as the evidence indicates, but the reason you can't discover him is that he is invisible, etc., not accessible to your senses or detectable by your instruments." But that cast-iron defense of the "hypothesis" only serves to make it idle, a kind of joke, like saying, "There is a green, three-legged, ten-foot tall woman in the middle of the road, only you can't detect her because she is invisible, intangible, etc." And one would still be left with the problem why any phenomena could be understood as evidence for this hypothesis.[4]

If Moore is right, the traditional theistic claims about God as a nonphysical, invisible reality is self-contradictory. Presumably to claim there is something with physical size, extension, and color is implicitly to claim there is something visible at a given location. A thing cannot be visible and invisible in the same respects.

The problem of individuation: Kai Nielsen argues that traditional theism falls apart because of the incompatibility of viewing God as an immaterial individual while at the same time thinking of God as infinite.

> [God] is said to be an infinite, purely spiritual individual transcendent to the world. But verificationist considerations aside, it is contradictory to speak of an "infinite individual" (or, though a little less clearly, of an "infinite person"). Consider just what it means to be an individual. Something could not be an *individual* unless she or it were differentiated from other individuals or things. But something that is infinite cannot (logically cannot) be so differentiated. She or it cannot, being infinite, be an individual distinct from other individuals, for something which is infinite is not bounded, is not, and cannot be, differentiated from other things in the way an individual can be. So "infinite individual" is self-contradictory: the idea does not make sense. "Infinite" and "individual" just do not go together.[5]

Nielsen thereby offers an argument against theism which takes issue with a conflict that is *internal* to theism. The problem is not that theism conflicts with some remote, independent, evident metaphysical principle, but that theism implodes from within. Theism collapses because of its own terms, which cannot stand together. The concept of an immaterial, infinite individual is as incoherent as the concept of a square circle. God is in worse shape than the griffin and goran, which at least *can* exist even if, as it happens, they do not.

Nielsen also presents what may be called the Problem of Transcendence. Nielsen thinks that theism is incoherent because it can make no sense for there to be a being that is "beyond the universe." God, qua nonphysical being who transcends the cosmos, makes no sense.

> What does or could "transcendent to the universe" mean? Perhaps being "beyond the universe"? But how could that be other than just more universe? Alternatively, if you do not want to say that, try – thinking carefully about the sense of "beyond" – to get a handle on "going beyond the universe." Is not language idling here?[6]

Nielsen uses the same term as Moore here: theistic language about God *idles* in the sense that it does not advance a conceivable, coherent state of affairs. In the earlier argument theism is flawed because the content of two of its crucial terms conflict, whereas here there is simply no content to a central theistic claim about God, as an immaterial reality, transcending the cosmos.

The Evidential Problem facing theism follows from the above arguments. If theism's central claim is incoherent, then of course issues of evidence are irrelevant. Moore, in a passage cited earlier (p. 241), suggests that theism would be in a muddle parallel with finding evidence for his three-legged, green and yet invisible person. Nielsen considers an extraordinary case: the stars in heaven spell out "God exists."

> We are no better off with the stars in the heavens spelling out GOD EXISTS than with their spelling out PROCRASTINATION DRINKS MELANCHOLY. We know that something has shaken our world [if "GOD EXISTS" appeared in the heavens], but we know not what; we know – or think we know, how could we tell which it was in such a circumstance? – that we heard a voice coming out of the sky and we know – or again think that we know – that the stars rearranged themselves right before our eyes and on several occasions to spell out GOD EXISTS. But are we wiser by observing this about what "God" refers to or what a pure disembodied spirit transcendent to the universe is or could be? At most we might think that maybe those religious people have something – something we know not what – going for them. But

we also might think it was some kind of big trick or some mass delusion. The point is that we wouldn't know what to think.[7]

Nielsen thinks our apoplectic reaction is due to our struggle to detect any content to the claim "God exists."

Replies

I shall first address the Problem of Observation. Nielsen, Moore, and the other philosophers cited earlier (Edwards, Kenny, Martin) appear to adopt the view that all physical objects are visible or observable in principle. I find this problematic. Perhaps there could be physical things with zero mass (similar to a magnetic field), possessing a location but no observable extension. For the sake of argument, however, I will assume that if something is physical, then it is spatially observable. Even so, the following stronger thesis seems less certain: if and only if something is physical, then it is spatially observable. Opponents of mind-body dualism and other philosophies which recognize nonphysical realities assume too quickly that something nonphysical must be invisible or unobservable.

Consider a dualist understanding of human nature, according to which human persons have material bodies as well as some nonphysical aspects. This nonphysical dimension may be any of the following: consciousness, sensory states, emotions, thoughts and beliefs, desires and intentions. More radical still is the conviction that the person is a substantial, nonphysical, individual subject (a mind or soul) which is causally embodied in a material substance. On either the radical account or the more modest forms of dualism, it makes perfect sense to claim that you can observe someone feeling pain, singing, speaking, expressing compassion, and so on. Presumably, in healthy, functioning human persons, their observable life reflects their interior, psychological, or mental life. Dualism also reserves the possibility that this functioning may break down. Someone's malice may not be observable. Perhaps there is a would-be Iago who never seizes the moment. And yet, under healthy, trustworthy circumstances, dualists would claim that you can observe someone's thinking even if the thinking itself is not metaphysically identical to bodily states and activities.[8]

Let us return to the Blackwell Dictionary entry and Moore's charge of incoherence. Both seem to assume that a nonphysical reality (God) cannot be manifested in visible, observable terms. But why assume this? In the early fifth century Augustine defended the classic incorporeal thesis with an analogy involving our thoughts being expressed in speech. My thinking about you, for example, is not the same thing as my reporting "I am thinking about you." The latter is an overt bodily event, but the thinking is not.

We ought not to be disturbed by the fact that, although he is invisible,

God is reported as having often shown himself in visible form to our ancestors. Just as the uttered sound which makes audible the thought that has its existence in the silence of the understanding, is not the same as that thought, so the visible form in which God – who exists in his invisible substance – became visible was not identical with God himself. For all that, he was seen in that material form, just as the thought is heard in the sound of the voice.[9]

I believe Augustine's example is effective. Just as our speaking to one another makes our ideas audible, so God may audibly and visibly be manifested in material terms. Behavioristic reductions of thought to behavior are highly implausible.

Probably the most famous twentieth-century attempt to collapse (or identify) thinking with physical, behavioral speaking was launched by J. B. Watson. "The behaviorist advances the view that what the psychologists have hitherto called thought is in short nothing but talking to ourselves."[10] "Thinking is merely talking, musculature."[11] To identify my thinking about you, with my saying to myself quietly (*sotto voce*) "I am thinking of you" seems discredited in all of our experience. Thinking is what makes the verbal utterance true, for the *mere utterance alone does not count as thinking*. Just as it appears that there can be thinking without utterances, there can be utterances without thinking. One may easily imagine someone *mindlessly* uttering all kinds of things where there is little, if any, thought. And the behaviorist case seems completely at odds with pre-linguistic thinking beings (children) and any complex intentional interaction. When you thoughtfully walk into a crowded room and take note of who is present and absent, are you making innumerable, quiet motions with your larynx?

There are more sophisticated attempts to identify the mental with the physical than J. B. Watson's larynx account. But none of these, in my view, is able to escape the overwhelmingly plausible conviction that our concepts of thoughts, consciousness, experience, etc., are distinct from our concepts of bodily movement, including our utterances. I am not proposing here that the truth of mind-body dualism is overwhelmingly obvious; I am, rather, making a point about concepts and meaning. An enthusiastic materialist can grant (as many do) that our *concepts* of thinking and of bodily movement are distinct even if thinking turns out to be identical with bodily movement. Both the materialist and dualist can recognize that our concept of someone declaring his intention to marry someone is complex: this involves auditions as well as an (ostensibly) conscious resolution of some kind. When these are in concord, the dualist as well as the materialist may claim to observe the exchange of vows. And both may allow that there can be a rupture when the utterances are made without the conscious resolution.

I believe the theist may allow that our language about God has its primary use in referring to observable cases of ourselves and others knowing, acting, and so on. The critic still needs an argument to the effect that it is *incoherent* or *self-contradictory* to think that something nonphysical knows, acts, and the like. No amount of evidence that we need brains and bodies to know, act, and so on, can secure the thesis that it is *impossible* for there to be a nonphysical being that does these things. Indeed, many atheistic and agnostic philosophers allow that there are nonphysical dimensions to ourselves so that our action and knowledge are not reducible to exclusively material terms (Colin McGinn, Thomas Nagel, Galen Strawson, Ned Block). At the beginning of the twenty-first century the prospects of a "pure" materialism with no mystery continue to be elusive. Bertrand Russell's comment in the 1960s still has purchase today: "I should have found intellectual satisfaction in becoming a [pure] materialist, but on grounds almost identical with those of Descartes . . . I came to the conclusion that consciousness is an undeniable datum, and therefore pure materialism is impossible."[12]

Moore and Nielsen may resist the dualistic tendencies of some contemporary philosophy of mind, and still claim that ordinary language supports their ruling out incorporeal, purposive life. But I suggest instead that even our commonplace concept of *embodiment* welcomes or suggests the thesis that something elusive, perhaps even immaterial, comes to have a bodily, observable reality it may lose. Injuries whereby one loses motor control or sensory awareness are sometimes described in terms of disembodiment.[13] It makes perfect sense in ordinary language to think that at death the person has either perished or gone on to an afterlife, leaving behind a corpse. Perhaps there is no afterlife and death marks the annihilation of persons. Even so, many scientifically literate people believe in an afterlife. Is this belief a contradiction or does it involve a massive misuse of language? I believe that any case for an affirmative answer faces a considerable burden of proof. I am not proposing that ordinary language about our embodiment is always consistent, nor that it always signals a dualist account of the mind-body relation! Still, talk of someone's embodiment in terms of certain functions, powers, and liabilities accommodates the idea that something has become realized or made present which would otherwise be absent. Many materialists concede that dualism is a common, ordinary philosophy of mind (Daniel Dennett, David Lewis, Tomas Nagel, Brian O'Shaughnessy, Richard Rorty, Michael Levin, Donald Davidson, William Lycan). In *The Elusive Mind, The Elusive Self* and elsewhere, H. D. Lewis has argued plausibly that a widespread attraction to dualism has found its way into our ordinary language with talk of embodiment. My point here is that while our commonplace use of language to describe ourselves does not presuppose dualism, it readily welcomes a dualist view according to which we may observe each other's thinking, acting and feelings – albeit these activities are not exclusively physical activities. Ordinary language is not sufficiently materialistic to rule out possible disembodied or immaterial agency.[14]

Let us now consider the Problem of Individuation. Nielsen's case against divine incorporeality rests on what I believe is a confused mischaracterization of theism. Few theists ever refer to God as "infinite" without some qualification or specification of just what is being referred to. "Infinite" means, literally, not finite. Theists have traditionally held that God's existence is without beginning or temporal end. God's power and knowledge are limitless in a respect that I will consider in the next section. God's omnipresence as an immaterial being is traditionally understood in terms of God's creating the cosmos, conserving it in existence, and there being no place where God is unable to act. With respect to each of these divine attributes there are conditions of differention and individuation. To give a banal example of differentiation, the claim that God is omnipotent implies that God is not capable of only moving tea cups. God's omniscience entails God's knowing more than you and me. Being omnipotent and omniscient involve unsurpassably perfect power and knowledge. God's having both attributes entails a personal being (as apposed to a set or process) distinguishable from individuals like you and me. God's omnipresence means God's creativity, power, and knowledge are not circumscribed the way our creativity, power, and knowledge are bounded. So far, there does not appear to be anything garbled or incoherent in theism.

Perhaps Nielsen's argument about *being infinite* and *being an individual* can be re-worked as a problem of nonspatial individuation. We tend to individuate material objects by virtue of their spatial relations. This page and my body are distinct, in part, by virtue of the fact that they occupy distinct spatial regions. Even if we had two things that shared all the same characteristics – Tweedledee and Tweedledum, the identical characters in *Alice in Wonderland* – they would still be distinguishable by their spatial distance. But if we imagine that there is a nonphysical, and thus nonspatial deity, recourse to spatial distance will not provide a principle of individuation.

Reply: we differentiate innumerable things without recourse to spatial relations. The number 7 qua abstract object is not some spatial distance from the concept of justice. The God of traditional theism is also not akin to Tweedledee, who might have a twin sibling. There is the classical Christian teaching of the Trinity but within the Godhead the three persons are distinguishable in terms of internal relations (the Son is said to be *begotten* of the Father, the Holy Spirit, *proceeds* from the Father, and so on). Moreover problems face an account of spatial relations as a principle of individuation. Two events may occupy the same space (my waving my hand and my expressing a greeting) without being the same thing; one could, for example, have one event without the other.

Leaning on a principle of individuation that only allows for spatial demarcation also poses this question: what distinguishes two regions of space? To say that material objects are distinct because of their occupying two distinct regions of space (or having two different spatial relations) invites this question: what makes two regions of space (or two spatial relations) different? The defender of spatial relations will have either to provide some further spatial basis (*this* spatial region occupies a different, more fundamental region than *that* spatial region) and thus risk an implausible regress or to simply claim that, as a basic feature of reality, spatial relations are different. If it comes to positing basic features of reality like that, why not claim that some nonphysical realities – whether we are talking about mathematical objects or God – are simply different? The individuation of nonphysical objects can take place along adequate lines without spatial reference. For example, the number 6 is not omniscient, whereas God is; the number 6 is the successor of 5, whereas God is not. Nonphysical objects are thereby distinguishable through our intentional attitudes (intentional attitudes include thinking, hoping, desiring). To think of the number 6 is distinct from thinking about the concept of a griffin or of God.[15]

Let us now consider the Problem of Transcendence. Nielsen seems to be using the concept of a universe to stand in for something like "everything that is." If we say God is beyond everything that is, well, presumably then God is nothing (or no thing). Perhaps Nielsen accuses theists of this confusion: because they believe God exists and God is different from the universe they must believe God is nothing. But Nielsen's argument seems to rest on a question-begging definition of "universe." Of course any theistic claim that God is "beyond" the universe or cosmos amounts to the traditional claim that God is not identical with this physical, contingent cosmos. God is believed to be omnipresent throughout the cosmos (and thus omnipresent or ubiquitous) but not, for all that, to *be* the cosmos.

The evidential problem: Nielsen's and Moore's claims about evidence are derived from their prior charge of incoherence. Once you are convinced that a nonphysical reality is possible (or you adopt the more modest view that it is not impossible), matters of evidence seem to fall into place. Return to Augustine's analogy of thought and language. Imagine you receive radio signals that are patterned and appear to have a syntax and semantics similar to English. They are generated at a particular point of space but there is no evident external physical source of them. Referring back to Nielsen's and Moore's examples but changing them slightly, imagine you *think* that this message is being sent through the waves: "It is not a good idea to drink if you are prone to procrastination and melancholy, and especially if you are a green, three-legged, ten-foot tall women in the middle of the road." Is this a random assortment of mere sound or does it express the relevant thoughts and bemused feelings about such matters? I see no reason why we cannot use an inference to the best explanation here. Someone is sending out a (not very funny) joke. If you exhaust the explanations for ongoing messages in material, physical terms, why not posit a nonphysical reality responsible for these peculiar jokes?

As for seeing Nielsen's stars spelling out "Procrastination drinks melancholy," I would be inclined to think that there is some kind of purposive agency behind the phenomena, but I would also think that if the one or more agents were trying to communicate in English, their grammar is appalling.[16] Although I seek to accommodate Moore's and Nielsen's "amusing" thought experiments here, in the final part of this paper I question their appropriateness.

The coherence of the divine attributes

> Bricks, for all practical purposes, hardly mind what other things they are put with. Meanings mind intensely – more indeed than any other sort of things.
>
> (I. A. Richards)[17]

Debate over divine attributes has had a long history in Jewish, Christian, and Islamic traditions. I shall highlight only one aspect of the debate: the *flexibility* of the terms involved.

Apart from incorporeality, the divine attributes most often singled out are the following: God's omniscience, omnipotence, goodness, necessity (or aseity), eternity, omnipresence, simplicity, impassibility, and freedom. Debate is typically occasioned by worries about the extensiveness of the attribute or the compatibility of one attribute with the others. *Apropos* divine omniscience, philosophers have debated whether God knows the future. This concerns the extension or scope of divine knowledge. Problems of compatibility arise when one considers whether, if God knows the future, God is still free. To some critics the problem with divine attributes is their compatibility or, in the spirit of I. A. Richard's colorful language, problems arise when the meanings of distinct divine attributes mind intensely when they are assembled into a composite idea of God.

An enormous amount of philosophical work has been dedicated to each of the divine attributes. Even a cursory glance at *Analytic Philosophy of Religion: A Bibliography, 1940–1996*,[18] edited by Robert Wolf, would bring anyone to despair who hopes to make any summary of this work. While more worthy scholars might hesitate, I will use the modest space allotted to offer a proposal of why this literature is so extensive, and why it is so difficult to show theism to be incoherent. I believe the key lies in what may be called the flexibility or elasticity of the metaphysics of theism. This flexibility is due, in part, to theistic convictions about God's perfection or excellence.

Theistic religious tradition often gives center place to God's perfection, or excellence – what may also be called God's greatness or goodness. This has an impact on how the divine attributes are identified. In part, it is because of the high value we recognize in knowledge and wisdom that God, as a being of unsurpassable value, is thought of as having unsurpassable knowledge. Because God's knowledge is of supreme excellence, theists need not have to choose between competing epistemological theories of knowledge which apply to beings with fallible, finite cognitive equipment. The traditional analysis of human knowledge as justified true belief was deemed a failure in recent years because it was pointed out that a subject may have a justified true belief in something and yet the justification involved a false premise. Many epistemologists hold that belief in a false premise undermines the subject's claim to know that the relevant belief is true even if it is true. With an omniscient being, however, there are (*ex hypothesi*) no false beliefs. Theists may therefore not feel compelled to choose between many of the accounts of knowledge that are hotly debated in *human* epistemology. Some theists retain the traditional model of justified true belief to depict God's knowledge, whereas others seek accounts of knowledge that far surpass our limited cognitive power. A similar freedom is in play when it comes to forging an understanding of God's power and agency. Contemporary philosophical accounts of agency offer competing theories of action in terms of mental and physical causation. Given that God does not have a material body, theists need not choose between competing human conceptions of embodied agency.[19]

The appeal to God's goodness or unsurpassable value has also pointed the way to resolving some of the problems involving the divine attributes. I shall illustrate this in relation to three divine attributes: omnipotence, omniscience, and eternity. I select these in order to show how, in the case of omnipotence, an appeal to God's supreme excellences leads one naturally to a refined analyses of the attribute. In the case of omniscience, concern with values naturally leads to a refined view of the scope of this attribute. I then turn to eternity, for I believe this attribute to be the least resolved and yet this does not at all threaten theism.

Case 1: the scope of omnipotence

Consider the following analysis of omnipotence:

> X is omnipotent = the scope of X's power is such that it is metaphysically impossible for there to be any being Y that has a greater scope of power.

I defended this analysis in the early 1980s.[20]

In his extensive book, *Atheism*, Michael Martin contends that this account is incompatible with other divine attributes. The God of Christian theism cannot bring about states of affairs like this: Hidden Valley's being flooded is brought about directly or indirectly by a being that has never been omniscient. Given that God is omniscient, God cannot do that, nor (to cite Martin's other cases) can God bring about Hidden Valley's being flooded by a being that has never been triune or infinitely good.[21] Two lines of defense are immediately apparent.

First one may argue that Martin's description of the state of affairs is skewed. In assessing the scope of a being's power, isn't the relevant object of dispute *bringing about a flood* and not *the way the flood is brought about*. Martin seems to improperly emphasize *the identity of an agent* over against the *object* of an act. Martin and I would be equally strong if he and I can lift the same weight even if I can never lift the following: a weight which is lifted by someone who has never been called Taliaferro.

A second strategy strikes me as more fruitful, involving an appeal to God's excellence or goodness. Imagine that as an essentially good being God cannot do something which another, morally unscrupulous being could, e.g. bring about an evil event for its own sake. Why think this latter "power" is indeed a bona fide power? Arguably, the ability to do evil may be the ability to act in weakness and corruption, not in strength and excellence. Historically Boethius, Anselm, and Aquinas have argued that the omnipotence of God involves God's essential goodness. In light of this tradition, I revise my earlier account of omnipotence to this: X is omnipotent = the scope of X's power is such that it is metaphysically impossible for there to be any being Y that has a more excellent scope of power. George Schlesinger and T. V. Morris are two of many prominent philosophers who adopt a similar strategy.[22]

Theistic tradition can also accommodate a middle position, according to which God could do something wicked but does not.

The literature on omnipotence displays a great deal of versatility for theists, but I suggest that it also exhibits a promising way to resolve matters by appeal to God's excellence.

Case 2: omniscience and freedom

Imagine you believe that if God is omniscient, then God knows all future facts. Imagine further you hold that if it is true *now* that some being will do such and such tomorrow, then it is not possible that act (call it "X") will not be done. X must, in some way be fixed. You also hold that being free to do X tomorrow involves the bona fide possibility of not doing X. On this view, X must not be fixed. You appear to face this problem: either God is not omniscient or there are no future free acts. This is a conflict involving two values: the one concerns divine sovereignty, the other the dignity and independence of creation.

What should a theist do? The theist can, first, bracket the question of God altogether and suggest that if it is in principle possible to make true statements about human actions in the future ("*E* will happen at time *t*,") then the non-theist faces the same problem as the theist. This is not solely the domain of the theist. But the benefit of this strategy (matters are just as bad for theists and atheists) is short-lived. Let us say that you cannot find a good objection to the original argument and conclude that if God knows the future there can be no future free acts. Most but not all theists are strongly committed to the belief that human beings have freedom. If you share this conviction (as I do) you may question the scope of omniscience. Many theists contend that God's omniscience involves knowing everything possible. Because future free acts cannot be known, God's not knowing what someone will do tomorrow is not a flaw in divine cognition. Most analyses of the divine attributes of omnipotence do not require that an omnipotent being be able to do something impossible (make $1 + 2 = 5$). A similar point needs to be made about omniscience. If it is not possible for anyone to know what someone will *freely* do tomorrow, then omniscience should not be seen as covering the free act. Some philosophers follow Aristotle in thinking that there is no truth of the matter now concerning future free action. J. R. Lucas, William Hasker, Richard Swinburne, and others, adopt the stance that omniscience does not include knowledge of future free action, whereas William Craig, Alfred Freddoso, Jonathan Kvanvig, and Thomas Flint argue for the traditional thesis that knowledge of future free action is possible. Perhaps Craig *et al.* are right, but if they are not, then there are back-up positions.[23]

Case 3: eternity

Theistic tradition has supported two views of God that appear to be in conflict. On the one hand God is portrayed as a person or person-like reality who loves and acts in history. On this view, God is in time upon creation; there is a "before," "during," and "after," for God. These theists often place great value on God's existential presence in creation. On the other hand, there is a rich, historical tradition which conceives of God as atemporal or outside of time. Augustine, Boethius, Anselm, and Aquinas endorse this position, adding that God enters time in the incarnation.

The literature on eternity and the relevant divine attributes is immense. It displays, in my view, that highly capable, if not brilliant, philosophers can line up on both sides as well as map out plausible middle positions. William Hasker, John Lucas, Richard Swinburne, Nicholas Wolterstorff, and others demonstrate that theists can deny God's atemporality and endorse instead God being *everlasting*, without beginning or end. I also suggest that Brian Leftow, Eleonore Stump, Norman Kretzmann, Paul Helm, and others demonstrate that there are cogent defenses of God's atemporality that are able to appreciate the personal, proximate values in God's presence in history. This extensive literature is evidence of the ways in which theism may admit of more than one philosophical analysis of a key divine attribute.[24]

Is the extensive debate over theistic attributes something unexpected or a sign of philosophical trouble? I doubt it. The philosophy of God involves philosophically reflecting on a reality believed to be unsurpassable in excellence. Presumably our best thinking in a host of areas of philosophy is relevant to the debate, including major work in metaphysics, epistemology, value theory, the philosophy of language, and so on. Insofar as there continues to be fruitful disagreements in each of these areas of philosophy, we may expect that they will enrich and broaden the scope of work on the philosophy of God. For example, there is not as yet consensus in the philosophy of time. On some views of time God may be atemporal, and the problem of God knowing the future is bypassed because these events are not known by a being in time before they occur. This is Boethius' famous strategy by which he seeks to resolve the tension between freedom and omniscience. I happen to think that God is in time and believe that God does not know future free acts, but I am not so confident about ruling out God's atemporal eternity. Until we gain greater certainty in our philosophy of time, the topic is open and sure to generate more attention. I now turn to consider the broader context of debating whether theism is coherent.

Naturalistic coherence and theistic coherence

What is the good of a philosophy with a major premise that isn't the rationalization of your feelings? If you've never had a religious experience, it's folly to believe in God. You might as well believe in the excellence of oysters; when you can't eat them without being sick.

(Aldous Huxley)[25]

The debate over the coherence of theism seems to me to be profoundly affected by one's background beliefs. Why, for example, are the cases cited in the first section, "Divine incorporeality," from works by Nielsen and Moore so bizarre – cases in which stars spell out "God exists" and we have a peculiar hypothesis of a three-legged woman? Although theistic tradition includes narratives in which God does address us in language and there are some unusual heavenly visions (Ezekiel), religious believers typically anchor their experience of the divine in very different terms. For example, God may be experienced through suffering or through the pursuit of justice or in meditation, in nature, and so on.[26] I suggest that Nielsen's and Moore's cases are so remote from the tradition they are critiquing because their background assumption are altogether at odds with entertaining the possibility of theism.

I do not suggest that one must be a theist or hold quasi-theistic beliefs to see the coherence of theism. But I do propose that if one is strongly motivated at the outset to rule out any reality which is not a constituent part of the physical cosmos, then a case for the coherence of theism will seem inconsequential at best. A bare commitment to a materialist account of human persons and animals is not enough to altogether eclipse a positive case for the coherence of theism, but a more robust form of materialism which seeks to eliminate all mental life (human and divine) is another story.

The ideal of what may be called materialist naturalism today works to render secondary, if not completely idle, our mental life of consciousness, beliefs, and desires. To varying degrees, this ideal form of materialism has been advanced by Willard Quine, Paul and Patricia Churchland, Stephen Stich, and Daniel Dennett. This passage from Dennett's work is representative: "If there is progress in psychology, it will inevitably be . . . in the direction of eliminating ultimate appeals to beliefs, desires, and other intentional items from our explanations."[27] If this is what counts as *progress*, then any sign of theism's plausibility with its ultimate appeals to God's intentional action will seem disastrous.

Early in the twentieth century there was a movement in the United States called "personalism," which privileged explanations in terms of persons, beliefs and desires over against impersonal causal relations. Most personalists were theists.[28] Today's more stringent forms of materialism may be thought of as "impersonalism." According to impersonalism, the complete description and explanation of all events in the cosmos are shorn of any reference to intentions, beliefs, and desires. Quine's dismisses personalist efforts to recognize mental states – "those who posit the mental states and events have no details of appropriate mechanisms to offer" – and he asks rhetorically: "The bodily states exist anyway; why add the others?"[29] The problem with this form of materialism is that it seems at odds with experience and it appears to conflict with our commonplace understanding of reason. I noted in Part I how a large number of materialists are finding it hard indeed to eliminate consciousness (Nagel, McGinn, Ned Block *et al.*) and today there are few friends of strict behaviorism *à la* Watson. The problem with reason comes in when materialists propose that intentional explanations must give way to non-intentional accounts. When we reason, whether deductively or inductively, we embrace conclusions by virtue of having beliefs and grasping rules of inference. I answer "6" when asked "What is the smallest perfect number?" by virtue of calculating that 6 is the smallest number equal to the sum of its devisors including 1 but not including itself. But if impersonalism holds, then this "by virtue of" is idle, for it does not have explanatory fore.

There is not space here to develop a refutation of "impersonalism." Stronger arguments which confront radical forms of materialism are referred to in the notes.[30] The point I want to raise is more modest: in assessing the coherence of a concept, we must assess it in the broadest terms, noting its link with other concepts and evaluating it over against competing metaphysical assumptions. Radical materialism may be a consistent view of the cosmos and in that respect be coherent, but it may not be coherent when measured by our experience or our exercise of reason. The history of philosophy hosts plenty of conceptual schemes that are self-consistent but run into major problems when it comes to cohering with experience. Psychological egoism, according to which all human action is motivated by believed self-interest, is simple and coherent in its formulation. Even so, psychological egoism faces a profoundly up-hill battle when one sizes up the vast amount of ostensibly non-self-interested action. The same is true, I suggest, of certain forms of skepticism and, more controversially, moral theories like utilitarianism.

There is a host of possible responses to the problems facing physicalism. My point here that the form of materialism today which is deemed most "pure" or ideal and most hostile to theism is also a threat (whether lethal or merely apparent) to our experience and reason. Not all materialists go as far as Lycan, Dennett, Quine, and others I am calling "impersonalists." Indeed, Nielsen explicitly repudiates the eliminative project of Dennett, and Moore also seems to be committed to resisting eliminativism. But materialism is often motivated by a drive for a unified explanation of the cosmos. A unified science requires that one not be left with two, radically distinguished types of explanation: personal and impersonal. Materialists, typically, blast their competition on the grounds that they leave the cosmos bifurcated or fragmented. You can see evidence of this strategy in Nielsen's rejection of any agency that does not exist bodily. Moore also seems to rule out any incorporeal theistic agency on the grounds that it is too dissimilar to our understanding of human agents. Schopenhauer once said that philosophical arguments are not like taxi cabs you can get out of whenever you like. Perhaps materialists can avoid a thoroughgoing impersonalism; all I observe here is that while a strong motive to reach such a destination will render theism a merely self-consistent concept of only antiquarian interest, reaching that end may also carry an intolerable cost.

Does theism face a similar problem? Arguably, an ideal theism may generate a view of the cosmos in which God does everything, except perhaps control the free will of creatures. Is idealism the complementary opposite of Dennett's and Lycan's impersonalism?

Although I believe idealism is a coherent philosophical system, theists have abundant reason not to accept it. Idealism, at least in most versions, has difficulties with offering the best explanation of the natural world, the success of science, and the status of nonhuman animals (my dog is *not* a collection of sense data). Still, theists can (and I think should) embrace idealism's portrait of God purposively willing the ongoing existence of the cosmos. The key to not being an idealist is that a theist may claim that, say, our solar system exists by virtue of God's will that it does, but that the solar system is not constituted by God's will, nor is the cosmos a state or mode of God. The comprehensive "personalism" in classical theism does not endanger impersonal causation. Explanations for why sugar dissolves in water are to be found in the relevant atomic structures involved, etc. Theism provides a framework for both kinds of explanation.

I believe that debate over the coherence of theism should take into account one's best philosophy of nature, and all relevant background convictions. Paul Churchland is a model of clarity on this point:

> Most scientists and philosophers would cite the presumed fact that humans have their origins in 4.5 billion years of purely chemical and biological evolution as a weighty consideration in favor of expecting mental phenomena to be nothing but a particularly exquisite articulation of the basic properties of matter and energy.[31]

Given such a physicalist framework, positing God may appear to be philosophically arduous, but not impossible. Matters shift, however, if one allows that the cosmos may or may not have its origin and continuation in divine intentions. If one does not rule out from the beginning a theistic overarching framework, theism may begin to look more promising than something which is merely internally consistent and coherent in only the most narrow, and arcane fashion.

Once one is open to the wider coherence of theism, cases in which one may acquire evidence of God look quite different from Nielsen's and Moore's thought experiments. Peter Donovan paints a more sympathetic picture of someone who sees the world in religious terms.

> A religious believer who looks on the world as a domain in which God may possibly manifest himself (in one way or another) has the potential for a whole range of significant experiences not open to the person without such a world-view. He does not just *view* the world in a religious way. He lives within it, and acts and responds and experiences its events and happenings (including his own feelings and states of mind) with the possibility in his mind that in doing so he may be coming in touch not just with the world and other people in it, but with the activity and manifestations of God.[32]

Since this chapter is mostly on coherence, not on positive argumentation for the truth of theism, I will resist amplifying Donovan's portrait and instead summarize the proposal of this third and final part of this chapter: in considering the coherence of theism, assess its coherence in the broadest terms with respect to background metaphysical assumptions and *then* see how evidence may be brought to bear on its truth.[33]

Conclusion

Thomas Nagel wrote on what he thinks is the actual widespread distribution of different kinds of conscious experiences: "No doubt it occurs in countless forms totally unimaginable to us, on other planets and in other solar systems throughout the universe."[34] Perhaps Nagel is wrong, but why rule out as *incoherent* levels of consciousness within and around the cosmos which vastly outstrip our imagination? As Franz Brentano wrote, some "obscurity is just what must be expected of our infinitely inferior mind when it tries to understand the work of an infinitely superior one."[35]

The difficulty of securing the incoherence of theism has led many of the prominent atheist philosophers of the late twentieth/early twenty-first centuries to concede that theism in indeed possible. The only disagreement with their theistic colleagues is over its truth.[36]

Notes

1 G. K. Chesterton, *Orthodoxy* (New York: Doubleday, 1990 [1908]), 11.
2 In what follows I shall treat the following terms synonymously: physical, corporeal, and material – their negations are also treated as synonyms: nonphysical, incorporeal, and immaterial.
3 T. Mautner (ed.) *A Dictionary of Philosophy* (Oxford: Blackwell, 1996), 416.
4 Gareth Moore, *Believing in God* (Edinburgh: T&T Clark, 1988), 17.
5 Kai Nielsen, *Naturalism and Religion* (New York: Prometheus, 2001), 473.
6 Nielsen, *Naturalism and Religion*, 474.
7 Ibid., 279.
8 I defend the observability of mental states, from a dualist perspective in *Consciousness and the Mind of God* (Cambridge, UK: Cambridge University Press, 1994) – henceforth *CMOG* – and in "The Virtues of Embodiment," *Philosophy* 76 (January 2001), 111–25.
9 Augustine of Hippo, *The City of God*, H. Bettenson (trans.) (London: Penguin, 1972) Book X, Ch. 13.
10 *Psychology from the Standpoint of a Behaviourist*, cited by Brand Blanshard, *The Nature of Thought* (New York: Macmillan, 1940), 317.
11 *Behaviourism*, also cited by Blanshard, 317. Blanshard offers a devastating critique of Watson.
12 Bertrand Russell, *The Autobiography of Bertrand Russell 1872–1914* (Boston: Little Brown, 1967), 47. I discuss the relevant arguments in *CMOG*.
13 See, for example, Oliver Sack's *The Man Who Mistook His Wife for a Hat* (New York: Summit Books, 1985).
14 See *CMOG*, 26, Chapters 1–3, for references. For a case for dualism that takes as its point of departure ordinary language and experience, see H. D. Lewis's *The Elusive Mind* (Philadelphia: Westminster Press, 1982).
15 See Joshua Hoffman and Gary Rosenkrantz, *Substance: Its Nature and Existence* (London: Routledge, 1997), especially 3–7, and Ch. 3 of *CMOG*. See also Hoffman and Rosenkrantz *Divine Attributes* (Oxord: Balckwell, 2002), Ch. 3.
16 For a clever treatment of inferences from patterns to intelligence, see Robert Hambourger's "The Argument from Design," in *Intentions and Intentionality*, C. Diamond (ed.) (Ithaca, NY: Cornell University Press, 1979).
17 I.A. Richards, *The Philosophy of Rhetoric* (Oxford: Oxford University Press, 1936), 10.
18 Robert G. Wolf, *Analytic Philosophy of Religion; 1940–1996* (Charlottesville, VA: Philosophy Documentation Center, 1998).
19 For a good overview of the breadth of work on the divine attributes, see P. Quinn and C. Taliaferro (eds) *A Companion to Philosophy of Religion* (Oxford:

Blackwell, 1997), and Brian Davies (ed.) *Philosophy of Religion: A Guide to the Subject* (London: Cassell, 1998).

20 Charles Taliaferro, "The Magnitude of Omnipotence," *The International Journal for Philosophy of Religion* 14 (1983), 99–106.

21 Michael Martin, *Atheism* (Philadelphia: Temple University Press, 1990), 309–11.

22 See Thomas V. Morris' *Anselmian Explanations* (Notre Dame, IN: University of Notre Dame Press, 1987); George Schlesinger's *New Perspectives on Old-Time Religion* (Oxford: Oxford University Press, 1988). See also Ch. 3 of *Contemporary Philosophy of Religion* (Oxford: Blackwell, 1998).

23 See John Lucas's *A Treatise on Time and Space* (London: Methuen, 1973); William Hasker's *God, Time and Knowledge* (Ithaca, NY: Cornell University Press, 1989); Richard Swinburne's *The Coherence of Theism* (Oxford: Clarendon Press, 1977); A. Freddoso's "Introduction" to *On Divine Foreknowledge* by L. Molina (Ithaca, NY: Cornell University Press, 1988); Thomas Flint's *Divine Providence* (Ithaca, NY: Cornell University Press, 1998); J. Kvanvig's *The Possibility of an All-Knowing God* (London: Macmillan); William Lane Craig's *The Problem of Divine Foreknowledge and Future Contingents from Aristotle to Suarez* (Leiden: Brill, 1988) and his *Divine Foreknowledge and Human Freedom: The Coherence of Theism I: Omniscience* (Leiden: Brill, 1990). For an interchange of views on the relationship of divine foreknowledge and human freedom, see James Beilby and Paul Eddy, *Divine Foreknowledge and Human Freedom: Four Views* (Downers Grove, IL: Intervarsity Press, 2001).

24 Hasker's *God, Time and Knowledge*; Lucas's *A Treatise on Time and Space*; Swinburne's *The Coherence of Theism*; Brian Leftow's *Time and Eternity* (Ithaca, NY: Cornell University Press, 1991); Eleonore Stump and Norman Kretzmann's "Eternity," *Journal of Philosophy* 78 (1981); Paul Helm's *Eternal God* (Oxford: Oxford University Press, 1988); William Craig, *The Tensed Theory of Time: A Critical Examination* (Dordrecht: Kluwer, 2000), *The Tenseless Theory of Time: A Critical Examination* (Dordrecht: Kluwer, 2000), and his *God, Time, and Eternity* (Dordrecht: Kluwer, 2001); Nicholas Wolterstorff, "God Everlasting," in *God and the Good*, C. Orlebeke and L. Smedes (eds) (Grand Rapids, MI: Eerdmans, 1975).

25 Aldous Huxley, *Point Counter Point* (New York: The Literary Guild of America, 1928), 13.

26 See Caroline Davis, *The Evidential Force of Religious Experience* (New York: Oxford University Press, 1989).

27 Daniel Dennett, *Brainstorms* (Cambridge: MIT Press, 1978), 61.

28 See "Personalism," in *A Companion to Philosophy of Religion*.

29 Willard Quine, *Word and Object* (Cambridge: MIT, 1960), 264.

30 See especially William Hasker's *The Emergent Self* (Ithaca, NY: Cornell University Press, 1999). Hasker articulates a variety of devastating anti-materialist arguments. Victor Reppert has developed the best anti-physicalist arguments on the grounds that physicalism undermines reason. See his "The Argument from Reason," *Philo* 2 (Spring–Summer, 1999); "Reply to Parsons and Lippard on the Argument from Reason," *Philo* 3 (Spring/Summer 2000); and "Causal Closure, Mechanism, and Rational Inference," *Philosophia Christi* 2, 2 (New series) (2001), 473–83.

31 Paul Churchland, *The Engine of Reason, the Seat of the Soul* (Cambridge, MA: MIT Press, 1995), 211.

32 Peter Donovan, *Interpreting Religious Experience* (New York: Seabury, 1979), 81.

33 The better philosophical works on the nature of religious experience takes this appeal to broader philosophical frameworks seriously. See, for example, work by William Alston, C. Davis, Alvin Plantinga, and Jerome Gellman. Also see Ch. 9 by Douglas Geivett.

34 Thomas Nagel, *Mortal Questions* (Cambridge, UK: Cambridge University Press, 1979), 10.

35 Franz Brentano, *On the Existence of God*, Susan Krantz (trans.) (Dordrecht: Martinus Nijhoff, 1987), 337.

36 I thank Cleo Granneman, Gretchen Ross, and Paul Copan for helpful comments on earlier drafts of this chapter.

13

GOD AND EVIL

Gregory E. Ganssle

Introduction

The problem of evil is, perhaps, the most common objection to theistic belief. There has been more written on this topic in recent years than any other
topic in the philosophy of religion.[1] Although it is difficult in one chapter to
make much progress, I will take this chapter to summarize the background
to the issue, and then I will turn to interact in more detail with what I think
is the most challenging form of the problem.

There are a few distinctions that are in order as we begin. The first distinction must be raised before we even begin to address the problem of evil
as a challenge to theism. This is the distinction between the *philosophical*
problem of evil and what we may call the *existential* problem of evil. When
philosophers talk about the problem of evil, they are discussing an argument – or, to be more precise, a family of arguments – against the existence
of God, taking evil as the starting point. It is argued that the existence,
amount, magnitude, or distribution of evil renders God's existence impossible or unlikely. So the philosophical problem of evil concerns certain
arguments against God's existence. The existential problem of evil is more
pervasive than the philosophical problem. Many people who rarely think
about arguments at all are faced with this problem. The existential problem
of evil is not an argument but a challenge. The challenge can be phrased in
the form of a question: *how can I make sense out of my life given the evil
that I suffer or that I witness?* Each human being encounters or, at least, is
aware of significant evil and thus faces the existential problem of evil. I face
the existential problem of evil when I am facing real suffering. I think about
the philosophical problem when I have the luxury of sitting back and theorizing about evil. It is rare that someone in the middle of deep suffering will
spin an argument against God. He might cry out against God or for God,
but there is generally little structuring of arguments going on.

It is important to make this distinction, because adequate answers to
these problems will be very different from one another. An answer to the
philosophical problem of evil will require that we pay careful attention to
the details of various arguments. We shall analyze them and try to find the

various strengths and weaknesses in them. This kind of academic work is not directly relevant to a person in the throes of suffering. When a person faces the existential problem of evil, she is not concerned with arguments at all. An answer to the existential problem of evil will be very personal. If I provide a detailed refutation of some argument to a person when she is struggling with her own experience of evil, I will miss her need entirely. We can help each other through difficulties by expressing our deep concern and by extending a listening ear and by providing what might be called *pastoral care*. It may be that either of these problems – or their combination – is at the heart of a person's rejection of theism. In this chapter, however, I will address only the philosophical problem of evil. I will try to determine whether it amounts to a cogent argument against the existence of God.

Almost before we make our first step, we must make another distinction. There are two basic kinds of arguments against God's existence that start with some facts about evil. The first has been called the *logical* or the *deductive* problem of evil, and the second is the *evidential* or *inductive* problem of evil. The logical or deductive argument from evil is an argument that purports to show that the existence of evil is logically incompatible with the existence of God. The names "logical" and "deductive" are not helpful names to pick out this kind of argument, for both kinds of arguments (at least versions of both kinds) can be framed as logically deductive arguments. I prefer to call the first kind of argument *the charge of contradiction*. The second type of argument is not always framed as an inductive argument, but it is fairly accurate to call it an evidential argument.

The charge of contradiction

Many people have thought that the existence of evil poses some kind of logical problem for belief in God. If God is wholly good and all-powerful, he ought to make sure that no evil enters the world. Since it is obvious that there is plenty of evil around, it must be the case that an all-powerful and wholly good God does not exist. The existence of evil, such people have argued, is logically incompatible with the existence of God. In what has become, perhaps, the most famous argument of this kind, John Mackie urged the following:

> I think, however, that a more telling criticism can be made by way of the traditional problem of evil. Here it can be shown, not that religious beliefs lack rational support, but that they are positively irrational, that the several parts of the essential theological doctrine are inconsistent with one another, so that the theologian can maintain his position as a whole only by a much more extreme rejection of reason than in the former case. He must now be prepared to believe, not merely what cannot be proved, but what can be *disproved* from other beliefs he holds.[2]

Mackie goes on to claim that the following three statements are inconsistent:

God is wholly good.
God is omnipotent.
Evil exists.

They are inconsistent, Mackie insists, because of what it means to claim that God is omnipotent and that God is good. If God is omnipotent, then there are no limits to what he can do. If he is wholly good, he will eliminate evil to the best of his ability. Therefore, if it was the case that God existed, there would be no evil. God and evil are logically incompatible.

In recent years, it has been largely agreed that the kind of argument Mackie presented cannot succeed. The reason is that his analysis of omnipotence and of goodness is not correct. It turns out that there are limits to what an omnipotent being can do. An omnipotent being cannot, for example, do logical impossibilities. So God cannot create a square circle. He cannot make a physical object that is, at some point in time, larger than itself. He cannot make contradictions true. He cannot, then, make a creature with a certain kind of freedom and then guarantee that the creature always chooses rightly. Furthermore, a being can be good while allowing evil. Sometimes a good person allows evil even when that person could prevent it. A good person can allow evil and still be good *if* he has good reason to allow it. So if God has a *sufficient reason* to allow evil, then the existence of evil is compatible with the existence of God.[3]

Atheist William Rowe comments on the fact that few philosophers will press the charge of contradiction any more:

> Some philosophers have contended that the existence of evil is *logically inconsistent* with the existence of the theistic God. No one, I think, has succeeded in establishing such an extravagant claim. Indeed, granted incompatibilism, there is a fairly compelling argument for the view that the existence of evil is logically consistent with the existence of the theistic God.[4]

Of course, this admission does not put to rest the problem of evil. Rowe has developed a different kind of argument against the existence of God based on evil. He put forward a version of the evidential problem of evil. I shall discuss Rowe's version of the argument briefly and then turn my attention to another version offered by Paul Draper.

The evidential problem of evil

Rowe's evidential argument

The answer to the charge of contradiction is based on the claim that God could have a good reason for allowing evil. If it is possible that God has a sufficient reason, then the co-existence of God and evil does not involve a contradiction. The evidential problem of evil takes up a different question. The question is *whether it is likely or probable* that God has a sufficient reason to allow the amount or the kinds of the evil that we see.

The kind of argument Rowe is putting forward begins with the hunch that there are certain evils that are so bad that it seems as though God could have no good reason to allow them. I write these words barely three months after the attacks on the World Trade Center. I am sure that there are many people who, upon reflection, will think that God could not have a good enough reason to allow that much suffering. Couldn't he, they might reason, accomplish whatever his purposes were if he had allowed fifty fewer people to be lost? If not fifty, why not five? It seems to us that he could. Rowe's argument gets going from such a hunch. He states his argument as follows:

1   There exist instances of intense suffering which an omnipotent, omniscient being could have prevented without thereby losing some greater good or permitting some evil equally bad or worse.
2   An omniscient, wholly good being would prevent the occurrence of any intense suffering it could, unless it could not do so without thereby losing some greater good or permitting some evil equally bad or worse.
3   There does not exist an omnipotent, omniscient, wholly good being.[5]

Just like Mackie's argument, this is a valid deductive argument. Rowe calls his approach an evidential argument because his support of premise 1 is not decisive. He thinks he can argue that premise 1 is probably true. If premise 1 is probably true, then the conclusion that follows will be a probabilistic conclusions as well. He can conclude, then, that *probably* there does not exist an omnipotent, omniscient, wholly good being.

Most theists will grant Rowe's second premise.[6] The major dispute is over the first premise. Rowe points out that "we are not in a position to prove that (1) is true . . . ."[7] We can, Rowe insists, support the claim that we have rational grounds for thinking it is true. Rowe takes a particular case of evil as his starting point. In this essay, he discusses a fawn suffering badly for several days after being burned in a forest fire caused by lightning. He claims that it is likely that there is no reason such that, if God exists, the reason would justify him in allowing this evil:

> Consider again the case of the fawn's suffering. Is it reasonable to believe that there is some greater good so intimately connected to that suffering that even an omnipotent, omniscient being could not have obtained that good without permitting that suffering or some evil at

least as bad? It certainly does not appear reasonable to believe this. Nor does it seem reasonable to believe that there is some evil at least as bad as the fawn's suffering such that an omnipotent being simply could not have prevented it without permitting the fawn's suffering. But even if it should somehow be reasonable to believe either of these things of the fawn's suffering, we must then ask whether it is reasonable to believe either of these things of *all* the instances of seemingly pointless human and animal suffering that occur daily in our world.[8]

Rowe's argument for the claim that we are rationally justified to think premise 1 is true is that it simply does not seem reasonable to deny its truth. In other words, he argues in the following way:

4   It *seems* as though there is no reason sufficient to justify God in allowing this evil.
5   Therefore, it is *probably true* that there is no reason sufficient to justify God in allowing this evil.

If premise 5 is true, then premise 1 of the original argument is probably true and it is probably true that there is no God. At first glance, this reasoning appears to be strong. After all, if we search for a justifying reason long enough, and we come up empty, we can begin to think that it is more likely that there is no justifying reason for the evil in question.

We can challenge Rowe's case, however. Following (and greatly simplifying) the work of Stephen Wykstra, we can argue that Rowe's grounds for thinking premise 1 probable are insufficient.[9] The inference from the claim that it seems as though there is no sufficient reason to be found to the conclusion that it is probably the case that there is no sufficient reason at all is not a strong inference. To support this criticism, let us consider what kind of inference we are asked to make here. The general form is the following:

6   It seems as though there is no x.
7   Therefore, probably there is no x.

Sometimes this kind of inference is a strong inference and sometimes it is not. Consider the following instantiation:

8   It seems as though there is no live elephant in this room.
9   Therefore, probably there is no live elephant in this room.

This is a good inference. You are perfectly reasonable to look around the room and say, "It seems as though there are no live elephants here; so probably there are not any." Consider, however, the following instantiation:

10 It seems as though there is no carbon 14 atom in the room.[10]
11 Therefore, probably there is no carbon 14 atom in the room.

This inference is fairly weak. The difference between an instantiation that yields a strong inference and one that yields a weak one turns on how reasonable it is for us to expect that we would detect the presence of whatever it is that we substitute for x. We get a strong inference when the same substitution makes the following sentence true:

12 If there were an x, we would probably know it.

Replacing x with "live elephant" results in a true sentence. When we replace x with "carbon 14 atom," we get a false one. Even if there were carbon 14 atoms in the room, I would have no way of detecting them. Is a reason that would justify God for allowing a particular instance of evil more like an elephant or more like a carbon 14 atom? Is it more reasonable to believe that I *would* be able to figure it out if it is there, or that I *would not* be able to figure it out? Is the following sentence true?

13 If God had a reason to allow this particular case of evil, we would probably know what it is.

Given that if God exists, he has a good reason to allow the evil he allows, how likely is it that we should *know* what his reasons are? I think we should expect to be able to discern some likely candidates in some cases but not in others. No one thinks that we should be able to figure out God's reasons in every case. By the same token, no one will argue that we cannot discern what his reasons very well could be in many cases. Where disagreement remains about Rowe's formulation of the argument is in the degree to which we ought to expect to be able to discern more justifying reasons than we can.[11] What level of expectation is reasonable in this regard? I think that those who press the argument against God's existence *overestimate* the percentage of cases in which we *ought* to be able to figure all of this out and they *underestimate* the percentage of cases in which we *actually can*.

Suppose we call some particular evil *mysterious* if the following is true of it. (a) After some careful reflection, we have no idea how any of the standard repertoire of reasons that might justify God to allow *some* evils apply to *this* particular evil event. For example, we cannot see how preserving the freedom of the will or preserving the regularity of cause and effect or other potential reasons are relevant to the evil in question. (b) We cannot think of any additional reasons (beyond the standard ones) that might justify God in allowing this evil. All other evils, then, we could call *non-mysterious*.

It is important to note that for an evil to count as non-mysterious, it is not necessary that we *know* what God's reasons actually are for allowing it.

We only need to see that it is *not clear* that certain reasons do not apply to it. The reason this last caveat is critical is that we are trying to determine not what God's reasons are but whether it is reasonable to think that there are reasons available that would justify God in allowing the evil. If some particular evil is non-mysterious in the sense I am using here, then we have some idea that some potential reason we know about just might apply to it.

I think most of the evils in the world fall into the category of the non-mysterious. It is only a small percentage of the evil things in the world that are such that we have no idea what kind of reasons might apply.[12] So when we ask whether statement 11 is true or false, we are asking about the relatively small subset of evil things that are mysterious. We are asking the following question of each mysterious evil we encounter: if God has sufficient reason to allow it, would we expect to be able to discern what it is? I think that the answer is clearly that we ought not. If God exists, we would expect that there would be significant stretches of reality which are beyond our grasp. Some of this, we would expect, would have to do with God's reasons for doing and allowing the things he does. The fact that there is mysterious evil is just what we would *expect* if there is a God. We ought to expect some significant mystery about his particular purposes especially in the darkest times of our lives. If this is about what we should expect, it cannot be counted as evidence against God's existence. So even though it might seem, at first glance, that there are no good reasons to allow certain evils we see, this does not provide strong evidence that these evils are really unjustified. Rowe's argument, then, need not be troubling to anyone weighing the rational grounds for believing in God.[13]

Draper's evidential argument

Paul Draper, in a series of papers, has presented what I think is the strongest version of the evidential argument from evil.[14] Rather than arguing directly for the conclusion that theism is unlikely given the amount or kinds of evil in the world, Draper provides a hypothesis that is an alternative to theism. He claims that this alternative hypothesis explains what we observe about evil better than theism. Since the alternative he provides is incompatible with theism, the alternative hypothesis is more likely to be true than theism is. As a result, it is more likely that theism is false than that it is true, given our observations about evil.

Draper calls his alternative hypothesis, the "Hypothesis of Indifference" (*HI*). He expresses it as follows:

> *HI*: neither the nature nor the condition of sentient beings on earth is the result of benevolent or malevolent actions performed by nonhuman persons.[15]

This hypothesis is, of course, incompatible with theism. Draper points out that theism does not involve only the existence of God but that God created the universe and cares in some sense for sentient beings in the universe as well.

Draper now turns his attention to evil. He uses the letter "O" to stand for "a statement reporting both the observations one has made of humans and animals experiencing pain and pleasure and the testimony one has encountered concerning the observations others have made of sentient beings experiencing pain and pleasure."[16] O is a statement that describes a situation requiring an explanation. Both HI and theism ought to explain why we see the distribution of pain and pleasure that we do. Draper's central argument, then, is for the following claim:

C: HI explains the facts O reports much better than theism does.[17]

If C is true, our observations give us a prima facie reason to prefer HI to theism. How does Draper argue for C? He looks at both the biological and the moral utility of pain and pleasure, and he argues that, given each of these, HI explains O better than theism. Actually, he argues that the biological utility of pain and pleasure is much better explained by HI than by theism, and the moral utility of pain and pleasure does not raise the probability of theism. Barring some other purpose for pain and pleasure, tipping the explanatory balance in favor of theism, Draper concludes that HI is in a much better position than theism regarding pain and pleasure.

The biological utility of pain and pleasure

Draper thinks that "it is the biological role played by both pain and pleasure that renders this claim [C] true."[18] He calls any part of a goal-directed biological system "biologically useful" if it contributes to the biological goals of the system in a way that is not accidental. His example is the pain felt by his cat when it jumps on the hot stove. Because the cat responds quickly to such pain, it avoids more serious damage. In this case, the pain contributes to the goal of survival and therefore is biologically useful.

Some pain or pleasure is biologically useful and some is not. Draper points out that O captures three kinds of observations about pain and pleasure. They are:

a   moral agents experiencing pain or pleasure that we know to be biologically useful,
b   sentient beings that are not moral agents experiencing pain or pleasure that we know to be biologically useful, and
c   sentient beings experiencing pain or pleasure that we do not know to be biologically useful.[19]

These categories exhaust all of the reports contained in O (and all of the possible reports of the experience of evil in the world). Draper argues that *HI* explains the pain or pleasure in each of these categories better than theism does. Draper's argument boils down to the claim that an omnipotent, omniscient being *could* "create goal-directed organic systems (including humans) without biologically useful pain and pleasure."[20] What shapes our expectations about what God *would* do concerning pain and pleasure is that these have intrinsic moral value. Pain is intrinsically bad and pleasure is intrinsically good. Therefore, we would expect that God would have reason to produce as much pleasure as possible, even if some of the pleasure is biologically gratuitous. By the same token, we would expect God to produce or allow little pain at all. Since he could create us without needing pain to achieve biological goals, we would expect that he would do so. Our statement of our observations concerning the kinds of pain and pleasure we see, however, includes (a) and (b) above. It includes biologically useful pain and pleasure. On the assumption that God exists, this is a surprise. If *HI* is true, however, the fact that pain and pleasure have intrinsic moral weight would not affect whether we would expect biologically useful pleasure or pain. Given the fact of biologically useful pain, *HI* explains O much better than theism does. Therefore our observations about evil confirm *HI* to a much higher degree than they do theism.

Morally useful pleasure and pain

Draper recognizes that pain and pleasure play more than biological roles. They also play moral roles in the lives of moral agents. It is here, he admits, that the theist is likely to attempt to win back some turf in the argument. While dismissing traditional theodicies, Draper does discuss some of the moral roles of pain that might raise the probability of theism in relation to O. There are various theistic resources that may shed light on the moral or spiritual usefulness of pain or pleasure. Some of these resources have provided that material for traditional theodicies. Two examples that Draper discusses are the appeals to the moral value of the freedom of the will and the importance of creaturely moral responsibility. Although some of these strategies may seem promising, Draper reminds us that they each appeal to resources that are themselves not very likely given theism. As a result, they do not raise the probability of theism enough to make a significant difference to Draper's main argument. For example, Draper explores a defense that appeals to something like the following principle:

T_1: God exists, and one of His final ends is a favorable balance of freely* performed right actions over wrong actions.[21]

The difficulty is that, given theism, the likelihood that T_1 is true is not significantly greater than the likelihood that the denial of T_1 is true. In other words, given that God exists, the probability that one of his goals involves a favorable balance of freely* performed right actions is not much greater than the probability that this is not one of his final ends. If T_1 is not very likely given theism, then it cannot provide resources adequate to raise the probability of theism given our observations of evil. Draper uses the same kind of argument against other attempts to explain evil by adding to theism some specification of God's purposes. Thus all of the appeals to the moral utility of pain or pleasure fail to undermine the argument that *HI* explains biologically useful pain and pleasure significantly better than theism. We are left with the conclusion that *HI* explains *all* of our observations about pain and pleasure better than theism does. Considering evil, then, theism is more likely to be false than to be true. Draper recognizes that it may be that some argument *for* theism will override the strength of this argument *against* theism. He is not very optimistic about this claim, however. Most of the arguments for theism, he thinks have been shown to be not very persuasive. What we observe about evil, then, makes it unlikely that theism is true.

Towards a theistic defense

Draper's argument raises the bar in the debate over the evidential argument. Unlike many arguments from the existence or nature of pain, he does not ignore the existence of pleasure. He also provides a deeper analysis of the various roles of pain and pleasure than is often discussed. I think, though, the biggest strength of his project is his presentation of the alternative hypothesis to theism. Although this strategy is not original to Draper, it marks a significant improvement in the contemporary discussion of the evidential argument from evil.[22] Whether some hypothesis is likely depends, in part, upon the range of available alternatives. By arguing that there is a ready, non-theistic alternative that offers a better explanation of pain and pleasure, Draper gains the needed leverage to argue that it is less than rational to hold to theism.

Although I think that Draper's is the strongest version of the evidential argument going, I do not find it persuasive. Furthermore, I do not think that anyone who is undecided with respect to God's existence ought to be moved by it. There are six issues that I want to raise by way of criticism.[23] Some of these issues overlap with one another.

Our expectations concerning biologically useful pain and pleasure

My first point is minor, but not unimportant. It seems to me that Draper is a bit too confident that God, if he existed, would create only a world without biologically useful pain and pleasure. Draper thinks that it is clear that God *could* create a sentient being without biologically useful pain and pleasure. It is not the capacity to experience pain in general that is the problem. Draper's real trouble is with the idea that God would make the pain and pleasure biologically useful. The special problem with biologically useful pain is that God, presumably, could accomplish his biological goals for organisms without having to use pain, and therefore he should do so.

First of all, it might be that sentience requires the ability to feel pain. If so, it would not be possible for God to make sentient creatures that are immune to all pain.[24] As far as biologically useful pain is concerned, a biological being that is sentient that does not experience biologically useful pain would be an odd creature. Biological goals largely have to do with eating, avoiding being eaten, staying away from danger, and successfully reproducing. All of these activities involve the various biological systems within the organism. Sentient animals employ a fairly complex nervous system in accomplishing all of these goals. The nervous system is what makes possible sentience itself.

Furthermore, the nervous system is also the pain system. To think that God might make sentient beings that are biological but that he would use some other non-biological means to prompt behavior that is conducive to survival seems a bit of a stretch. It is hard to imagine how biological organisms could be prompted without the use of the nervous system. In addition, urgent biological needs require severe prompting. If God is going to make sentient biological organisms, employing pain and pleasure to achieve biological goals makes sense. We can ask whether God, if he exists, would make biological beings at all, but given that he does, it is no real surprise that these creatures experience biologically useful pain and pleasure. I call this point minor simply because I am not very confident about all of this. Draper's confidence to the contrary, however, ought to be challenged.

The status of the hypothesis of indifference

My second concern is with the hypothesis of indifference. What exactly is *HI*? Draper holds that it is a hypothesis that is an alternative to theism. He argues that it provides a better explanation for what we observe about pain and pleasure than does theism. If we look closely, we can see that *HI*, by itself, is *not* a hypothesis that explains anything. It is simply the *denial of theism*.[25] To claim that the nature and conditions of sentient beings are not the result of the action of nonhuman persons is not to explain anything about the nature and condition of sentient beings. *HI*, then is not a hypothesis about what the explanations of pain, pleasure, or other kinds of evils *are*. It is a hypothesis about what their explanations *are not*. It is the claim that whatever explanation is the right one for the universe and its creatures, it is not one that appeals to nonhuman persons.

Of course there are many ways one could try to explain the nature and conditions of sentient beings that are *consistent with HI*. Some of these ways might even be plausible. *HI* itself, though, is not an explanation. Only if *HI* is coupled with one of these particular theories can we begin to have anything like an explanation of pain and pleasure. Since *HI* is not an alternative explanation, it cannot play the role of the alternative explanation to theism that Draper needs it to play. He needs much more by way of an explanatory theory. Draper needs to specify what sort of theory, consistent with *HI*, he is putting forward as a better explanation for our observations of pain and pleasure. Picking any particular theory will land Draper in some other difficulties, as we shall see in the next section.

The role of expansions to theism

Draper's discussion of the attempts by theists to raise the probability of theism by appeal to things like the freedom of the will brings up what I think is an extremely important issue. This issue is related to that of the previous section. Draper proceeds with the presumed demand upon the theist: to defend a position we can call "minimalistic theism." I call this position "minimalistic" because there is not much to it. It contains the bare minimum necessary for any position to be correctly characterized as theistic. What Draper calls theism, I am calling here minimalistic theism. It is, then, the claim that an omnipotent, omniscient, morally perfect person exists and created the universe. Draper sets up the discussion as though the theist's position develops as follows. First, he is committed primarily to minimalistic theism. When he encounters various difficult objections, he adds other ingredients to his minimalistic theism. He then claims that theism can answer the challenge. What he winds up with is some form of expanded theism. It looks as if the theist develops his original position simply to put into theism the resources to answer various challenges.[26]

In reality, however, few thinkers begin by holding only to minimalistic theism. Most begin with some particular version of a rather expanded theism and aim to defend this more robust position against the challenge of evil. (I will call this type of view "particularistic theism.") For example, most of the philosophers who are defending theism today are Christian theists. Although minimalistic theism is entailed by Christian theism, it is not the position that primarily is defended. Nor should it be.

The fact that most theistic philosophers hold some particular theism ought to affect how an argument from evil is pressed and challenged. Otherwise, arguments from evil turn out to have as their targets a position that few people hold in isolation from a fuller theistic system. Restricting the discussion to minimalistic theism limits the resources the theist may draw upon to address the challenge of evil. Each version of "particularistic theism" (e.g. Christian theism or Islamic theism) has far greater resources available. Christian theism, for example, requires the existence of pervasive moral and natural evil if it is to be true. The whole Christian story is about the human fall into sin that affected the entire created order and brought evil into the world and about God's actions to redeem us and all creation from that evil. If there were no evil at all or only a small amount of evil, Christian theism would be known to be false. Furthermore, the depth of evil in the world required by Christian theism is significant enough to warrant the highest sacrifice – in the person of Jesus Christ – in order for it to be redeemed. Pervasive moral and natural evil, then, will not be surprising if Christian theism is true.

Draper will point out, rightly, two problems. First, Christian theism (CT) entails theism (T) and, therefore, the antecedent probability of CT cannot exceed the probability of T. Second, there are many different, mutually incompatible kinds of particular theisms that entail T so the probability that CT is true is antecedently fairly low. The Christian theist can readily accept both the challenge of the lower antecedent probability of any particular theism and the challenge of the plurality of theisms in the following manner.

Regarding the first challenge, there are analogous difficulties concerning the hypotheses of indifference. As we saw above, HI by itself is not an explanation. We need for HI to be combined with some particular theory to explain our observations about pain and pleasure. There are many explanations that might fit the bill. Each "particular HI" entails the minimal HI and therefore is antecedently less probable than HI. So whatever actual alternative explanation that Draper proposes will have a significantly lower antecedent probability than the minimal HI. Regarding the second challenge, the plurality of incompatible robust hypotheses plagues HI as much as it does theism.

Some philosophers will, at first glance, be tempted to think that the problem of the plurality of HI may seem not to be as severe as that of the plurality of theisms. The idea may be that scientific opinion tends to converge concerning the big theories about the universe and life within it. I think that, on the contrary, the plurality of HIs turns out to be more severe than the plurality of theisms for two basic reasons. First (and less important), there is actually less convergence than is advertised in scientific theories. We have evolutionists who hold to gradual transitions, and those who hold to punctuated equilibrium. Many think that the universe is uncaused while some think it was caused by a timeless point.[27] The second, more important, problem is that a particular HI must explain not only what we might call *scientific facts*; it must also explain other sorts of facts such as moral facts and aesthetic facts. Each particular HI has its own theory of morality and a theory of beauty. Once we consider these other facts, the idea that particular HIs converge more than theisms do is seen to be fictitious. There turn out to be many different but incompatible particular theories, each entailing HI. Such considerations, at the least, show us that Christian theism is in no worse a position than any particular HI as far as the effect of pluralism on antecedent probability is concerned.[28] The Christian theist does not, then, weaken his case by appealing to the parts of the Christian story that shape what a Christian's expectation concerning our observation of pain and pleasure ought to be.

What ought to be included in a statement of our observations of pain and pleasure?

Draper's argument is for the conclusion that *HI* explains *O* much better than theism. He uses *O* to stand for "a statement reporting both the observations one has made of humans and animals experiencing pain and pleasure and the testimony one has encountered concerning the observations others have made of sentient beings experiencing pain and pleasure."[29] What counts as the evidence from which the argument is to be launched, then, is what we observe about the experience of pain and pleasure. What we observe about the experience of pain and pleasure, Draper claims, is exhausted by sentient beings, moral or not, experiencing evil that we know to be biologically useful or evil that we do not know to be so. Why ought we restrict what counts as evidence to *these* observations of pain and pleasure? Alvin Plantinga points out that Christians have beliefs about pain and pleasure that go far beyond the observations that Draper considers. He mentions the belief in eternal life as one candidate here.[30]

A stronger challenge to Draper's restriction that does not appeal to anything held only by theists is that there are observations, critical to Draper's argument, which he leaves out of his summary of O. If his argument is to be an argument from our observations concerning pleasure and pain, then *everything* we observe about pain and pleasure ought to be put into our statement to be explained by *HI* and by theism. Draper's argument depends upon the facts that pain is intrinsically bad and pleasure is intrinsically good, but he leaves these observations out of his characterization of what needs explanation. These facts too ought to be included.

Which of the two theories, *HI* or theism, provides a better explanation for the intrinsic moral nature of pain and pleasure? The prospects for *HI* in this respect are not bright. If the moral nature of pain is real and objective and intrinsic, as Draper insists, the range of particular *HI*s that have a chance at providing a plausible explanation for pain is diminished greatly. Some of the relevant material is discussed in Chapter 8 of this volume. I have discussed one particular attempt to explain objective moral value in a way consistent with *HI* elsewhere.[31]

Now, one might object that I am simply trying to bring in a completely different argument for God's existence to try to raise the overall probability of theism. I am not doing this. I am arguing that an explanatory argument about evil ought to consider all of the relevant facts about evil that need to be explained. Draper's argument is an explanatory argument, but he restricts what he wants to have explained to the *experience* of pain and pleasure and not to what they are in themselves. Since Draper agrees that pain and pleasure have intrinsic moral weight, this observation is not a matter of dispute between us.

One other consideration is relevant here. It is hard to see how Draper can be confident that pain and pleasure have moral properties intrinsically unless he has some rough characterization of evil in mind. Douglas Geivett has recently noted that few atheists or agnostics writing on the problem of evil even mention the task of characterizing evil and that those who do generally dismiss the task as unimportant. That Draper does not state or explain his characterization is not a serious problem. The problem is that it is extremely difficult to formulate any plausible characterization of evil (one that is not ad hoc) that does not have theistic implications. Draper's characterization of evil must capture the intrinsic badness of pain. Geivett has put forward a minimalistic sort of characterization. "Crudely stated," he writes, "I consider evil to be *a departure from the way things ought to be.*"[32] This characterization of evil will work for Draper because it accounts for the fact that pain is intrinsically bad. Creatures, we feel, ought not experience pain. Pain is a departure from the way things ought to be. Of course, if this characteristic is correct, it implies that there is a way things ought to be, and this raises the probability that there is a designer. Draper must have some characterization in mind, and it must be robust enough to account for the intrinsic badness of pain yet, for him, it cannot have theistic implications. The task of coming up with such a characteristic will be difficult.

If Draper is to construct an argument that begins with what we observe about pain and pleasure, he needs to include all of our observations. It turns out that a fuller account of our observations about pain and pleasure actually raises the probability of theism and reduces the probability of *HI*.

Connecting Draper's argument with other chapters in this book

Although in the previous section I denied that I was trying to bring in other arguments for God's existence, I think there are two ways that these arguments are relevant to Draper's version of the evidential argument. First, they purport to show that *HI* is less adequate than theism to explain the existence and nature of the universe. Since a necessary condition for the existence of evil is that certain kinds of creatures exist and the existence of these creatures requires that a certain kind of universe exists, theism, prima facie, provides a better explanation for the possibility of evil. Three examples will suffice. In Chapter 7 of this book, Robin Collins argues for the claim that the existence of a universe that is capable of sustaining sentient life is much less likely on *HI* than it is on theism. Since the existence of sentient beings that experience biologically useful pain and pleasure is required for Draper's argument and this entails that the universe *can* sustain sentient creatures, the teleological argument is relevant to the problem of evil. The probability of the *actual* existence of creatures which can experience such evil is lower than the probability that the universe is able to sustain such creatures *whether or not they exist*. The probability of a universe suitable to these kinds of creatures is too small to allow that it came to be solely by chance. Theism, then, is more likely than *HI* given the kind of universe required for our observations of pain and pleasure.

In Chapter 6, William Lane Craig argues that the existence of any universe at all is much less likely on some kind of *HI* than it is on theism. Of course, the existence of creatures that experience pain and pleasure entails the existence of a universe. Again, theism turns out to be more likely than *HI* given what is required for our observations about pain and pleasure.

In Chapter 10, J. P. Moreland argues that the existence of conscious beings is highly unlikely if theism is false. Consciousness is required for much of the evil we see to be considered truly evil. For example, much moral evil consists in or, at least, necessarily involves evil mental states. The intention to harm someone is evil and it requires consciousness. If consciousness cannot be adequately explained without the existence of God, much of the evil we observe is such that its very possibility points to the existence of God.

The second way in which these arguments are relevant to the problem of evil is that, if reasonably successful, they raise the antecedent probability of theism. Therefore, *HI* and theism do not start off on an equal plane. The probability of *HI* given some subsequent evidence will have to be much greater than the probability of theism in order to even out the odds. These arguments can serve to stack the deck against atheism prior to any argument against theism.

Regardless of whether we bring in other arguments for God's existence, Draper's case against theism has been seen to be unpersuasive. Although it is the best argument of its type, it does not render belief in God less rational than his choice alternative.

Conclusion

Although arguments from evil are popular and sometimes difficult, the ones we have investigated have been seen to be less than cogent. To be sure, many have been persuaded that belief in God is rationally sub-par based on such arguments. I think there is good reason not to be swayed by them. Furthermore, a careful investigation of these arguments shows that many facts about evil raise the probability of theism relative to the probability of its best rivals. If evil presents the most challenging objection to belief in God, then theism is secure indeed.[33]

Notes

1 Daniel Howard-Snyder reports that over 4,200 philosophical and theological items were published on the problem of evil between 1960 and 1990. See his

preface in *The Evidential Argument from Evil*, Daniel Howard-Snyder (ed.) (Bloomington, IN: Indiana University Press, 1996), ix.

2　John Mackie, "Evil and Omnipotence," *Mind* 64 (1955), 200–12; reprinted in *The Problem of Evil*, Robert Merrihew Adams and Marilyn McCord Adams (eds) (Oxford: Oxford University Press, 1990), 25–37; citation on 25.

3　I have omitted many important details in my summary. For a more detailed account, see Alvin Plantinga, *God, Freedom and Evil* (Grand Rapids, MI: Eerdmans, 1977), 7–64.

4　William Rowe, "The Problem of Evil and Some Varieties of Atheism," *American Philosophical Quarterly* 16 (1979); reprinted in *The Evidential Argument from Evil*, Daniel Howard-Snyder (ed.), 1–11. All citations to Rowe's paper are to this printing. Citation in note 10.

5　Ibid., 2.

6　William Hasker challenges it in "The Necessity of Gratuitous Evil," *Faith and Philosophy* 9 (1992), 23–44.

7　Rowe, "Problem of Evil," 4.

8　Ibid., 5.

9　See Stephen J. Wykstra, "The Humean Obstacle to Evidential Arguments from Suffering: On Avoiding the Evils of 'Appearance,' " *International Journal for the Philosophy of Religion* 16 (1974), 73–93. Reprinted in Adams and Adams (eds) *The Problem of Evil*, 138–60. I will be relying on Wykstra for much of what follows regarding Rowe's argument.

10　Someone might think that we are not in a position even to make the claim that it *seems* as though there is no carbon 14 atom in the room. Wykstra presses his criticism of Rowe's argument in precisely this way. We cannot be in a position, he argues, to say that it seems as though there could not be a justifying reason for God to allow the particular evil situation in question. I think Wykstra is right, but I try to put the same idea in terms of an inference.

11　It is not just a matter of whether we should expect to grasp the reasons that God might have to allow the instance of evil in question. It is also a matter of whether we should expect to figure out whether reasons we already know about apply to the particular case. For an important discussion of this issue, see William P. Alston, "The Inductive Argument from Evil and the Human Cognitive Condition," *Philosophical Perspectives 5, Philosophy of Religion* James Tomberlin (ed.) (Ridgeview, NJ: Ridgeview Publishing, 1991); reprinted in Daniel Howard-Snyder (ed.) *The Evidential Argument From Evil*, 97–125.

12　Upon reflection I am confident that the overwhelming percentage of particular evils I encounter are connected to my own choices, the choices of others or the regularity of cause and effect or other reasons about which I have some idea. It is instructive that Rowe's example of the fawn has to be constructed carefully to try to fit it into the mysterious category. Even so, it is not clear to me that it is mysterious.

13　Two points ought to be made here. First, it would be unfair not to mention that there are many who are persuaded by Rowe's argument. These philosophers do not see the "relative percentages" and what our expectations ought to be in the way I see these things. Because of this disagreement, Rowe's argument is still a real challenge to theism for many people. Second, I must point out that I have only discussed Rowe's first paper on this topic. My purpose was to show the kinds of moves that are being made in this kind of argument and to set up my discussion of Draper's work. Anyone wishing to take up the worthwhile endeavor of thinking through the entirety of Rowe's project must consult his many other papers including, "Evil and the Theistic Hypothesis: A Response to S. Wykstra," *International Journal for the Philosophy of Religion* 16 (1984),

95–100; "The Empirical Argument from Evil," in *Rationality Religious Belief, and Moral Commitment*, Robert Audi and William J. Wainwright (eds) (Ithaca, NY: Cornell University Press, 1986); "The Evidential Argument from Evil: A Second Look" in *The Evidential Argument from Evil*, Howard-Snyder (ed.) 262–85; and "William Alston on the Problem of Evil," in *The Rationality of Belief and the Plurality of Faiths*, Thomas Senor (ed.) (Ithaca, NY: Cornell University Press, 1994).

14 See, especially, Paul Draper, "Pain and Pleasure: An Evidential Problem for Theists," *Nous* 23 (1989), 331–50. Reprinted in Daniel Howard-Snyder (ed.) *The Evidential Argument from Evil*, 12–29. See also "Evil and the Proper Basicality of Belief in God," *Faith and Philosophy* 8 (1991), 135–47; and "Probabilistic Arguments from Evil," *Religious Studies* 28 (1993), 303–17.

15 Paul Draper, "Pain and Pleasure," 13.

16 Ibid.

17 Ibid., 14.

18 Ibid., 15.

19 Ibid., 16.

20 Ibid., 17.

21 Ibid., 21. A "freely*" performed action is one that is free in the incompatiblist sense and, if it is a moral choice, the agent has at least two alternatives that are within his power to actualize at the time of choosing such that at least one alternative is morally right and at least one is morally wrong.

22 Draper rightly credits David Hume with pursuing this same strategy in *Dialogues Concerning Natural Religion*.

23 The following discussion has points in common with the following essays. Peter van Inwagen, "The Problem of Evil, the Problem of Air, the Problem of Silence," *Philosophical Perspectives 5: Philosophy of Religion*, James E. Tomberlin (ed.) (Ridgeview, 1991), reprinted in *The Evidential Argument from Evil*, Howard-Snyder (ed.) 151–74; Peter van Inwagen, "Reflections on the Chapters by Draper, Russell, and Gale," *The Evidential Argument from Evil*: 219–33; Alvin Plantinga, "On Being Evidentially Challenged," in *The Evidential Argument from Evil*, Howard-Snyder (ed.), 244–61; and Daniel Howard-Snyder, "Theism, The Hypothesis of Indifference, and the Biological Role of Pain and Pleasure," *Faith and Philosophy* 11 (1994), 452–66. See also Draper's response to van Inwagen and others in "The Skeptical Theist," in *The Evidential Argument from Evil*, Howard-Snyder (ed.), 175–92.

24 As Alvin Plantinga points out, there may well be sentient beings that are not biological, such as angels and Cartesian egos: "On Being Evidentially Challenged," 252. These may still experience pain, although it will not be biologically useful. It will not be physical pain at all.

25 Peter van Inwagen also makes this observation in "The Problem of Evil, the Problem of Air, and the Problem of Silence," 170.

26 Draper is not alone here. Most others who discuss the problem of evil proceed in a similar way.

27 See Quentin Smith, "Time was Created by a Timeless Point: An Atheist Explanation of Spacetime," in *God and Time: Essays on the Nature of God,* Gregory E. Ganssle and David M. Woodruff (eds) (New York: Oxford University Press, 2002), 95–128.

28 The moral of the story might be that the challenge of the plurality of theories on either side is too complex to make our worry over antecedent probabilities fruitful or relevant to the argument.

29 Draper, "Pain and Pleasure," 13.

30 Alvin Plantinga, "On Being Evidentially Challenged," 257.

31 "Necessary Moral Truths and the Need for Explanation," *Philosophica Christi* 2, 1 (New series) (2000), 105–12.
32 R. Douglas Geivett, "A Neglected Aspect of the Problem of Evil." Paper delivered at the Evangelical Philosophical Society meeting in Orlando, Florida (November 1998), 6.
33 I would like to thank Paul Copan for helpful comments on an earlier draft of this chapter.

BIBLIOGRAPHY

General

Baillie, John. *Our Knowledge of God*. New York: Scribner's Sons, 1959.

Brown, Alexandra. *The Cross and Human Transformation*. Minneapolis: Fortress, 1995.

Brunner, Emil. *Revelation and Reason: The Christian Doctrine of Faith and Knowledge*. Philadelphia: Westminster, 1946.

Camfield, F. W. *Revelation and the Holy Spirit*. New York: Scribner's Sons, 1934.

Carnell, Edward. *Christian Commitment*. New York: Macmillan, 1957.

Craig, William Lane (ed.) *Philosophy of Religion: a Reader and Guide*. Trenton: Rutgers University Press, 2001.

Craig, William Lane and Moreland, J. P. (eds) *Naturalism: A Critical Analysis*. London: Routledge, 2000.

Davis, Stephen T. *God, Reason, and Theistic Proofs*. Edinburgh: Edinburgh University Press, 1997.

Farmer, Herbert H. *Towards Belief in God*. New York: Macmillan, 1947.

Hardy, Daniel and Ford, David. *Praising and Knowing God*. Philadelphia: Westminster, 1985.

Haught, John. *Mystery and Promise*. Collegeville, MN: Liturgical, 1993.

Hick, John. *Faith and Knowledge*. Ithaca, NY: Cornell University Press, 1957.

Morris, Thomas V. *Anselmian Explorations*. Notre Dame, IN: University of Notre Dame Press, 1987.

—— *Making Sense of It All: Pascal and the Meaning of Life*. Grand Rapids, MI: Eerdmans, 1992.

Pascal, Blaise. *Pensées* (various editions).

Plantinga, Alvin. *Warranted Christian Belief*. Oxford: Oxford University Press, 2000.

Quinn, P. L. and Taliaferro, C. (eds) *A Companion to Philosophy of Religion*. Oxford: Basil Blackwell, 1997.

Solberg, Mary. *Compelling Knowledge*. Albany: State University of New York Press, 1997.

Stump, Eleonore and Murray, Michael J. (eds) *Philosophy of Religion: The Big Questions*. Oxford: Basil Blackwell, 1999.

Taliaferro, Charles. *Contemporary Philosophy of Religion*. Oxford: Basil Blackwell, 1998.

Religious language and verificationism

Ayer, A. J. *Language, Truth, and Logic*, 2nd edn. London: Victor Gollancz, 1948, Introduction and Chs. 1, 6.

Heimbeck, Raeburne S. *Theology and Meaning*. Stanford, CA: Stanford University Press, 1969.

Hempel, Carl G. "Empiricist Criteria of Cognitive Significance: Problems and Changes," in *Aspects of Scientific Explanation*, 99–122. New York: Free Press, 1965.

Hick, John. "Theology and Verification," *Theology Today* 27 (1960), 12–31.

Plantinga, Alvin, *God and Other Minds*, 2nd edn. Ithaca: Cornell University Press, 1990, Ch. 7

Swinburne, Richard. *The Coherence of Theism*. Oxford: Clarendon Press, 1977, Ch. 1.

Faith and foundationalism

Alston, William. *Perceiving God: The Epistemology of Religious Experience*. Ithaca, NY: Cornell University Press, 1991.

BonJour, Laurence. "The Dialectic of Foundationalism and Coherentism," in *The Blackwell Guide to Epistemology*. John Greco and Ernest Sosa (eds). Oxford: Blackwell Publishers, 1999.

Clark, Kelly James. *Return to Reason: A Critique of Enlightenment Evidentialism, and a Defense of Reason and Belief in God*. Grand Rapids, MI: Eerdmans, 1990.

DePaul, Michael (ed.) *Resurrecting Old-Fashioned Foundationalism*. New York: Rowman & Littlefield, 2001.

Martin, Michael. *Atheism: A Philosophical Justification*. Philadelphia: Temple University Press, 1990.

Nielsen, Kai. *Naturalism without Foundations*. Amherst, NY: Prometheus Books, 1996.

Plantinga, Alvin. *Warranted Christian Belief*. Oxford: Oxford University Press, 2000.

Cognitive inspiration and knowledge of God

Baillie, John. *Our Knowledge of God*. New York: Scribner's Sons, 1959.

Baker, John Austin. *The Foolishness of God*. Atlanta: John Knox Press, 1970.

Brown, Alexandra. *The Cross and Human Transformation*. Minneapolis: Fortress, 1995.

Brunner, Emil. *Revelation and Reason: The Christian Doctrine of Faith and Knowledge*. Philadelphia: Westminster, 1946.

Camfield, F. W. *Revelation and the Holy Spirit*. New York: Scribner's Sons, 1934.

Carnell, Edward. *Christian Commitment*. New York: Macmillan, 1957.

Craig, William Lane and Moreland, J. P. (eds) *Naturalism: A Critical Analysis*. London: Routledge, 2000.

Farmer, Herbert H. *Towards Belief in God*. New York: Macmillan, 1947.

Hardy, Daniel and Ford, David. *Praising and Knowing God*. Philadelphia: Westminster, 1985.

Haught, John. *Mystery and Promise*. Collegeville, MN: Liturgical, 1993.
Hick, John. *Faith and Knowledge*. Ithaca, NY: Cornell University Press, 1957.
Howard-Snyder, Daniel and Moser, Paul K. (eds) *Divine Hiddenness*. New York: Cambridge University Press, 2002.
Pascal, Blaise. *Pensées* (various editions).
Solberg, Mary. *Compelling Knowledge*. Albany: State University of New York Press, 1997.

Science and theism: concord, not conflict

Craig, William Lane and Moreland, J. P. (eds) *Naturalism: A Critical Appraisal*. London: Routledge, 2000.
Kaiser, Christopher. *Creation and the History of Science*. Grand Rapids, MI: Eerdmans, 1981.
Koons, Robert C. *Realism Regained: An Exact Theory of Causation, Teleology and the Mind*. New York: Oxford University Press, 2000.
Pearcey, Nancy and Thaxton, Charles. *The Soul of Science: Christian Faith & Natural Philosophy*. Wheaton, IL: Crossway Books, 1994.
Plantinga, Alvin. *Warrant and Proper Function*. New York: Oxford University Press, 1993.
Steiner, Mark. *The Applicability of Mathematics as a Philosophical Problem*. Cambridge, MA: Harvard University Press, 1998.

The ontological argument

Charlesworth, M. J. (trans. and ed.) *St Anselm's Proslogion*. Notre Dame, IN: University of Notre Dame Press, 1979.
Davis, Stephen T. *God, Reason, and Theistic Proofs*. Edinburgh: Edinburgh University Press, 1997, 15–45.
Mackie, J. L. *The Miracle of Theism*. Oxford: Oxford University Press, 1982, 41–63.
Martin, Michael. *Atheism: A Philosophical Justification*. Philadelphia: Temple University Press, 1990, 79–95.
Plantinga, Alvin. *God, Freedom and Evil*. New York: Harper and Row, 1974, 85–112.
—— *The Nature of Necessity*. Oxford: Oxford University Press, 1974, 197–221.

The cosmological argument

Beck, W. David. "The Cosmological Argument: A Current Bibliographical Appraisal." *Philosophia Christi* 2 (2000), 283–304.
Burrill, Donald R. *The Cosmological Arguments*. Garden City, NY: Doubleday, 1967.
Craig, William Lane. *The Cosmological Argument from Plato to Leibniz*. New York: Barnes & Noble, 1980.
—— "Naturalism and Cosmology," in *Naturalism: a Critical Appraisal*, William. L. Craig and J. P. Moreland (eds). London: Routledge, 2000, 215–52.

Craig, William Lane and Smith, Quentin. *Theism, Atheism, and Big Bang Cosmology*. Oxford: Clarendon Press, 1993.

Davis, Stephen T. *God, Reason, and Theistic Proofs*. Grand Rapids, MI: Eerdmans, 1997.

Gale, Richard M. *On the Existence and Nature of God*. New York: Cambridge University Press, 1991.

Harrison, Jonathan. *God, Freedom, and Immortality*. Avebury Series in Philosophy. Burlington, VT: Ashgate Publishing, 1999.

Hick, John. *Arguments for the Existence of God*. London: Macmillan, 1971.

Mackie, John L. *The Miracle of Theism*. Oxford: Clarendon Press, 1982.

Martin, Michael. *Atheism: A Philosophical Justification*. Philadelphia: Temple University Press, 1990.

Rowe, William L. "Circular Explanations, Cosmological Arguments, and Sufficient Reasons." *Midwest Studies in Philosophy* 21 (1997), 188–99.

Swinburne, Richard. *The Existence of God*, revised edn. Oxford: Clarendon Press, 1991.

Vallicella, William. "On an Insufficient Argument against Sufficient Reason." *Ratio* 10 (1997), 76–81.

The teleological argument

Collins, Robin. "The Argument from Design and the Many-Worlds Hypothesis," in *Philosophy of Religion: A Reader and Guide*. William Lane Craig (eds). Trenton: Rutgers University Press, 2002.

Guth, Alan. *The Inflationary Universe: The Quest for a New Theory of Cosmic Origins*. New York: Helix Books, 1997.

Leslie, John. *Universes*. London: Routledge, 1989.

Manson, Neil (ed.) *God and Design*. London: Routledge, forthcoming.

Rees, Martin. *Just Six Numbers: The Deep Forces that Shape the Universe* (New York: Basic Books, 2000).

Weinberg, Steven. "A Designer Universe?" *The New York Review of Books* 46, 14 (1999), 46–8.

The moral argument

Adams, Robert M. *Finite and Infinite Goods: A Framework for Ethics*. Oxford: Oxford University Press, 1999.

—— *The Virtue of Faith and Other Essays in Philosophical Theology*. Oxford: Oxford University Press, 1987.

Alston, William. "Some Suggestions for Divine Command Theorists," in *Christian Theism and the Problems of Philosophy*, Michael D. Beaty (ed.). Notre Dame, IN: University Press, 1990, 304–20.

Evans, C. Stephen, "Moral Arguments," in *A Companion to Philosophy of Religion*, P. L. Quinn and C. Taliaferro (eds). Oxford: Blackwell, 1997, 345–51.

Graham, Gordon. *Evil and Christian Ethics*. Cambridge: Cambridge University Press, 2001.

Hasker, William. "Humanness as the Mirror of God," *Philosophia Christi* (New Series) 1 (1999), 105–10.

Mavrodes, George I. "Religion and the Queerness of Morality," in *Rationality, Religious Belief and Moral Commitment*, R. Audi and W. J. Wainwright (eds). Ithaca, NY: Cornell University Press, 1986, 213–26.

Quinn, Philip L. *Divine Commands and Moral Requirements*. Oxford: Oxford University Press, 1978.

Rist, John M. *Real Ethics*. Cambridge: Cambridge University Press, 2002.

Sorley, William R. *Moral Values and the Idea of God*. New York: Macmillan, 1921.

The evidential value of religious experience

Alston, William P. *Perceiving God: The Epistemology of Religious Experience*. Ithaca, NY: Cornell University Press, 1991.

Franks Davis, Caroline. *The Evidential Force of Religious Experience*. Oxford: Clarendon Press, 1989.

Gellman, Jerome I. *Experience of God and the Rationality of Theistic Belief*. Ithaca, NY: Cornell University Press, 1997.

—— *Mystical Experience: A Philosophical Inquiry*. Aldershot, UK: Ashgate, 2001.

Smith, John E. *Experience and God*. New York, NY: Oxford University Press, 1968.

—— *The Analogy of Experience: An Approach to Understanding Religious Truth*. New York: Harper & Row, 1973.

Swinburne, Richard. "The Argument from Religious Experience," in *The Existence of God*. Oxford: Clarendon Press. 1979, Ch. 13.

Wainwright, William J. *Mysticism: A Study of its Nature, Cognitive Value and Moral Implications*. Madison: The University of Wisconsin Press, 1981.

Yandell, Keith E. *The Epistemology of Religious Experience*. Cambridge, UK: Cambridge University Press, 1993.

The argument from consciousness

Hasker, William. *The Emergent Self*. Ithaca, NY: Cornell University Press, 1999.

Jackson, Frank. *From Metaphysics to Ethics*. Oxford: Oxford University Press, 1998.

McGinn, Colin. *The Mysterious Flame*. New York: Basic Books, 1999.

Moreland, J. P. "Searle's Biological Naturalism and the Argument from Consciousness," *Faith and Philosophy* 15 (January 1998), 68–91.

Searle, John. *The Rediscovery of the Mind*. Cambridge: MIT Press, 1992.

Swinburne, Richard. *The Existence of God*. Oxford: Clarendon Press, 1979.

—— *The Evolution of the Soul*, revised edn. Oxford: Clarendon, 1997,

Theism, miracles, and the modern mind

Beckwith, Francis J. "Hume's Evidential/Testimonial Epistemology, Probability, and Miracles," in *Faith In Theory and Practice: Essays on Justifying Religious Belief*, Elizabeth S. Radcliffe and Carol J. White (eds). Chicago: Open Court, 1993, 117–40.

Flew, Antony. "Miracles," in *Encyclopedia of Philosophy*, Paul Edwards (ed.). New York: Macmillan/Free Press, 1967, 346–53.

Gaskin, J. C. A. *Hume's Philosophy of Religion*, 2nd edn. Atlantic Heights, NJ: Humanities Press, 1988.

Geivett, R. Douglas and Habermas, Gary R. (eds) *In Defense of Miracles: A Comprehensive Case for God's Action in History*. Downers Grove, IL: InterVarsity Press, 1997.

Hume, David. *Of Miracles*, Antony Flew (ed.) LaSalle, IL: Open Court, 1985.

Martin, Michael. *Atheism: A Philosophical Justification*. Philadelphia: Temple University Press, 1990, 188–209.

Swinburne, Richard. *The Concept of Miracle*. New York: MacMillan, 1970.

—— (ed.) *Miracles*. New York: Macmillan, 1989.

The possibility of God: the coherence of theism

Hughes, G. J. *The Nature of God*. London: Routledge, 1996.

Swinburne, Richard. *The Coherence of Theism*, 2nd edn. Oxford: Clarendon Press, 1993.

Taliaferro, Charles. *Consciousness and the Mind of God*. Cambridge, UK: Cambridge University Press, 1994.

—— *Contemporary Philosophy of Religion*. Oxford: Basil Blackwell, 1999.

Wierenga, Edward R. *The Nature of God*. Ithaca, NY: Cornell University Press, 1989.

God and evil

Adams, Marilyn McCord and Adams, Robert Merrihew (eds). *The Problem of Evil*. Oxford: Oxford University Press, 1990.

Geivett, R. Douglas. *Evil and the Evidence for God*. Philadelphia: Temple University Press, 1993.

Howard-Snyder, Daniel (ed.) *The Evidential Argument from Evil*. Bloomington, IN: Indiana University Press, 1996.

Plantinga, Alvin. *God, Freedom and Evil*. Grand Rapids, MI: Eerdmans, 1977.

NAME INDEX

Abraham 56, 57, 150
Adams, R. M. 166, 172, 206, 218
Agrippa 49
Al-Ghazali 112
Alston, W. P. 10, 17–34, 41, 121, 131, 173, 183–4, 185, 186–8, 199, 201, 201, 202, 258, 275
Anselm, 93–105, 109, 110, 111, 112, 250, 251
Aquinas, T. 7, 33, 112, 113, 116, 129, 131, 132, 133, 250, 251
Archimedes 78
Aristotle 79, 80, 83, 112, 113, 124, 132
Armstrong, D. M. 209, 211, 219
Audi, R. 53, 151, 165, 168, 172
Augustine 243–4, 247, 251, 256
Ayala, F. J. 88
Ayer, A. J. 17, 175, 200

Bach, J. S. 169
Bacon, R. 78, 83, 87
Baillie, J. 57, 71
Barbour, I. G. 34
Baker, J. A. 71
Barr, J. 71
Barrow, J. 145
Basil of Caesarea 82
Beckwith, F. J. 12, 90, 221–36
Berger, P. L. 4, 14, 168
Bin Laden, O. 223
Bishop, J. 211, 219
Block, N. 245, 253
Boethius 121, 250, 251, 252
Bohm, D. 118
Boltzman, L. 147
BonJour, Laurence 53, 203
Boyd, R. 158–9, 169, 171

Boyle, R. 80–1
Bradley, R. 111
Bradwardine, T. 87
Braithwaite, R. G. 26, 34
Brandt, R. B. 167–8, 174
Brantano, F. 256, 258
Brink, D. O. 152, 156, 158, 169, 170
Bruno, G. 88
Buber, M. 203
Buffon, G. L. L. 80
Byrne, P. 174, 202

Calvin, John 36
Camus, A. 233
Cantor, G. 120
Carnap, R. 17, 136, 146, 175, 200
Carr, B. 140, 145, 146
Carson, T. L. 165, 168, 172, 174
Chalmers, D. 216, 219
Chesterton, G. K. 217, 239, 256
Churchland, Patricia 253
Churchland, Paul 210, 211, 219, 253, 255, 257
Clark, D. K. 10, 35–54
Clark, K. J. 13, 53, 203
Clark, S. R. L. 219
Clifford, W. K. 10, 35, 53
Collins, R. 11–12, 132–48, 200, 273
Copan, P. 1–14, 89, 149–74, 235
Copernicus 73
Copleston, F. 130
Craig, E. 13
Craig, W. L. 11, 14, 37, 53, 112–31, 200, 235, 251, 274
Crick, F. 160, 162, 172
Crombie, A. C. 87
Crombie, I. 34

284

SUBJECT INDEX

simplicity (divine) 33, 113, 116, 130, 142, 248
Stoicism 132; World-Soul 81
string theory 143
suffering *see* problem of evil
sufficient reason 112, 113–4, 261; principle of 113–4, 117, 119, 129
supervenience: consciousness 155, 156, 157–8, 212–4; moral values 153, 155–6, 157–8
teleological argument 9, 11, 132–48, 177, 218; objections 140–2
teleology 79, 80, 82, 88, 132
time 118, 119, 122–3, 126 tensed vs. tenseless 118, 119, 122–3
timelessness (divine) 23, 33, 116, 128, 251–2; God and time 239, 248, 251–2
theism: coherence 6–10, 12, 101–2, 239–58; explanatory power 2–4; particularistic vs. minimalistic 270–1; psychology of belief 4–6;

realism 1-4; recent resurgence 1–2, 17, 175–6
theistic proofs *see* natural theology
thermodynamics 28, 30, 79, 127–8; second law 127–8
tolerance 169
Trinity 23, 24, 246; naturalistic trinity 24
Tristram Shandy example 123–5, 131

Uncaused Cause *see* First Cause
universals 108

vacuum fluctuation universe 126
verificationist principle 10, 17–34, 73, 74–7, 175–6; "bridge principles" 28–32; problems 26–32
verificationism *see* verificationist principle
Vienna Circle 17, 200
Voluntarism (theological) 80

Zeno's paradoxes 124